Clashing Views in

Science, Technology, and Society

SEVENTH EDITION

TAKING SIDES

Clashing Views in

Science, Technology, and Society

SEVENTH EDITION

Selected, Edited, and with Introductions by

Thomas A. Easton
Thomas College

Mc Graw Hill **Contemporary Learning Series**
A Division of The McGraw-Hill Companies

Photo Acknowledgment
Cover image: Chad Baker/Ryan McVay/Getty Images

Cover Acknowledgment
Maggie Lytle

Library of Congress Cataloging-in-Publication Data
Main entry under title:
Taking sides: clashing views on controversial issues in science, technology, and society/
selected, edited, and with introductions by Thomas A. Easton.—7th ed.
Includes bibliographical references and index.
1. Science—Social aspects. 2. Technology—Social aspects. I. Easton, Thomas A., *comp.*
306.45
0-07-351493-4
ISSN: 1098-5417

Printed on Recycled Paper

Preface

Those who must deal with scientific and technological issues—scientists, politicians, sociologists, business managers, and anyone who is concerned about a neighborhood dump or power plant, government intrusiveness, expensive space programs, or the morality of medical research, among many other issues—must be able to consider, evaluate, and choose among alternatives. Making choices is an essential aspect of the scientific method. It is also an inescapable feature of every public debate over a scientific or technological issue, for there can be no debate if there are no alternatives.

The ability to evaluate and to select among alternatives—as well as to know when the data do not permit selection—is called critical thinking. It is essential not only in science and technology but in every other aspect of life as well. *Taking Sides: Clashing Views in Science, Technology, and Society* is designed to stimulate and cultivate this ability by holding up for consideration 19 issues that have provoked substantial debate. Each of these issues has at least two sides, usually more. However, each issue is expressed in terms of a single question in order to draw the lines of debate more clearly. The ideas and answers that emerge from the clash of opposing points of view should be more complex than those offered by the students before the reading assignment.

The issues in this book were chosen because they are currently of particular concern to both science and society. They touch on the nature of science and research, the relationship between science and society, the uses of technology, and the potential threats that technological advances can pose to human survival. And they come from a variety of fields, including computer and space science, biology, environmentalism, law enforcement, and public health.

Organization of the book For each issue, I have provided an *issue introduction,* which provides some historical background and discusses why the issue is important. I then present two selections, one pro and one con, in which the authors make their cases. Each issue concludes with a *postscript* that brings the issue up to date and adds other voices and viewpoints. I have also provided relevant Internet site addresses (URLs) on the *On the Internet* page that accompanies each part opener. At the back of the book is a listing of all the *contributors to this volume,* which gives information on the scientists, technicians, professors, and social critics whose views are debated here.

Which answer to the issue question—yes or no—is the correct answer? Perhaps neither. Perhaps both. Students should read, think about, and discuss the readings and then come to their own conclusions without letting my or their instructor's opinions (which perhaps show at least some of the time!) dictate theirs. The additional readings mentioned in both the introductions and the postscripts should prove helpful. It is worth stressing that the issues covered in this book are all *live* issues; that is, the debates they represent are active and ongoing.

Changes to this edition This seventh edition represents a considerable revision. There are three completely new issues: "Does Politics Come Before Science in Current Government Decision Making?" (Issue 1); "Is It Time to Revive Nuclear Power?" (Issue 5); And "Should Potential Risks Slow the Development of Nanotechnology?" (Issue 10). The issue on population (Issue 7) has been retitled and given two new essays to reflect the change in the projections of future population. The issue on manned space exploration (Issue 13) has also been retitled and given two new essays to sharpen the debate.

In addition, for ten of the issues retained from the previous edition, one reading has been replaced to bring the debate up to date: "Should Society Restrict the Publication of Unclassified but "Sensitive" Research?" (Issue 2); "Should Creationism and Evolution Get Equal Time in Schools?" (Issue 3); "Should Society Act Now to Halt Global Warming?" (Issue 4); "Will Hydrogen Replace Fossil Fuels for Cars?" (Issue 6); "Is There Sufficient Scientific Research to Conclude that Cell Phones Cause Cancer?" (Issue 8); "Should DDT Be Banned Worldwide?" (Issue 9); "Is The Search for Extraterrestrial Life Doomed to Fail?" (Issue 12); "Does the Spread of Surveillance Technology Threaten Privacy?" (Issue 15); "Is the Use of Animals in Research Justified?" (Issue 17); and "Should Genetically Modified Foods Be Banned?" (Issue 18). The issue on the use of animals in research (Issue 17) has been given two new essays. In all, there are 21 new selections. The book's introduction and the issue introductions and postscripts in the retained issues have been revised and updated where necessary.

A word to the instructor An *Instructor's Manual with Test Questions* (multiple-choice and essay) is available through the publisher for the instructor using *Taking Sides* in the classroom. It includes suggestions for stimulating in-class discussion for each issue. A general guidebook, *Using Taking Sides in the Classroom*, which discusses methods and techniques for integrating the pro-con approach into any classroom setting, is also available. An online version of *Using Taking Sides in the Classroom* and a correspondence service for *Taking Sides* adopters can be found at http://www.mhcls.com/usingts/.

Taking Sides: Clashing Views in Science, Technology, and Society is only one title in the Taking Sides series. If you are interested in seeing the table of contents for any of the other titles, please visit the Taking Sides Web site at http://www.mhcls.com/takingsides/.

Thomas A. Easton
Thomas College

Contents In Brief

Contents

Richard J. Clifford, a professor of biblical studies, argues that although modern creationism is flawed, excluding the Bible and religion from American public education is indefensible. He maintains that schools should be places where religious beliefs are treated with respect. Journalist Evan Ratliff describes the current debate over introducing creationism, in its "Intelligent Design" guise, into the schools and concludes that "in science, not all theories are equal." Science education should not be decided by rhetoric, but by scientific scrutiny.

PART 2   THE ENVIRONMENT   63

Issue 4.   Should Society Act Now to Halt Global Warming?   64

The Intergovernmental Panel on Climate Change states that global warming appears to be real, with strong effects on sea level, ice cover, and rainfall patterns to come, and that human activities—particularly emissions of carbon dioxide—are to blame. The Bush administration's plan for dealing with global warming insists that short-term economic health must come before reducing emissions of greenhouse gases. It is more useful to reduce "greenhouse gas intensity" or emissions per dollar of economic activity than to reduce total emissions.

Issue 5.   Is It Time to Revive Nuclear Power?   88

Peter Schwartz and Spencer Reiss argue that nuclear power should be encouraged as the one practical answer to global warming and forthcoming shortages of fossil fuels. Professor of journalism Karl Grossman argues that to encourage the use of nuclear power is reckless. It would be wiser to promote renewable energy and energy efficiency.

Issue 6.   Will Hydrogen Replace Fossil Fuels for Cars?   106

Social activist Jeremy Rifkin asserts that fossil fuels are approaching the end of their usefulness and that hydrogen fuel holds the potential not only to replace them but also to reshape society. Michael Behar argues that the public has been misled about the prospects of the "hydrogen economy." We must overcome major technological, financial, and political obstacles before hydrogen can be a viable alternative to fossil fuels.

PART 3   HUMAN HEALTH AND WELFARE   123

Michael Meyer argues that when world population begins to decline after about 2050, economies will no longer continue to grow, government benefits will decline, young people will have to support an elderly population, and despite some environmental benefits, quality of life will suffer. David Nicholson-Lord argues that the economic problems of population decline all have straightforward solutions. A less-crowded world will not suffer from the environmental ills attendant on overcrowding and will, overall, be a roomier, gentler, less materialistic place to live, with cleaner air and water.

Public health scientist George Carlo and journalist Martin Schram argue that there is a definite risk that the electromagnetic radiation generated by cell phone antennae can cause cancer and other health problems. The National Radiation Protection Board (now the Radiation Protection Division, http://www.hpa.org.uk/radiation/, of the United Kingdom's Health Protection Agency) argues that there is no clear indication of adverse health effects, including cancer, from the use of mobile phones, but precautions are nevertheless in order.

Anne Platt McGinn, a senior researcher at the Worldwatch Institute, argues that although DDT is still used to fight malaria, there are other, more effective and less environmentally harmful methods. She maintains that DDT should be banned or reserved for emergency use. Alexander

Julian Savulescu, director of the Ethics Program of the Murdoch Institute at the Royal Children's Hospital in Melbourne, Australia, argues that it is not only permissible but morally required to use human cloning to create embryos as a source of tissue for transplantation. Biochemist Leon R. Kass argues that human cloning is "so repulsive to contemplate" that it should be prohibited entirely.

Introduction

Analyzing Issues in Science and Technology

As civilization enters the twenty-first century, it cannot escape science and technology. Their fruits—the clothes we wear, the foods we eat, the tools we use—surround us. They also fill us with both hope and dread for the future, for although new discoveries promise us cures for diseases and other problems, new insights into the wonders of nature, new gadgets, new industries, and new jobs (among other things), the past has taught us that technological developments can have unforeseen and terrible consequences.

Those consequences do *not* belong to science, for science is nothing more (or less) than a systematic approach to gaining knowledge about the world. Technology is the application of knowledge (including scientific knowledge) to accomplish things we otherwise could not. It is not just devices such as hammers and computers and jet aircraft, but also management systems and institutions and even political philosophies. And it is of course such *uses* of knowledge that affect our lives for good and ill.

We cannot say, "for good *or* ill." Technology is neither an unalloyed blessing nor an unmitigated curse. Every new technology offers both new benefits and new problems, and the two sorts of consequences cannot be separated from each other. Automobiles provide rapid, convenient personal transportation, but precisely because of that benefit, they also create suburbs, urban sprawl, crowded highways, air pollution, and even global climate change.

Optimists vs. Pessimists

The inescapable pairing of good and bad consequences helps to account for why so many issues of science and technology stir debate in our society. Optimists focus on the benefits of technology and are confident that we will be able to cope with any problems that arise. Pessimists fear the problems and are sure their costs will outweigh any possible benefits.

Sometimes the costs of new technologies are immediate and tangible. When new devices—steamship boilers or space shuttles—fail or new drugs prove to have unforeseen side-effects, people die. Sometimes the costs are less obvious.

The proponents of technology answer that if a machine fails, it needs to be fixed, not banned. If a drug has side-effects, it may need to be refined or its permitted recipients may have to be better defined (the banned tranquilizer thalidomide is famous for causing birth defects when taken early in pregnancy; it is apparently quite safe for men and nonpregnant women).

Certainty vs. Uncertainty

Another root for the debates over science and technology is uncertainty. Science is by its very nature uncertain. Its truths are provisional, open to revision.

Unfortunately, most people are told by politicians, religious leaders, and newspaper columnists that truth is certain. They therefore believe that if someone admits uncertainty, their position is weak and they need not be heeded. This is, of course, an open invitation for demagogues to prey upon fears of disaster or side-effects or upon the wish to be told that the omens of greenhouse warming and ozone holes (etc.) are mere figments of the scientific imagination.

Is Science Just Another Religion?

Science and technology have come to play a huge role in human culture, largely because they have led to vast improvements in nutrition, health care, comfort, communication, transportation, and humanity's ability to affect the world. However, science has also enhanced understanding of human behavior and of how the universe works, and in this it frequently contradicts what people have long thought they knew. Furthermore, it actively rejects any role of God in scientific explanation.

Many people therefore reject what science tells us. They see science as just another way of explaining how the world and humanity came to be; in this view, science is no truer than religious accounts. Indeed, some say science is just another religion, with less claim on followers' allegiance than other religions that have been divinely sanctioned and hallowed by longer traditions. Certainly, they see little significant difference between the scientist's faith in reason, evidence, and skepticism as the best way to achieve truth about the world and the religious believer's faith in revelation and scripture. This becomes very explicit in connection with the debates between creationists and evolutionists. Even religious people who do not favor creationism may reject science because they see it as denying both the existence of God and the importance of "human values" (meaning behaviors that are affirmed by traditional religion). This leads to a basic antipathy between science and religion, especially conservative religion, and especially in areas—such as human origins—where science and scripture seem to be talking about the same things but are contradicting each other. This point can be illustrated by mentioning the Italian physicist Galileo Galilei (1564–1642) who in 1616 was attacked by the Roman Catholic Church for teaching Copernican astronomy and thus contradicting the teachings of the Church. Another example arose when evolutionary theorist Charles Darwin first published *On the Origin of Species by Means of Natural Selection* in 1859. Mano Singham notes in "The Science and Religion

Wars," *Phi Delta Kappan* (February 2000), that "In the triangle formed by science, mainstream religion, and fringe beliefs, it is the conflict between science and fringe beliefs that is usually the source of the most heated, acrimonious, and public debate." Michael Ruse takes a more measured tone when he asks "Is Evolution a Secular Religion?" *Science* (March 7, 2003); his answer is that, "Today's professional evolutionism is no more a secular religion than is industrial chemistry" but there is also a "popular evolutionism" that treads on religious ground and must be carefully distinguished.

Even if religion does not enter the debate, some people reject new developments in science and technology (and in other areas) because they seem "unnatural." For most people, "natural" seems to mean any device or procedure to which they have become accustomed. Very few realize how "unnatural" are such ordinary things as circumcision and horseshoes and baseball.

Yet new ideas are inevitable. The search for and the application of knowledge is perhaps the human species' single most defining characteristic. Other creatures also use tools, communicate, love, play, and reason. Only humans have embraced change. We are forever creating variations on our religions, languages, politics, and tools. Innovation is as natural to us as building dams is to a beaver.

Voodoo Science

Public confusion over science and technology is increased by several factors. One is the failure of public education. In 2002, the Committee on Technological Literacy of the National Academy of Engineering and the National Research Council published a report (*Technically Speaking: Why All Americans Need to Know More about Technology*) that said that although the United States is defined by and dependent on science and technology, "its citizens are not equipped to make well-considered decisions or to think critically about technology. As a society, we are not even fully aware of or conversant with the technologies we use every day."

A second factor is the willingness of some to mislead. Alarmists stress awful possible consequences of new technology without paying attention to actual evidence, they demand certainty when it is impossible, and they reject the new because it is untraditional or even "unthinkable." And then there are the marketers, hypesters, fraudsters, activists, and even legitimate scientists and critics who oversell their claims. Robert L. Park, author of *Voodoo Science: The Road from Foolishness to Fraud* (Oxford University Press, 2002) lists seven warning signs "that a scientific claim lies well outside the bounds of rational scientific discourse" and should be viewed warily:

- The discoverer pitches his claim directly to the media, without permitting peer review.
- The discoverer says that a powerful establishment is trying to suppress his or her work.
- The scientific effect involved is always at the very limit of detection.
- Evidence for a discovery is only anecdotal.

- The discoverer says a belief is credible because it has endured for centuries.
- The discoverer has worked in isolation.
- The discoverer must propose new laws of nature to explain an observation.

The Soul of Science

The standard picture of science—a world of observations and hypotheses, experiments and theories, a world of sterile white coats and laboratories and cold, unfeeling logic—is a myth of our times. It has more to do with the way science is presented by both scientists and the media than with the way scientists actually do their work. In practice, scientists are often less orderly, less logical, and more prone to very human conflicts of personality than most people suspect.

The myth remains because it helps to organize science. It provides labels and a framework for what a scientist does; it may thus be especially valuable to student scientists who are still learning the ropes. In addition, it embodies certain important ideals of scientific thought. It is these ideals that make the scientific approach the most powerful and reliable guide to truth about the world that human beings have yet devised.

The Ideals of Science: Skepticism, Communication, and Reproducibility

The soul of science is a very simple idea: *Check it out.* Scholars used to think that all they had to do to do their duty by the truth was to say "According to . . . " some ancient authority such as Aristotle or the Bible. If someone with a suitably illustrious reputation had once said something was so, it was so. Arguing with authority or holy writ could get you charged with heresy and imprisoned or burned at the stake.

This attitude is the opposite of everything that modern science stands for. As Carl Sagan says in *The Demon-Haunted World: Science as a Candle in the Dark* (Random House, 1995, p. 28), "One of the great commandments of science is, 'Mistrust arguments from authority.'" Scientific knowledge is based not on authority but on reality itself. Scientists take nothing on faith. They are *skeptical.* When they want to know something, they do not look it up in the library or take others' word for it. They go into the laboratory, the forest, the desert—wherever they can find the phenomena they wish to know about—and they ask those phenomena directly. They look for answers in the book of nature. And if they think they know the answer already, it is not of books that they ask, "Are we right?" but of nature. This is the point of "scientific experiments"—they are how scientists ask nature whether their ideas check out.

This "check it out" ideal is, however, an ideal. No one can possibly check everything out for himself or herself. Even scientists, in practice, look things up in books. They too rely on authorities. But the authorities they rely on are other scientists who have studied nature and reported what they learned. In principle, everything those authorities report can be checked. Observations in the lab or in the field can be repeated. New theoretical or computer models can be designed. What is in the books can be confirmed.

In fact, a good part of the official "scientific method" is designed to make it possible for any scientist's findings or conclusions to be confirmed. Scientists do not say, "Vitamin D is essential for strong bones. Believe me. I know." They say, "I know that vitamin D is essential for proper bone formation because I raised rats without vitamin D in their diet, and their bones turned out soft and crooked. When I gave them vitamin D, their bones hardened and straightened. Here is the kind of rat I used, the kind of food I fed them, the amount of vitamin D I gave them. Go thou and do likewise, and you will see what I saw."

Communication is therefore an essential part of modern science. That is, in order to function as a scientist, you must not keep secrets. You must tell others not just what you have learned by studying nature, but how you learned it. You must spell out your methods in enough detail to let others repeat your work.

Scientific knowledge is thus *reproducible* knowledge. Strictly speaking, if a person says, "I can see it, but you can't," that person is not a scientist. Scientific knowledge exists for everyone. Anyone who takes the time to learn the proper techniques can confirm it. They don't have to believe in it first.

ᴄᴀⵙᵣ

As an exercise, devise a way to convince a red-green colorblind person, who sees no difference between red and green, that such a difference really exists. That is, show that a knowledge of colors is reproducible, and therefore scientific, knowledge, rather than something more like belief in ghosts or telepathy.

Here's a hint: Photographic light meters respond to light hitting a sensor. Photographic filters permit light of only a single color to pass through.

ᴄᴀⵙᵣ

The Standard Model of the Scientific Method

As it is usually presented, the scientific method has five major components. They include *observation, generalization* (identifying a pattern), stating a *hypothesis* (a tentative extension of the pattern or explanation for why the pattern exists), and *experimentation* (testing that explanation). The results of the tests are then *communicated* to other members of the scientific community, usually by publishing the findings. How each of these components contributes to the scientific method is discussed briefly below.

Observation

The basic units of science—and the only real facts the scientist knows—are the individual *observations*. Using them, we look for patterns, suggest explanations, and devise tests for our ideas. Our observations can be casual, as when we notice a black van parked in front of the fire hydrant on our block. They may also be more deliberate, as what a police detective notices when he or she sets out to find clues to who has been burglarizing apartments in our neighborhood.

Generalization

After we have made many observations, we try to discern a pattern among them. A statement of such a pattern is a *generalization*. We might form a generalization if we realized that every time there was a burglary on the block, that black van was parked by the hydrant.

Cautious experimenters do not jump to conclusions. When they think they see a pattern, they often make a few more observations just to be sure the pattern holds up. This practice of strengthening or confirming findings by *replicating* them is a very important part of the scientific process. In our example, the police would wait for the van to show up again and for another burglary to happen. Only then might they descend on the alleged villains.

The Hypothesis

A tentative explanation suggesting why a particular pattern exists is called a *hypothesis*. In our example, the hypothesis that comes to mind is obvious: The burglars drive to work in that black van.

The mark of a good hypothesis is that it is *testable*. The best hypotheses are *predictive*. Can you devise a predictive test for the "burglars use the black van" hypothesis?

Unfortunately, tests can fail even when the hypothesis is perfectly correct. How might that happen with our example?

Many philosophers of science insist on *falsification* as a crucial aspect of the scientific method. That is, when a test of a hypothesis shows the hypothesis to be false, the hypothesis must be rejected and replaced with another.

The Experiment

The *experiment* is the most formal part of the scientific process. The concept, however, is very simple: An experiment is nothing more than a test of a hypothesis. It is what a scientist—or a detective—does to check an idea out.

If the experiment does not falsify the hypothesis, that does not mean the hypothesis is true. It simply means that the scientist has not yet come up with the test that falsifies it. The more times and the more different ways that falsification fails, the more probable it is that the hypothesis is true. Unfortunately, because it is impossible to do all the possible tests of a hypothesis, the scientist can never *prove* it is true.

Consider the hypothesis that all cats are black. If you see a black cat, you don't really know anything at all about all cats. If you see a white cat, though, you certainly know that not all cats are black. You would have to look at every cat on Earth to prove the hypothesis. It takes just one to disprove it.

This is why philosophers of science say that *science is the art of disproving,* not proving. If a hypothesis withstands many attempts to disprove it, then it may be a good explanation of what is going on. If it fails just one test, it is clearly wrong and must be replaced with a new hypothesis.

However, researchers who study what scientists actually do point out that the truth is a little different. Almost all scientists, when they come up with what strikes them as a good explanation of a phenomenon or pattern, do *not* try to disprove their hypothesis. Instead, they design experiments to *confirm* it. If an experiment fails to confirm the hypothesis, the researcher tries another experiment, not another hypothesis.

Police detectives may do the same thing. Think of the one who found no evidence of wrongdoing in the black van but arrested the suspects anyway. Armed with a search warrant, he later searched their apartments. He was saying, in effect, "I *know* they're guilty. I just have to find the evidence to prove it."

The logical weakness in this approach is obvious, but that does not keep researchers (or detectives) from falling in love with their ideas and holding onto them as long as possible. Sometimes they hold on so long, even without confirmation of their hypothesis, that they wind up looking ridiculous. Sometimes the confirmations add up over the years and whatever attempts are made to disprove the hypothesis fail to do so. The hypothesis may then be elevated to the rank of a *theory, principle,* or *law.* Theories are explanations of how things work (the theory of evolution *by means of* natural selection). Principles and laws tend to be statements of things that happen, such as the law of gravity (masses attract each other, or what goes up comes down) or the gas law (if you increase the pressure on an enclosed gas, the volume will decrease and the temperature will increase).

Communication

Each scientist is obligated to share her or his hypotheses, methods, and findings with the rest of the scientific community. This sharing serves two purposes. First, it supports the basic ideal of skepticism by making it possible for others to say, "Oh, yeah? Let me check that." It tells those others where to see what the scientist saw, what techniques to use, and what tools to use.

Second, it gets the word out so that others can use what has been discovered. This is essential because science is a cooperative endeavor. People who work thousands of miles apart build with and upon each other's discoveries, and some of the most exciting discoveries have involved bringing together information from very different fields, as when geochemistry, paleontology, and astronomy came together to reveal that what killed off the dinosaurs 65 million years ago was apparently the impact of a massive comet or asteroid with the Earth.

Scientific cooperation stretches across time as well. Every generation of scientists both uses and adds to what previous generations have discovered. As Isaac Newton said, "If I have seen further than [other men], it is by standing upon the shoulders of Giants" (Letter to Robert Hooke, February 5, 1675/6).

The communication of science begins with a process called "peer review," which typically has three stages. The first occurs when a scientist seeks funding—from government agencies, foundations, or other sources—to carry out a research program. He or she must prepare a report describing the intended work, laying out background, hypotheses, planned experiments, expected results, and even the broader impacts on other fields. Committees of other scientists then go over the report to see whether the scientist knows his or her area, has the necessary abilities, and is realistic in his or her plans.

Once the scientist has the needed funding, has done the work, and has written a report of the results, that report will go to a scientific journal. Before publishing the report, the journal's editors will show it to other workers in the same or related fields and ask whether the work was done adequately, the conclusions are justified, and the report should be published.

The third stage of peer review happens after publication, when the broader scientific community gets to see and judge the work.

This three-stage quality-control filter can, of course, be short-circuited. Any scientist with independent wealth can avoid the first stage quite easily, but such scientists are much, much rarer today than they were a century or so ago. Those who remain are the object of envy. Surely it is fair to say that they are not frowned upon as are those who avoid the later two stages of the "peer review" mechanism by using vanity presses and press conferences.

On the other hand, it is certainly possible for the standard peer review mechanisms to fail. By their nature, these mechanisms are more likely to approve ideas that do not contradict what the reviewers think they already know. Yet unconventional ideas are not necessarily wrong, as Alfred Wegener proved when he tried to gain acceptance for the idea of continental drift in the early twentieth century. At the time, geologists believed the crust of the Earth—which was solid rock, after all—did not behave like liquid. Yet Wegener was proposing that the continents floated about like icebergs in the sea, bumping into each other, tearing apart (to produce matching profiles like those of South America and Africa), and bumping again. It was not until the 1960s that most geologists accepted his ideas as genuine insights instead of hare-brained delusions.

The Need for Controls

Many years ago, I read a description of a wish machine. It consisted of an ordinary stereo amplifier with two unusual attachments. The wires that would normally be connected to a microphone were connected instead to a pair of copper plates. The wires that would normally be connected to a speaker were connected instead to a whip antenna of the sort we usually see on cars.

To use this device, one put a picture of some desired item between the copper plates. It could be a photo of a person with whom one wanted a date, a lottery ticket, a college, anything. One test case used a photo of a pest-infested cornfield. One then wished fervently for the date, a winning ticket, a college acceptance, or whatever else one craved. In the test case, that meant wishing that all the cornfield pests should drop dead.

Supposedly the wish would be picked up by the copper plates, amplified by the stereo amplifier, and then sent via the whip antenna wherever wish-orders have to go. Whoever or whatever fills those orders would get the message, and then. . . . Well, in the test case, the result was that when the testers checked the cornfield, there was no longer any sign of pests.

What's more, the process worked equally well whether the amplifier was plugged in or not.

I'm willing to bet that you are now feeling very much like a scientist—skeptical. The true, dedicated scientist, however, does not stop with saying, "Oh, yeah? Tell me another one!" Instead, he or she says something like, "Mmm. I wonder. Let's check this out." (Must we, really? After all, we can be quite sure that the wish machine does not work because if it did, it would be on the market. Casinos would then be unable to make a profit for their backers. Deadly diseases would not be deadly. And so on.)

Where must the scientist begin? The standard model of the scientific method says the first step is observation. Here, our observations (as well as our necessary generalization) are simply the description of the wish machine and the claims for its effectiveness. Perhaps we even have an example of the physical device itself.

What is our hypothesis? We have two choices, one consistent with the claims for the device, one denying those claims: The wish machine always works, or the wish machine never works. Both are equally testable, but perhaps one is more easily falsifiable. (Which one?)

How do we test the hypothesis? Set up the wish machine, and perform the experiment of making a wish. If the wish comes true, the device works. If it does not, it doesn't.

Can it really be that simple? In essence, yes. But in fact, no.

Even if you don't believe that wishing can make something happen, sometimes wishes do come true by sheer coincidence. Therefore, if the wish machine is as nonsensical as most people think it is, sometimes it will *seem* to work. We therefore need a way to shield against the misleading effects of coincidence. We need a way to *control* the possibilities of error.

Coincidence is not, of course, the only source of error we need to watch out for. For instance, there is a very human tendency to interpret events in such a way as to agree with our preexisting beliefs, our prejudices. If we believe in wishes, we therefore need a way to guard against our willingness to interpret near misses as not quite misses at all. There is also a human tendency not to look for mistakes when the results agree with our prejudices. That cornfield, for instance, might not have been as badly infested as the testers said it was, or a farmer might have sprayed it with pesticide whether the testers had wished or not, or the field they checked might have been the wrong one.

We would also like to check whether the wish machine does indeed work equally well plugged in or not, and then we must guard against the tendency to wish harder when we know it's plugged in. We would like to know whether the photo between the copper plates makes any difference, and then we must guard against the tendency to wish harder when we know the wish matches the photo.

Coincidence is easy to protect against. All that is necessary is to repeat the experiment enough times to be sure we are not seeing flukes. This is one major purpose of replication.

Our willingness to shade the results in our favor can be defeated by having someone else judge the results of our wishing experiments. Our eagerness to overlook "favorable" errors can be defeated by taking great care to avoid any errors at all; peer reviewers also help by pointing out such problems.

The other sources of error are harder to avoid, but scientists have developed a number of helpful *control* techniques. One is "blinding." In essence, it means setting things up so the scientist does not know what he or she is doing.

In the pharmaceutical industry, this technique is used whenever a new drug must be tested. A group of patients are selected. Half of them—chosen randomly to avoid any unconscious bias that might put sicker, taller, shorter, male, female, homosexual, black, or white patients in one group instead of the other—are given the drug. The others are given a dummy pill, or a sugar pill, also known as a placebo. In all other respects, the two groups are treated exactly the same. Drug (and other) researchers take great pains to be sure groups of experimental subjects are alike in every way but the one way being tested. Here that means the only difference between the groups should be which one gets the drug and which one gets the placebo.

Unfortunately, placebos can have real medical effects, apparently because we *believe* our doctors when they tell us that a pill will cure what ails us. We have faith in them, and our minds do their best to bring our bodies into line. This mind-over-body "placebo effect" seems to be akin to faith healing.

Single Blind.   The researchers therefore do not tell the patients what pill they are getting. The patients are "blinded" to what is going on. Both placebo and drug then gain equal advantage from the placebo effect. If the drug seems to work better or worse than the placebo, then the researchers can be sure of a real difference between the two.

Double Blind.   Or can they? Unfortunately, if the researchers know what pill they are handing out, they can give subtle, unconscious cues. Or they may interpret any changes in symptoms in favor of the drug. It is therefore best to keep the researchers in the dark too; since both researchers and patients are now blind to the truth, the experiment is said to be "double blind." Drug trials often use pills that differ only in color or in the number on the bottle, and the code is not broken until all the results are in. This way nobody knows who gets what until the knowledge can no longer make a difference.

Obviously, the double-blind approach can work only when there are human beings on both sides of the experiment, as experimenter and as experimental subject. When the object of the experiment is an inanimate object such as a wish machine, only the single-blind approach is possible.

With suitable precautions against coincidence, self-delusion, wishful thinking, bias, and other sources of error, the wish machine could be convincingly tested. Yet it cannot be perfectly tested, for perhaps it works only sometimes, when the aurora glows green over Copenhagen, in months without an "r," or when certain people use it. It is impossible to rule out all the possibilities, although we can rule out enough to be pretty confident as we call the gadget nonsense.

Very similar precautions are essential in every scientific field, for the same sources of error lie in wait wherever experiments are done, and they serve very much the same function. However, we must stress that no controls and no peer review system, no matter how elaborate, can completely protect a scientist—or science—from error.

Here, as well as in the logical impossibility of proof (experiments only fail to disprove) and science's dependence on the progressive growth of knowledge (its requirement that each scientist make his or her discoveries while standing on the shoulders of the giants who went before, if you will) lies the uncertainty that is the hallmark of science. Yet it is also a hallmark of science that its methods guarantee that uncertainty will be reduced (not eliminated). Frauds and errors will be detected and corrected. Limited understandings of truth will be extended.

Those who bear this in mind will be better equipped to deal with issues of certainty and risk.

Something else to bear in mind is that argument is an inevitable part of science. The combination of communication and skepticism very frequently leads scientists into debates with each other. The scientist's willingness to be skeptical about and hence to challenge received wisdom leads to debates with everyone else. A book like this one is an unrealistic portrayal of science only because it covers such a small fraction of all the arguments available.

Is Science Worth It?

What scientists do as they apply their methods is called *research*. Scientists who perform *basic or fundamental research* seek no specific result. Basic research is motivated essentially by curiosity. It is the study of some intriguing aspect of nature for its own sake. Basic researchers have revealed vast amounts of detail about the chemistry and function of genes, explored the behavior of electrons in semiconductors, revealed the structure of the atom, discovered radioactivity, and opened our minds to the immensity in both time and space of the universe in which we live.

Applied or strategic research is more mission-oriented. Applied scientists turn basic discoveries into devices and processes, such as transistors, computers, antibiotics, vaccines, nuclear weapons and power plants, and communications and weather satellites. There are thousands of such examples, all of which are answers to specific problems or needs, and many of which were quite surprising to the basic researchers who first gained the raw knowledge that led to these developments.

It is easy to see what drives the movement to put science to work. Society has a host of problems that cry out for immediate solutions. Yet there is also a need for research that is not tied to explicit need because such research undeniably supplies a great many of the ideas, facts, and techniques that problem-solving researchers then use in solving society's problems. Basic researchers, of course, use the same ideas, facts, and techniques as they continue their probings into the way nature works.

In 1945—after the scientific and technological successes of World War II—Vannevar Bush argued in *Science, the Endless Frontier* (Washington, DC:

National Science Foundation, 1990) that science would continue to benefit society best if it were supported with generous funding but not controlled by society. On the record, he was quite right, for the next half-century saw an unprecedented degree of progress in medicine, transportation, computers, communications, weapons, and a great deal more.

There have been and will continue to be problems that emerge from science and its applications in technology. Some people respond like Bill Joy, who argues in "Why the Future Doesn't Need Us," *Wired* (April 2000), that some technologies—notably robotics, genetic engineering, and nanotechnology—are so hazardous that we should refrain from developing them. On the whole, however, argue those like George Conrades ("Basic Research: Long-Term Problems Facing a Long-Term Investment," *Vital Speeches of the Day*, May 15, 1999), the value of the opportunities greatly outweighs the hazards of the problems. Others are less sanguine. David H. Guston and Kenneth Keniston ("Updating the Social Contract for Science," *Technology Review*, November/December 1994) argue that despite the obvious successes of science and technology, public attitudes toward scientific research also depend on the vast expense of the scientific enterprise and the perceived risks. As a result, the public should not be "excluded from decision making about science." That is, decisions should not be left to the experts alone.

Conflict also arises over the function of science in our society. Traditionally, scientists have seen themselves as engaged in the disinterested pursuit of knowledge, solving the puzzles set before them by nature with little concern for whether the solutions to these puzzles might prove helpful to human enterprises such as war, health care, and commerce, among many more. Yet again and again the solutions found by scientists have proved useful. They have founded industries. And scientists love to quote Michael Faraday who, when asked by politicians what good the new electricity might be, replied: "Someday, sir, you will tax it."

Not surprisingly, society has come to expect science to be useful. When asked to fund research, it feels it has the right to target research on issues of social concern, to demand results of immediate value, and to forbid research it deems dangerous or disruptive.

Private interests such as corporations often feel that they have similar rights in regard to research they have funded. For instance, tobacco companies have displayed a strong tendency to fund research that shows tobacco to be safe and to cancel funding for studies that come up with other results, which might interfere with profits.

One argument for public funding is that it avoids such conflict-of-interest issues. Yet politicians have their own interests, and their control of the purse strings—just like a corporation's—can give their demands a certain undeniable persuasiveness.

Public Policy

The question of targeting research is only one way in which science and technology intersect the broader realm of public policy. Here the question becomes how society should allocate its resources in general: toward education or prisons? health care or welfare? research or trade? encouraging new technologies or cleaning up after old ones?

The problem is that money is finite. Faced with competing worthy goals, we must make choices. We must also run the risk that our choices will turn out to have been foolish.

The Purpose of This Book

Is there any prospect that the debates over the proper function of science, the acceptability of new technologies, or the truth of forecasts of disaster will soon fall quiet? Surely not, for some of the old issues will forever refuse to die (think of evolution vs. creationism), and there will always be new issues to debate afresh. Some of the new issues will strut upon the stage of history only briefly, but they will in their existence reflect something significant about the way human beings view science and technology. Some will remain controversial as long as has evolution or the population explosion (which has been debated ever since Thomas Malthus' 1798 "Essay on the Principle of Population"). Some will flourish and fade and return to prominence; early editions of this book included the debate over whether the last stocks of smallpox virus should be destroyed; they were not, and the war on terrorism has brought awareness of the virus and the need for smallpox vaccine back onto the public stage. The loss of the space shuttle *Columbia* reawakened the debate over whether space should be explored by people or machines. Some issues will remain live but change their form, as has the debate over government interception of electronic communications. And there will always be more issues than can be squeezed into a book like this one—think, for instance, of the debate over whether elections should use electronic voting machines (discussed by Steve Ditlea, "Hack the Vote," *Popular Mechanics*, November 2004).

Since almost all of these science and technology issues can or will affect the conditions of our daily lives, we should know something about them. We can begin by examining the nature of science and a few of the current controversies over issues in science and technology. After all, if one does not know what science, the scientific mode of thought, and their strengths and limitations are, one cannot think critically and constructively about any issue with a scientific or technological component. Nor can one hope to make informed choices among competing scientific, technological, or political and social priorities.

On the Internet . . .

Union of Concerned Scientists

The Union of Concerned Scientists is an independent nonprofit alliance of more than 100,000 concerned citizen and scientist advocates dedicated to building a cleaner, healthier environment and a safer world.

http://www.ucsusa.org/

Science and Technology Policy

The Federal Office of Science and Technology Policy advises the President on how science and technology affects domestic and international affairs.

http://www.ostp.gov/

Institute for Creation Research

According to the developers of this site, the Institute for Creation Research (ICR) is a major center of scientific creationism.

http://www.icr.org

Committee for the Scientific Investigation of Claims of the Paranormal

The Committee for the Scientific Investigation of Claims of the Paranormal encourages the critical investigation of paranormal and fringe-science claims from a responsible, scientific point of view and disseminates factual information about the results of such inquiries to the scientific community and the public. It also promotes science and scientific inquiry, critical thinking, science education, and the use of reason in examining important issues, and it also publishes the *Skeptical Inquirer.*

http://www.csicop.org

Science and Creationism

The National Academy of Sciences maintains this page of links and resources on science and creationism.

http://www.nationalacademies.org/evolution/

PART 1

The Place of Science and Technology in Society

*T*he partnership between human society and science and technology is an uneasy one. Science and technology offer undoubted benefits, in both the short and long term, but they also challenge wisdom and political ideology. They also present us with new worries, especially when they fall into the wrong hands. The issues in this section deal with whether public policy should follow science or ideology, whether access to scientific and technological information should be controlled, and the debate over creationism versus evolution.

- Does Politics Come Before Science in Current Government Decision Making?

- Should Society Restrict the Publication of Unclassified but "Sensitive" Research?

- Should Creationism and Evolution Get Equal Time in Schools?

ISSUE 1

Does Politics Come Before Science in Current Government Decision Making?

YES: Union of Concerned Scientists, from *Scientific Integrity in Policymaking: An Investigation into the Bush Administration's Misuse of Science* (Union of Concerned Scientists, 2004)

NO: John H. Marburger III, "Statement on Scientific Integrity in the Bush Administration" (April 2, 2004)

ISSUE SUMMARY

YES: The Union of Concerned Scientists argues that the Bush administration displays a clear pattern of suppression and distortion of scientific findings across numerous federal agencies. These actions have consequences for human health, public safety, and community well-being.

NO: Speaking for the Bush administration, John H. Marburger III argues that the Bush administration strongly supports science and applies the highest scientific standards in decision making, but science is only one input to the policy-making process.

The history of science is also the history of struggle against those who insist—from religious, political, or other motives—that truth is what they say it is. Scientists insist on evidence and reason rather than creed or ideology, and the monuments on the field of battle between the two opposing forces include the tombstones of Galileo and Lysenko, among others.

Galileo Galilei used an early telescope to discover that Venus showed phases like Earth's moon and to find moons around Jupiter. The Roman Catholic Church, upset that Galileo's discoveries contradicted traditional teachings of the Church, demanded in 1633 that he recant. (See The Galileo Project at http://galileo.rice.edu/index.html.) Trofim Lysenko concluded that plants could be, in effect, trained to grow in inhospitable conditions. This view found favor with Soviet dictator Josef Stalin (whose ideology insisted on the "trainability" of human nature), who put Lysenko in charge of Soviet genetic and agricultural research and thereby set Soviet progress in these fields back by decades. (See http://www.wsws.org/articles/1999/feb1999/sov-gen.shtml.)

In the United States, science has enjoyed a very special relationship with government. Largely because science has generated answers to many pressing problems in areas ranging from war to medicine, the government has chosen to fund science with a liberal hand and, as well, to sponsor organizations such as the National Academies of Science, Engineering, and Medicine (http://www.nas.edu/) to provide objective advice to Congress and government agencies. Historically, the role of government has been to pose questions to be answered, or to offer money for research into specific problem areas. Government has *not* specified the answers sought or required that scientists belong to a particular political party or religion.

There have been exceptions. Robert Buderi, in "Technological McCarthyism," *Technology Review* (July/August 2003), reminds us that in 1954, J. Robert Oppenheimer, who played a crucial role in the development of the atomic bomb, was investigated for his opposition to the hydrogen bomb and for his "alleged left-wing associations." Oppenheimer lost his security clearance and was thereby barred from further work in his field. "Scientific McCarthyism" has become the term of choice for using a scientist's political or religious beliefs to judge their scientific work. It arises in connection with research into sexual behavior, AIDS, environmental science, and many other areas, notably where the conservative and religious right already "know" the answers the scientists seek in their research. (For example, do abstinence-only sex education programs keep young people from contracting HIV, or should they be taught about condoms?)

Another method of avoiding the scientific evidence and the need to make decisions that conflict with political or corporate agendas is to create the appearance of doubt. According to David Michaels, "Doubt Is Their Product," *Scientific American* (June 2005), "this administration has tried to facilitate and institutionalize the corporate strategy of manufacturing uncertainty," in part by putting industry representatives or industry-funded scientists on advisory panels. "Instead of allowing uncertainty to be an excuse for inaction," he says, "regulators . . . should use the best science available."

In February 2004, and again in March, the Union of Concerned Scientists (UCS) released a report that assembled numerous charges that the Bush administration had repeatedly and on an unprecedented scale used political "litmus tests" to choose members of scientific advisory panels, suppressed and distorted scientific findings, and otherwise tried to stack the scientific deck in favor of its policies, with important consequences for human health, public safety, and community well-being. In April 2004, the President's science advisor, John H. Marburger III, responded with a point-by-point rebuttal of the UCS report. He argued that the Bush administration strongly supports science and applies the highest scientific standards in decision making, but he also stressed that science is only one input in the policy process. He did not say that other factors can override scientific input, but that is an inescapable implication of his words.

Union of Concerned Scientists  **YES**

Scientific Integrity in Policymaking: An Investigation into the Bush Administration's Misuse of Science

Executive Summary

Science, like any field of endeavor, relies on freedom of inquiry; and one of the hallmarks of that freedom is objectivity. Now more than ever, on issues ranging from climate change to AIDS research to genetic engineering to food additives, government relies on the impartial perspective of science for guidance.

—President George H.W. Bush, 1990

The U.S. government runs on information—vast amounts of it. Researchers at the National Weather Service gather and analyze meteorological data to know when to issue severe-weather advisories. Specialists at the Federal Reserve Board collect and analyze economic data to determine when to raise or lower interest rates. Experts at the Centers for Disease Control examine bacteria and viral samples to guard against a large-scale outbreak of disease. The American public relies on the accuracy of such governmental data and upon the integrity of the researchers who gather and analyze it.

Equally important is the analysis of fact-based data in the government's policy-making process. When compelling evidence suggests a threat to human health from a contaminant in the water supply, the federal government may move to tighten drinking water standards. When data indicate structural problems in aging bridges that are part of the interstate highway system, the federal government may allocate emergency repair funds. When populations of an animal species are found to be declining rapidly, officials may opt to seek protection for those animals under the federal Endangered Species Act.

Given the myriad pressing problems involving complex scientific information—from the AIDS pandemic to the threat of nuclear proliferation—the American public expects government experts and researchers to provide more data and analysis than ever before, and to do so in an impartial and accurate way.

However, at a time when one might expect the federal government to increasingly rely on impartial researchers for the critical role they play in gathering and analyzing specialized data, there are numerous indications that the opposite is occurring. A growing number of scientists, policy makers, and technical specialists both inside and outside the government allege that the current Bush administration has suppressed or distorted the scientific analyses of federal agencies to bring these results in line with administration policy. In addition, these experts contend that irregularities in the appointment of scientific advisors and advisory panels are threatening to upset the legally mandated balance of these bodies.

The quantity and breadth of these charges warrant further examination, especially given the stature of many of the individuals lodging them. Toward this end, the Union of Concerned Scientists (UCS) undertook an investigation of many of the allegations made in the mainstream media, in scientific journals, and in overview reports issued from within the federal government and by nongovernmental organizations. To determine the validity of the allegations, UCS reviewed the public record, obtained internal government documents, and conducted interviews with many of the parties involved (including current and former government officials).

Findings of the Investigation

1. *There is a well-established pattern of suppression and distortion of scientific findings by high-ranking Bush administration political appointees across numerous federal agencies. These actions have consequences for human health, public safety, and community well-being.* Incidents involve air pollutants, heat-trapping emissions, reproductive health, drug resistant bacteria, endangered species, forest health, and military intelligence.

2. *There is strong documentation of a wide-ranging effort to manipulate the government's scientific advisory system to prevent the appearance of advice that might run counter to the administration's political agenda.* These actions include: appointing under-qualified individuals to important advisory roles including childhood lead poisoning prevention and reproductive health; applying political litmus tests that have no bearing on a nominee's expertise or advisory role; appointing a non-scientist to a senior position in the president's scientific advisory staff; and dismissing highly qualified scientific advisors.

3. *There is evidence that the administration often imposes restrictions on what government scientists can say or write about "sensitive" topics.* In this context, "sensitive" applies to issues that might provoke opposition from the administration's political and ideological supporters.

4. *There is significant evidence that the scope and scale of the manipulation, suppression, and misrepresentation of science by the Bush administration are unprecedented.*

Restoring Scientific Integrity to Federal Policymaking

This report calls on the president, Congress, scientists, and the public to take immediate steps to restore the integrity of science in the federal policymaking process.

The president should immediately request his science advisor to prepare a set of recommendations for executive orders and other actions to prohibit further censorship and distortion of scientific information from federal agencies, and put an end to practices that undermine the integrity of scientific advisory panels.

Congress should ensure that this administration and future administrations reverse this dangerous trend. To this end, Congress should: hold oversight hearings to investigate and assess the allegations raised in this report; ensure that the laws and rules that govern scientific advisory appointments require that all appointees meet high professional standards, and protect against the domination of such panels by individuals tied to entities that have a vested interest at stake; guarantee public access to government scientific studies and the findings of scientific advisory panels; and re-establish an organization able to independently assess and provide guidance to Congress on technical questions that have a bearing on public policy, similar to the former Office of Technology Assessment.

Scientists must encourage their professional societies and colleagues to become engaged in this issue, discuss their concerns directly with elected representatives, and communicate the importance of this issue to the public, both directly and through the media. And the *public* must also voice its concern about this issue to its elected representatives, letting them know that censorship and distortion of scientific knowledge are unacceptable in the federal government and must be halted.

Suppression and Distortion of Research Findings at Federal Agencies

> *Tinkering with scientific information, either striking it from reports or altering it, is becoming a pattern of behavior. It represents the politicizing of a scientific process, which at once manifests a disdain for professional scientists working for our government and a willingness to be less than candid with the American people.*

> —Roger G. Kennedy, Former Director of the National Park Service, Responding to the Doctoring of Findings on Yellowstone National Park.

Political partisans have long disagreed over each administration's politics and policy. But there is little disagreement about the need for elected and appointed officials to have access to rigorous, objective scientific research and analysis, and to fully understand its implications for addressing the problems they are trying to solve. To be sure, politics plays an unavoidable and, at times, valuable role in policymaking because many factors in addition to science and technology must be weighed in decision making. To make policy choices, government officials must frequently balance the needs of one constituency against another. Consider, for instance, the policy quandary over nuclear waste from the nation's nuclear power plants. Politics and science both play a crucial role as policy makers try to balance the risk to public health and the environment from the proposed spent fuel repository at Yucca Mountain in Nevada versus the long-term health risks to people living near one of the country's numerous current nuclear spent fuel storage facilities. In health care, decision makers must weigh the funding of research on rare serious diseases against broad public health issues such as funding cholesterol screening or childhood vaccinations.

There is, however, a crucial difference between political fights over policy and the manipulation of the scientific underpinnings of the policy-making process itself. Distorting that process runs the risk that decision makers will not have access to the factual information needed to help them make informed decisions that affect human health, public safety, and the well-being of our communities.

The following section details the results of a UCS investigation into numerous allegations that the current administration has undermined the quality of the science that informs policy making by suppressing, distorting, or manipulating the work done by scientists at federal agencies.

Distorting and Suppressing Climate Change Research

Since taking office, the Bush administration has consistently sought to undermine the public's understanding of the view held by the vast majority of climate scientists that human-caused emissions of carbon dioxide and other heat-trapping gases are making a discernible contribution to global warming.

After coming to office, the administration asked the National Academy of Sciences (NAS) to review the findings of the Intergovernmental Panel on Climate Change (IPCC) and provide further assessment of what climate science could say about this issue. The NAS panel rendered a strong opinion, which, in essence, confirmed that of the IPCC. The American Geophysical Union, the world's largest organization of earth scientists, has also released a strong statement describing human-caused disruptions of Earth's climate. Yet Bush administration spokespersons continue to contend that the uncertainties in climate projections and fossil fuel emissions are too great to warrant mandatory action to slow emissions.

In May 2002, President Bush expressed disdain for a State Department report to the United Nations that pointed to a clear human role in the accumulation of heat-trapping gases and detailed the likely negative consequences of climate change; the president called it "a report put out by the bureaucracy." In September 2002, the administration removed a section on climate change from the Environmental Protection Agency's (EPA) annual air pollution report, even though the climate issue had been discussed in the report for the preceding five years.

Then, in one well-documented case, the Bush administration blatantly tampered with the integrity of scientific analysis at a federal agency when, in June 2003, the White House tried to make a series of changes to the EPA's draft Report on the Environment.

A front-page article in *The New York Times* broke the news that White House officials tried to force the EPA to substantially alter the report's section on climate change. The EPA report, which referenced the NAS review and other studies, stated that human activity is contributing significantly to climate change. . . .

In a political environment now-departed EPA Administrator Christine Todd Whitman has since described as "brutal," the entire section on climate change was ultimately deleted from the version released for public comment. According to internal EPA documents and interviews with EPA researchers, the agency staff chose this path rather than compromising their credibility by misrepresenting the scientific consensus. Doing otherwise, as one current, high-ranking EPA official puts it, would "poorly represent the science and ultimately undermine the credibility of the EPA and the White House."

The EPA's decision to delete any mention of global warming from its report drew widespread criticism. Many scientists and public officials—Republicans and Democrats alike—were moved to decry the administration's political manipulation in this case. Notably, the incident drew the ire of Russell Train, who served as EPA administrator under Presidents Nixon and Ford. In a letter to *The New York Times,* Train stated that the Bush administration's actions undermined the independence of the EPA and were virtually unprecedented for the degree of their political manipulation of the agency's research. As Train put it, the "interest of the American people lies in having full disclosure of the facts." Train also noted that, "In all my time at the EPA, I don't recall any regulatory decision that was driven by political considerations. More to the present point, never once, to my best recollection, did either the Nixon or Ford White House ever try to tell me how to make a decision."

Were the case an isolated incident, it could perhaps be dismissed as an anomaly. On the contrary, the Bush administration has repeatedly intervened to distort or suppress climate change research findings despite promises by the president that, "my Administration's climate change policy will be science-based."

Despite the widespread agreement in the scientific community that human activity is contributing to global climate change, as demonstrated by the consensus of international experts on the IPCC, the Bush administration has sought to exaggerate uncertainty by relying on disreputable and fringe science reports and preventing informed discussion on the issue. As one current EPA scientist puts it, the Bush administration often "does not even invite the EPA into the discussion" on climate change issues. "This administration seems to want to make environmental policy at the White House," the government scientist explains. "I suppose that is their right. But one has to ask: on the basis of what information is this policy being promulgated? What views are being represented? Who is involved in the decision making? What kind of credible expertise is being brought to bear?"

Dr. Rosina Bierbaum, a Clinton administration appointee to the Office of Science and Technology Policy (OSTP) who also served during the first year of the Bush administration, offers a disturbing window on the process. From the start, Bierbaum contends, "The scientists [who] knew the most about climate change at OSTP were not allowed to participate in deliberations on the issue within the White House inner circle."

Through such consistent tactics, the Bush administration has not only distorted scientific and technical analysis on global climate change and suppressed the dissemination of research results, but has avoided fashioning any policies that would significantly reduce the threat implied by those findings. . . .

Censoring Information on Air Quality

Mercury Emissions from Power Plants
The Bush administration has long attempted to avoid issuing new standards to regulate mercury emissions by coal-fired power plants based on Maximum Achievable Control Technology (MACT), as required by the Clean Air Act. Mercury is a neurotoxin that can cause brain damage and harm reproduction in women and wildlife; coal-fired power plants are the nation's largest source of mercury air emissions, emitting about 48 tons annually.

As a prelude to the current debate, published accounts to date have documented that senior Bush officials suppressed and sought to manipulate government information about mercury contained in an EPA report on children's health and the environment. As the EPA readied the report for completion in May 2002, the White House Office of Management and Budget and the OSTP began a lengthy review of the document. In February 2003, after nine months of delay by the White House, a frustrated EPA official leaked the draft report to the *Wall Street Journal*, including its finding that including that finding that 8 percent of women between the ages of 16 and 49 have mercury levels in the blood that could lead to reduced IQ and motor skills in their offspring.

The finding provides strong evidence in direct contradiction to the administration's desired policy of reducing regulation on coal-fired power plants and was, many sources suspect, the reason for the lengthy suppression by the White House. On February 24, 2003, just days after the leak, the EPA's report was finally released to the public. Perhaps most troubling about this incident is that the report may never have surfaced at all had it not been leaked to the press. . . .

Distorting Scientific Knowledge on Reproductive Health Issues

Abstinence-only Education
Since his tenure as governor of Texas, President Bush has made no secret of his view that sex education should teach teenagers "abstinence only" rather than including information on other ways to avoid sexually transmitted diseases and pregnancy. Unfortunately, despite spending more than $10 million on abstinence-only programs in Texas alone, this strategy has not been shown to be effective at curbing teen pregnancies or halting the spread of HIV and other

sexually transmitted diseases. During President Bush's tenure as governor of Texas from 1995 to 2000, for instance, with abstinence-only programs in place, the state ranked last in the nation in the decline of teen birth rates among 15- to 17-year-old females. Overall, the teen pregnancy rate in Texas was exceeded by only four other states.

The American Medical Association, the American Academy of Pediatrics, the American Public Health Association, and the American College of Obstetricians and Gynecologists all support comprehensive sex education programs that encourage abstinence while also providing adolescents with information on how to protect themselves against sexually transmitted diseases. In fact, a recent systematic analysis of pregnancy prevention strategies for adolescents found that, far from reducing unwanted pregnancies, abstinence programs actually "may increase pregnancies in partners of male participants."

The fact that the Bush administration ignores the scientific evidence, troubling though that is, is not the primary concern of this report. Rather, it is the fact that the Bush administration went further by distorting science-based performance measures to test whether abstinence-only programs were proving effective, such as charting the birth rate of female program participants. In place of such established measures, the Bush administration has required the government to track only participants' program attendance and attitudes, measures designed to obscure the lack of efficacy of abstinence-only programs.

In addition to distorting performance measures, the Bush administration has suppressed other information at odds with its preferred policies. At the behest of higher-ups in the Bush administration, according to a source inside the CDC, the agency was forced to discontinue a project called "Programs that Work," which identified sex education programs found to be effective in scientific studies. All five of the programs identified in 2002 involved comprehensive sex education for teenagers and none were abstinence-only programs. In ending the project, the CDC removed all information about these programs from its website. One scientist, recently departed from a high-ranking position at CDC, recounts that, on one occasion, even top staff scientists at the agency were required by the administration to attend a day-long session purportedly devoted to the "science of abstinence." As this source puts it, "out of the entire session, conducted by a nonscientist, the only thing resembling science was one study reportedly in progress and another not even begun." Despite the absence of supporting data, this source and others contend, CDC scientists were regularly reminded to push the administration's abstinence-only stance. As he puts it, "The effect was very chilling."

HIV/AIDS

Along similar lines, at the instigation of higher-ups in the administration, fact-based information on the CDC's website has been altered to raise scientifically questionable doubt about the efficacy of condoms in preventing the spread of HIV/AIDS.

A fact sheet on the CDC website that included information on proper condom use, the effectiveness of different types of condoms, and studies showing that condom education does not promote sexual activity was replaced in October 2002 with a document that emphasizes condom failure rates and the effectiveness of abstinence. When a source inside the CDC questioned the actions, she was told that the changes were directed by Bush administration officials at the Department of Health and Human Services.

Breast Cancer

Similarly, in a case *The New York Times* labeled "an egregious distortion of the evidence," information suggesting a link between abortion and breast cancer was posted on the National Cancer Institute website despite objections from CDC staff, who noted that substantial scientific study has long refuted the connection. After public outcry on the matter, the information has since been revised and no longer implies a connection. While the correct information is currently available on the website, it is troubling that public pressure was necessary to halt this promotion of scientifically inaccurate information to the public.

Suppressing Analysis on Airborne Bacteria

One particularly dramatic and well-documented case involves Dr. James Zahn, a research microbiologist at the USDA who asserts that he was prohibited on no fewer than 11 occasions from publicizing his research on the potential hazards to human health posed by airborne bacteria resulting from farm wastes.

Zahn's research had discovered significant levels of antibiotic-resistant bacteria in the air near hog confinement operations in Iowa and Missouri. But, as Zahn recounts, he was repeatedly barred by his superiors from presenting his research at scientific conferences in 2002. In at least one instance, a message from a supervisor advised Zahn that, "politically sensitive and controversial issues require discretion." . . .

Manipulation of Science Regarding the Endangered Species Act

A wide array of scientists, government officials, and environmental groups has charged that the Bush administration is engaged in a systematic attempt to weaken the Endangered Species Act. The administration has supported pending amendments before Congress that would make it harder to list threatened and endangered species, in particular by greatly limiting the use of population modeling. This technique is the most credible way to assess the likelihood that a small species population will survive in a given habitat. Perhaps most troubling, however, has been the way in which the Bush administration has suppressed or even attempted to distort the scientific findings of its own agencies to further its political agenda. These actions go well beyond a policy fight over the Endangered Species Act and represent a manipulation of the scientific underpinnings of the policymaking process itself. . . .

Manipulating the Scientific Process on Forest Management

In an incident involving the management of national forests, the Bush administration created a "review team" made up of predominantly nonscientists who proceeded to overrule a $12 million science-based plan for managing old-growth forest habitat and reducing the risk of fire in 11 national forests. This so-called Sierra Nevada Framework, which was adopted by the Clinton administration in 2001 after nine years of research by more than 100 scientists from the Forest Service and academia, had been viewed by the experts who reviewed it as an exemplary use of credible science in forest policy.

The Bush administration's proposed changes to the plan include harvesting more of the large trees, which may double or triple harvest levels over the first 10 years of the plan. Other changes call for relaxing restrictions on cattle grazing in some areas where the original plan significantly reduced grazing due to the potentially critical impact on sensitive species.

Forest Service officials justified these changes in part by stating that the original plan relies too much on prescribed burning and would fail to " . . . effectively protect the general forest areas from fire." Indeed, ecologically sustainable thinning that minimizes risks to threatened and endangered species may also be an appropriate tool for reducing risk of catastrophic fire in these forests. The Forest Service claims that these changes are "grounded in the best available scientific information." However, a scientific review panel put together by the Forest Service found that the revisions failed to consider key scientific information regarding fire, impacts on forest health, and endangered species. . . .

An Unprecedented Pattern of Behavior

No administration has been above inserting politics into science from time to time. However, a considerable number of individuals who have served in positions directly involved in the federal government's use of scientific knowledge and expertise have asserted that the Bush administration is, to an unprecedented degree, distorting and manipulating the science meant to assist the formation and implementation of policy. The following are accounts from a number of authoritative sources including political appointees from past Republican administrations, senior science advisors who have served both Republican and Democratic administrations, and long-term civil servants from federal agencies.

Disseminating Research from Federal Agencies

William Ruckelshaus, the first EPA administrator under President Nixon, and his successor, Russell Train, have spoken out about the matter. Specifically, Ruckelshaus told the press, "Is the analysis flawed? That is a legitimate reason for not releasing [a science-based analysis]. But if you don't like the outcome that might result from the analysis, that is not a legitimate reason." Train commented, "My sense is that, from the beginning of the Bush administration, the White House has constantly injected itself into the way the EPA approaches and decides the critical issues before it. The agency has had little or no independence. I think that is a very great mistake, and one for which the American people could pay over the long run in compromised health and reduced quality of life."

Scientific advisors to government also weigh in on this matter. Dr. Wolfgang K.H. Panofsky, a distinguished physicist who worked on the Manhattan Project and served on the Presidential Scientific Advisory Committee and in other high-level scientific advisory roles in the Eisenhower, Kennedy, Johnson, and Nixon administrations, states that the current administration has isolated itself from independent scientific advice to an unprecedented degree. Dr. Marvin Goldberger, a former president of the California Institute of Technology who has advised both Republican and Democratic administrations on nuclear weapons issues, compares the attitude of this administration to those he has served by stating, "Politics plays no role in scientists' search for understanding and applications of the laws of nature. To ignore or marginalize scientific input to policy decisions, where relevant, on the basis of politics is to endanger our national economic and military security."

According to Dr. Margaret Scarlett, a former CDC staff member who served in the agency for 15 years, most recently in the Office of HIV/AIDS Policy, "The current administration has instituted an unheard-of level of micromanagement in the programmatic and scientific activities of CDC. We're seeing a clear substitution of ideology for science and it is causing many committed scientists to leave the agency." Scarlett also points out that, "Ronald Reagan was very uncomfortable with the issue of sex education and the transmission of HIV, which was still largely stigmatized at the time. Nonetheless, with the help of CDC, his administration got factual information out to every household in the country about the problem. His actions stand in dramatic contrast to the sorry record of the current administration on informing the public about issues related to sex education and HIV transmission."

REP America, the national grassroots organization of Republicans for Environmental Protection, has also raised concerns about the administration's approach to scientific research: "Withholding of vital environmental information is getting to be a bad habit with the Bush administration."

Irregularities in Appointments to Scientific Advisory Panels

Donald Kennedy, editor of the journal *Science*, former president of Stanford University, and a former FDA commissioner, remarked in early 2003, "I don't think any administration has penetrated so deeply into the advisory committee structure as this one, and I think it matters. If you start picking people by their ideology instead of their scientific credentials you are inevitably reducing the quality of the advisory group."

Dr. D. Allan Bromley, science advisor in the first Bush administration, noted at a meeting of former OSTP directors that nominees are likely to face detailed questioning about their positions on issues ranging from global warming to stem cell research. "There are too many litmus tests," Bromley asserts.

Professor Lewis M. Branscomb is a highly regarded scientist who served as director of the National Bureau of Standards (now the National Institute of Standards and Technology) in the Nixon administration, vice president and chief scientist at IBM, and president of the American Physical Society. Dr. Branscomb recently stated, "I'm not aware that [Nixon] ever hand-picked ideologues to serve on advisory committees, or dismissed from advisory committees very well-qualified people if he didn't like their views. . . . What's going on now is in many ways more insidious. It happens behind the curtain. I don't think we've had this kind of cynicism with respect to objective scientific advice since I've been watching government, which is quite a long time."

Dr. Lynn Goldman, a pediatrician and professor at the Bloomberg School of Public Health at Johns Hopkins University and former assistant administrator of the EPA, makes the same point emphatically about policymaking in the previous administration: "The Clinton administration did not do this. . . . They did not exclude people based on some sort of litmus test." She adds that this kind of activity represents "a threat to the fundamental principle that we want to make decisions based on the best available science."

Statement of the Honorable John H. Marburger, III On Scientific Integrity in the Bush Administration April 2, 2004

President Bush believes policies should be made with the best and most complete information possible, and expects his Administration to conduct its business with integrity and in a way that fulfills that belief. I can attest from my personal experience and direct knowledge that this Administration is implementing the President's policy of strongly supporting science and applying the highest scientific standards in decision-making.

The Administration's strong commitment to science is evidenced by impressive increases devoted to Federal research and development (R&D) budgets. With the President's FY 2005 budget request, total R&D investment during this Administration's first term will have increased 44 percent, to a record $132 billion in FY 2005, as compared to $91 billion in FY 2001. President Bush's FY 2005 budget request commits 13.5 percent of total discretionary outlays to R&D—the highest level in 37 years.

In addition to enabling a strong foundation of scientific research through unprecedented Federal funding, this Administration also believes in tapping the best scientific minds—both inside and outside the government—for policy input and advice. My office establishes interagency working groups under the aegis of the National Science and Technology Council for this purpose. In addition, this Administration has sought independent advice, most often through the National Academies, on many issues. Recent National Academies reviews of air pollution policy, fuel economy standards, the use of human tests for pesticide toxicity, and planned or ongoing reviews on dioxin and perchlorate in the environment are examples. The Administration's climate change program is based on a National Academies report that was requested by the Administration in the spring of 2001, and the National Academies continues to review our programs and strategic research planning in this field. The frequency of such referrals, and the high degree to which their advice has been incorporated into the policies of this Administration, is consistent with a desire to strengthen technical input into decision-making.

Statement on Scientific Integrity in the Bush Administration, April 2, 2004. Notes deleted.

Climate change has proven to be a contentious science-related issue. President Bush clearly acknowledged the role of human activity in increased atmospheric concentrations of greenhouse gases in June 2001, stating "concentration of greenhouse gases, especially CO_2, have increased substantially since the beginning of the industrial revolution. And the National Academy of Sciences indicates that the increase is due in large part to human activity." That speech launched programs to accelerate climate change science and technology to address remaining uncertainties in the science, develop adaptation and mitigation mechanisms, and invest in clean energy technologies to reduce the projected growth in global greenhouse gas emissions. In 2004, the U.S. will spend approximately $4 billion in climate change science and technology research.

The President created the new U.S. Climate Change Science Program (CCSP) to refocus a disorganized interagency activity into a cohesive program, oriented at resolving key uncertainties and enhancing decision making capabilities. The Strategy was heartily endorsed by the National Academies in its recent review. Their report, *Implementing Climate and Global Change Research— A Review of the Final U.S. Climate Change Science Program Strategic Plan*, stated "In fact, the approaches taken by the CCSP to receive and respond to comments from a large and broad group of scientists and stakeholders, including a two-stage independent review of the plan, set a high standard for government research programs. . . . Advancing science on all fronts identified by the program will be of vital importance to the Nation."

In this Administration, science strongly informs policy. It is important to remember, however, that even when the science is clear—and often it is not— it is but one input into the policy process.

Regulatory decisions provide the trigger for some of the most contentious policy debates. Science can play an important role in these policy decisions, and this Administration has sought to strengthen, not undermine, this role. In fact, the Office of Management and Budget (OMB) has for the first time hired toxicologists, environmental engineers, and public health scientists to review regulations and help agencies strengthen their scientific peer review processes. This increased attention to science in the regulatory process is providing a more solid foundation for regulatory decisions. As several recent examples demonstrate, emerging scientific data has prompted swift action by the Bush Administration to protect public health, strongly guided by advanced scientific knowledge:

- On May 23, 2003 the Environmental Protection Agency (EPA) proposed a new regulation to reduce by 90 percent the amount of pollution from off-road diesel engines used in mining, agriculture, and construction. This proposed rule stemmed from collaboration between EPA and OMB. Recent scientific data from the Harvard School of Public Health indicates that diesel engine exhaust is linked to the development of cardiopulmonary problems and also aggravates respiratory health problems in children and the elderly.
- On July 11, 2003 the Food and Drug Administration required that food labels for consumers contain new information on trans-fat

content in addition to existing information on saturated fat content. This rule, requested by the White House via a public OMB letter, responded to emerging scientific data indicating that intake of trans-fats (found in margarine and other foods) is linked to coronary heart disease.

- On December 29, 2003, the Department of Transportation requested public comment on ideas for potential reform of the CAFE program. Several potential reform ideas contained in that request for comment come directly from a 2002 National Academies report on the effectiveness of the current CAFE program.

Regarding the document that was released on February 18, 2004 by the Union of Concerned Scientists (UCS), I believe the UCS accusations are wrong and misleading. The accusations in the document are inaccurate, and certainly do not justify the sweeping conclusions of either the document or the accompanying statement. I believe the document has methodological flaws that undermine its own conclusions, not the least of which is the failure to consider publicly available information or to seek and reflect responses or explanations from responsible government officials. Unfortunately, these flaws are not necessarily obvious to those who are unfamiliar with the issues, and the misleading, incomplete, and even personal accusations made in the document concern me deeply. It is my hope that the detailed response I submit today will allay the concerns of the scientists who signed the UCS statement.

I can say from personal experience that the accusation of a litmus test that must be met before someone can serve on an advisory panel is preposterous. After all, President Bush sought me out to be his Science Advisor—the highest-ranking S&T official in the federal government—and I am a lifelong Democrat. . . .

Response to the Union of Concerned Scientists' February 2004 Document

I. The UCS' Claim of "Suppression and Distortion of Research Findings at Federal Agencies"

The UCS' Claims on "Distorting and Suppressing Climate Change Research"

- The UCS document claims that "the Bush administration has consistently sought to undermine the public's understanding of the view held by the vast majority of climate scientists that human-caused emissions of carbon dioxide and other heat-trapping gases are making a discernible contribution to global warming."

This statement is not true. In his June 11, 2001, Rose Garden speech on climate change, the President stated that the "[c]oncentration of greenhouse gases, especially CO_2, have increased substantially since the beginning of the Industrial Revolution. And the National Academy of Sciences indicate that the increase is due in large part to human activity. . . . While scientific uncertainties remain, we can now begin to address the factors that contribute to climate change." In this speech, the President cited the National Academy's Climate Change Science report that was initiated at the Administration's request, and launched a major, prioritized scientific effort to improve our understanding of global climate change.

Moreover, the President's Climate Change Science Program (CCSP) has developed its plans through an open and transparent process. In the development of its Strategic Plan, released in July 2003, the CCSP incorporated comments and advice from hundreds of scientists both from the U.S. and around the world. The CCSP Strategic Plan received a strong endorsement from the National Academy of Sciences in a February 2004 review, which commended the work of the CCSP.

- The UCS claims that the "Bush administration blatantly tampered with the integrity of scientific analysis at a Federal agency when, in June 2003, the White House tried to make a series of changes to the EPA's draft Report on the Environment."

This statement is false. In fact, the Administrator of the EPA decided not to include a short summary on climate change. An ordinary review process indicated that the complexity of climate change science was not adequately addressed in EPA's draft document. Instead, the final EPA report referred readers to the far more expansive and complete exposition of climate change knowledge, the Climate Change Science Program (CCSP) Strategic Plan. The Administration chose, appropriately, to present information in a single, more expansive and far more complete format. This choice of presentation format did not influence the quality or integrity of the scientific analysis or its dissemination.

- The UCS quotes an unnamed EPA scientist as saying that the Administration "does not even invite the EPA into the discussion" on climate change issues, and cites a previous Clinton Administration OSTP official, Dr. Rosina Bierbaum, as claiming that the Administration excluded OSTP scientists from the climate change discussions.

These accusations are wrong. The EPA, in fact, is a key participant in the development and implementation of climate change policy in the Bush Administration. The EPA participates in the development of Administration policy on climate change through the cabinet-level Committee on Climate Science and Technology Integration, which was created in February 2002. The EPA is also a member of subsidiary bodies, such as the Interagency Working Group on Climate Change Science and Technology, the Climate Change Science Program and the Climate Change Technology Program. (A table illustrating the Bush Administration's climate change program's organization can be found on page 9 of the CCSP Strategic Plan (2003)). Moreover, the EPA is a co-chair of the National Science and Technology Council's Committee on Environment and Natural Resources (CENR). CENR has oversight of and responsibility for the Subcommittee on Global Change Research. (This subcommittee holds the same membership and is functionally the same entity as the Climate Change Science Program, noted above.)

Dr. Bierbaum's claim refers to cabinet-level discussions that led to the development of the Administration's climate change organization described above. The cabinet-level discussions referenced by Dr. Bierbaum included numerous, respected Federal career scientists including Dr. David Evans, former Assistant Administrator for Oceanic and Atmospheric Research at NOAA, Dr. Ari Patrinos, Associate Director of the Office of Biological and Environmental Research at the Department of Energy, and Dr. Dan Albritton, Director of the Aeronomy Laboratory of Oceanic and Atmospheric Research at NOAA. Starting with these early discussions, the Bush Administration's climate change organization has fully involved climate change experts from throughout the Federal government.

As already noted, subsequent to its initial internal discussions, the Administration submitted the draft CCSP Strategic Plan to some of the Nation's most qualified scientists at the National Academy of Sciences for review. The Academy made numerous recommendations, which the CCSP incorporated. The CCSP then resubmitted its plans to the Academy for further review, and just recently, the NAS returned a highly favorable review. The Administration developed the climate change science strategic plan through an open, back-and-forth process. . . .

The UCS' Claims on "Censoring Information on Air Quality"

- The UCS claims that the Administration was withholding the publication of an EPA report on children's health and the environment in order to avoid the issue of mercury emissions by coal-fired power plants. The UCS also claims that the Administration suppressed and sought to manipulate government information about mercury contained in the EPA report.

This is not true. The interagency review of the EPA report on children's health and the environment occurred independently of the Administration's deliberations on mercury emissions from power plants. The interagency review process is the standard operating procedure for reports that include areas of scientific and policy importance to multiple agencies. As such, the report was reviewed by a number of scientists and analysts across Federal agencies. During this review, other agencies expressed concerns about the report. OSTP worked collaboratively with EPA staff on addressing interagency comments to make certain that the proposed indicators had a robust scientific basis and were presented in an understandable manner.

The report contained a statement that 8% of women of child-bearing age had at least 5.8 ppb of mercury in their blood in 1999–2000 and therefore children born to these women are at some increased risk. This information was available well before the EPA report both in raw form through the CDC and in an interagency analysis (CDC's Morbidity and Mortality Weekly Review, 2001) that indicated that approximately 10% of women of child-bearing age had blood mercury levels above the EPA reference dose, as opposed to the 8% level noted in EPA's report. The updated analysis in EPA's report and later published in the scientific literature (Journal of the American Medical Association, 2003) included an additional year of data and found the level to be 8%. These updated risk levels were used by the Administration in the preparation of its two regulatory proposals to reduce mercury emissions from coal-fired power plants.

The final report was released in February 2003, as soon as the inter-agency review process was completed.

- The UCS states that "the new rules the EPA has finally proposed for regulating power plants' mercury emissions were discovered to have no fewer than 12 paragraphs lifted, sometimes verbatim, from a legal document prepared by industry lawyers."

The UCS' implication that industry is writing government regulations is wrong. The reference here is to a preamble of a proposed EPA rule to control (for the first time) mercury emissions from power plants. The text in question is in the preamble, not the proposed rule itself. The preamble is intended to engage the public and encourage comments, including both assenting and dissenting viewpoints. All agencies, including EPA, openly seek public comment during rulemaking proceedings in order to obtain useful information and advice that is accepted or rejected or used in part.

Such direct use of submitted memoranda should not have occurred. However, the text at issue was taken from memoranda that were publicly presented to an advisory group made up of environmental activists, State officials, and industry representatives. These documents are openly available in the public docket. The UCS' allegations are based on text that had nothing to do with the integrity of the science used by EPA. . . .

The UCS' Claims on "Distorting Scientific Knowledge on Reproductive Health Issues"

- The UCS claims that the Administration distorted the U.S. Centers for Disease Control and Prevention's (CDC's) science-based performance measures to test whether abstinence-only programs were proving effective, and attempted to obscure the lack of efficacy of such programs.

This accusation is false. The UCS mischaracterizes the program, its performance measures, and the reasons behind changes that were made to those performance measures. There were no CDC science-based performance measures associated with this program. Currently, the Federal government funds abstinence-only education programs through the Health Resources and Services Administration, not CDC. The program was never designed as a scientific study, and so even if the original performance measures had been kept, little or no scientifically useable data would be obtained. However, other independent evaluation efforts are underway that *are* intended to address questions of the effectiveness of abstinence only programs.

- The UCS claims that a CDC condom fact sheet posted on its web site was removed and replaced with a document that emphasizes condom failure rates and the effectiveness of abstinence.

This accusation is a distortion of the facts. The CDC routinely takes information off its website and replaces it with more up-to-date information. Recently updated topics include anthrax, West Nile Virus, and other health issues for which new information had become available. The condom fact sheet was removed from the website for scientific review and was subsequently updated to reflect the results of a condom effectiveness review conducted by the National Institutes of Health, as well as new research from other academic institutions. The condom information sheet was re-posted with the new information.

The "Programs That Work" website was also removed because the programs it listed were limited. CDC is exploring new and appropriate means to identify and characterize interventions that have scientifically credible evidence of effectiveness. In addition, CDC is currently working on a new initiative that is aimed at better addressing the needs of schools and communities by providing assistance in selecting health education curricula based on the best evidence available.

- The UCS alleges that information suggesting a link between abortion and breast cancer was posted on the National Cancer Institute (NCI) website despite substantial scientific study refuting the connection, and only revised after a public outcry.

This claim distorts the facts. The NCI fact sheet "Abortion and Breast Cancer" has been revised several times since it was first written in 1994. NCI temporarily removed the fact sheet from the website when it became clear that there was conflicting information in the published literature. In order to clarify the issue, in February 2003 a workshop of over 100 of the world's leading experts who study pregnancy and breast cancer risk was convened. Workshop participants reviewed existing population-based, clinical, and animal studies on the relationship between pregnancy and breast cancer risk, including studies of induced and spontaneous abortions. They concluded that having an abortion or miscarriage does not increase a woman's subsequent risk of developing breast cancer. A summary of their findings, titled *Summary Report: Early Reproductive Events and Breast Cancer Workshop*, can be found at http://cancer.gov/cancerinfo/ere-workshop-report. A revised fact sheet was posted on the NCI website shortly after the workshop reflecting the findings.

The UCS' Claims on "Suppressing Analysis on Airborne Bacteria"

- The UCS claims that a former Agricultural Research Service (ARS) scientist at Ames, Iowa, Dr. James Zahn, was prohibited on no fewer than 11 occasions from publicizing his research on the potential hazards to human health posed by airborne bacteria resulting from farm wastes.

This accusation is not true. Dr. Zahn did not have any scientific data or expertise in the scientific area in question. Dr. Zahn's assigned research project, as part of the Swine Odor and Manure Management Research Unit, dealt with the chemical constituency of volatiles from swine manure and ways to abate odors. In the course of this research, Dr. Zahn observed incidentally that when dust was collected from a hog feeding operation, some of the "dust" emitted from these facilities contained traces of antibiotic resistant bacteria. The recorded data were severely limited in scope and quantity, and did not represent a scientific study of human health threats.

In February 2002, Dr. Zahn was invited to speak at the Adair (Iowa) County Board of Health meeting in Greenfield, Iowa. Permission was initially granted by ARS management for Dr. Zahn to speak because it was thought that he was being invited to speak on his primary area of scientific expertise and government work, management of odors from hog operations. Permission for Dr. Zahn to speak representing the ARS at the meeting was withdrawn when it was learned that Dr. Zahn was expected to speak on health risks of hog confinement operations, an area in which Dr. Zahn did not have any scientific data or expertise.

The accusation of "no fewer than 11 occasions" of ARS denials to Dr. Zahn for him to present or publicize his research is not accurate. He was approved to report on his preliminary observations of dust borne antibiotic resistant bacteria at the 2001 meeting of the American Society of Animal Science and at a 2001 National Pork Board Symposium. He also was approved on numerous occasions to present and publish his research on volatiles and odors from swine manure. However, on five occasions he was not authorized to discuss the public health ramifications of his observations on the spread of resistant bacteria, because he had no data or expertise with respect to public health. Three of these occasions were local Iowa public community meetings; two others were professional scientific meetings.

- The UCS also claims that the USDA has issued a directive to staff scientists to seek prior approval before publishing any research or speaking publicly on "sensitive issues."

This is not true. USDA-ARS headquarters has had a long-standing, routine practice (at least 20 years) that has spanned several Administrations to require review of research reports of high-visibility topics (called the "List of Sensitive Issues"). ARS headquarters review, when required, do not censor, or otherwise deny publication of, the research findings, but may aid in the interpretation and communication of the results, including providing advance alert to others. The purpose of this review is to keep ARS Headquarters officials informed before publication and in an otherwise timely way of new developments on cutting-edge research, controversial subjects, or other matters of potential special interest to the Secretary's Office, Office of Communications, USDA agency heads (particularly those other agencies in USDA that depend on ARS for the scientific basis for policy development and program operations), scientific collaborators, the news media, and/or the general public. This practice deals with research reporting only and does not relate to the initial research priority setting process or to determining which studies will be undertaken. To the contrary, the "special issues" are mostly high-priority items and receive considerable research attention. . . .

The UCS' Claims on "Manipulation of Science Regarding the Endangered Species Act"

- The UCS claims that the Administration is attempting to weaken the Endangered Species Act.

This accusation is false. The current listing situation results from Fish and Wildlife Service (FWS) practices in place *before the Bush Administration took office*. The FWS listing budget is currently consumed by court-ordered listings and critical habitat designations. These court orders result from pre-2001 FWS decisions to list endangered species but not to designate associated critical habitat as required by the Act as well as to ignore pending petitions to list species. This practice resulted in a flood of litigation forcing FWS to act on petitions that had been languishing for years as well as to designate critical habitat for already listed species. Fulfilling the resulting court mandates expends all of FWS's listing budget (the Administration has taken steps to redirect additional funds to this budget account, and the President's FY05 Budget requests an increase of more than 50 percent). With respect to the critical habitat designations, officials from both the current and prior administrations have said that these lawsuits prevent FWS from taking higher priority actions such as listing new species. Moreover, without regard to the current court-driven budgetary situation, the number of new species listed as endangered during a particular time period varies over time for numerous reasons, and as such is not an appropriate measure of the success of the Act.

This Administration is committed to working in partnership with States, local governments, tribes, landowners, conservation groups, and others to conserve species through voluntary agreements and grant programs in addition to ESA procedures. For FY 2005, the President's proposed budget includes more than $260 million in the Interior Department budget alone for cooperative conservation programs for endangered species and other wildlife. The President created the new Landowner Incentive Program and the Private Stewardship Initiative grant programs to help private landowners conserve endangered species habitat on their property. In early March 2004, for example, Secretary Norton announced $25.8 million in cost-share grants to help private landowners conserve and restore the habitat of endangered species and other at-risk plants and animals. These grants are going to support projects in 40 states and the Virgin Islands.

Because the large majority of threatened and endangered species depend on habitat on private lands, this Administration believes it is vitally important that the Federal government provide incentives for landowners to engage in conservation efforts. The incentive programs implemented during this Administration have shown returns in the form of voluntary contributions of time and effort by landowners. These contributions provide far more to species conservation than the government could ever compel through regulatory action. This Administration is focusing on enhancing and restoring habitats of threatened and candidate species populations—thus keeping them off the list by preventing these species from becoming threatened in the first place. . . .

The UCS' Claims on "Manipulating the Scientific Process on Forest Management"

- The UCS claims that the USDA manipulated the scientific process on forest management, and used a "Review Team" made up primarily of non-scientists to "overrule" an existing forest management plan.

This claim is false. This case actually highlights how aggressive the Administration has been in using input from the scientific community to inform its forest management decisions. The UCS claim demonstrates a lack of understanding of the NEPA processes used to update the Sierra Nevada Forest Plan Amendment (SNFPA) Record of Decision. In fact, the Forest Service received over 200 appeals of the SNFPA and had to review and respond to them. To address these appeals, the Regional Forester (Region Five—California) established the five-person Review Team to evaluate any needed changes to the SNFPA Record of Decision. One scientist provided scientific support to this team. Once the Review Team completed its work, a Draft Supplemental EIS (DSEIS) was completed. This was developed using an interdisciplinary team of 31 people, which included four individuals with PhDs and nine additional individuals with master's degrees in scientific fields.

A Science Consistency Review (SCR) was conducted to assess the DSEIS from a scientific perspective. The Forest Service uses the SCR process infrequently and only when the additional level of thoroughness is judged necessary to ensure that decisions are consistent with the best available science. Controversy is not a consideration in the SCR process. The SCR is accomplished by judging whether scientific information of appropriate content, rigor, and applicability has been considered, evaluated, and synthesized in the draft documents that underlie and implement land management decisions. This SCR included 13 members, with 11 being scientists, nine external to the Forest Service and seven of these external to the government, including those from universities, the Nature Conservancy, and an independent firm. The results of the SCR were provided to a group of Forest Service professionals (including those experienced in NEPA, science, writing, and resource management) who prepared the final NEPA documents.

It would be highly unusual for all SCR comments to be reflected in the final NEPA documents, since these are prepared in the face of significant scientific uncertainty and a diversity of values. Nevertheless, the draft documents, the science consistency review, the response to the science consistency review, the responses to public comments, and the final SEIS are all available on the web so that scientific information used and the process that utilized this information is transparent. How uncertainty and risk are handled in the decision have both scientific and policy elements. In addition, a paper discussing the risk and uncertainty issues around the decision was developed by four additional university scientists. These documents are all available at http://www.fs.fed.us/r5/snfpa/.

III. The UCS' Claims of "An Unprecedented Pattern of Behavior"

The UCS' Claims on "Disseminating Research from Federal Agencies"
Part III closes the UCS "investigation" and contains two sections—one on "Disseminating Research from Federal Agencies" and one on "Irregularities in Appointments to Scientific Advisory Panels." Here, the UCS does not provide a single instance of an actual suppression of agency research or an appointment irregularity occurring. Both sections consist entirely of quotations from various individuals and one organization.

Individual opinions are not actual events with facts that can be determined. With no context, one must assume these opinions are based upon the type of misinformation presented throughout the UCS document.

The stated opinions do not reflect the views of many outstanding scientists who have worked with this Administration. In particular, the National Academy of Sciences has been closely involved in various aspects of the Bush Administration's science policies. The Academy of Sciences has graciously accepted numerous requests to conduct research program reviews, and have gained first-hand knowledge of the Administration's commitment to independent scientific advice, a commitment that extends to all areas of science under Federal support. The most prominent example is the National Academy's review of the Climate Change Science Program's recently released Strategic Plan. If there has ever been an area of contention about this Administration's commitment to science, climate change science is it. Yet the Academy says about the Strategic Plan that:

> "The *Strategic Plan for the U.S. Climate Change Science Program* articulates a guiding vision, is appropriately ambitious, and is broad in scope. It encompasses activities related to areas of long-standing importance, together with new or enhanced cross-disciplinary efforts. It appropriately plans for close integration with the complementary Climate Change Technology Program. The CCSP has responded constructively to the National Academies review and other community input in revising the strategic plan. In fact, the approaches taken by the CCSP to receive and respond to comments from a large and broad group of scientists and stakeholders, including a two-stage independent review of the plan, set a high standard for government research programs. As a result, the revised strategic plan is much improved over its November 2002 draft, and now includes the elements of a strategic management framework that could permit it to effectively guide research on climate and associated global changes over the next decades. . . . Advancing science on all fronts identified by the program will be of vital importance to the nation."

POSTSCRIPT

Does Politics Come Before Science in Current Government Decision Making?

The Union of Concerned Scientists' report was followed by a number of press reports, including Jeffrey Brainerd, "How Sound Is Bush's 'Sound Science'?" *The Chronicle of Higher Education* (March 5, 2004), Eric Alterman and Mark Green, "The New Scopes Trials," *The Nation* (March 8, 2004) (which noted that "we risk an era of Lysenkoism in America"), and Andrew C. Revkin, "Bush vs. the Laureates: How Science Became a Partisan Issue," *The New York Times* (October 19, 2004). Robert Costanza, "When Scoundrels Rule," *Bioscience* (May 2005), notes in reviewing David W. Orr's *The Last Refuge: Patriotism, Politics, and the Environment in an Age of Terror* (Island Press, 2004), that "scientists abhor (as well they should) faith-based or politically driven conclusions to important questions of science and policy" and asks "But what happens when these rules of conduct are disrespected, as they have been in the last four years? What happens when religious beliefs and political power are allowed to influence science and policy?"

In July 2004, the Union of Concerned Scientists published a riposte to Marburger's defense of the Bush administration's approach to science policy. *Scientific Integrity in Policy Making: Further Investigation of the Bush Administration's Misuse of Science* charged that "the White House document was filled with largely irrelevant information and arguments unrelated to the scientists' charges" and adduced new examples to support the UCS argument.

In April 2004, the U.S. Department of Health and Human Services (HHS) announced that henceforth, when the World Health Organization (WHO) invited scientists employed by the HHS (including scientists at the National Institutes of Health and the Centers for Disease Control), it could no longer send invitations directly to those scientists whom it deemed experts in particular fields (such as avian flu, carcinogenic chemicals, and SARS) and whose assistance it particularly desired. Instead, WHO must send invitations to the office of William Steiger, the HHS global health chief, who would then choose the appropriate experts. There was no suggestion that "appropriate" would mean anything other than scientific expertise, but Steiger did note in a letter to WHO that "regulations require HHS experts to serve as representatives of the U.S. government at all times and advocate U.S. government policies." See "Politics Manipulating Scientific Decisions, Recent Report Shows," *Nation's Health* (September 2004).

In the wake of the Union of Concerned Scientists report, as well as an earlier restriction in the number of government scientists allowed to travel to overseas scientific meetings on such topics as AIDS, there was immediate concern that the change in policy indicated an attempt to establish political control over what government scientists had the opportunity to tell the world. On April 28, 2005, the eleven Democrats on the House Science Committee sent a letter to the new HHS Secretary, Michael Leavitt, asking him to rescind or justify the "counterproductive" and "potentially dangerous" WHO-advisor policy (reported by Jocelyn Kaiser, "Democrats Protest Limits on WHO Advisory Panels," *Science* [May 6, 2005]).

About the same time, the Committee on Ensuring the Best Presidential and Federal Advisory Committee Science and Technology Appointments, of the National Academy of Sciences, National Academy of Engineering, and Institute of Medicine, published *Science and Technology in the National Interest: Ensuring the Best Presidential and Federal Advisory Committee Science and Technology Appointments* (National Academy Press, 2005) (see http://www.nap.edu/catalog/11152.html). This report stated that: "When a federal advisory committee requires scientific or technical proficiency, persons nominated to provide that expertise should be selected on the basis of their scientific and technical knowledge and credentials and their professional and personal integrity. It is inappropriate to ask them to provide nonrelevant information, such as voting record, political-party affiliation, or position on particular policies." The reason is simple:

> "The nation is in need of exceptionally able scientists, engineers, and health professionals to serve in executive positions in the federal government and on federal advisory committees. Such persons, when serving as presidential appointees, make key programmatic and policy decisions that will affect our lives and those of our children. Similarly, skilled scientists and engineers are needed for advisory committees to provide advice on the myriad issues with complex technologic dimensions that confront government decision makers. Our nation has long been served by its ability to draw qualified S&T candidates to government service because of the opportunities for intellectually challenging work that affects the world in which we live and that encourages and protects the scientific process. We must continue to enlist the best candidates for these important positions and ensure that the obstacles to their service are minimized."

See also Kelly Field, "Keep Selection Process for Panels Free of Politics, Report Urges," *Chronicle of Higher Education* (November 26, 2004). On February 16, 2005, Demcratic Representatives Henry A. Waxman and Bart Gordon introduced the "Restore Scientific Integrity to Federal Research and Policymaking Act" (H.R. 839) to prohibit interference with science, among other things; see http://www.democrats.reform.house.gov/Documents/20050216175029-74858.pdf.

Is science the only or chief factor to consider in making public policy decisions? John F. Kavanaugh, "The Values Vote," *America* (November 29, 2004), argues that there is a place for morality or ethics, but neither the Republicans nor the Democrats have suitable versions of either. Tibor R. Machan, "Faith and Public Controversy," *The Humanist* (May/June 2005), disagrees, arguing that resting public policy on faith "places it on wobbly foundations."

ISSUE 2

Should Society Restrict the Publication of Unclassified but "Sensitive" Research?

YES: Lewis M. Branscomb, from "The Changing Relationship between Science and Government Post-September 11," in Albert H. Teich, Stephen D. Nelson, and Stephen J. Lita, eds., *Science and Technology in a Vulnerable World* (Committee on Science, Engineering, and Public Policy, American Association for the Advancement of Science, 2002)

NO: The Royal Society and Wellcome Trust, from "Do No Harm: Reducing the Potential for the Misuse of Life Science Research," Report of a Royal Society (October 7, 2004)

ISSUE SUMMARY

YES: Lewis M. Branscomb asserts that because the results of much scientific research have the potential to aid terrorists, there is a need to control the publication and distribution of "sensitive but unclassified" information.

NO: Scientists and others who met under the aegis of the U.K.'s Royal Society and the Wellcome Trust concluded that the issue is real, but self-governance by the scientific community is much preferred over new legislation.

T he fall of 2001 was remarkable for two events. One was the al Qaeda use of hijacked airliners to destroy the World Trade Towers in New York City. The other was the still-mysterious appearance of anthrax spores in the mail. The two do not seem to have been related, but together they created a climate of fear and mistrust. Part of that fear and mistrust was aimed at science and technology, for the al Qaeda terrorists had used computers and the Internet for communicating with each other, and whoever was responsible for the anthrax scare obviously knew too much about anthrax. One response was the Bush Administration's March 2002 declaration that some information—notably the results of scientific research, especially in the life sciences—might not be classified in the ways long familiar to researchers in nuclear physics (for instance), but it could still be considered "sensitive" and thus worthy of restrictions on publication and dissemination. The Department of Defence (DoD) announced—and promptly dropped—plans to restrict the use and spread of unclassified DoD-funded research. However, a National Academy of Sciences report on agricultural bioterrorism that contained no classified information was censored on the insistence of the Department of Agriculture "to keep potentially dangerous information away from enemies of the United States." National security experts warned "that the current system of openness in science could lead to dire consequences." [See Richard Monastersky, "Publish and Perish?" *Chronicle of Higher Education* (October 11, 2002).] However, many have objected to inventing and attempting to restrict the new "sensitive but unclassified" category of information.

In July 2002, researchers announced that they had successfully assembled a polio virus from biochemicals and the virus's gene map. Members of Congress called for more care in releasing such information, and the American Society for Microbiology (ASM) began to debate voluntary restrictions on publication. By August, the ASM had policy guidelines dictating that journal submissions that contain "information . . . that could be put to inappropriate use" be carefully reviewed and even rejected. The ASM policy has met surprisingly little active resistance, for though "New Antiterrorism Tenets Trouble Scientists," [Peg Brickley, *The Scientist* (October 28, 2002)], many researchers see the need for restraint. However, many say, there is a need for new rules to be very clear [see David Malakoff, "Researchers See Progress in Finding the Right Balance," *Science* (October 18, 2002)]. On the other hand, Charles M. Vest, in "Response and Responsibility: Balancing Security and Openness in Research and Education," *Report of the President for the Academic Year 2001–2002* (Massachusetts Institute of Technology, 2002), argued that openness in science must preempt fears of the consequences of scientific knowledge falling into the wrong hands.

In April 2002, the American Association for the Advancement of Science (AAAS) held its annual Colloquium on Science and Technology Policy. The papers in the resulting book [*Science and Technology in a Vulnerable World*, Albert H. Teich, Stephen D. Nelson, and Stephen J. Lita, eds. (AAAS, 2002)] included Lewis M. Branscomb's argument that because the results of much scientific research have the potential to aid terrorists, there is a need to control the publication and distribution of "sensitive but unclassified" information. The debate has continued. On October 7, 2004, the U.K.'s Royal Society and the Wellcome Trust held a meeting of practicing scientists and policy makers who concluded that although there are real risks of misuse of scientific information, the answer lies more in self-governance by the scientific community than in new legislation. "Do No Harm: Reducing the Potential for the Misuse of Life Science Research" is a summary of the key issues and challenges that emerged from the October 2004 meeting. It's not necessarily an expression of the views of the Royal Society or the Wellcome Trust. The full report may be found at http://www.royalsoc.ac.uk/document.asp?tip=0&id=2830.

Lewis M. Branscomb

 **YES**

The Changing Relationship between Science and Government Post-September 11

The events of September 11, 2001 came as a great shock to the American people. But the anticipation of that day goes back a long time. Exactly 25 years ago Harvard professor Gerald Holton . . . describe[d] three kinds of terrorism. Type I is traditional terrorism by an individual or small group of people who are determined to wreak havoc for reasons of their own. It is not connected with any government. Type II terrorism is conducted by a dysfunctional state, unable to deal with the rest of the world through normal interstate relationships. This state engages in terrorism either against its own people or against others. Type III terrorism occurs when the Type I terrorist (a stateless terrorist group) finds that it can get resources and technical support from a Type II terrorist state.

We now face Type III terrorism. We must understand that the source of our vulnerability to terrorism is not the terrorists themselves. Our vulnerability is generated by our economic, social, and political systems. . . . If you have a highly competitive market economy, everyone is driven to greater efficiency. But the public also wants stability. Stability, with only small perturbations, is built into the system. But this does not work unless you have a peaceful, obedient society that does not threaten to exploit these vulnerabilities. This society cannot avoid threats to leverage that very hyper-efficiency.

University-Government Relationships

University-government relationships have changed with every major war. Before and during World War II, and even for some time after, everyone understood that you dropped what you were doing when your country needed you. The science and technology community was totally dedicated to defeating the enemy, which was known and identifiable. Everyone pulled together in the expectation of unconditional surrender by the enemy. The war would have an end point, after which there would be peaceful life and civil society again.

The Cold War was somewhat different, in that it was of indefinite duration. But it was similar because the opponent was a state, which was well-known and well-recognized. We produced an unresilient (but effective) strategy called mutually assured destruction (MAD). The military and foreign policy people had the responsibility to manage that problem. Society had to support it, but it did not really upset our civil life. The military-industrial complex ran the "war." Academic support was primarily through the basic research agencies (such as the Office of Naval Research, the Air Force Office of Scientific Research, the Army Research Office, and the Defense Advanced Research Projects Agency).

The war on terrorism is different. We have an unknown enemy in our midst, and the duration is indefinite. We are creating vulnerabilities all the time. Unless we do something different, it is going to get worse.

The universities need to support the nation in this war, building on their traditional values. But we need some significant changes. Catastrophic terrorism is the ultimate in asymmetric warfare. We depended on S&T [science and technology] to compensate for the asymmetry in the Cold War, when Soviet forces greatly outnumbered ours. We compensated by having our forces technically superior. But, now, each terrorist threat is in some ways a new war. Terrorists are technically competent and may be armed with weapons of mass destruction. To what extent can S&T compensate for this asymmetry? What is the role of and the effect on the universities? . . .

Countering Terrorism

There are three ways to counter terrorism. One, you can reduce the incentives that create and motivate terrorists. This approach clearly falls in the category of foreign and military policies, international relations and alliances, and intelligence. S&T can certainly contribute here, through technical means and gathering intelligence and through social science studies. The ideal solution would be to make this a peaceful world in which the number of individuals willing to kill themselves to destroy societies was greatly reduced. But that is very hard to do.

Another way is to detect and arrest the terrorists. This is essentially a police function. This may be the cheapest of the three, but it is the one that bears most heavily on civil rights and civil liberties.

The third way is to harden the target society, that is, make it more difficult for the terrorists to attack. We do this by detecting their preparations, intercepting their plans, making the targets less vulnerable, limiting the damage they can do, and enhancing the recovery. Industry has a role to play in this area. But we must motivate industry to reduce the vulnerabilities inherent in our society.

The Nature of the Vulnerabilities

We credit science and technology not only for creating an efficient economy, but also for creating the weapons that terrorists use. These weapons are based on the same technologies we use domestically for beneficial purposes. Our S&T strategy to address this has to be very sophisticated. It has to use the very S&T that creates the vulnerabilities to lessen those vulnerabilities.

One of our biggest problems is that the critical elements of our infrastructure are deeply linked. When one part is attacked, we see a domino effect on the other parts. The three most obvious infrastructure elements are energy, communications, and transportation. If you bring down any one of these three, the other two are affected. For example, if you bring the energy sector down, you cannot communicate and you cannot travel. There is a lot you cannot do. Terrorists understand that, and we must deal with this reality. We have to consider the threat of multiple, simultaneous attacks on our infrastructure.

Another problem was brought on by deregulation, by getting the federal government out of the markets. Over the last decade, we have introduced more competition, particularly in the energy area, by deregulating. One result of that is a significant increase in vulnerability.

The threats are now more varied than simply the weapons of mass destruction. They include bioterrorism, chemical warfare, nuclear attack, and radiation contamination. All of these threats affect infrastructure issues. They come together in the cities where people are, because people are the targets. In cities we face the key issue of managing the warnings of an attack, as well as the attack itself. We also have to support the first responders.

And, finally, of course, our defense has to address the issues of intelligence and borders. One of the unfortunate characteristics of almost every feature of security and defense, whether security against crime or against minor acts of terrorism, is based on a single, thin wall. We try to check people coming into the country, but once they are legally in, they are in. We can put a fence around a critical facility, but if you can overcome it, you are in. That is characteristic of most of our systems, even in the computer area. Computer security has the same thin wall, and it does not work. We need a lot of technical tools to address this. They include sensor systems, data systems and networks, biomedical vaccines, chemical warfare treatments, and biometrics for efficient identification. Some of these involve cross-cutting issues and human factors-decision systems.

Terrorism, to a greater degree than any problem before, calls for a new way of thinking about the nature of the threats and how to deal with them. It calls for systems engineering and analysis. It calls for strategy-driven goals for the research program and the creation of new capabilities. Basic research will help us develop the strategy we need. It will not give us the answers to the current problem, but it will tell us how to change the questions.

Basic Research

Basic research, if it removes ignorance in critical areas, can give us a whole new way to approach this problem and make it easier to solve. That, in my view, is the critical role of basic research. But when you think about it, the government is not well-structured to do anything that is built on a systems strategy that cuts across all the current missions and areas of technical activity in the country. Countering terrorism is going to touch on every discipline in the universities, not just technical areas. Importantly, this time we have to pay attention to what the social sciences and humanities have to contribute.

Many different fields will need to address the many requirements of the war on terrorism. Developing sensors and dealing with hazardous materials will involve chemistry, physics, and engineering. Nuclear and radiological threats will be addressed by nuclear science. Bioterrorism will need the biomedical sciences and medical services. Threats against energy will be on the agenda of the physical facilities themselves, their infrastructure links, engineering, and information technology. Transportation and distribution are in the realm of engineering. Protecting our water, food, and agriculture will need people from biology and chemistry. Cyberattacks will be met by information science and engineering. Cities and people will be protected by the social and behavioral sciences. Infrastructure linkages will be taken care of by systems analysis and systems engineering people.

The political world has always been skeptical about the contributions of the social sciences and humanities. There are areas of which social science cannot give actionable advice, but there are many other areas where it absolutely can. Social scientists have studied the terrorism problem in great detail and have things to tell us that are very important.

R&D Capability and Mobilization

The big difficulty is that the government and the universities are "stovepiped," with different areas in technical work segregated into different organizations; financed by specific agencies. In the government, we do not have to create an S&T capability. We have fabulous S&T capability. It is nurtured by agencies born out of World War II and the Cold War. These agencies have massive capability to mobilize American science and technology. They are well-known: the National Institutes of Health [NIH], the National Science Foundation [NSF], the U.S. Departments of Energy (DOE), Defense and the National Aeronautics and Space Administration. These are big organizations devoted to a technical enterprise. But they do not, with the possible exception of the Department of Defense and some of DOE, have the mission of domestic security against terrorism. That mission is in agencies like the Federal Emergency Management Agency, the U.S. Customs Service, the Immigration and Naturalization Service, the U.S. Coast Guard, and the U.S. Department of Transportation. The latter is a technical agency, but it has never had a very strong research and development (R&D) capability. There are many other agencies, as well as state and local governments, in this situation. So the customers for science and technology are agencies with very little R&D experience.

Most of the U.S. R&D capability is in the hands of agencies that do not have the mission of countering terrorism. So how can we put all that together? When you go to the universities to get work done in physics, you know where to go. But if you want to solve a more complex problem, the universities are not internally structured, in most cases, to work on it. The implementation of any strategy depends on the federal government, which is capable of deploying most of the nation's capability (except that in the private sector).

We do not want to disrupt the present S&T capability. Instead, we are going to have to create an architecture for defining not only a strategy for using S&T in counterterrorism and managing its execution, but we also have to help the President manage that process. This requires linked-systems approaches and intersectional collaboration (involving the federal government, states, cities, and industry). It will be a challenge. We are not very experienced in this area. But most counterterrorism research must be interdisciplinary and in a systems context. We have our work cut out for us. As I said above, government science agencies tend to be stovepiped. Interdisciplinary work is hard to peer review. But many counterterrorism problems cut across agency lines. The university structure is also poorly adapted to a systems context and multidisciplinary work. We may need some institutional innovations, both in government and in the universities.

The universities have many resources. They have research capability for creating new options and competencies. They have links to local government and industry. They have access to students and colleagues around the world. And they have relevant capability in the social sciences and humanities. But the universities have needs too. They need more research resources. They need to continue to have access to foreign resources and students, the freedom to share technical information, and acceptable levels of security. They need to be able to admit students and collaborate with foreign scientists without irrational restrictions. And they need to be able to handle and deal with the very difficult and unclear question of how sensitive information should be handled in the research community.

Possible Effects of a New Strategy

Positive effects could come out of all this. . . . Important agencies of the government may learn how to use the research capacity of the country. We could also broaden the base of support, with new sources and levels of funding. . . .

[T]he right research strategy will benefit "dual use" technologies. We can define problems to address civil as well as security needs. For example, we could develop better ways to detect an infection prior to seeing clinical symptoms. We can also develop ways to make needed capabilities affordable. New probes and sensors that identify and track containers reduce costs in time and money in normal commercial shipping. This has wide application. We can also find new ways to deal with natural disasters. This would include advancements in communications, robotics, and even clothing for firefighters and hazardous materials specialists. We could also improve threat characterization for first responders. . . .

The good news is that basic research may emerge out of this to be seen as a strategic necessity. We may see a new balance between the physical and health sciences. Because the problem is so ill defined, we need an open-ended, imaginative, creative way of thinking about it. This will only come out of the basic research community, which has been substantially funded by the traditional civilian agencies (NSF, NIH, DOE, etc.).

The bad news is that as agencies re-label a large part of their programs as counterterrorism, they invite constraints. The research may be the same, but it may now be labeled as defending the country, and, therefore, critically important to national security. So Congress, knowing that the universities are so important, may put constraints on communication, publication, and the like, beyond what ought to be done. Legislation and agency policy may place information restrictions on grants. Indeed, counterterrorism is a preempting budget priority. So if you cannot re-label your program as counterterrorism, then that part of your budget may suffer. I hope this will not be the case.

We must look seriously at the government's inability to manage cross-cutting research programs. Counterterrorism requires a systems approach. The systems approach demands capability at the top level of government to develop national research programs. This will help with maximizing interdisciplinary research, but it is going to put additional burdens on the White House Office of Science and Technology Policy, the Office of Homeland Security, and others. But it is very important that we have a strong, visionary capability to lead the definition of how S&T can help in this area. If successful, we can apply this approach to sustainable development, climate change, and other areas that challenge our quality of life.

Control of Information

The control of sensitive information is a big issue. This is a quote from *The Economist,* which I think is very perceptive.

> Knowledge is power. Those who possess it have always sought to deny it to their enemies. . . . But exactly what knowledge needs to be controlled depends on who those enemies are. Nor is the control of knowledge without cost.
>
> A free society should regard it as a last resort. Scientists cannot build on each other's results if they do not know them. And governments are frequently tempted to hide not only what is dangerous, but also what is embarrassing. That can result in dangers of its own.[1]

Unfortunately, the present state of government controls on information is chaotic. The system of military secret classification is not adapted to the terrorist threat. The U.S. Department of Health and Human Services has no legal authority to classify information as "secret." This means that information that could be extraordinarily dangerous if it were publicly known to the terrorists is not protected. We have to protect this information in some way until the rules are worked out as to how this will be done routinely. The term "sensitive but unclassified" is likely to be applied to much university work, even though it has no clear definition.

We see serious, legitimate dilemmas about what should, in fact, be published. Add to this the Patriot Act (PL 107-56), which authorizes intrusion into the Internet, servers, answering machines, and other telecommunication equipment. (It also requires colleges to turn over student records, and requires the National Center for Education Statistics to turn over data in response to a warrant.)

This poses the question, but it does not give the answer, of how this will be done. Ultimately, we need to resolve a lot of open issues with respect to the government's view of sensitive information.

Security and intelligence on university campuses is a much more difficult problem now than during the Cold War. Public interest in security lapses at universities, real or imagined, will be intense. Terrorist threats are extraordinarily diverse and of indefinite duration. The public will expect research universities to track students who may be perceived as threats.

Conclusion

I think the scientific community is going to have to engage in a long debate. It should have started before September 11 because this debate has to do with things besides terrorism. It has to do with the moral and ethical responsibility of individual scientists and engineers. We all must think about how they can relate our activity in science, our communication, and all the things we do in a way that we believe benefits the long-term public interest.

Must the culture of science evolve to discourage its misuse? If so, in what ways? Is there a consensus on the expectations scientists place on themselves now? I believe that thoughtful self-constraint is the only way to maintain the creativity of science and still protect the country.

Note

1.   Secrets and lives. 2002. *The Economist,* March 9.

Do No Harm: Reducing the Potential for the Misuse of Life Science Research

Summary

The threat of advances in the life sciences being used for harmful purposes is a real one. The challenge that the scientific community faces is to identify what measures can be taken to manage or reduce this risk without jeopardising the enormous potential benefits from research advances. The aim of the joint Royal Society—Wellcome Trust meeting was to bring together practising life scientists with policy makers, funders and other interested parties to identify what the issues were and how they might be addressed. This report presents a summary of the key issues and challenges that emerged from the meeting and is not necessarily an expression of the views of the Royal Society or the Wellcome Trust.

The key points arising from the meeting and possible next steps were:

- Research institutions and funding agencies need to consider how to build on existing processes for reviewing research projects to ensure that risks of misuse are assessed in an appropriate and timely manner.
- Preventing publication of basic research would not prevent the misuse of advances in the life sciences.
- Self governance by the scientific community was favoured, rather than new legislation.
- Although some scepticism was expressed about the value of codes of conduct, it was suggested that the scientific community should take the lead in determining any codes of conduct or good practice, to preempt their introduction through legislation or other 'top down' approaches. National guidelines for good practice could provide the basis for individual organisations and employers generating their own codes. There was a call for the wider scientific community to be bought together to discuss the merits of producing guidelines for good practice, and then to start the process of drafting such guidelines if appropriate.

- Education and awareness-raising training are needed to ensure that scientists at all levels are aware of their legal and ethical responsibilities and consider the possible consequences of their research. University department heads, research institute directors, vice chancellors and Universities UK would be ideally placed to take this forward for the academic community. However, these bodies would need to be co-ordinated. The Association of British Pharmaceutical Industries and the BioIndustry Association could take the lead for industrial training.

1. Introduction

Following the September 2001 Washington DC and New York terrorist attacks and the US anthrax letters of autumn 2001 there has been increased concern that life sciences research could be misused enhancing the threat of bioterrorist attacks. The increased political attention to this issue was illustrated by the House of Commons Science and Technology Select Committee inquiry into the scientific response to terrorism. The UK Government will be chairing the 2005 Annual Meeting of the Biological Weapons Convention, which will focus on how the Convention could be strengthened through the content, promulgation and adoption of codes of conduct for scientists.

The Royal Society has a long standing interest in reducing the threat from biological weapons and strengthening the Biological Weapons Convention, and has produced a number of reports and statements on these subjects. The Wellcome Trust published their position statement on bioterrorism and biomedical research stating that the Trust was keen to work with other scientific organisations to identify how the scientific community could best address concerns regarding the potential misuse of life science research. Consequently, the Royal Society and Wellcome Trust agreed to bring together practising life scientists with policy makers, funders and other interested parties to discuss these issues.

The meeting was attended by 66 people, including academic, Government and industry scientists, representatives of funding bodies and learned societies, scientific publishers, scientific journalists, Government policy makers and other interested individuals. . . .

2. What Are the Issues?

A range of opinions was expressed on the size of the threat from misuse of life science research. Some believed that natural outbreaks of emerging diseases (such as SARS) are much more likely to occur than bioterrorist attacks, with greater impact in terms of loss of life. However, others commented that there was a considerable risk of the deliberate misuse of life science research.

It was noted that bioterrorism incidents had generated considerable political interest, disproportionate to the size of the events. For example, it was suggested that the geopolitical impact from the US anthrax letters in autumn 2001, which resulted in 22 cases and five deaths, was of a similar scale to the 2002–2003 SARS outbreak, which caused an estimated 8098 cases and 774 deaths. Public perception of the risk posed by bioterrorism is vital, as this feeds into the geopolitical response to incidents. This echoes the Royal Society's report on biological weapons which stated that the main negative impact of a biological weapons attack may be panic, with consequent disruption of civilian services.

Currently, the threat is most likely to be from known biological agents and easily accessible 'low tech' approaches. These involve knowledge, expertise and processes that are already in the public domain. However, in the future technological advances might make novel or non-conventional agents (and the means of delivering them) more attractive to terrorists and other individuals wishing to use them.

The challenge is to think beyond the obvious and identify those avenues of research and technologies that present risks of being misused for harmful purposes that are quite distinct from the original aims of the work. This needs imaginative thinking as the vast majority of work falls into the grey area of having some potential for misuse.

It was argued that the 'life sciences' should not be considered in isolation from other scientific disciplines, as the development and weaponisation of biological agents can involve techniques from fields such as mathematics, engineering, physics and computer science. . . .

3. How Can These Issues Be Addressed?

3.1. Research Funding

There was discussion about weighing up the risks of misuse of research proposals against the potential benefits. Some felt this 'risk-benefit' approach had the advantage of building on existing procedures, such as those for dangerous pathogens, genetically modified organisms and animal experiments, and that it was an appropriate tool for assessing whether research proposals should be undertaken. However, some participants commented that the difficulties in quantifying the potential risks undermined the 'risk-benefit' approach. It was noted that Nobel laureate Joshua Lederberg commented in 1975 regarding the then-fledgling technology of DNA splicing that it gave uncertain peril and certain benefit. It was suggested that this was equally applicable in assessing the potential for misuse of work in relation to the development of biological weapons. To address these concerns a framework for assessing risk would need to be developed. It was noted that there are currently no criteria for such assessing risks, so existing processes rely on the wisdom of those assessing research proposals.

The key roles to be played by funding bodies and research institutions were stressed, with both needing to consider how to build on existing processes for reviewing research projects to ensure that risks of misuse are assessed in an appropriate and timely manner. It was felt that funding bodies already have strong existing processes in place to assess the scientific merit and ethical implications of research proposals. These processes could be built upon to ensure that risks of misuse are considered during the review of applications;

for example through including a specific question on application forms and introducing explicit guidance for referees and funding committees. It was suggested that institutions need to take responsibility for assessing and monitoring risks of misuse associated with ongoing research programmes. The processes for conducting risk assessments on genetically-modified organisms introduced by the previous UK Health and Safety Executive Genetics Modification Advisory Group (GMAG) were suggested as a potential model upon which to base such institutional systems.

Communication between funding bodies and research institutions is vital for any workable research funding based solution. For the majority of funding schemes the money is given to the institution rather than the individual. This means that university and institute department heads must engage in discussion about what systems and procedures might work in practice.

3.2. Communicating Research Results

The very strongly and widely held belief was expressed that preventing publication of basic research would not prevent its misuse. The reasons for this include:

- Information is likely to be published elsewhere such as in other journals, websites or conference proceedings, or communicated informally via e-mail, telephone or face-to-face discussion.
- Similar research will often be undertaken by others within two years.
- Publishing work allows developments to be used in work on countermeasures to biological agents, such as vaccines, and for use in strengthening public health measures. Suppressing publication would stop this happening, with the potential to hinder work with beneficial applications.
- Publishing makes others aware of unintended results. For example, the publication of the paper on the insertion of the interleukin-4 gene into mousepox made a large number of researchers aware of the surprising discovery that the insertion of this gene enabled the virus to overcome both genetic resistance and immunisation to the disease.
- Publication is a vital method of communicating results amongst the international scientific community.
- Full methodological and experimental details must be published to allow peer reviewers and readers to evaluate the research.

In very rare cases consideration could be given to delaying publication of highly sensitive information, or releasing only some of the information into the public domain. However, in these cases there would need to be a very clear benefit in delaying publication.

3.3. Existing and Possible Future Controls and Oversight

It was agreed that existing regulatory processes did not assess whether experiments should be undertaken. Many of the current systems, such as those for dangerous pathogens, genetically modified organisms and animal experiments, address whether an experiment can be conducted safely, rather than whether the experiment should be conducted at all based on a consideration of the potential misuse of the research. For example, an experiment to reconstruct the 1918 influenza virus would be permitted providing it was conducted in a category 4 laboratory to ensure the required level of containment. However, there would not be any discussion of whether it would be wise to undertake the experiment.

It was noted that funding bodies, such as Higher Education Funding Council for England (HEFCE), currently audit educational establishments and it was suggested that these processes could be expanded to cover the examination of procedures for assessing potential concerns of research misuse.

During the discussion about the role of regulation and oversight, the clear preference was expressed for self governance by the scientific community, rather than new legislation. For any system of self governance to work, it must have a high degree of transparency in order to ensure public trust.

3.4. Responsibilities of Scientists and the Utility of An Ethical Code of Conduct for Life Scientists

There was no consensus on what the main justification would be for introducing an ethical code of conduct. The principal value of both ethical codes and codes of practice was seen to be in reinforcing norms and as educational and training tools. It is difficult to produce a code that is both specific enough to have a positive effect and sufficiently flexible to deal with changes in technology or wider applications. Consequently, there is the distinct possibility of a large number of codes being produced for very small, specific groups rather than a few broad codes.

Contracts of employment are currently used to enforce good practice. These could be expanded, and lessons learnt from industry for use in academia and Government research institutes. It was noted that there are many existing codes that could form the basis of future codes. For example, the criteria for chartered scientist or chartered engineer status could be expanded to cover the misapplication of their work. Consideration would need to be given to what would happen if there was a conflict between different codes that an individual had signed up to. For example, if a scientist's professional society's code did not agree with their contract of employment, which would take precedence?

A range of views was expressed on the merit of accreditation or registration of scientists. Some believed that it is inevitable that scientists will have to receive some form of accreditation. Others saw a fundamental problem that scientists do not have a clearly identified 'customer', unlike currently registered professions such as doctors or lawyers, and hence have no clear duties of care that could be codified.

Despite some scepticism being expressed about the value of codes of conduct, there was broad support for the proposal that the scientific community should take the lead in determining any codes, to pre-empt their introduction through legislation or other 'top down' approaches. National guidelines for good practice could provide the basis for individual organisations and employers generating their own codes of practice. Producing national guidelines for good practice would need an organisation (with the Royal Society being suggested) to take the lead in bringing together key stakeholders, and coordinating the necessary wider consultation.

3.5. Training and Education of Life Scientists

It was widely agreed that it was essential to inform students of their legal and ethical responsibilities and to ensure that they consider the possible consequences of their research; although it was thought that it was rare for such training to occur at the moment. Opinion varied about the utility of teaching this to undergraduates: it was suggested that it would be difficult to introduce such subjects that would not be directly assessed into already full syllabuses. This was countered by noting that educating undergraduates who do not stay in science was a vital part of increasing understanding amongst the wider public. It was strongly agreed that as part of their induction all researchers at postgraduate level should be told about the legal and ethical responsibilities relating to their work. This could be included in existing induction courses that deal with health, safety and other general laboratory training. This training would apply to all incoming students, both national and international. Outlining the implications for researchers of international treaties, such as the Biological Weapons Convention, would be an integral part of the training.

In addition to student training, education would be needed for established researchers, as many current workers have not received any training. This would also need to be undertaken if other measures were implemented, such as altering funding application processes, as staff would need a good understanding of the potential misapplications of their work, to be able to complete an additional box on application forms outlining any possible misuses of their research. University department heads, research institute directors, vice chancellors and Universities UK would be ideally placed to take this forward for the academic community. However, these bodies would need to be co-ordinated.

In the same way, training at the induction stage was also suggested for those joining industry or public research facilities, particularly those at graduate level. Rather than being prescriptive it should be left to employers to judge the likelihood of misuse and the relevance to individual workers. Recommendations of best practice should be issued to employers, possibly through organisations such as the Association of British Pharmaceutical Industries (ABPI) and the BioIndustry Association.

Whilst the need for training and education was stressed, it was suggested that awareness raising approaches could proceed in an incremental fashion: a suitably aware core of workers would be able to raise awareness and promote good practice amongst their colleagues and act as whistleblowers.

It was noted that training and education have associated costs that need to be factored into organisations' budgets and resource requirements and that even with considerable funding and resources awareness might not become as widespread as desired. . . .

POSTSCRIPT

Should Society Restrict the Publication of Unclassified but "Sensitive" Research?

$\mathbf{A}$ paper by Lawrence M. Wein and Yifan Liu, "Analyzing a Bioterror Attack on the Food Supply: The Case of Botulinum Toxin in Milk," on how terrorists might attack the U.S.'s milk supply and on how to safeguard it, was scheduled for the May 30, 2005, issue of the *Proceedings of the National Academy of Sciences* (*PNAS*) (see Lawrence M. Wein, "Got Toxic Milk?" *New York Times* [May 30, 2005], for an op-ed version of the paper). However, Stewart Simonson, assistant secretary of the Department of Health and Human Services, asked the NAS (National Academy of Sciences) not to publish the paper on the grounds that it provides "a road map for terrorists and publication is not in the interests of the United States." The journal put the paper on hold while it studied the issue; it appeared on-line (http://www.pnas.org/cgi/content/abstract/0408526102v1) on June 28, 2005, and in print in the July 12, 2005, issue of *PNAS*. The Department of Health and Human Services continues to believe publication is a mistake, for the "consequences could be dire."

It is a frustrating truth that science and technology offer both threat and promise, even in the context of terrorism. William B. Bonvillian and Kendra V. Sharp ["Homeland Security Technology," *Issues in Science and Technology* (Winter 2001–2002)] note that the need to detect terrorists before they can do damage requires "accelerated technology development and deployment." Yet the same science and technology, in the wrong hands, can aid the terrorists.

It is worth noting that "Even before the terrorist attacks of 2001, White House directives and agencies used the label SBU [sensitive but unclassified] to safeguard from public disclosure information that does not meet the standards for classification." [See Genevieve J. Knezo, "'Sensitive but Unclassified' and Other Federal Security Controls on Scientific and Technical Information: History and Current Controversy" (Congressional Research Service Report for Congress, April 2, 2003).] Yet, says Ronald M. Atlas, ["National Security and the Biological Research Community," *Science* (October 25, 2002)], the controversy is far from settled and "is likely to continue until we have a national debate and reach consensus on how to balance the traditional openness of science with national security in the new age of bioterrorism." The presidents of the National Academies of Sciences and Engineering and the Institute of Medicine issued a statement that same month that said that although "No restrictions may be placed upon the conduct or reporting of federally funded fundamental research that has not received national security classification,"

43

the research community should work closely with the federal government to determine which presently unclassified research should be classified. Early in 2003, the National Academies and the Center for Strategic and International Studies hosted a meeting that concluded researchers had better exercise self-restraint before the government imposes restraint. At the workshop, the editors of a number of major scientific journals indicated that they were following the American Society for Microbiology's lead in watching for security issues, and a group of editors and prominent scientists issued a "Statement on Scientific Publication and Security" that stressed that while both editors and authors bear responsibility to the public for the consequences of publication, scientific publication must include sufficient details for replication of the work; the very research that may be most helpful to terrorists is also likely to be most helpful to fighting terrorists; and when "on occasion an editor may conclude that the potential harm of publication outweighs the potential societal benefits . . . the paper should be modified, or not be published." [See Donald Kennedy, "Two Cultures" (editorial), *Science* (February 21, 2003).] James B. Petro and David A. Relman, "Understanding Threats to Scientific Openness," *Science* (December 12, 2003), added that life scientists should assist the security community with identifying "research of concern." In October 2003, the National Research Council issued a report calling for increased oversight of unclassified research with the potential to aid terrorists. Within a few months, one of the report's recommendations—a new advisory panel for the National Institutes of Health, the National Science Advisory Board for Biosecurity—was already being implemented. The government was "so far seeking only voluntary guidelines to control research and the dissemination of results that could conceivably aid bioterrorists." See Jennifer Couzin, "U.S. Agencies Unveil Plan for Biosecurity Peer Review," *Science* (March 12, 2004).

Are there other possible answers besides restricting—voluntarily or otherwise—publication of potentially hazardous work? John D. Steinbruner and Elisa D. Harris ["Controlling Dangerous Pathogens," *Issues in Science and Technology* (Spring 2003)] call for a global body that could oversee and regulate potentially dangerous disease research. Robert H. Sprinkle proposes "The Biosecurity Trust" (*Bioscience,* March 2003): The Trust would be "a transnational, nongovernmental life-sciences organization" whose goals would be "First, to keep safe, or to make safe, the work of well-intentioned life scientists. Second, to maximize the chance that directors of malicious research-and-development efforts worldwide would cite as chief among their frustrations chronic trouble attracting and retaining, or even successfully coercing, sufficient numbers of life scientists willing to pursue illegal and immoral ends or to keep completely quiet about the true purpose of efforts assisted or observed. Third, to complement existing and evolving legal safeguards, rather than to replace or preempt them. Fourth, to foster the adaptation of the most forceful elements of the modern life-sciences ethical tradition, the Nuremberg principles, to non-medical situations, specifically to weaponeering by life scientists and to environmental endangerment. Fifth, to enrich the capacity to understand and manage biosecurity compromise, such as through the promotion of microbial-ecological education and research."

ISSUE 3

Should Creationism and Evolution Get Equal Time in Schools?

YES: Richard J. Clifford, from "Creationism's Value?" *America* (March 11, 2000)

NO: Evan Ratliff, from "The Crusade Against Evolution," *Wired* (October 2004)

ISSUE SUMMARY

YES: Richard J. Clifford, a professor of biblical studies, argues that although modern creationism is flawed, excluding the Bible and religion from American public education is indefensible. He maintains that schools should be places where religious beliefs are treated with respect.

NO: Journalist Evan Ratliff describes the current debate over introducing creationism, in its "Intelligent Design" guise, into the schools and concludes that "in science, not all theories are equal." Science education should not be decided by rhetoric, but by scientific scrutiny.

It has long been an article of faith for scientists that teleological questions ("why" questions that presume there is an intent behind the phenomena they study) should not be asked, largely because "intent" implies an intender, which is generally taken to mean divine will. As a result, there is a continuing conflict between the forces of faith and the forces of reason. Conservative Christians in the southern United States, Texas, and California have mounted vigorous campaigns to require public school biology classes to give equal time to both biblical creationism and Darwinian evolution. For many years, this meant that evolution was hardly mentioned in high school biology textbooks.

For a time, it looked like evolution had scored a decisive victory. In 1982 federal judge William K. Overton struck down an Arkansas law that would have required the teaching of straight biblical creationism, with its explicit talk of God the Creator, as an unconstitutional intrusion of religion into a government activity: education. But the creationists have not given up. They have returned to the fray with something they call "scientific creationism" or "Intelligent Design" (ID), and they have shifted their campaigns from state legislatures and school boards to local school boards, where it is harder for lawyers and biologists to mount effective counterattacks. "Scientific creationism" tries to show that the evolutionary approach is incapable of providing satisfactory explanations. For one thing, it says that natural selection relies on random chance to produce structures whose delicate intricacy really could only be the product of deliberate design. Therefore, there must have been a designer. There is no mention of God—but, of course, that is the only possible meaning of "designer" (unless one believes in ancient extraterrestrial visitors). For an excellent presentation of the various threads in the debate over intelligent design, see Robert T. Pennock, *Intelligent Design Creationism and Its Critics: Philosophical, Theological, and Scientific Perspectives* (MIT Press, 2001), and Eugenie C. Scott and Glenn Branch, "Antievolutionism Changes and Continuities," *BioScience* (March 2003).

William Johnson, associate dean of academic affairs at Ambassador University in Big Sandy, Texas, offered another argument for replacing the theory of evolution in a 1994 speech reprinted in "Evolution: The Past, Present, and Future Implications," *Vital Speeches of the Day* (February 15, 1995). He argued that the triumph of Darwin's theory "meant the end of the traditional belief in the world as a purposeful created order . . . and the consequent elimination of God from nature has played a decisive role in the secularization of Western society. Darwinian theory broke man's link with God and set him adrift in a cosmos without purpose or end." Johnson suggested that evolution—and perhaps the entire scientific approach to nature—should be abandoned in favor of a return to religion because of the untold damage it has done to the human values that underpin society.

In the following selections, Richard J. Clifford argues that modern creationism is flawed in that it fails to recognize both that the Bible holds many versions of creation and that those who composed those versions did not think the same way as modern scientists. However, he maintains that excluding the Bible and religion from American public education is indefensible. Evan Ratliff describes the current debate over introducing creationism, in its "Intelligent Design" guise, into the schools and concludes that "in science, not all theories are equal." What is taught in science education should be those ideas that have survived scientific scrutiny, not those supported by rhetoric alone.

YES

Richard J. Clifford

Creationism's Value?

The whole battle is hotting up," declared Ken Ham to The New York Times (12/1/99). A disillusioned science teacher turned creationist, Ham opposes the theory of evolution. He proposes instead a literal reading of the first chapter of the Book of Genesis: God created the world in six days. This interpretation has broader implications, for there is "a culture war hotting up in America between Christian morality and relative morality, which is really the difference between a creation-based philosophy and an evolution-based one." To a creationist like Ken Ham, even the common conservative view that a "day" in Genesis 1 stands for a time-span of eons is unacceptable, for it would attribute error to the Bible and reduce morality to human whim.

Creationists, who have been in and out of the public eye since the Scopes trial in 1925, had some major successes [recently]. In August 1999 the Kansas Board of Education deleted almost every mention of evolution from the state's science curriculum, and in October the Kentucky Board of Education voted to substitute the phrase "change over time" for "evolution." Oklahoma officials recently decreed that textbooks must include a disclaimer on the certainty of evolution.

What, then, should be thought of creationism? Is it a courageous stand for open-mindedness toward the Bible in an educational culture that excludes the biblical perspective? Or is it an attempt to impose an idiosyncratic view of the Bible and of science? At first glance, the creationist proposal seems reasonable: Present students with two theories, evolution and creationism, and let them make up their own minds. A second look, however, shows that the proposal contains two assumptions that virtually all professionally trained biblical scholars and scientists completely reject: that Genesis 1, interpreted literally, is the only or at least the standard biblical creation account, and that the six-day creation story in Genesis 1 is a rival to the modern theory of evolution. These assumptions show that creationism fundamentally misunderstands the Bible and the relation of science and religion.

The majority of biblical scholars, theologians of the mainstream churches, and philosophers of science hold an alternative view that will be summarized here under three headings: creation in the Bible, the differences between biblical and modern views of creation and the relation of religion and science.

Creation in the Bible

The strongest biblical argument against creationism is that Genesis 1 is only one of many creation accounts in the Bible, and these biblical accounts are too distinctive to be harmonized. The cosmogony found in the second and third chapters of Genesis tells a very different story than Genesis 1. Here are a few of these differences. Creation in Genesis 2 proceeds at an unspecified pace that surely lasts longer than a week, whereas in Genesis 1 all takes place within six days. In Genesis 1, the man and the woman are created at the same time, whereas in Genesis 2 the man is created earlier than the woman. In Genesis 1, the animals are created before the man, which is the opposite of the order in Genesis 2.

Other creation accounts—in the Psalms, Isaiah 40–66, Job and Proverbs—also differ from one another and from Genesis 1. Psalms 77, 89 and 93, for example, depict creation as a cosmic battle with the forces of chaos; God's victory is the act of creation. Isaiah 40–55 uses creation-by-combat to interpret the reconstruction of Israel after the sixth-century exile. Israel's new creation is portrayed through a grand analogy—just as in olden times God brought Israel into being by vanquishing Sea (the Red or Reed Sea) and bringing the people to Canaan, so today he is bringing Israel into being by vanquishing Desert and bringing the people to Zion (see especially Isa. 43:16–21). Creation-by-combat is common in the Bible (and in the literature of Israel's neighbors). The creation-by-word in Genesis 1 is unique in the Old Testament and to make it the biblical standard, as creationists do, is gratuitous on purely biblical grounds.

Biblical and Modern Views of Creation

As the above examples suggest, creation in the Bible differs markedly from modern conceptions—a point that is neglected by creationism. There are important differences in the process, in the world that emerges and in the manner of reporting.

1. *The process of creation.* Ancient Near Eastern writers imagined creation on the model of human making or of natural activity. For example, the gods formed the world as an artisan works clay, or as a king's word makes things happen, or as a warrior defeats an enemy. Biblical writers did not draw the modern dichotomous distinction between "nature" and human beings, and they used psychic and social analogies to explain non-human phenomena. Today, influenced by scientific and evolutionary thinking, we understand creation as the (impersonal) interaction of physical forces extending over eons.
2. *The product or world that emerges.* For the ancients, creation issued in a *populated* universe. Human society was normally the term of biblical

accounts. Ancient cosmogonies explained the institutions and practices of contemporary society. The first appearance of a reality was a privileged time when the imprint of the divine maker was freshest. Hence, to know the origin of a thing was in some sense to know its essence. For moderns, on the other hand, creation is usually thought of in terms of the planets and stars. If life is mentioned, it is usually life in its most primitive forms. Human society and culture do not usually come into consideration.

3. *The manner of reporting and the criteria of truth.* The Bible often describes creation as a drama, whereas contemporary thinkers write scientific reports. The description in each case follows upon a particular conceptualization of creation, either "impersonal" or "dramatic." Each has its own criteria of truth. Scientific reports explain new data by new hypotheses, discarding old hypotheses when they do not adequately explain the data. There can be only *one* true account. Ancients, on the other hand, had many cosmogonies. They were not bothered, for example, by the impossibility of harmonizing the first and second chapters of Genesis. Their only requirement was verisimilitude—does the cosmogony make sense as a story? Ancients were less interested in how creation happened than in what the gods or God intended.

The Bible must be read in light of its difference—"The past is a foreign country; they do things differently there." Biblical cosmologists were not scientists or historians in the current meaning of those terms. They were people of faith seeking understanding by exploring the *origins* of their world. Instead of using the genre of the scientific essay that we would employ, they told and retold stories of origin, altering details or even recasting them entirely for the one purpose of explaining the world that God made. To read their stories of origins as if they were modern scientific reports is to misinterpret both the Bible and science.

Relation of Science and Theology

The third problem with creationism is that it reads biblical cosmogonies and scientific reports with the same literalness. Ian G. Barbour, who is professor of physics, professor of religion and Bean Professor of Science, Technology and Society at Carleton College in Minnesota, criticized such undifferentiated reading in his Gifford Lectures of 1989–91, published as *Religion and Science: Historical and Contemporary Issues* (1997, Part II, No. 4). Barbour argues that the models for relating science and religion are ultimately four: 1) conflict, 2) independence, 3) dialogue and 4) integration. Under the conflict model, Barbour groups both creationism and its great nemesis, the scientific materialism that holds that the scientific method is the *only* method and that matter is the fundamental reality. Each of these claims that science and theology make competing literal statements about the same domain, the history of nature. But, says Barbour, this mixes different levels of discourse. Scientific materialism starts from science but ends up making broad philosophical claims without acknowledging its shift. Biblical creationism moves from theology to make claims about science, again without recognizing its jump to a new level of discourse. Neither school owns up to its shifting methodology.

The models most commonly used in mainstream Christian theology are the third and the fourth, dialogue and integration. It turns out that dialogue is the model favored by many contemporary Roman Catholic thinkers—for example, John Paul II, Ernan McMullin, David Tracy, and the late Karl Rahner. Dialogue notices the presuppositions and the limit-questions of each area, and it is careful about methodology. Integration goes a step further, seeking some kind of integration between the content of theology and the content of science. The writings of Pierre Teilhard de Chardin (1881–1955) provide examples of this model. Whether we prefer the model of dialogue or integration, we have to be aware of the differences between the aims and methods of science and of theology. We cannot flatten out these differences as creationists do, nor can we do away with the differences between biblical literature and our own.

Value of Creationism

What ought one to think, then, of creationists and their project? First of all, we should recognize that creationists are human beings like ourselves, who earnestly seek religious meaning in the Bible. Moreover, if we are to be practical, we need to be aware that criticizing them will likely have no effect whatsoever. Creationists are constantly attacked and have become inured to it. The best approach, therefore, is positive—to show how a non-fundamentalist reading of the creation accounts can be religiously meaningful. Biblical creation stories reveal a God who is intent on making the world beautiful for the human race and also reveal what the world will be like at the end of time. God defeats chaos and is shown as the God of life, order and beauty.

Nonetheless, we must criticize the creationist project, even as we recognize its sincerity. This criticism will have a political dimension in addition to its epistemological one. As George Marsden has pointed out in *Fundamentalism and American Culture: The Shaping of Twentieth-Century Evangelicalism 1870–1925* (1980), American fundamentalism has a political goal—the preservation or restoration of a nondenominational conservative Christian culture. It is clear from the pressure they have exerted on state school boards that creationists share that political agenda. Opponents of creationism must, therefore, not only criticize it as an idea but also actively oppose creationists' strategy of imposing their religious views on others.

The debate about creationism in public schools can, however, have a happy outcome. American public education has traditionally excluded the Bible and religion from its curriculum. This exclusion of so central an aspect of human life and history has always been indefensible on purely academic grounds. The attempt to force schools to teach creationism can be a wake-up call to public educators. In November 1999 the National Bible Association and the First Amendment Center, with the support of 20 national organizations, ranging from the American Association of School Administrators to the Union of American Hebrew Congregations, published a booklet on teaching the Bible in public schools. Avoiding what it calls "two failed models"—advocacy of one religion or making schools into "religion-free zones"—the booklet suggests an approach in which "public schools neither inculcate nor inhibit religion but become places where religion and religious conviction are treated with fairness and respect." That approach is the best response to creationism.

The Crusade Against Evolution

On a spring day two years ago, in a downtown Columbus auditorium, the Ohio State Board of Education took up the question of how to teach the theory of evolution in public schools. A panel of four experts—two who believe in evolution, two who question it—debated whether an antievolution theory known as intelligent design should be allowed into the classroom.

This is an issue, of course, that was supposed to have been settled long ago. But 140 years after Darwin published *On the Origin of Species*, 75 years after John Scopes taught natural selection to a biology class in Tennessee, and 15 years after the US Supreme Court ruled against a Louisiana law mandating equal time for creationism, the question of how to teach the theory of evolution was being reopened here in Ohio. The two-hour forum drew chanting protesters and a police escort for the school board members. Two scientists, biologist Ken Miller from Brown University and physicist Lawrence Krauss from Case Western Reserve University two hours north in Cleveland, defended evolution. On the other side of the dais were two representatives from the Discovery Institute in Seattle, the main sponsor and promoter of intelligent design: Stephen Meyer, a professor at Palm Beach Atlantic University's School of Ministry and director of the Discovery Institute's Center for Science and Culture, and Jonathan Wells, a biologist, Discovery fellow, and author of *Icons of Evolution,* a 2000 book castigating textbook treatments of evolution. Krauss and Miller methodically presented their case against ID. "By no definition of any modern scientist is intelligent design science," Krauss concluded, "and it's a waste of our students' time to subject them to it."

Meyer and Wells took the typical intelligent design line: Biological life contains elements so complex—the mammalian blood-clotting mechanism, the bacterial flagellum—that they cannot be explained by natural selection. And so, the theory goes, we must be products of an intelligent designer. Creationists call that creator God, but proponents of intelligent design studiously avoid the G-word—and never point to the Bible for answers. Instead, ID believers speak the language of science to argue that Darwinian evolution is crumbling.

The debate's two-on-two format, with its appearance of equal sides, played right into the ID strategy—create the impression that this very complicated issue could be seen from two entirely rational yet opposing views. "This is a controversial subject," Meyer told the audience. "When two groups of experts disagree about a controversial subject that intersects with the public-school science curriculum, the students should be permitted to learn about both perspectives. We call this the 'teach the controversy' approach."

Since the debate, "teach the controversy" has become the rallying cry of the national intelligent-design movement, and Ohio has become the leading battleground. Several months after the debate, the Ohio school board voted to change state science standards, mandating that biology teachers "critically analyze" evolutionary theory. This fall, teachers will adjust their lesson plans and begin doing just that. In some cases, that means introducing the basic tenets of intelligent design. One of the state's sample lessons looks as though it were lifted from an ID textbook. It's the biggest victory so far for the Discovery Institute. "Our opponents would say that these are a bunch of know-nothing people on a state board," says Meyer. "We think it shows that our Darwinist colleagues have a real problem now."

But scientists aren't buying it. What Meyer calls "biology for the information age," they call creationism in a lab coat. ID's core scientific principles—laid out in the mid-1990s by a biochemist and a mathematician—have been thoroughly dismissed on the grounds that Darwin's theories can account for complexity, that ID relies on misunderstandings of evolution and flimsy probability calculations, and that it proposes no testable explanations.

As the Ohio debate revealed, however, the Discovery Institute doesn't need the favor of the scientific establishment to prevail in the public arena. Over the past decade, Discovery has gained ground in schools, op-ed pages, talk radio, and congressional resolutions as a "legitimate" alternative to evolution. ID is playing a central role in biology curricula and textbook controversies around the country. The institute and its supporters have taken the "teach the controversy" message to Alabama, Arizona, Minnesota, Missouri, Montana, New Mexico, and Texas.

The ID movement's rhetorical strategy—better to appear scientific than holy—has turned the evolution debate upside down. ID proponents quote Darwin, cite the Scopes monkey trial, talk of "scientific objectivity," then in the same breath declare that extraterrestrials might have designed life on Earth. It may seem counterintuitive, but the strategy is meticulously premeditated, and it's working as planned. The debate over Darwin is back, and coming to a 10th-grade biology class near you.

❦

At its heart, intelligent design is a revival of an argument made by British philosopher William Paley in 1802. In Natural Theology, the Anglican archdeacon suggested that the complexity of biological structures defied any explanation but a designer: God. Paley imagined finding a stone and a watch in a field. The watch, unlike the stone, appears to have been purposely assembled and wouldn't function without its precise combination of parts. "The inference," he wrote, "is inevitable, that the watch must have a maker." The same logic, he concluded, applied to biological structures like the vertebrate eye. Its complexity implied design.

Fifty years later, Darwin directly answered Paley's "argument to complexity." Evolution by natural selection, he argued in *Origin of Species,* could create the appearance of design. Darwin—and 100-plus years of evolutionary science after him—seemed to knock Paley into the dustbin of history.

In the American public arena, Paley's design argument has long been supplanted by biblical creationism. In the 1970s and 1980s, that movement recast the Bible version in the language of scientific inquiry—as "creation science"—and won legislative victories requiring "equal time" in some states. That is, until 1987, when the Supreme Court struck down Louisiana's law. Because creation science relies on biblical texts, the court reasoned, it "lacked a clear secular purpose" and violated the First Amendment clause prohibiting the establishment of religion. Since then, evolution has been the law of the land in US schools—if not always the local choice.

Paley re-emerged in the mid-1990s, however, when a pair of scientists reconstituted his ideas in an area beyond Darwin's ken: molecular biology. In his 1996 book *Darwin's Black Box,* Lehigh University biochemist Michael Behe contended that natural selection can't explain the "irreducible complexity" of molecular mechanisms like the bacterial flagellum, because its integrated parts offer no selective advantages on their own. Two years later, in *The Design Inference,* William Dembski, a philosopher and mathematician at Baylor University, proposed that any biological system exhibiting "information" that is both "complex" (highly improbable) and "specified" (serving a particular function) cannot be a product of chance or natural law. The only remaining option is an intelligent designer—whether God or an alien life force. These ideas became the cornerstones of ID, and Behe proclaimed the evidence for design to be "one of the greatest achievements in the history of science."

The scientific rationale behind intelligent design was being developed just as antievolution sentiment seemed to be bubbling up. In 1991, UC Berkeley law professor Phillip Johnson published *Darwin On Trial,* an influential anti-evolution book that dispensed with biblical creation accounts while uniting antievolutionists under a single, secular-sounding banner: intelligent design. In subsequent books, Johnson presents not just antievolution arguments but a broader opposition to the "philosophy of scientific materialism"—the assumption (known to scientists as "methodological materialism") that all events have material, rather than supernatural, explanations. To defeat it, he offers a strategy that would be familiar in the divisive world of politics, called "the wedge." Like a wedge inserted into a tree trunk, cracks in Darwinian theory can be used to "split the trunk," eventually overturning scientific materialism itself.

That's where Discovery comes in. The institute was founded as a conservative think tank in 1990 by longtime friends and former Harvard roommates Bruce Chapman—director of the census bureau during the Reagan administration—and technofuturist author George Gilder. "The institute is futurist and rebellious, and it's prophetic," says Gilder. "It has a science and technology orientation in a contrarian spirit." In 1994, Discovery added ID to its list of contrarian causes, which included everything from transportation to bioethics. Chapman hired Meyer, who studied origin-of-life issues at Cambridge University, and the institute signed Johnson—whom Chapman calls "the real godfather of the intelligent design movement"—as an adviser and adopted the wedge.

For Discovery, the "thin end" of the wedge—according to a fundraising document leaked on the Web in 1999—is the scientific work of Johnson, Behe, Dembski, and others. The next step involves "publicity and opinion-making." The final goals: "a direct confrontation with the advocates of material science" and "possible legal assistance in response to integration of design theory into public school science curricula."

Step one has made almost no headway with evolutionists—the near-universal majority of scientists with an opinion on the matter. But that, say Discovery's critics, is not the goal. "Ultimately, they have an evangelical Christian message that they want to push," says Michael Ruse, a philosopher of science at Florida State. "Intelligent design is the hook."

It's a lot easier to skip straight to steps two and three, and sound scientific in a public forum, than to deal with the rigor of the scientific community. "It starts with education," Johnson told me, referring to high school curricula. "That's where the public can have a voice. The universities and the scientific world do not recognize freedom of expression on this issue." Meanwhile, like any champion of a heretical scientific idea, ID's supporters see themselves as renegades, storming the gates of orthodoxy. "We all have a deep sense of indignation," says Meyer, "that the wool is being pulled over the public's eyes."

The buzz phrase most often heard in the institute's offices is *academic freedom*. "My hackles go up on the academic freedom issue," Chapman says. "You should be allowed in the sciences to ask questions and posit alternative theories."

None of this impresses the majority of the science world. "They have not been able to convince even a tiny amount of the scientific community," says Ken Miller. "They have not been able to win the marketplace of ideas."

And yet, the Discovery Institute's appeals to academic freedom create a kind of catch-22. If scientists ignore the ID movement, their silence is offered as further evidence of a conspiracy. If they join in, they risk reinforcing the perception of a battle between equal sides. Most scientists choose to remain silent. "Where the scientific community has been at fault," says Krauss, "is in assuming that these people are harmless, like flat-earthers. They don't realize that they are well organized, and that they have a political agenda."

Taped to the wall of Eugenie Scott's windowless office at the National Center for Science Education on the outskirts of Oakland, California, is a chart titled "Current Flare-Ups." It's a list of places where the teaching of evolution is under attack, from California to Georgia to Rio de Janeiro. As director of the center, which defends evolution in teaching controversies around the country, Scott has watched creationism up close for 30 years.

ID, in her view, is the most highly evolved form of creationism to date. "They've been enormously effective compared to the more traditional creationists, who have greater numbers and much larger budgets," she says.

Scott credits the blueprint laid out by Johnson, who realized that to win in the court of public opinion, ID needed only to cast reasonable doubt on evolution. "He said, 'Don't get involved in details, don't get involved in fact claims,'" says Scott. "'Forget about the age of Earth, forget about the flood, don't mention the Bible.'" The goal, she says, is "to focus on the big idea that evolution is inadequate. Intelligent design doesn't really explain anything. It says that evolution can't explain things. Everything else is hand-waving."

The movement's first test of Johnson's strategies began in 1999, when the Kansas Board of Education voted to remove evolution from the state's science standards. The decision, backed by traditional creationists, touched off a fiery debate, and the board eventually reversed itself after several antievolution members lost reelection bids. ID proponents used the melee as cover to launch their own initiative. A Kansas group called IDNet nearly pushed through its own textbook in a local school district.

Two years later, the Discovery Institute earned its first major political victory when US senator Rick Santorum (R-Pennsylvania) inserted language written by Johnson into the federal No Child Left Behind Act. The clause, eventually cut from the bill and placed in a nonbinding report, called for school curricula to "help students understand the full range of scientific views" on topics "that may generate controversy (such as biological evolution)."

As the institute was demonstrating its Beltway clout, a pro-ID group called Science Excellence for All Ohioans fueled a brewing local controversy. SEAO—consisting of a few part-time activists, a Web site, and a mailing list—began agitating to have ID inserted into Ohio's 10th-grade-biology standards. In the process, they attracted the attention of a few receptive school board members.

When the board proposed the two-on-two debate and invited Discovery, Meyer and company jumped at the opportunity. Meyer, whom Gilder calls the institute's resident "polymath," came armed with the Santorum amendment, which he read aloud for the school board. He was bringing a message from Washington: Teach the controversy. "We framed the issue quite differently than our supporters," says Meyer. The approach put pro-ID Ohioans on firmer rhetorical ground: Evolution should of course be taught, but "objectively." Hearing Meyer's suggestion, says Doug Rudy, a software engineer and SEAO's director, "we all sat back and said, Yeah, that's the way to go."

❦

Back in Seattle, around the corner from the Discovery Institute, Meyer offers some peer-reviewed evidence that there truly is a controversy that must be taught. "The Darwinists are bluffing," he says over a plate of oysters at a downtown seafood restaurant. "They have the science of the steam engine era, and it's not keeping up with the biology of the information age."

Meyer hands me a recent issue of *Microbiology and Molecular Biology Reviews* with an article by Carl Woese, an eminent microbiologist at the University of Illinois. In it, Woese decries the failure of reductionist biology—the tendency to look at systems as merely the sum of their parts—to keep up with the developments of molecular biology. Meyer says the conclusion of Woese's argument is that the Darwinian emperor has no clothes.

It's a page out of the antievolution playbook: using evolutionary biology's own literature against it, selectively quoting from the likes of Stephen Jay Gould to illustrate natural selection's downfalls. The institute marshals journal articles discussing evolution to provide policymakers with evidence of the raging controversy surrounding the issue.

Woese scoffs at Meyer's claim when I call to ask him about the paper. "To say that my criticism of Darwinists says that evolutionists have no clothes," Woese says, "is like saying that Einstein is criticizing Newton, therefore Newtonian physics is wrong." Debates about evolution's mechanisms, he continues, don't amount to challenges to the theory. And intelligent design "is not science. It makes no predictions and doesn't offer any explanation whatsoever, except for 'God did it.'"

Of course Meyer happily acknowledges that Woese is an ardent evolutionist. The institute doesn't need to impress Woese or his peers; it can simply co-opt the vocabulary of science—"academic freedom," "scientific objectivity," "teach the controversy"—and redirect it to a public trying to reconcile what appear to be two contradictory scientific views. By appealing to a sense of fairness, ID finds a place at the political table, and by merely entering the debate it can claim victory. "We don't need to win every argument to be a success," Meyer says. "We're trying to validate a discussion that's been long suppressed."

This is precisely what happened in Ohio. "I'm not a PhD in biology," says board member Michael Cochran. "But when I have X number of PhD experts telling me this, and X number telling me the opposite, the answer is probably somewhere between the two."

An exasperated Krauss claims that a truly representative debate would have had 10,000 pro-evolution scientists against two Discovery executives. "What these people want is for there to *be* a debate," says Krauss. "People in the audience say, Hey, these people sound reasonable. They argue, 'People have different opinions, we should present those opinions in school.' That is nonsense. Some people have opinions that the Holocaust never happened, but we don't teach that in history."

Eventually, the Ohio board approved a standard mandating that students learn to "describe how scientists continue to investigate and critically analyze aspects of evolutionary theory." Proclaiming victory, Johnson barnstormed Ohio churches soon after notifying congregations of a new, ID-friendly standard. In response, anxious board members added a clause stating that the standard "does not mandate the teaching or testing of intelligent design." Both sides claimed victory. A press release from IDNet trumpeted the mere inclusion of the phrase *intelligent design*, saying that "the implication of the statement is that the 'teaching or testing of intelligent design' is permitted." Some pro-evolution scientists, meanwhile, say there's nothing wrong with teaching students how to scrutinize theory. "I don't have a problem with that," says Patricia Princehouse, a professor at Case Western Reserve and an outspoken opponent of ID. "Critical analysis is exactly what scientists do."

The good feelings didn't last long. Early this year, a board-appointed committee unveiled sample lessons that laid out the kind of evolution questions students should debate. The models appeared to lift their examples from Wells' book *Icons of Evolution*. "When I first saw it, I was speechless," says Princehouse.

With a PhD in molecular and cell biology from UC Berkeley, Wells has the kind of cred that intelligent design proponents love to cite. But, as ID opponents enjoy pointing out, he's also a follower of Sun Myung Moon and once declared that Moon's prayers "convinced me that I should devote my life to destroying Darwinism." *Icons* attempts to discredit commonly used examples of evolution, like Darwin's finches and peppered moths. Writing in *Nature*, evolutionary biologist Jerry Coyne called *Icons* stealth creationism that "strives to debunk Darwinism using the familiar rhetoric of biblical creationists, including scientific quotations out of context, incomplete summaries of research, and muddled arguments."

After months of uproar, the most obvious *Icons*-inspired lessons were removed. But scientists remain furious. "The ones they left in are still arguments for special creation—but you'd have to know the literature to understand what they are saying. They've used so much technical jargon that anybody who doesn't know a whole lot of evolutionary biology looks at it and says 'It sounds scientific to me, what's the matter with it?'" says Princehouse. "As a friend of mine said, it takes a half a second for a baby to throw up all over your sweater. It takes hours to get it clean."

As Ohio teachers prepare their lessons for the coming year, the question must be asked: Why the fuss over an optional lesson plan or two? After all, both sides agree that the new biology standards—in which 10 evolution lessons replace standards that failed to mention evolution at all—are a vast improvement. The answer: In an era when the government is pouring billions into biology, and when stem cells and genetically modified food are front-page news, spending even a small part of the curriculum on bogus criticisms of evolution is arguably more detrimental now than any time in history. Ironically, says Ohio State University biology professor Steve Rissing, the education debate coincides with Ohio's efforts to lure biotech companies. "How can we do that when our high school biology is failing us?" he says. "Our cornfields are gleaming with GMO corn. There's a fundamental disconnect there."

Intelligent design advocates say that teaching students to "critically analyze" evolution will help give them the skills to "see both sides" of all scientific issues. And if the Discovery Institute execs have their way, those skills will be used to reconsider the philosophy of modern science itself—which they blame for everything from divorce to abortion to the insanity defense. "Our culture has been deeply influenced by materialist thought," says Meyer.

"We think it's deeply destructive, and we think it's false. And we mean to overturn it."

It's mid-July, and the Ohio school board is about to hold its final meeting before classes start this year. There's nothing about intelligent design on the agenda. The debate was settled months ago. And yet, Princehouse, Rissing, and two other scientists rise to speak during the "non-agenda" public testimony portion.

One by one, the scientists recite their litany of objections: The model lesson plan is still based on concepts from ID literature; the ACLU is considering to sue to stop it; the National Academy of Sciences opposes it as unscientific. "This is my last time," says Rissing, "as someone who has studied science and the process of evolution for 25 years, to say I perceive that my children and I are suffering injuries based on a flawed lesson plan that this board has passed."

During a heated question-and-answer session, one board member accuses the scientists of posturing for me, the only reporter in the audience. Michael Cochran challenges the scientists to cite any testimony that the board hadn't already heard "ad infinitum." Another board member, Deborah Owens-Fink, declares the issue already closed. "We've listened to experts on both sides of this for three years," she says. "Ultimately, the question of what students should learn "is decided in a democracy, not by any one group of experts."

The notion is noble enough: In a democracy, every idea gets heard. But in science, not all theories are equal. Those that survive decades—centuries—of scientific scrutiny end up in classrooms, and those that don't are discarded. The intelligent design movement is using scientific rhetoric to bypass scientific scrutiny. And when science education is decided by charm and stage presence, the Discovery Institute wins.

POSTSCRIPT

Should Creationism and Evolution Get Equal Time in Schools?

In 1999, the Kansas Board of Education deleted evolution—as well as much other science that would support the idea of an Earth and universe older than 6,000 years—from coverage in state competency tests. Since most teachers could be expected to focus their efforts on material, their students would need to score well on the tests, and since the board had vocal anti-evolution, pro-creation members, the board's move was widely seen as supporting the anti-evolution, pro-creation agenda. See Marjorie George, "And Then God Created Kansas . . . ," *University of Pennsylvania Law Review* (January 2001). Early in 2001, a new Kansas Board of Education took office and promptly put evolution back in the curriculum. See Eugene Russo, "Fighting Darwin's Battles," *The Scientist* (March 19, 2001). Yet the battle is hardly won. Not even Pope John Paul II's 1996 announcement that "new knowledge leads us to recognize that the theory of evolution is more than a hypothesis" had much impact. Indeed, in November 2004, the balance of power on the Kansas Board of Education had changed again, and an effort to move "Intelligent Design" into the curriculum was growing. See Yudhijit Bhattacharjee, "Kansas Gears Up for Another Battle Over Teaching Evolution," *Science* (April 29, 2005). A similar battle was raging in Dover, Pennsylvania; see Jeffrey Mervis, "Dover Teachers Want No Part of Intelligent-Design Statement," *Science* (January 28, 2005).

The debate has at times turned abusive, as it did in May 1996, when biologists attempting to inform the Ohio House Education Committee of how thoroughly the evidence supports the theory of evolution were heckled, jeered, and shouted down. See Karen Schmidt, "Creationists Evolve New Strategy," *Science* (July 26, 1996). The rhetoric on the other side is not always much better. Virginia Barbour, "Science and Myth," *Lancet* (April 20, 2002), says that "intellectual laziness is the most charitable explanation for not accepting the evidence for evolution." See also John Rennie, "15 Answers to Creationist Nonsense" (*Scientific American*, July 2002).

The late Stephen Jay Gould, in "The Persistently Flat Earth," *Natural History* (March 1994), makes the point that irrationality and dogmatism serve the adherents of neither science nor religion well: "The myth of a war between science and religion remains all too current and continues to impede a proper bonding and conciliation between these two utterly different and powerfully important institutions of human life."

Many Americans appear to agree with Gould. For example, Dudley Barlow, in "The Teachers' Lounge: Kansas Junta Repudiated," *Education Digest* (May 2000), contends that most Americans are willing to give creationism space in public education because "it is good to expose students to several different ways of thinking about complex ideas." However, the battle continues (see Mano Singham, "The Science and Religion Wars," *Phi Delta Kappan* [February 2000] and Randy Moore, "The Revival of Creationism in the United States," *Journal of Biological Education* [Winter 2000]) and even shows sign of spreading abroad. In Turkey, for instance, teachers of evolution are receiving e-mailed death threats, and a legislator is trying to get evolution taken out of the schools. See Robert Koenig, "Creationism Takes Root Where Europe, Asia Meet," *Science* (May 18, 2001).

Among recent books on this issue, Thomas Woodward's *Doubts About Darwin: A History of Intelligent Design* (Baker Books, 2003) argues the case in favor of "Intelligent Design." Michael Ruses *Darwin and Design: Does Evolution Have a Purpose?* (Harvard University Press, 2003) also covers the history but concludes that those who study evolution have an almost religious response to the marvels they find. More critical efforts include Niall Shanks, *God, the Devil, and Darwin: A Critique of Intelligent Design Theory* (Oxford University Press, 2004); Barbara Forrest and Paul R. Gross, *Creationism's Trojan Horse: The Wedge of Intelligent Design* (Oxford University Press, 2004); and Matt Young and Taner Edis, eds., *Why Intelligent Design Fails: A Scientific Critique of the New Creationism* (Rutgers University Press, 1984).

Worldwatch Institute

The Worldwatch Institute is dedicated to fostering the evolution of an environmentally sustainable society, one in which human needs are met in ways that do not threaten the health of the natural environment or the prospects of future generations.

http://www.worldwatch.org

Department of Energy

The U.S. Department of Energy provides information on nuclear power, hydrogen, and other energy sources, as well as such energy-related issues as global warming.

http://www.energy.gov/engine/content.doc

Global Warming

The Environmental Protection Agency maintains this site to summarize the current state of knowledge about global warming.

http://www.epa.gov/globalwarming/

Intergovernmental Panel on Climate Change

The Intergovernmental Panel on Climate Change (IPCC) was formed by the World Meteorological Organization (WMO) and the United Nations Environment Programme (UNEP) to assess any scientific, technical, and socioeconomic information that is relevant to the understanding of the risk of human-induced climate change.

http://www.ipcc.ch

National Renewable Energy Laboratory

The National Renewable Energy Laboratory (NREL) is the leading center for renewable energy research in the United States.

http://www.nrel.gov

Heritage Foundation

The Heritage Foundation is a think tank whose mission is to formulate and promote conservative public policies based on the principles of free enterprise, limited government, individual freedom, traditional American values, and a strong national defense.

http://www.heritage.org

PART 2

The Environment

*A*s the damage that human beings do to their environment in the course of obtaining food, wood, ore, fuel, and other resources has become clear, many people have grown concerned. Some of that concern is for the environment—the landscapes and living things with which humanity shares its world. Some of that concern is more for human welfare; it focuses on the ways in which environmental damage threatens human health or even human survival.

Among the major environmental issues are those related to energy. By releasing vast amounts of carbon dioxide, fossil fuels threaten to change the world's climate. Potential solutions include greatly expanding the use of nuclear power and changing our automobile fuel from gasoline to hydrogen.

- Should Society Act Now to Halt Global Warming?

- Is It Time to Revive Nuclear Power?

- Will Hydrogen Replace Fossil Fuels for Cars?

ISSUE 4

Should Society Act Now to Halt Global Warming?

YES: Intergovernmental Panel on Climate Change, from "Climate Change 2001: The Scientific Basis," A Report of Working Group I of the Intergovernmental Panel on Climate Change (2001)

NO: Bush Administration, from "Global Climate Change Policy Book," http://www.whitehouse.gov/news/releases/2002/02/climatechange.html (February 2002)

ISSUE SUMMARY

YES: The Intergovernmental Panel on Climate Change states that global warming appears to be real, with strong effects on sea level, ice cover, and rainfall patterns to come, and that human activities—particularly emissions of carbon dioxide—are to blame.

NO: The Bush administration's plan for dealing with global warming insists that short-term economic health must come before reducing emissions of greenhouse gases. It is more useful to reduce "greenhouse gas intensity" or emissions per dollar of economic activity than to reduce total emissions.

$\mathbf{S}$cientists have known for more than a century that carbon dioxide and other "greenhouse gases" (including water vapor, methane, and chlorofluorocarbons) help prevent heat from escaping the earth's atmosphere. In fact, it is this "greenhouse effect" that keeps the earth warm enough to support life. Yet there can be too much of a good thing. Ever since the dawn of the industrial age, humans have been burning vast quantities of fossil fuels, releasing the carbon they contain as carbon dioxide. Because of this, some estimate that by the year 2050, the amount of carbon dioxide in the air will be double what it was in 1850. By 1982 an increase was apparent. Less than a decade later, many researchers were saying that the climate had already begun to warm. Now the scientific consensus is that the global climate is warming and will continue to warm (see Naomi Oreskes, "The Scientific Consensus on Climate Change," *Science* [December 3, 2004]). There is less agreement on just how much it will warm or what the impact of the warming will be on human (and other) life.

The debate has been heated. The June 1992 issue of *The Bulletin of the Atomic Scientists* carries two articles on the possible consequences of the greenhouse effect. In "Global Warming: The Worst Case," Jeremy Leggett says that although there are enormous uncertainties, a warmer climate will release more carbon dioxide, which will warm the climate even further. As a result, soil will grow drier, forest fires will occur more frequently, plant pests will thrive, and methane trapped in the world's seabeds will be released and will increase global warming much further. Leggett also hints at the possibility that polar ice caps will melt and raise sea levels by hundreds of feet.

Taking the opposing view, in "Warming Theories Need Warning Label," S. Fred Singer emphasizes the uncertainties in the projections of global warming and their dependence on the accuracy of the computer models that generate them, and he argues that improvements in the models have consistently shrunk the size of the predicted change. There will be no catastrophe, he argues, and money spent to ward off the climate warming would be better spent on "so many pressing—and real—problems in need of resources." See Stephen Goode, "Singer Cool on Global Warming," *Insight* (April 27–May 10, 2004).

Global warming, says the UN Environment Programme, will do some $300 billion in damage each year to the world economy by 2050. In March 2001 President George W. Bush announced that the United States would not take steps to reduce greenhouse emissions—called for by the international treaty negotiated in 1997 in Kyoto, Japan—because such reductions would harm the American economy (the U.S. Senate has not ratified the Kyoto treaty). Since the Intergovernmental Panel on Climate Change (IPCC) had just released its third report saying that past forecasts were, in essence, too conservative, Bush's stance provoked immense outcry.

The analysis of data and computer simulations described by the IPCC in the following selection indicates that global warming is a genuine problem. According to the IPCC, climate warming is already apparent and will get worse than previous forecasts had suggested. Sea level will rise, ice cover will shrink, rainfall patterns will change, and human activities—particularly emissions of carbon dioxide—are to blame. The report excerpt reprinted here does not suggest that anything in particular should be done, but other writers, such as Stephen H. Schneider and Kristin Kuntz-Duriseti ("Facing Global Warming," *The World & I* [June 2001]), pull no punches: "Nearly all knowledgeable scientists agree that some global warming is inevitable, that major warming is quite possible, and that for the bulk of humanity the net effects are more likely to be negative than positive. This will hold true particularly if global warming is allowed to increase beyond a few degrees, which is likely to occur by the middle of this century if no policies are undertaken to mitigate emissions."

The Bush administration's plan for dealing with global warming insists that short-term economic health must come before reducing emissions of greenhouse gases. It is more useful to reduce "greenhouse gas intensity" or emissions per dollar of economic activity, which will not interfere with continued economic growth the way reducing total emissions would surely do. Unfortunately, if greenhouse gas intensity is reduced and the economy grows, total emissions may well increase dramatically.

 **YES**

Summary for Policymakers

The Third Assessment Report of Working Group I of the Intergovernmental Panel on Climate Change (IPCC) builds upon past assessments and incorporates new results from . . . five years of research on climate change. Many hundreds of scientists from many countries participated in its preparation and review.

This Summary for Policymakers (SPM), which was approved by IPCC member governments in Shanghai in January 2001, describes the current state of understanding of the climate system and provides estimates of its projected future evolution and their uncertainties. . . .

An increasing body of observations gives a collective picture of a warming world and other changes in the climate system.

Since the release of the Second Assessment Report (SAR), additional data from new studies of current and palaeoclimates, improved analysis of data sets, more rigorous evaluation of their quality, and comparisons among data from different sources have led to greater understanding of climate change.

The global average surface temperature has increased over the 20th century by about 0.6°C.

- The global average surface temperature (the average of near surface air temperature over land, and sea surface temperature) has increased since 1861. Over the 20th century the increase has been 0.6 ± 0.2°C. This value is about 0.15°C larger than that estimated by the SAR for the period up to 1994, owing to the relatively high temperatures of the additional years (1995 to 2000) and improved methods of processing the data. These numbers take into account various adjustments, including urban heat island effects. The record shows a great deal of variability; for example, most of the warming occurred during the 20th century, during two periods, 1910 to 1945 and 1976 to 2000.
- Globally, it is very likely that the 1990s was the warmest decade and 1998 the warmest year in the instrumental record, since 1861.

- New analyses of proxy data for the Northern Hemisphere indicate that the increase in temperature in the 20th century is likely to have been the largest of any century during the past 1,000 years. It is also likely that, in the Northern Hemisphere, the 1990s was the warmest decade and 1998 the warmest year. Because less data are available, less is known about annual averages prior to 1,000 years before present and for conditions prevailing in most of the Southern Hemisphere prior to 1861.
- On average, between 1950 and 1993, night-time daily minimum air temperatures over land increased by about 0.2°C per decade. This is about twice the rate of increase in daytime daily maximum air temperatures (0.1°C per decade). This has lengthened the freeze-free season in many mid- and high latitude regions. The increase in sea surface temperature over this period is about half that of the mean land surface air temperature.

Temperatures have risen during the past four decades in the lowest 8 kilometres of the atmosphere.

- Since the late 1950s (the period of adequate observations from weather balloons), the overall global temperature increases in the lowest 8 kilometres of the atmosphere and in surface temperature have been similar at 0.1°C per decade.
- Since the start of the satellite record in 1979, both satellite and weather balloon measurements show that the global average temperature of the lowest 8 kilometres of the atmosphere has changed by $+0.05 \pm 0.10$°C per decade, but the global average surface temperature has increased significantly by $+0.15 \pm 0.05$°C per decade. The difference in the warming rates is statistically significant. This difference occurs primarily over the tropical and sub-tropical regions.
- The lowest 8 kilometres of the atmosphere and the surface are influenced differently by factors such as stratospheric ozone depletion, atmospheric aerosols, and the El Niño phenomenon. Hence, it is physically plausible to expect that over a short time period (e.g., 20 years) there may be differences in temperature trends. In addition, spatial sampling techniques can also explain some of the differences in trends, but these differences are not fully resolved.

Snow cover and ice extent have decreased.

- Satellite data show that there are very likely to have been decreases of about 10% in the extent of snow cover since the late 1960s, and ground-based observations show that there is very likely to have been a reduction of about two weeks in the annual duration of lake and river ice cover in the mid- and high latitudes of the Northern Hemisphere, over the 20th century.
- There has been a widespread retreat of mountain glaciers in non-polar regions during the 20th century.
- Northern Hemisphere spring and summer sea-ice extent has decreased by about 10 to 15% since the 1950s. It is likely that there

has been about a 40% decline in Arctic sea-ice thickness during late summer to early autumn in recent decades and a considerably slower decline in winter sea-ice thickness.

Global average sea level has risen and ocean heat content has increased.

- Tide gauge data show that global average sea level rose between 0.1 and 0.2 metres during the 20th century.
- Global ocean heat content has increased since the late 1950s, the period for which adequate observations of sub-surface ocean temperatures have been available.

Changes have also occurred in other important aspects of climate.

- It is very likely that precipitation has increased by 0.5 to 1% per decade in the 20th century over most mid- and high latitudes of the Northern Hemisphere continents, and it is likely that rainfall has increased by 0.2 to 0.3% per decade over the tropical (10°N to 10°S) land areas. Increases in the tropics are not evident over the past few decades. It is also likely that rainfall has decreased over much of the Northern Hemisphere sub-tropical (10°N to 30°N) land areas during the 20th century by about 0.3% per decade. In contrast to the Northern Hemisphere, no comparable systematic changes have been detected in broad latitudinal averages over the Southern Hemisphere. There are insufficient data to establish trends in precipitation over the oceans.
- In the mid- and high latitudes of the Northern Hemisphere over the latter half of the 20th century, it is likely that there has been a 2 to 4% increase in the frequency of heavy precipitation events. Increases in heavy precipitation events can arise from a number of causes, e.g., changes in atmospheric moisture, thunderstorm activity and large-scale storm activity.
- It is likely that there has been a 2% increase in cloud cover over mid- to high latitude land areas during the 20th century. In most areas the trends relate well to the observed decrease in daily temperature range.
- Since 1950 it is very likely that there has been a reduction in the frequency of extreme low temperatures, with a smaller increase in the frequency of extreme high temperatures.
- Warm episodes of the El Niño-Southern Oscillation (ENSO) phenomenon (which consistently affects regional variations of precipitation and temperature over much of the tropics, sub-tropics and some mid-latitude areas) have been more frequent, persistent and intense since the mid-1970s, compared with the previous 100 years.
- Over the 20th century (1900 to 1995), there were relatively small increases in global land areas experiencing severe drought or severe wetness. In many regions, these changes are dominated by inter-decadal and multi-decadal climate variability, such as the shift in ENSO towards more warm events.
- In some regions, such as parts of Asia and Africa, the frequency and intensity of droughts have been observed to increase in recent decades.

Some important aspects of climate appear not to have changed.

- A few areas of the globe have not warmed in recent decades, mainly over some parts of the Southern Hemisphere oceans and parts of Antarctica.
- No significant trends of Antarctic sea-ice extent are apparent since 1978, the period of reliable satellite measurements.
- Changes globally in tropical and extra-tropical storm intensity and frequency are dominated by inter-decadal to multi-decadal variations, with no significant trends evident over the 20th century. Conflicting analyses make it difficult to draw definitive conclusions about changes in storm activity, especially in the extra-tropics.
- No systematic changes in the frequency of tornadoes, thunder days, or hail events are evident in the limited areas analysed.

Emissions of greenhouse gases and aerosols due to human activities continue to alter the atmosphere in ways that are expected to affect the climate.

Changes in climate occur as a result of both internal variability within the climate system and external factors (both natural and anthropogenic). The influence of external factors on climate can be broadly compared using the concept of radiative forcing. A positive radiative forcing, such as that produced by increasing concentrations of greenhouse gases, tends to warm the surface. A negative radiative forcing, which can arise from an increase in some types of aerosols (microscopic airborne particles) tends to cool the surface. Natural factors, such as changes in solar output or explosive volcanic activity, can also cause radiative forcing. Characterisation of these climate forcing agents and their changes over time is required to understand past climate changes in the context of natural variations and to project what climate changes could lie ahead.

Concentrations of atmospheric greenhouse gases and their radiative forcing have continued to increase as a result of human activities.

- The atmospheric concentration of carbon dioxide (CO_2) has increased by 31% since 1750. The present CO_2 concentration has not been exceeded during the past 420,000 years and likely not during the past 20 million years. The current rate of increase is unprecedented during at least the past 20,000 years.
- About three-quarters of the anthropogenic emissions of CO_2 to the atmosphere during the past 20 years is due to fossil fuel burning. The rest is predominantly due to land-use change, especially deforestation.
- Currently the ocean and the land together are taking up about half of the anthropogenic CO_2 emissions. On land, the uptake of anthropogenic CO_2 very likely exceeded the release of CO_2 by deforestation during the 1990s.
- The rate of increase of atmospheric CO_2 concentration has been about 1.5 ppm (0.4%) per year over the past two decades. During the 1990s the year to year increase varied from 0.9 ppm (0.2%) to

2.8 ppm (0.8%). A large part of this variability is due to the effect of climate variability (e.g., El Niño events) on CO_2 uptake and release by land and oceans.

- The atmospheric concentration of methane (CH_4) has increased by 1060 ppb (151%) since 1750 and continues to increase. The present CH_4 concentration has not been exceeded during the past 420,000 years. The annual growth in CH_4 concentration slowed and became more variable in the 1990s, compared with the 1980s. Slightly more than half of current CH_4 emissions are anthropogenic (e.g., use of fossil fuels, cattle, rice agriculture and landfills). In addition, carbon monoxide (CO) emissions have recently been identified as a cause of increasing CH_4 concentration.
- The atmospheric concentration of nitrous oxide (N_2O) has increased by 46 ppb (17%) since 1750 and continues to increase. The present N_2O concentration has not been exceeded during at least the past thousand years. About a third of current N_2O emissions are anthropogenic (e.g., agricultural soils, cattle feed lots and chemical industry).
- Since 1995, the atmospheric concentrations of many of those halocarbon gases that are both ozone-depleting and greenhouse gases (e.g., $CFCl_3$ and CF_2Cl_2), are either increasing more slowly or decreasing, both in response to reduced emissions under the regulations of the Montreal Protocol and its Amendments. Their substitute compounds (e.g., CHF_2Cl and CF_3CH_2F) and some other synthetic compounds (e.g., perfluorocarbons (PFCs) and sulphur hexafluoride (SF_6)) are also greenhouse gases, and their concentrations are currently increasing. . . .

Confidence in the ability of models to project future climate has increased.

Complex physically-based climate models are required to provide detailed estimates of feedbacks and of regional features. Such models cannot yet simulate all aspects of climate (e.g., they still cannot account fully for the observed trend in the surface-troposphere temperature difference since 1979) and there are particular uncertainties associated with clouds and their interaction with radiation and aerosols. Nevertheless, confidence in the ability of these models to provide useful projections of future climate has improved due to their demonstrated performance on a range of space and time-scales.

- Understanding of climate processes and their incorporation in climate models have improved, including water vapour, sea-ice dynamics, and ocean heat transport.
- Some recent models produce satisfactory simulations of current climate without the need for non-physical adjustments of heat and water fluxes at the ocean-atmosphere interface used in earlier models.
- Simulations that include estimates of natural and anthropogenic forcing reproduce the observed large-scale changes in surface temperature over the 20th century. However, contributions from some

additional processes and forcings may not have been included in the models. Nevertheless, the large-scale consistency between models and observations can be used to provide an independent check on projected warming rates over the next few decades under a given emissions scenario.

- Some aspects of model simulations of ENSO, monsoons and the North Atlantic Oscillation, as well as selected periods of past climate, have improved.

There is new and stronger evidence that most of the warming observed over the last 50 years is attributable to human activities.

The SAR concluded: "The balance of evidence suggests a discernible human influence on global climate." That report also noted that the anthropogenic signal was still emerging from the background of natural climate variability. Since the SAR, progress has been made in reducing uncertainty, particularly with respect to distinguishing and quantifying the magnitude of responses to different external influences. Although many of the sources of uncertainty identified in the SAR still remain to some degree, new evidence and improved understanding support an updated conclusion.

- There is a longer and more closely scrutinised temperature record and new model estimates of variability. The warming over the past 100 years is very unlikely to be due to internal variability alone, as estimated by current models. Reconstructions of climate data for the past 1,000 years also indicate that this warming was unusual and is unlikely to be entirely natural in origin.
- There are new estimates of the climate response to natural and anthropogenic forcing, and new detection techniques have been applied. Detection and attribution studies consistently find evidence for an anthropogenic signal in the climate record of the last 35 to 50 years.
- Simulations of the response to natural forcings alone (i.e., the response to variability in solar irradiance and volcanic eruptions) do not explain the warming in the second half of the 20th century. However, they indicate that natural forcings may have contributed to the observed warming in the first half of the 20th century.
- The warming over the last 50 years due to anthropogenic greenhouse gases can be identified despite uncertainties in forcing due to anthropogenic sulphate aerosol and natural factors (volcanoes and solar irradiance). The anthropogenic sulphate aerosol forcing, while uncertain, is negative over this period and therefore cannot explain the warming. Changes in natural forcing during most of this period are also estimated to be negative and are unlikely to explain the warming.
- Detection and attribution studies comparing model simulated changes with the observed record can now take into account uncertainty in the magnitude of modelled response to external forcing, in particular that due to uncertainty in climate sensitivity.
- Most of these studies find that, over the last 50 years, the estimated rate and magnitude of warming due to increasing concentrations of

greenhouse gases alone are comparable with, or larger than, the observed warming. Furthermore, most model estimates that take into account both greenhouse gases and sulphate aerosols are consistent with observations over this period.

- The best agreement between model simulations and observations over the last 140 years has been found when all the above anthropogenic and natural forcing factors are combined. These results show that the forcings included are sufficient to explain the observed changes, but do not exclude the possibility that other forcings may also have contributed.

In the light of new evidence and taking into account the remaining uncertainties, most of the observed warming over the last 50 years is likely to have been due to the increase in greenhouse gas concentrations.

Furthermore, it is very likely that the 20th century warming has contributed significantly to the observed sea level rise, through thermal expansion of sea water and widespread loss of land ice. Within present uncertainties, observations and models are both consistent with a lack of significant acceleration of sea level rise during the 20th century.

Human influences will continue to change atmospheric composition throughout the 21st century.

Models have been used to make projections of atmospheric concentrations of greenhouse gases and aerosols, and hence of future climate, based upon emissions scenarios from the IPCC Special Report on Emission Scenarios (SRES). These scenarios were developed to update the IS92 series, which were used in the SAR and are shown for comparison here in some cases.

Greenhouse Gases

- Emissions of CO_2 due to fossil fuel burning are virtually certain to be the dominant influence on the trends in atmospheric CO_2 concentration during the 21st century.
- As the CO_2 concentration of the atmosphere increases, ocean and land will take up a decreasing fraction of anthropogenic CO_2 emissions. The net effect of land and ocean climate feedbacks as indicated by models is to further increase projected atmospheric CO_2 concentrations, by reducing both the ocean and land uptake of CO_2.
- By 2100, carbon cycle models project atmospheric CO_2 concentrations of 540 to 970 ppm for the illustrative SRES scenarios (90 to 250% above the concentration of 280 ppm in the year 1750). These projections include the land and ocean climate feedbacks. Uncertainties, especially about the magnitude of the climate feedback from the terrestrial biosphere, cause a variation of about –10 to +30% around each scenario. The total range is 490 to 1260 ppm (75 to 350% above the 1750 concentration).
- Changing land use could influence atmospheric CO_2 concentration. Hypothetically, if all of the carbon released by historical land-use changes could be restored to the terrestrial biosphere over

the course of the century (e.g., by reforestation), CO_2 concentration would be reduced by 40 to 70 ppm.

- Model calculations of the concentrations of the non-CO_2 greenhouse gases by 2100 vary considerably across the SRES illustrative scenarios, with CH_4 changing by –190 to +1,970 ppb (present concentration 1,760 ppb), N_2O changing by +38 to +144 ppb (present concentration 316 ppb), total tropospheric O_3 changing by –12 to +62%, and a wide range of changes in concentrations of HFCs, PFCs and SF_6, all relative to the year 2000. In some scenarios, total tropospheric O_3 would become as important a radiative forcing agent as CH_4 and, over much of the Northern Hemisphere, would threaten the attainment of current air quality targets.
- Reductions in greenhouse gas emissions and the gases that control their concentration would be necessary to stabilise radiative forcing. For example, for the most important anthropogenic greenhouse gas, carbon cycle models indicate that stabilisation of atmospheric CO_2 concentrations at 450, 650 or 1,000 ppm would require global anthropogenic CO_2 emissions to drop below 1990 levels, within a few decades, about a century, or about two centuries, respectively, and continue to decrease steadily thereafter. Eventually CO_2 emissions would need to decline to a very small fraction of current emissions.

Aerosols

The SRES scenarios include the possibility of either increases or decreases in anthropogenic aerosols (e.g., sulphate aerosols, biomass aerosols, black and organic carbon aerosols) depending on the extent of fossil fuel use and policies to abate polluting emissions. In addition, natural aerosols (e.g., sea salt, dust and emissions leading to the production of sulphate and carbon aerosols) are projected to increase as a result of changes in climate.

Radiative Forcing over the 21st Century

For the SRES illustrative scenarios, relative to the year 2000, the global mean radiative forcing due to greenhouse gases continues to increase through the 21st century, with the fraction due to CO_2 projected to increase from slightly more than half to about three quarters. The change in the direct plus indirect aerosol radiative forcing is projected to be smaller in magnitude than that of CO_2.

Global average temperature and sea level are projected to rise under all IPCC SRES scenarios.

In order to make projections of future climate, models incorporate past, as well as future emissions of greenhouse gases and aerosols. Hence, they include estimates of warming to date and the commitment to future warming from past emissions.

Temperature

- The globally averaged surface temperature is projected to increase by 1.4 to 5.8°C over the period 1990 to 2100. These results are for the full range of 35 SRES scenarios, based on a number of climate models.
- Temperature increases are projected to be greater than those in the SAR, which were about 1.0 to 3.5°C based on the six IS92 scenarios. The higher projected temperatures and the wider range are due primarily to the lower projected sulphur dioxide emissions in the SRES scenarios relative to the IS92 scenarios.
- The projected rate of warming is much larger than the observed changes during the 20th century and is very likely to be without precedent during at least the last 10,000 years, based on palaeoclimate data.
- By 2100, the range in the surface temperature response across the group of climate models run with a given scenario is comparable to the range obtained from a single model run with the different SRES scenarios.
- On timescales of a few decades, the current observed rate of warming can be used to constrain the projected response to a given emissions scenario despite uncertainty in climate sensitivity. This approach suggests that anthropogenic warming is likely to lie in the range of 0.1 to 0.2°C per decade over the next few decades under the IS92a scenario. . . .
- Based on recent global model simulations, it is very likely that nearly all land areas will warm more rapidly than the global average, particularly those at northern high latitudes in the cold season. Most notable of these is the warming in the northern regions of North America, and northern and central Asia, which exceeds global mean warming in each model by more than 40%. In contrast, the warming is less than the global mean change in south and southeast Asia in summer and in southern South America in winter.
- Recent trends for surface temperature to become more El Niño-like in the tropical Pacific, with the eastern tropical Pacific warming more than the western tropical Pacific, with a corresponding eastward shift of precipitation, are projected to continue in many models.

Precipitation

Based on global model simulations and for a wide range of scenarios, global average water vapour concentration and precipitation are projected to increase during the 21st century. By the second half of the 21st century, it is likely that precipitation will have increased over northern mid- to high latitudes and Antarctica in winter. At low latitudes there are both regional increases and decreases over land areas. Larger year to year variations in precipitation are very likely over most areas where an increase in mean precipitation is projected. . . .

El Niño

- Confidence in projections of changes in future frequency, amplitude, and spatial pattern of El Niño events in the tropical Pacific is tempered by some shortcomings in how well El Niño is simulated in complex models. Current projections show little change or a small increase in amplitude for El Niño events over the next 100 years.
- Even with little or no change in El Niño amplitude, global warming is likely to lead to greater extremes of drying and heavy rainfall and increase the risk of droughts and floods that occur with El Niño events in many different regions.

Monsoons

It is likely that warming associated with increasing greenhouse gas concentrations will cause an increase of Asian summer monsoon precipitation variability. Changes in monsoon mean duration and strength depend on the details of the emission scenario. The confidence in such projections is also limited by how well the climate models simulate the detailed seasonal evolution of the monsoons.

Thermohaline Circulation

Most models show weakening of the ocean thermohaline circulation which leads to a reduction of the heat transport into high latitudes of the Northern Hemisphere. However, even in models where the thermohaline circulation weakens, there is still a warming over Europe due to increased greenhouse gases. The current projections using climate models do not exhibit a complete shut-down of the thermohaline circulation by 2100. Beyond 2100, the thermohaline circulation could completely, and possibly irreversibly, shut-down in either hemisphere if the change in radiative forcing is large enough and applied long enough.

Snow and Ice

- Northern Hemisphere snow cover and sea-ice extent are projected to decrease further.
- Glaciers and ice caps are projected to continue their widespread retreat during the 21st century.
- The Antarctic ice sheet is likely to gain mass because of greater precipitation, while the Greenland ice sheet is likely to lose mass because the increase in runoff will exceed the precipitation increase.
- Concerns have been expressed about the stability of the West Antarctic ice sheet because it is grounded below sea level. However, loss of grounded ice leading to substantial sea level rise from this source is now widely agreed to be very unlikely during the 21st century, although its dynamics are still inadequately understood, especially for projections on longer time-scales.

Sea Level

Global mean sea level is projected to rise by 0.09 to 0.88 metres between 1990 and 2100, for the full range of SRES scenarios. This is due primarily to thermal expansion and loss of mass from glaciers and ice caps. The range of sea level rise presented in the SAR was 0.13 to 0.94 metres based on the IS92 scenarios. Despite the higher temperature change projections in this assessment, the sea level projections are slightly lower, primarily due to the use of improved models, which give a smaller contribution from glaciers and ice sheets.

Anthropogenic climate change will persist for many centuries.

- Emissions of long-lived greenhouse gases (i.e., CO_2, N_2O, PFCs, SF_6) have a lasting effect on atmospheric composition, radiative forcing and climate. For example, several centuries after CO_2 emissions occur, about a quarter of the increase in CO_2 concentration caused by these emissions is still present in the atmosphere.
- After greenhouse gas concentrations have stabilised, global average surface temperatures would rise at a rate of only a few tenths of a degree per century rather than several degrees per century as projected for the 21st century without stabilisation. The lower the level at which concentrations are stabilised, the smaller the total temperature change.
- Global mean surface temperature increases and rising sea level from thermal expansion of the ocean are projected to continue for hundreds of years after stabilisation of greenhouse gas concentrations (even at present levels), owing to the long timescales on which the deep ocean adjusts to climate change.
- Ice sheets will continue to react to climate warming and contribute to sea level rise for thousands of years after climate has been stabilised. Climate models indicate that the local warming over Greenland is likely to be one to three times the global average. Ice sheet models project that a local warming of larger than 3°C, if sustained for millennia, would lead to virtually a complete melting of the Greenland ice sheet with a resulting sea level rise of about 7 metres. A local warming of 5.5°C, if sustained for 1,000 years, would be likely to result in a contribution from Greenland of about 3 metres to sea level rise.
- Current ice dynamic models suggest that the West Antarctic ice sheet could contribute up to 3 metres to sea level rise over the next 1,000 years, but such results are strongly dependent on model assumptions regarding climate change scenarios, ice dynamics and other factors.

Further action is required to address remaining gaps in information and understanding.

Further research is required to improve the ability to detect, attribute and understand climate change, to reduce uncertainties and to project future climate changes. In particular, there is a need for additional systematic and sustained observations, modelling and process studies. A serious concern is the decline of observational networks. The following are high priority areas for action.

- Systematic observations and reconstructions:

  - Reverse the decline of observational networks in many parts of the world.
  - Sustain and expand the observational foundation for climate studies by providing accurate, long-term, consistent data including implementation of a strategy for integrated global observations.
  - Enhance the development of reconstructions of past climate periods.
  - Improve the observations of the spatial distribution of greenhouse gases and aerosols.

- Modelling and process studies:

  - Improve understanding of the mechanisms and factors leading to changes in radiative forcing.
  - Understand and characterise the important unresolved processes and feedbacks, both physical and biogeochemical, in the climate system.
  - Improve methods to quantify uncertainties of climate projections and scenarios, including long-term ensemble simulations using complex models.
  - Improve the integrated hierarchy of global and regional climate models with a focus on the simulation of climate variability, regional climate changes and extreme events.
  - Link more effectively models of the physical climate and the biogeochemical system, and in turn improve coupling with descriptions of human activities.
  - Cutting across these foci are crucial needs associated with strengthening international co-operation and co-ordination in order to better utilise scientific, computational and observational resources. This should also promote the free exchange of data among scientists. A special need is to increase the observational and research capacities in many regions, particularly in developing countries. Finally, as is the goal of this assessment, there is a continuing imperative to communicate research advances in terms that are relevant to decision making.

Global Climate Change Policy Book

Executive Summary

> "Addressing global climate change will require a sustained effort, over many generations. My approach recognizes that sustained economic growth is the solution, not the problem—because a nation that grows its economy is a nation that can afford investments in efficiency, new technologies, and a cleaner environment."
>
> —President George W. Bush

The President announced a new approach to the challenge of global climate change. This approach is designed to harness the power of markets and technological innovation. It holds the promise of a new partnership with the developing world. And it recognizes that climate change is a complex, long-term challenge that will require a sustained effort over many generations. As the President has said, "The policy challenge is to act in a serious and sensible way, given the limits of our knowledge. While scientific uncertainties remain, we can begin now to address the factors that contribute to climate change."

While investments today in science will increase our understanding of this challenge, our investments in advanced energy and sequestration technologies will provide the breakthroughs we need to dramatically reduce our emissions in the longer term. In the near term, we will vigorously pursue emissions reductions even in the absence of complete knowledge. Our approach recognizes that sustained economic growth is an essential part of the solution, not the problem. Economic growth will make possible the needed investment in research, development, and deployment of advanced technologies. This strategy is one that should offer developing countries the incentive and means to join with us in tackling this challenge together. Significantly, the President's plan will:

- **Reduce the Greenhouse Gas Intensity of the U.S. Economy by 18 Percent in the Next Ten Years.** Greenhouse gas intensity measures the ratio of greenhouse gas (GHG) emissions to economic output. This

Global Climate Change Policy Book, February 2002.

new approach focuses on reducing the growth of GHG emissions, while sustaining the economic growth needed to finance investment in new, clean energy technologies. It sets America on a path to slow the growth of greenhouse gas emissions, and—as the science justifies—to stop and then reverse that growth:

- In efficiency terms, the 183 metric tons of emissions per million dollars GDP that we emit today will be lowered to 151 metric tons per million dollars GDP in 2012.
- Existing trends and efforts in technology improvement will play a significant role. Beyond that, the President's commitment will achieve 100 million metric tons of reduced emissions in 2012 alone, with more than 500 million metric tons in cumulative savings over the entire decade.
- This goal is comparable to the average progress that nations participating in the Kyoto Protocol are required to achieve.
- **Substantially Improve the Emission Reduction Registry.** The President directed the Secretary of Energy, in consultation with the Secretary of Commerce, the Secretary of Agriculture, and the Administrator of the Environmental Protection Agency, to propose improvements to the current voluntary emission reduction registration program under section 1605(b) of the 1992 Energy Policy Act within 120 days. These improvements will enhance measurement accuracy, reliability and verifiability, working with and taking into account emerging domestic and international approaches.
- **Protect and Provide Transferable Credits for Emissions Reduction.** The President directed the Secretary of Energy to recommend reforms to ensure that businesses and individuals that register reductions are not penalized under a future climate policy, and to give transferable credits to companies that can show real emissions reductions.
- **Review Progress Toward Goal and Take Additional Action if Necessary.** If, in 2012, we find that we are not on track toward meeting our goal, and sound science justifies further policy action, the United States will respond with additional measures that may include a broad, market-based program as well as additional incentives and voluntary measures designed to accelerate technology development and deployment.
- **Increase Funding for America's Commitment to Climate Change.** The President's FY '03 budget seeks $4.5 billion in total climate spending—an increase of $700 million. This commitment is unmatched in the world, and is particularly notable given America's focus on international and homeland security and domestic economic issues in the President's FY '03 budget proposal.
- **Take Action on the Science and Technology Review.** The Secretary of Commerce and Secretary of Energy have completed their review of the federal government's science and technology research portfolios and recommended a path forward. As a result of their review, the President has established a new management structure to advance and coordinate climate change science and technology research.
  - The President has established a Cabinet-level Committee on Climate Change Science and Technology Integration to oversee this effort. The Secretary of Commerce and Secretary of Energy will lead the effort, in close coordination with the President's Science Advisor. The

research effort will continue to be coordinated through the National Science and Technology Council in accordance with the Global Change Research Act of 1990.

- The President's FY '03 budget proposal dedicates $1.7 billion to fund basic scientific research on climate change and $1.3 billion to fund research on advanced energy and sequestration technologies.
- This includes $80 million in new funding dedicated to implementation of the Climate Change Research Initiative (CCRI) and the National Climate Change Technology Initiative (NCCTI) announced last June. This funding will be used to address major gaps in our current understanding of the natural carbon cycle and the role of black soot emissions in climate change. It will also be used to promote the development of the most promising "breakthrough" technologies for clean energy generation and carbon sequestration.

- **Implement a Comprehensive Range of New and Expanded Domestic Policies, Including:**
  - *Tax Incentives for Renewable Energy, Cogeneration, and New Technology.* The President's FY '03 budget seeks $555 million in clean energy tax incentives, as the first part of a $4.6 billion commitment over the next five years ($7.1 billion over the next 10 years). These tax credits will spur investments in renewable energy (solar, wind, and biomass), hybrid and fuel cell vehicles, cogeneration, and landfill gas conversion. Consistent with the National Energy Policy, the President has directed the Secretary of the Treasury to work with Congress to extend and expand the production tax credit for electricity generation from wind and biomass, to develop a new residential solar energy tax credit, and to encourage cogeneration projects through investment tax credits.
  - *Business Challenges.* The President has challenged American businesses to make specific commitments to improving the greenhouse gas intensity of their operations and to reduce emissions. Recent agreements with the semi-conductor and aluminum industries and industries that emit methane already have significantly reduced emissions of some of the most potent greenhouse gases. We will build upon these successes with new agreements, producing greater reductions.
  - *Transportation Programs.* The Administration is promoting the development of fuel-efficient motor vehicles and trucks, researching options for producing cleaner fuels, and implementing programs to improve energy efficiency. The President is committed to expanding federal research partnerships with industry, providing market-based incentives and updating current regulatory programs that advance our progress in this important area. This commitment includes expanding fuel cell research, in particular through the "FreedomCAR" initiative. The President's FY '03 budget seeks more than $3 billion in tax credits over 11 years for consumers to purchase fuel cell and hybrid vehicles. The Secretary of Transportation has asked the Congressional leadership to work with him on legislation that would authorize the Department of Transportation to reform the Corporate Average Fuel Economy (CAFE) program, fully considering the recent National Academy Sciences report, so that we can safely improve fuel economy for cars and trucks.

- *Carbon Sequestration.* The President's FY '03 budget requests over $3 billion—a $1 billion increase above the baseline—as the first part of a ten year (2002–2011) commitment to implement and improve the conservation title of the Farm Bill, which will significantly enhance the natural storage of carbon. The President also directed the Secretary of Agriculture to provide recommendations for further, targeted incentives aimed at forest and agricultural sequestration of greenhouse gases. The President further directed the Secretary of Agriculture, in consultation with the Environmental Protection Agency and the Department of Energy, to develop accounting rules and guidelines for crediting sequestration projects, taking into account emerging domestic and international approaches.
- **Promote New and Expanded International Policies to Complement Our Domestic Program.** The President's approach seeks to expand cooperation internationally to meet the challenge of climate change, including:
  - *Investing $25 Million in Climate Observation Systems in Developing Countries.* In response to the National Academy of Sciences' recommendation for better observation systems, the President has allocated $25 million and challenged other developed nations to match the U.S. commitment.
  - *Tripling Funding for "Debt-for-Nature" Forest Conservation Programs.* Building upon recent Tropical Forest Conservation Act (TFCA) agreements with Belize, El Salvador, and Bangladesh, the President's FY '03 budget request of $40 million to fund "debt for nature" agreements with developing countries nearly triples funding for this successful program. Under TFCA, developing countries agree to protect their tropical forests from logging, avoiding emissions and preserving the substantial carbon sequestration services they provide. The President also announced a new agreement with the Government of Thailand, which will preserve important mangrove forest in Northeastern Thailand in exchange for debt relief worth $11.4 million.
  - *Fully Funding the Global Environmental Facility.* The Administration's FY '03 budget request of $178 million for the GEF is more than $77 million above this year's funding and includes a substantial $70 million payment for arrears incurred during the prior administration. The GEF is the primary international institution for transferring energy and sequestration technologies to the developing world under the United Nations Framework Convention on Climate Change (UNFCCC).
    - *Dedicating Significant Funds to the United States Agency for International Development (USAID).* The President's FY '03 budget requests $155 million in funding for USAID climate change programs. USAID serves as a critical vehicle for transferring American energy and sequestration technologies to developing countries to promote sustainable development and minimize their GHG emissions growth.
    - *Pursue Joint Research with Japan.* The U.S. and Japan continue their High-Level Consultations on climate change issues. Later this month, a team of U.S. experts will meet with their Japanese counterparts to discuss specific projects within the various areas of climate science and technology, to identify the highest priorities for collaborative research.

- *Pursue Joint Research with Italy.* Following up on a pledge of President Bush and Prime Minister Berlusconi to undertake joint research on climate change, the U.S. and Italy convened a Joint Climate Change Research Meeting in January 2002. The delegations for the two countries identified more than 20 joint climate change research activities for immediate implementation, including global and regional modeling.
- *Pursue Joint Research with Central America.* The United States and Central American Heads of Government signed the Central American-United States of America Joint Accord (CONCAUSA) on December 10, 1994. The original agreement covered cooperation under action plans in four major areas: conservation of biodiversity, sound use of energy, environmental legislation, and sustainable economic development. On June 7, 2001, the United States and its Central American partners signed an expanded and renewed CONCAUSA Declaration, adding disaster relief and climate change as new areas for cooperation. The new CONCAUSA Declaration calls for intensified cooperative efforts to address climate change through scientific research, estimating and monitoring greenhouse gases, investing in forestry conservation, enhancing energy efficiency, and utilizing new environmental technologies.

National Goal

The President set a national goal to reduce the greenhouse gas intensity of the U.S. economy by 18 percent over the next ten years. Rather than pitting economic growth against the environment, the President has established an approach that promises real progress on climate change by tapping the power of sustained economic growth.

- **The President's Yardstick—Greenhouse Gas Intensity—Is a Better Way to Measure Progress Without Hurting Growth.** A goal expressed in terms of declining greenhouse gas intensity, measuring greenhouse gas emissions relative to economic activity, quantifies our effort to reduce emissions through conservation, adoption of cleaner, more efficient, and emission-reducing technologies, and sequestration. At the same time, an intensity goal accommodates economic growth.
- **Reducing Greenhouse Gas Intensity by 18 Percent Over the Next Ten Years Is Ambitious but Achievable.** The United States will reduce the 183 metric tons of emissions per million dollars GDP that we emit today to 151 metric tons per million dollars GDP in 2012. We expect existing trends and efforts in technology improvement to play a significant role. Beyond that, our commitment will achieve 100 million metric tons of reduced emissions in 2012 alone, with more than 500 million metric tons in cumulative savings over the entire decade.
- **Focusing on Greenhouse Gas Intensity Sets America on a Path to Slow the Growth of Greenhouse Gas Emissions, and—as the Science Justifies—to Stop and Then Reverse That Growth.** As we learn more about the science of climate change and develop new technologies to mitigate emissions, this annual decline can be accelerated. When the annual decline in intensity equals the economic growth rate (currently,

about 3% per year), emission growth will have stopped. When the annual decline in intensity exceeds the economic growth rate, emission growth will reverse. Reversing emission growth will eventually stabilize atmospheric concentrations as emissions decline.

- **As We Advance Science and Develop Technology to Substantially Reduce Greenhouse Gas Emissions in the Long Term, We Do Not Want to Risk Harming the Economy in the Short Term.** Over the past 20 years, greenhouse gas emissions have risen with economic growth, as our economy benefited from inexpensive, fossil-fuel based—and greenhouse gas emitting—energy. While new technologies promise to break this emission-economy link, a rapid reduction in emissions would be costly and threaten economic growth. Sustained economic growth is essential for any long-term solution: Prosperity is what allows us to dedicate more resources to solving environmental problems. History shows that wealthier societies demand—and can afford—more environmental protection.

- **The Intensity Based Approach Promotes Near-Term Opportunities to Conserve Fossil Fuel Use, Recover Methane, and Sequester Carbon.** Until we develop and adopt breakthrough technologies that provide safe and reliable energy to fuel our economy without emitting greenhouse gases, we need to promote more rapid adoption of existing, improved energy efficiency and renewable resources that provide cost-effective opportunities to reduce emissions. Profitable methane recovery from landfills, coal mines and gas pipelines offers another opportunity—estimated by the EPA at about 30 million tons of carbon equivalent emissions. Finally, carbon sequestration in soils and forests can provide tens of millions of tons of emission reductions at very low costs.

- **The Intensity Based Approach Advances a Serious, but Measured Mitigation Response.** The President recognizes America's responsibility to reduce emissions. At the same time, any long-term solution—one that stabilizes atmospheric concentrations of greenhouse gases at safe levels—will require the development and deployment of new technologies that are not yet cost-effective. The President's policy balances the desire for immediate reductions with the need to protect the economy and to take advantage of developing science and technology.

The President's Goal Is Ambitious and Responsible

- **Reducing Greenhouse Gas Intensity by 18 Percent Over the Next Ten Years Is Comparable to the Average Progress that Nations Participating in the Kyoto Protocol Are Required to Achieve.** Our goal translates into a 4.5 percent reduction beyond forecasts of the progress that America is expected to make based on existing programs and private activity. Forecasts of the average reductions required by nations implementing the Kyoto Protocol range from zero to 7 percent.

- **While Producing Results Similar to What the Kyoto Protocol Participants Are Required to Achieve on Average, the President's Approach Protects the Economy and Develops Institutions for a Long-Term Solution.** The focus on greenhouse gas intensity separates the goal of reducing emissions from the potential economic harm associated with a rigid emission cap. By measuring greenhouse gas emissions relative to economic activity, we have a solid yardstick against which we can measure progress as we pursue a range of programs to reduce emissions. As we develop technologies to produce more goods with fewer greenhouse gas emissions, this yardstick does not penalize economic growth.

- **Greenhouse Gas Intensity Is a More Practical Way to Discuss Goals with Developing Countries.** The close connection between economic growth, energy use and greenhouse gas emissions implies that fixed appropriate emission limits are hard to identify when economic growth is uncertain and carbon-free, breakthrough energy technologies are not yet in place. Such targets are also hard to identify for developing countries where the future rate of emissions is even more uncertain. Given its neutrality with regard to economic growth, greenhouse gas intensity solves or substantially reduces many of these problems.

Enhanced National Registry for Voluntary Emissions Reductions

The Administration will improve the current federal GHG Reduction and Sequestration Registry that recognizes greenhouse gas reductions by non-governmental organizations, businesses, farmers, and the federal, state and local governments. Registry participants and the public will have a high level of confidence in the reductions recognized by this Registry, through capture and sequestration projects, mitigation projects that increase energy efficiency and/or switch fuels, and process changes to reduce emissions of potent greenhouse gases, such as methane. An enhanced registry will promote the identification and expansion of innovative and effective ways to reduce greenhouse gases. The enhanced registry will encourage participation by removing the risk that these actions will be penalized—or inaction rewarded—by future climate policy.

- **Improve the Quality of the Current Program.** A registry is a tool for companies to publicly record their progress in reducing emissions, providing public recognition of a company's accomplishments, and a record of mitigation efforts for future policy design. This tool goes hand-in-hand with voluntary business challenges, described below, by providing a standardized, credible vehicle for reporting and recognizing progress.
  - Although businesses can already register emission reductions under section 1605(b) of the 1995 Energy Policy Act, participation has been limited.
  - The President directed the Secretary of Energy, in consultation with the Secretary of Commerce, Secretary of Agriculture, and the Administrator of the Environmental Protection Agency, to propose improvements to the current voluntary emissions reduction registration program within 120 days.
  - These improvements will enhance measurement accuracy, reliability and verifiability, working with and taking into account emerging domestic and international approaches.
- **Protect and Provide Transferable Credits for Emissions Reduction.** The President directed the Secretary of Energy to recommend reforms

to ensure that businesses and individuals that register reductions are not penalized under a future climate policy, and to give transferable credits to companies that can show real emissions reductions. These protections will encourage businesses and individuals to pursue innovative strategies to reduce or sequester greenhouse gas emissions, without the risk that future climate policy will disadvantage them.

- **Background on Current Registry Program.** The Energy Policy Act of 1992 directed the Department of Energy (with EIA as the implementing agency) to develop a program to document voluntary actions that reduce emissions of greenhouse gases or remove greenhouse gases from the atmosphere.
  - Under the Energy Policy Act, EIA was directed to issue "procedures for the accurate reporting of information on annual reductions of greenhouse gas emissions and carbon fixation achieved through any measures, including fuel switching, forest management practices, tree planting, use of renewable energy, manufacture or use of vehicles with reduced greenhouse gas emissions, appliance efficiency, methane recovery, cogeneration, chlorofluorocarbon capture and replacement, and power plant heat rate improvement."
  - In 1999, 207 companies and other organizations, representing 24 different industries or services, reported on 1,722 projects that achieved 226 million metric tons of carbon dioxide equivalent reductions— equal to 3.4 percent of national emissions. Participating companies included Clairol, AT&T, Dow Chemical, Johnson & Johnson, IBM, Motorola, Pharmacia, Upjohn, Sunoco, Southern, General Motors and DuPont.
  - EIA released a February 2002 report demonstrating that this program continues to expand. In 2000, 222 companies had undertaken 1,882 projects to reduce or sequester greenhouse gases. These achieved 269 million metric tons of carbon dioxide equivalent reductions—equal to 3.9 percent of national emissions.
  - A number of proposals to reform the existing registry—or create a new registry—have appeared in energy and/or climate policy bills introduced in the past year. The Administration will fully explore the extent to which the existing authority under the Energy Policy Act is adequate to achieve these reforms.

Progress Check in 2012

The domestic programs proposed by the President allow consumers and businesses to make flexible decisions about emission reductions rather than mandating particular control options or rigid targets. If, however, by 2012, our progress is not sufficient, and sound science justifies further action, the United States will respond with additional measures that may include a broad, market-based program, as well as additional incentives and voluntary measures designed to accelerate technology development and deployment.

POSTSCRIPT

Should Society Act Now to Halt Global Warming?

The United Nations Conference on Environment and Development in Rio de Janeiro, Brazil, took place in 1992. High on the agenda was the problem of global warming, but despite widespread concern and calls for reductions in carbon dioxide releases, the United States refused to consider rigid deadlines or set quotas. The uncertainties seemed too great, and some thought the economic costs of cutting back on carbon dioxide might be greater than the costs of letting the climate warm.

The nations that signed the UN Framework Convention on Climate Change in Rio de Janeiro in 1992 met again in Kyoto, Japan, in December 1997 to set carbon emissions limits for the industrial nations. The United States agreed to reduce its annual greenhouse gas emissions 7 percent below the 1990 level between 2008 and 2012 but still has not ratified the Kyoto treaty. In November 1998 they met in Buenos Aires, Argentina, to work out practical details (see Christopher Flavin, "Last Tango in Buenos Aires," *World Watch* [November/December 1998]). Unfortunately, developing countries, where carbon emissions are growing most rapidly, face few restrictions, and political opposition in developed nations—especially in the United States—remains strong. Ross Gelbspan, in "Rx for a Planetary Fever," *American Prospect* (May 8, 2000), blames much of that opposition on "big oil and big coal [which] have relentlessly obstructed the best-faith efforts of government negotiators." Nor do some portions of the industry seem interested in acting on their own. In May 2003, Exxon Mobil rejected proposals that it address global warming and develop renewable energy. CEO Lee Raymond, who had previously denounced the Kyoto Protocol, said the company does not "make social statements at the expense of shareholder return."

The opposition remains, despite the latest IPCC report. Critics stress uncertainties in the data and the potential economic impacts of attempting to reduce carbon dioxide emissions. However, when the National Commission on Energy Policy published its report, *Ending the Energy Stalemate: A Bipartisan Strategy to Meet America's Energy Challenges* in December 2004 (http://64.70.252.93/newfiles/Final_Report/index.pdf), the Energy Information Administration promptly analyzed its economic impact in *Impacts of Modeled Recommendations of the National Commission on Energy Policy* (April 2005) (http://www.eia.doe.gov/oiaf/servicerpt/bingaman/index.html) and concluded that increasing automobile fuel efficiency, encouraging alternate energy sources, and increasing oil production and clean coal technology would cost the "U.S. economy . . . no more than 0.15% of GDP or about $78 per household per year, while overall GDP is projected to grow by 87%."

However, there is a problem with any plan that includes increasing oil production; according to Kenneth S. Deffeyes, *Beyond Oil: The View from Hubbert's Peak* (Hill and Wang, 2005), world oil production will peak as soon as November 2005 and will thereafter decline despite efforts to combat the trend. See also Robert L. Hirsch, Roger H. Bezdek, and Robert M. Wendling, "Peaking Oil Production: Sooner Rather than Later?" *Issues in Science and Technology* (Spring 2005).

There is also opposition based on the view that the methods of reducing greenhouse gas emissions called for in the Kyoto treaty are, at root, unworkable. See Frank N. Laird, "Just Say No to Greenhouse Gas Emissions Targets," *Issues in Science and Technology* (Winter 2000–2001). However, researchers have proposed a number of innovative ways to keep from adding carbon dioxide to the atmosphere, such as by capturing carbon dioxide and storing it deep underground. See Robert H. Socolow, "Can We Bury Global Warming?" *Scientific American* (July 2005). Fred Krupp, President of Environmental Defense, "Global Warming and the USA," *Vital Speeches of the Day* (April 15, 2003), recommends a market-based approach to finding and developing innovative approaches. Thomas J. Wilbanks, Sally M. Kane, Paul N. Leiby, Robert D. Perlack, Chad Settle, Jason F. Shogren, and Joel B. Smith, "Possible Responses to Global Climate Change: Integrating Mitigation and Adaptation," *Environment* (June 2003), note that many mitigation techniques are under study around the world, but people will also have to adapt to a warming world.

In June 2002 the U.S. Environmental Protection Agency (EPA) issued its *U.S. Climate Action Report—2002* (available at http://www.epa.gov/globalwarming/publications/car/index.html) to the United Nations. In it, the EPA admits for the first time that global warming is real and that human activities are most likely to blame. President George W. Bush immediately dismissed the report as "put out by the bureaucracy" and said he still opposes the Kyoto Protocol. He insists more research is necessary before we can even begin to plan a proper response. Unfortunately, the latest studies warn that the consequences of global warming may be much more severe than even the IPCC has forecast. See, for instance, Richard A. Kerr, "Climate Modelers See Scorching Future as a Real Possibility," *Science* (January 28, 2005), and *Meeting the Climate Challenge: Recommendations of the International Climate Change Taskforce* (January 2005) (http://www.americanprogress.org/atf/cf/%7BE9245FE4-9A2B-43C7-A521-5D6FF2E06E03%7D/CLIMAT-ECHALLENGE.PDF), which warns that the world may already be on the verge of irreversible disaster, including "widespread agricultural failure, water shortages and major droughts, increased disease, sea-level rise and the death of forests."

ISSUE 5

Is It Time to Revive Nuclear Power?

YES: Peter Schwartz and Spencer Reiss, from "Nuclear Now!" *Wired* (February 2005)

NO: Karl Grossman, from "The Push to Revive Nuclear Power," *Synthesis/Regeneration 28* (Spring 2002)

ISSUE SUMMARY

YES: Peter Schwartz and Spencer Reiss argue that nuclear power should be encouraged as the one practical answer to global warming and forthcoming shortages of fossil fuels.

NO: Professor of journalism Karl Grossman argues that to encourage the use of nuclear power is reckless. It would be wiser to promote renewable energy and energy efficiency.

The technology of releasing for human use the energy that holds together the atom did not get off to an auspicious start. Its first significant application was military, and the deaths associated with the Hiroshima and Nagasaki explosions have ever since tainted the technology with negative associations. It did not help that for the ensuing half-century, millions of people grew up under the threat of nuclear armageddon. But almost from the beginning, nuclear physicists and engineers wanted to put nuclear energy to more peaceful uses, largely in the form of power plants. Touted in the 1950s as an astoundingly cheap source of electricity, nuclear power soon proved to be more expensive than conventional sources, largely because safety concerns caused delays in the approval process and prompted elaborate built-in precautions. Safety measures have worked well when needed—Three Mile Island, often cited as a horrific example of what can go wrong, released very little radioactive material to the environment. The Chernobyl disaster occurred when safety measures were ignored. In both cases, human error was more to blame than the technology itself. The related issue of nuclear waste has also raised fears and proved to add expense to the technology.

From this very brief overview, it is clear that two factors—fear and expense—impede the wide adoption of nuclear power. If both could somehow be alleviated, it might become possible to gain the benefits of the technology. Among those benefits are that nuclear power does not burn oil, coal, or any other fuel, does not emit air pollution and thus contribute to smog and haze, does not depend on foreign sources of fuel and thus weaken national independence, and does not emit carbon dioxide. Avoiding the use of fossil fuels is an important benefit; see Robert L. Hirsch, Roger H. Bezdek, and Robert M. Wendling, "Peaking Oil Production: Sooner Rather than Later?" *Issues in Science and Technology* (Spring 2005). But avoiding carbon dioxide emissions may be more important at a time when society is concerned about global warming, and this is the benefit that prompted James Lovelock, creator of the Gaia Hypothesis and hero to environmentalists everywhere, to say, "If we had nuclear power we wouldn't be in this mess now, and whose fault was it? It was [the anti-nuclear environmentalists]." See his autobiography, *Homage to Gaia: The Life of an Independent Scientist* (Oxford University Press, 2001). Others have also seen this point. The OECD's Nuclear Energy Agency ("Nuclear Power and Climate Change," [Paris, France, 1998, http://www.nea.fr/html/ndd/climate/climate.pdf]) found that a greatly expanded deployment of nuclear power to combat global warming was both technically and economically feasible. Robert C. Morris published *The Environmental Case for Nuclear Power: Economic, Medical, and Political Considerations* (Paragon House) in 2000. "The time seems right to reconsider the future of nuclear power," say James A. Lake, Ralph G. Bennett, and John F. Kotek in "Next-Generation Nuclear Power," *Scientific American* (January 2002). Stephen Ansolabehere, et al., "The Future of Nuclear Power: An Interdisciplinary MIT Study" (MIT 2003), argue that greatly expanded use of nuclear power should not be excluded as a way to meet future energy needs and reduce the carbon emissions that contribute to global warming, although due attention must be paid to reducing costs and risks. Stewart Brand, long a leading environmentalist, predicts in "Environmental Heresies," *Technology Review* (May 2005), that nuclear power will soon be seen as the "green" energy technology. And this is not just a Western sentiment, for nuclear power and its anti-warming effects may have special meaning in developing countries; see R. Ramachandran, "The Case for Nuclear Power," *Frontline* (November 26–December 3, 2002).

In the following selections, Peter Schwartz and Spencer Reiss argue that nuclear power should be encouraged as the one practical answer to global warming and coming shortages of fossil fuels. The risks are much less than those associated with fossil fuels. Professor of journalism Karl Grossman argues that to encourage the use of nuclear power is reckless. "Instead of promoting dangerous and dirty forms of energy, the United States should be a world leader in promoting renewable energy and energy efficiency."

Peter Schwartz and
Spencer Reiss

 **YES**

Nuclear Now!: How Clean, Green Atomic Energy Can Stop Global Warming

On a cool spring morning a quarter century ago, a place in Pennsylvania called Three Mile Island exploded into the headlines and stopped the US nuclear power industry in its tracks. What had been billed as the clean, cheap, limitless energy source for a shining future was suddenly too hot to handle.

In the years since, we've searched for alternatives, pouring billions of dollars into windmills, solar panels, and biofuels. We've designed fantastically efficient lightbulbs, air conditioners, and refrigerators. We've built enough gas-fired generators to bankrupt California. But mainly, each year we hack 400 million more tons of coal out of Earth's crust than we did a quarter century before, light it on fire, and shoot the proceeds into the atmosphere.

The consequences aren't pretty. Burning coal and other fossil fuels is driving climate change, which is blamed for everything from western forest fires and Florida hurricanes to melting polar ice sheets and flooded Himalayan hamlets. On top of that, coal-burning electric power plants have fouled the air with enough heavy metals and other noxious pollutants to cause 15,000 premature deaths annually in the US alone, according to a Harvard School of Public Health study. Believe it or not, a coal-fired plant releases 100 times more radioactive material than an equivalent nuclear reactor—right into the air, too, not into some carefully guarded storage site. (And, by the way, more than 5,200 Chinese coal miners perished in accidents last year.)

Burning hydrocarbons is a luxury that a planet with 6 billion energy-hungry souls can't afford. There's only one sane, practical alternative: nuclear power.

We now know that the risks of splitting atoms pale beside the dreadful toll exacted by fossil fuels. Radiation containment, waste disposal, and nuclear weapons proliferation are manageable problems in a way that global warming is not. Unlike the usual green alternatives—water, wind, solar, and biomass—nuclear energy is here, now, in industrial quantities. Sure, nuke plants are expensive to build—upward of $2 billion apiece—but they start to look cheap when you factor in the true cost to people and the planet of burning fossil fuels. And nuclear is our best hope for cleanly and efficiently generating hydrogen, which would end our other ugly hydrocarbon addiction—dependence on gasoline and diesel for transport.

Some of the world's most thoughtful greens have discovered the logic of nuclear power, including Gaia theorist James Lovelock, Greenpeace cofounder Patrick Moore, and Britain's Bishop Hugh Montefiore, a longtime board member of Friends of the Earth. Western Europe is quietly backing away from planned nuclear phaseouts. Finland has ordered a big reactor specifically to meet the terms of the Kyoto Protocol on climate change. China's new nuke plants—26 by 2025—are part of a desperate effort at smog control.

Even the shell-shocked US nuclear industry is coming out of its stupor. The 2001 report of Vice President Cheney's energy task force was only the most high profile in a series of pro-nuke developments. Nuke boosters are especially buoyed by more efficient plant designs, streamlined licensing procedures, and the prospect of federal subsidies.

In fact, new plants are on the way, however tentatively. Three groups of generating companies have entered a bureaucratic maze expected to lead to formal applications for plants by 2008. If everything breaks right, the first new reactors in decades will be online by 2014. If this seems ambitious, it's not; the industry hopes merely to hold on to nuclear's current 20 percent of the rapidly growing US electric power market.

That's not nearly enough. We should be shooting to match France, which gets 77 percent of its electricity from nukes. It's past time for a decisive leap out of the hydrocarbon era, time to send King Coal and, soon after, Big Oil shambling off to their well-deserved final resting places—maybe on a nostalgic old steam locomotive.

Besides, wouldn't it be a blast to barrel down the freeway in a hydrogen Hummer with a clean conscience as your copilot? Or not to feel like a planet killer every time you flick on the A/C? That's how the future could be, if only we would get over our fear of the nuclear bogeyman and forge ahead—for real this time—into the atomic age.

The granola crowd likes to talk about conservation and efficiency, and surely substantial gains can be made in those areas. But energy is not a luxury people can do without, like a gym membership or hair gel. The developed world built its wealth on cheap power—burning firewood, coal, petroleum, and natural gas, with carbon emissions the inevitable byproduct.

Indeed, material progress can be tracked in what gets pumped out of smokestacks. An hour of coal-generated 100-watt electric light creates 0.05 pounds of atmospheric carbon, a bucket of ice makes 0.3 pounds, an hour's car ride 5. The average American sends nearly half a ton of carbon spewing into the atmosphere every month. Europe and Japan are a little more economical, but even the most remote forest-burning peasants happily do their part.

And the worst—by far—is yet to come. An MIT study forecasts that worldwide energy demand could triple by 2050. China could build a Three Gorges Dam every year forever and still not meet its growing demand for electricity. Even the carbon reductions required by the Kyoto Protocol—which pointedly exempts developing countries like China—will be a drop in the atmospheric sewer.

What is a rapidly carbonizing world to do? The high-minded answer, of course, is renewables. But the notion that wind, water, solar, or biomass will save the day is at least as fanciful as the once-popular idea that nuclear energy would be too cheap to meter. Jesse Ausubel, director of the human environment program at New York's Rockefeller University, calls renewable energy sources "false gods"—attractive but powerless. They're capital- and land-intensive, and solar is not yet remotely cost-competitive. Despite all the hype, tax breaks, and incentives, the proportion of US electricity production from renewables has actually fallen in the past 15 years, from 11.0 percent to 9.1 percent.

The decline would be even worse without hydropower, which accounts for 92 percent of the world's renewable electricity. While dams in the US are under attack from environmentalists trying to protect wild fish populations, the Chinese are building them on an ever grander scale. But even China's autocrats can't get past Nimby. Stung by criticism of the monumental Three Gorges project—which required the forcible relocation of 1 million people—officials have suspended an even bigger project on the Nu Jiang River in the country's remote southwest. Or maybe someone in Beijing questioned the wisdom of reacting to climate change with a multibillion-dollar bet on rainfall.

Solar power doesn't look much better. Its number-one problem is cost: While the price of photovoltaic cells has been slowly dropping, solar-generated electricity is still four times more expensive than nuclear (and more than five times the cost of coal). Maybe someday we'll all live in houses with photovoltaic roof tiles, but in the real world, a run-of-the-mill 1,000-megawatt photovoltaic plant will require about 60 square miles of panes alone. In other words, the largest industrial structure ever built.

Wind is more promising, which is one reason it's the lone renewable attracting serious interest from big-time equipment manufacturers like General Electric. But even though price and performance are expected to improve, wind, like solar, is inherently fickle, hard to capture, and widely dispersed. And wind turbines take up a lot of space; Ausubel points out that the wind equivalent of a typical utility plant would require 300 square miles of turbines plus costly transmission lines from the wind-scoured fields of, say, North Dakota. Alternatively, there's California's Altamont Pass, where 5,400 windmills slice and dice some 1,300 birds of prey annually.

What about biomass? Ethanol is clean, but growing the amount of cellulose required to shift US electricity production to biomass would require farming—no wilting organics, please—an area the size of 10 Iowas.

Among fossil fuels, natural gas holds some allure; it emits a third as much carbon as coal. That's an improvement but not enough if you're serious about rolling back carbon levels. Washington's favorite solution is so-called clean coal, ballyhooed in stump speeches by both President Bush (who offered a $2 billion research program) and challenger John Kerry (who upped the ante to $10 billion). But most of the work so far has been aimed at reducing acid rain by cutting sulphur dioxide and nitrogen oxide emissions, and more recently gasifying coal to make it burn cleaner. Actual zero-emissions coal is still a lab experiment that even fans say could double or triple generating costs. It would also leave the question of what to do with 1 million tons of extracted [Sulphur] each year.

By contrast, nuclear power is thriving around the world despite decades of obituaries. Belgium derives 58 percent of its electricity from nukes, Sweden 45 percent, South Korea 40, Switzerland 37 percent, Japan 31 percent, Spain 27 percent, and the UK 23 percent. Turkey plans to build three plants over the next several years. South Korea has eight more reactors coming, Japan 13, China at least 20. France, where nukes generate more than three-quarters of the country's electricity, is privatizing a third of its state-owned nuclear energy group, Areva, to deal with the rush of new business.

The last US nuke plant to be built was ordered in 1973, yet nuclear power is growing here as well. With clever engineering and smart management, nukes have steadily increased their share of generating capacity in the US. The 103 reactors operating in the US pump out electricity at more than 90 percent of capacity, up from 60 percent when Three Mile Island made headlines. That increase is the equivalent of adding 40 new reactors, without bothering anyone's backyard or spewing any more carbon into the air.

So atomic power is less expensive than it used to be—but could it possibly be cost-effective? Even before Three Mile Island sank, the US nuclear industry was foundering on the shoals of economics. Regulatory delays and billion-dollar construction-cost overruns turned the business into a financial nightmare. But increasing experience and efficiency gains have changed all that. Current operating costs are the lowest ever—1.82 cents per kilowatt-hour versus 2.13 cents for coal-fired plants and 3.69 cents for natural gas. The ultimate vindication of nuclear economics is playing out in the stock market: Over the past five years, the stocks of leading nuclear generating companies such as Exelon and Entergy have more than doubled. Indeed, Exelon is feeling so flush that it bought New Jersey's Public Service Enterprise Group in December, adding four reactors to its former roster of 17.

This remarkable success suggests that nuclear energy realistically could replace coal in the US without a cost increase and ultimately lead the way to a clean, green future. The trick is to start building nuke plants and keep building them at a furious pace. Anything less leaves carbon in the climatic driver's seat.

A decade ago, anyone thinking about constructing nuclear plants in the US would have been dismissed as out of touch with reality. But today, for the first time since the building of Three Mile Island, new nukes in the US seem possible. Thanks to improvements in reactor design and increasing encouragement from Washington, DC, the nuclear industry is posed for unlikely revival. "All the planets seem to be coming into alignment," says David Brown, VP for congressional affairs at Exelon.

The original US nuclear plants, built during the 1950s and '60s, were descended from propulsion units in 1950s-vintage nuclear submarines, now known as generation I. During the '80s and '90s, when new construction halted in the US, the major reactor makers—GE Power Systems, British-owned

Westinghouse, France's Framatome (part of Areva), and Canada's AECL—went after customers in Europe. This new round of business led to system improvements that could eventually, after some prototyping, be deployed back in the US.

By all accounts, the latest reactors, generation III+, are a big improvement. They're fuel-efficient. They employ passive safety technologies, such as gravity-fed emergency cooling rather than pumps. Thanks to standardized construction, they may even be cost-competitive to build—$1,200 per kilowatt-hour of generating capacity versus more than $1,300 for the latest low-emission (which is not to say low-carbon) coal plants. But there's no way to know for sure until someone actually builds one. And even then, the first few will almost certainly cost more.

Prodded by the Cheney report, the US Department of Energy agreed in 2002 to pick up the tab of the first hurdle—getting from engineering design to working blueprints. Three groups of utility companies and reactor makers have stepped up for the program, optimistically dubbed Nuclear Power 2010. The government's bill to taxpayers for this stage of development could top $500 million, but at least we'll get working reactors rather than "promising technologies."

But newer, better designs don't free the industry from the intense public oversight that has been nuclear power's special burden from the start. Believe it or not, Three Mile Island wasn't the ultimate nightmare; that would be Shoreham, the Long Island power plant shuttered in 1994 after a nine-year legal battle, without ever having sold a single electron. Construction was already complete when opponents challenged the plant's application for an operating license. Wall Street won't invest billions in new plants ($5.5 billion in Shoreham's case) without a clear path through the maze of judges and regulators.

Shoreham didn't die completely in vain. The 1992 Energy Policy Act aims to forestall such debacles by authorizing the Nuclear Regulatory Commission to issue combined construction and operating licenses. It also allows the NRC to pre-certify specific reactor models and the energy companies to bank preapproved sites. Utility executives fret that no one has ever road-tested the new process, which still requires public hearings and shelves of supporting documents. An idle reactor site at Browns Ferry, Alabama, could be an early test case; the Tennessee Valley Authority is exploring options to refurbish it rather than start from scratch.

Meanwhile, Congress looks ready to provide a boost to the nuclear energy industry. Pete Domenici (R-New Mexico), chair of the Senate's energy committee and the patron saint of nuclear power in Washington, has vowed to revive last year's energy bill, which died in the Senate. Earlier versions included a 1.85 cent per-kilowatt-hour production tax credit for the first half-dozen nuke plants to come online. That could add up to as much as $8 billion in federal outlays and should go a long way toward luring Wall Street back into the fray. As pork goes, the provision is easy to defend. Nuclear power's extraordinary startup costs and safety risks make it a special case for government intervention. And the amount is precisely the same bounty Washington spends annually in tax credits for wind, biomass, and other zero-emission kilowattage.

Safer plants, more sensible regulation, and even a helping hand from Congress—all are on the way. What's still missing is a place to put radioactive waste. By law, US companies that generate nuclear power pay the Feds a tenth of a cent per kilowatt-hour to dispose of their spent fuel. The fund—currently $24 billion and counting—is supposed to finance a permanent waste repository, the ill-fated Yucca Mountain in Nevada. Two decades ago when the payments started, opening day was scheduled for January 31, 1998. But the Nevada facility remains embroiled in hearings, debates, and studies, and waste is piling up at 30-odd sites around the country. Nobody will build a nuke plant until Washington offers a better answer than "keep piling."

At Yucca Mountain, perfection has been the enemy of adequacy. It's fun to discuss what the design life of an underground nuclear waste facility ought to be. One hundred years? Two hundred years? How about 100,000? A quarter of a million? Science fiction meets the US government budgeting process. In court!

But throwing waste into a black hole at Yucca Mountain isn't such a great idea anyway. For one thing, in coming decades we might devise better disposal methods, such as corrosion-proof containers that can withstand millennia of heat and moisture. For another, used nuclear fuel can be recycled as a source for the production of more energy. Either way, it's clear that the whole waste disposal problem has been misconstrued. We don't need a million-year solution. A hundred years will do just fine—long enough to let the stuff cool down and allow us to decide what to do with it.

The name for this approach is interim storage: Find a few patches of isolated real estate—we're not talking about taking it over for eternity—and pour nice big concrete pads; add floodlights, motion detectors, and razor wire; truck in nuclear waste in bombproof 20-foot-high concrete casks. Voilà: safe storage while you wait for either Yucca Mountain or plan B.

Two dozen reactor sites around the country already have their own interim facilities; a private company has applied with the NRC to open one on the Goshute Indian reservation in Skull Valley, Utah. Establishing a half-dozen federally managed sites is closer to the right idea. Domenici says he'll introduce legislation this year for a national interim storage system.

A handful of new US plants will be a fine start, but the real goal has to be dethroning King Coal and—until something better comes along—pushing nuclear power out front as the world's default energy source. Kicking carbon cold turkey won't be easy, but it can be done. Four crucial steps can help increase the momentum: Regulate carbon emissions, revamp the fuel cycle, rekindle innovation in nuclear technology, and, finally, replace gasoline with hydrogen.

- **Regulate carbon emissions.** Nuclear plants have to account for every radioactive atom of waste. Meanwhile, coal-fired plants dump tons of deadly refuse into the atmosphere at zero cost. It's time for that free ride to end, but only the government can make it happen.

The industry seems ready to pay up. Andy White, CEO of GE Energy's nuclear division, recently asked a roomful of US utility executives what they thought about the possibility of regulating carbon emissions. The idea didn't faze them. "The only question any of them had," he says, "was when and how much."

A flat-out carbon tax is almost certainly a nonstarter in Washington. But an arrangement in which all energy producers are allowed a limited number of carbon pollution credits to use or sell could pass muster; after all, this kind of cap-and-trade scheme is already a fact of life for US utilities with a variety of other pollutants. Senators John McCain and Joe Lieberman have been pushing legislation such a system. This would send a clear message to utility executives that fossil energy's free pass is over.

- **Recycle nuclear fuel.** Here's a fun fact: Spent nuclear fuel—the stuff intended for permanent disposal at Yucca Mountain—retains 95 percent of its energy content. Imagine what Toyota could do for fuel efficiency if 95 percent of the average car's gasoline passed through the engine and out the tailpipe. In France, Japan, and Britain, nuclear engineers do the sensible thing: recycle. Alone among the nuclear powers, the US doesn't, for reasons that have nothing to do with nuclear power.

Recycling spent fuel—the technical word is reprocessing—is one way to make the key ingredient of a nuclear bomb, enriched uranium. In 1977, Jimmy Carter, the only nuclear engineer ever to occupy the White House, banned reprocessing in the US in favor of a so-called once-through fuel cycle. Four decades later, more than a dozen countries reprocess or enrich uranium, including North Korea and Iran. At this point, hanging onto spent fuel from US reactors does little good abroad and real mischief at home.

The Bush administration has reopened the door with modest funding to resume research into the nuclear fuel cycle. The president himself has floated a proposal to provide all comers with a guaranteed supply of reactor fuel in exchange for a promise not to reprocess spent fuel themselves. Other proposals would create a global nuclear fuel company, possibly under the auspices of the International Atomic Energy Agency. This company would collect, reprocess, and distribute fuel to every nation in the world, thus keeping potential bomb fixings out of circulation.

In the short term, reprocessing would maximize resources and minimize the problem of how to dispose of radioactive waste. In fact, it would eliminate most of the waste from nuclear power production. Over decades, it could also ease pressure on uranium supplies. The world's existing reserves are generally reckoned sufficient to withstand 50 years of rapid nuclear expansion without a significant price increase. In a pinch, there's always the ocean, whose 4.5 billion tons of dissolved uranium can be extracted today at 5 to 10 times the cost of conventional mining.

Uranium is so cheap today that reprocessing is more about reducing waste than stretching the fuel supply. But advanced breeder reactors, which create more fuel as they generate power, could well be the economically competitive choice—and renewable as well.

- **Rekindle innovation.** Although nuclear technology has come a long way since Three Mile Island, the field is hardly a hotbed of innovation. Government-funded research—such as the DOE's Next Generation Nuclear Plant program—is aimed at designing advanced reactors, including high temperature, gas-cooled plants of the kind being built in China and South Africa and fast-breeder reactors that will use uranium 60 times more efficiently than today's reactors. Still, the nuclear industry suffers from its legacy of having been born under a mushroom cloud and raised by your local electric company. A tight leash on nuclear R&D may be good, even necessary. But there's nothing like a little competition to spur creativity. That's reason enough to want to see US companies squarely back on the nuclear power field—research is great, but more and smarter buyers ultimately drive quality up and prices down.

In fact, the possibility of a nuclear gold rush—not just a modest rebirth—depends on economics as much as technology. The generation IV pebble-bed reactors being developed in China and South Africa get attention for their meltdown-proof designs. . . . But it's their low capital cost and potential for fast, modular construction that could blow the game open, as surely as the PC did for computing. As long as investments come in $2 billion increments, purchase orders will be few and far between. At $300 million a pop for safe, clean energy, watch the floodgates open around the world.

- **Replace gasoline with hydrogen.** If a single change could truly ignite nuclear power, it's the grab bag of technologies and wishful schemes traveling under the rubric of the hydrogen economy. Leaving behind petroleum is as important to the planet's future as eliminating coal. The hitch is that it takes energy to extract hydrogen from substances like methane and water. Where will it come from?

Today, the most common energy source for producing hydrogen is natural gas, followed by oil. It's conceivable that renewables could do it in limited quantities. By the luck of physics, though, two things nuclear reactors do best—generate both electricity and very high temperatures—are exactly what it takes to produce hydrogen most efficiently. Last November, the DOE's Idaho National Engineering and Environmental Laboratory showed how a single next-gen nuke could produce the hydrogen equivalent of 400,000 gallons of gasoline every day. Nuclear energy's potential for freeing us not only from coal but also oil holds the promise of a bright green future for the US and the world at large.

The more seriously you take the idea of global warming, the more seriously you have to take nuclear power. Clean coal, solar-powered roof tiles, wind farms in North Dakota—they're all pie in the emissions-free sky. Sure, give them a shot. But zero-carbon reactors are here and now. We know we can build them. Their price tag is no mystery. They fit into the existing electric grid without a hitch. Flannel-shirted environmentalists who fight these realities run the risk of ending up with as much soot on their hands as the slickest coal-mining CEO.

America's voracious energy appetite doesn't have to be a bug—it can be a feature. Shanghai, Seoul, and São Paolo are more likely to look to Los Angeles or Houston as a model than to some solar-powered idyll. Energy technology is no different than any other; innovation can change all the rules. But if the best we can offer the developing world is bromides about energy independence, we'll deserve the carbon-choked nightmare of a planet we get.

Nuclear energy is the big bang still reverberating. It's the power to light a city in a lump the size of a soda can. Peter Huber and Mark Mills have written an iconoclastic new book on energy, *The Bottomless Well*. They see nuclear power as merely the latest in a series of technologies that will gradually eliminate our need to carve up huge swaths of the planet. "Energy isn't the problem. Energy is the solution," they write. "Energy begets more energy. The more of it we capture and put to use, the more readily we will capture still more."

The best way to avoid running out of fossil fuels is to switch to something better. The Stone Age famously did not end for lack of stones, and neither should we wait for the last chunk of anthracite to flicker out before we kiss hydrocarbons good-bye. Especially not when something cleaner, safer, more efficient, and more abundant is ready to roll. It's time to get real.

NO

Karl Grossman

The Push to Revive Nuclear Power

The [George W.] Bush administration and the nuclear industry are making an intense push to "revive" nuclear power in the United States. Diane D'Arrigo of the Nuclear Information and Resource Service (NIRS) says "relapse" is the better term: "It's the push to relapse," she says.

As Bob Alvarez, executive director of the group Standing for Truth About Radiation says, "It's like reviving Frankenstein—this is the sequel." For years— ever since the accidents at Three Mile Island and Chernobyl shattered public trust in atomic power—nuclear power advocates in government and industry have been laying the groundwork for a comeback in the US.

As Bush's Secretary of Treasury Paul O'Neill told *The Wall Street Journal*: "If you set aside Three Mile Island and Chernobyl, the safety record of nuclear is really good." (Yes, Mrs. Lincoln, apart from that, how did you enjoy the show?) The Bush administration struck a close working relationship with the nuclear industry well before taking office. The energy "transition" advisors included Joseph Colvin, president of the Nuclear Energy Institute, the self-described "policy organization of the nuclear energy and technologies industry," and other nuclear industry biggies. There was no one representing renewable energy or environmental organizations.

Two weeks after being sworn in, Bush set up a "National Energy Policy Development Group" and appointed Vice President [Dick] Cheney as its chairman. The group included O'Neill. Behind closed doors, it huddled with fat energy industry cats—indeed, the General Accounting Office is now in the process of pursuing an unprecedented lawsuit because of Cheney's refusal to disclose who this government panel met with before setting policy.

The panel, 10 weeks after being organized, issued its report declaring how it "supports the expansion of nuclear energy in the United States." The National Energy Policy plan would substantially increase the use of nuclear power in the US both by building new nuclear power plants—many to be constructed on existing nuclear plant sites—and extending the 40-year licenses of currently operating plants by another 20 years.

The National Energy Policy says: "Many US nuclear plants sites were designed to host 4 to 6 reactors, and most operate only 2 or 3; many sites across the country could host additional plants." Further, "Building new generators on existing sites avoids many complex issues associated with building plants on new sites." It would also magnify the impacts of an accident—if one nuclear plant in a cluster of plants undergoes a catastrophic accident resulting in a site evacuation and abandonment of control rooms, there is then the potential for a "cascading loss" involving additional plants, stresses Paul Gunter, who heads NIRS' Reactor Watchdog Project.

"No one foresaw" nuclear plants "running for more than 40 years," says Alvarez, who was senior policy advisor to the DOE [U.S. Department of Energy] secretary from 1993 to 1999. "These reactors are just like old machines but they are ultra-hazardous," he says, and by pushing their operating span to 60 years, "disaster is being invited." The Bush-Cheney administration National Energy Policy supports purportedly "new and improved" nuclear plants, "advanced" nukes. It says, "Advanced reactor technology promises to improve nuclear safety." The administration is especially bullish on the gas-cooled, pebble bed reactor, which it claims has inherent safety features. In fact, says Gunter, the pebble bed reactor is not new, it's just "old wine in a new bottle." It's a "hybrid" of the gas-cooled high-temperature design that "has appeared and been rejected in England, Germany and the United States." And far from being "inherently safe," a reactor of similar design, a THTR300 in the Ruhr Valley in Germany, spewed out substantial amounts of radioactivity in a 1986 accident leading to its permanent closure.

The new nuclear push would be pursued through what's called "one-step" licensing. This was part of an Energy Policy Act bill approved by a Democratic-controlled Congress in 1992—381 to 37—and signed into law by the first President George Bush.

"One-step" licensing allows the Nuclear Regulatory Commission (NRC) to hold a single hearing for a "combined construction and operating license." No longer can nuclear plant projects be slowed down or stopped at a separate operating license proceeding at which evidence of construction defects is revealed. As *The New York Times* described passage of the Energy Policy Act in a back-of-the paper story in 1992, "Nuclear power lobbyists called the bill their biggest victory in Congress since the Three Mile Island accident." As NIRS reported in its *Nuclear Monitor* in 1992: "As the bill wound its way through the Senate and House, the nuclear industry won nearly every vote that mattered, proving that Congress remains captive to industry lobbying and political contributions over public opinion." That has not changed.

Public Citizen's Critical Mass Energy and Environment Program has documented how the nuclear industry regularly showers Congress—and this includes members of both major parties—with political contributions. Likewise, nuclear industry money pours into presidential campaigns.

The website of the Nuclear Energy Institute—www.nei.org—includes a page of "Endorsements of Nuclear Energy" and among those quoted are Al Gore: "Nuclear power, designed well, regulated properly, cared for meticulously, has a place in the world's energy supply."

Gore's running mate, Senator Joseph Lieberman, is quoted as saying at a Senate hearing in 1998: "I am a supporter of nuclear energy." To make sure the public hardly participates even in the "one-step" process, the NRC is now involved in a "rulemaking" to undo what it through the years interpreted as the public's right to formal trial-type hearings on nuclear plant licensing. It seeks to "deformalize" the hearings, eliminating due process procedures. Documents would be restricted to what the NRC staff and company deem relevant, and instead of cross-examining witnesses, people will have to submit written questions as suggestions to the NRC presiding officer for he or she to ask—at their discretion—at a hearing.

Also to help in a nuclear power comeback is the effort to alter the standards for radiation exposure. As more and more has been learned about radioactivity, the realization came that any amount can kill, that there is no "safe" level. This is called the "linear no-threshold theory." Now nuclear advocates in government and industry want to alter the standards premised on a contention that low doses of radiation are not so bad after all. There is even interest in a long-rejected notion called "hormesis"—that a little radiation is good for people, that it helps exercise the immune system. The instrument for making the changes is a new Biological Effects of Ionizing Radiation (BEIR) panel of the National Academy of Sciences that is to make recommendations to the federal government. It is "stacked," notes Diane D'Arrigo of NIRS, with "radiation advocates."

Nuclear waste is another obstacle the nuclear proponents in government and industry are seeking to get around. The Bush administration is now moving to open Yucca Mountain in Nevada as a repository and also use Utah's Skull Valley Goshute Reservation and possibly other Native American reservations. For what is considered "low-level" waste, the strategy is to "recycle" it—to smelt metals down and incorporate irradiated material into consumer items.

The huge problem with using Yucca Mountain, which the government began exploring as a high-level nuclear waste repository in the 1980s, is that it is on or near 32 earthquake faults and, notes D'Arrigo, has a "history and prospects of volcanoes and a likelihood of flooding and leakage." In 1997, tribal leaders of the Goshute Reservation, as the Goshute's website notes, "leased land to a private group of electrical utilities for the temporary storage of 40,000 metric tons of spent nuclear fuel." Some members of the tribe are fighting the deal in court demanding to know who got what for what. To nuclear advocates in government and industry, collaborating with Indian reservations as sovereign nations is a way to unload atomic garbage. Critics describe it as a new form of environmental racism"—"nuclear racism"—seeking to take advantage of the poverty of Native Americans.

The drive to "recycle" nuclear waste has been percolating for years. In 1980, the NRC first proposed that irradiated "metal scrap could be converted," that "radioactive waste burial costs could be avoided [and] the smelted scrap could be made into any number of consumer or capital equipment products such as automobiles, appliances, furniture, utensils, personal items and coins." Some thought that the push for radioactive quarters and hot Pontiacs was too crazy to be true.

Meanwhile, those behind the nuclear push have moved to extend a key piece of US law that facilitated the nuclear power industry in the first place: the Price-Anderson Act, the law that drastically limits the amount of money people can collect as a result of a nuclear power plant disaster. It was enacted in 1957 as a temporary measure to give a boost to setting up a nuclear power industry. It originally limited in the event of a nuclear plant accident to $560 million with the federal government paying the first $500 million. Price-Anderson has been extended and extended, and now it's being extended once more—to provide a financial umbrella for the push to revive nuclear power. As Michael Mariotte has pointed out: "The renewal of Price-Anderson is only to build new reactors. That's the issue. Existing nuclear plants are covered by the present law." The new Price-Anderson liability limit would be $8.6 billion, a fraction of what the NRC itself has concluded would be the financial consequences of a nuclear plant accident. Those figures are contained in a 1982 report done for the NRC by the DOE's Sandia National Laboratories and titled "Calculation of Reactor Accident Consequences for US Nuclear Power Plants." It calculates—in 1980 dollars—costs as a result of a nuclear plant disaster as high as $274 billion for Indian Point 2 and $314 billion at the Indian Point 3 nuclear plants. The number of "early fatalities"—46,000 as a result of Indian Point 2 undergoing a meltdown with breach of containment, 50,000 for Indian Point 3.

And what are the chances of such a disaster occurring? In 1985, the NRC was asked by a House oversight committee to determine the "probability" of a "severe core melt accident" in the "next 20 years for those reactors now operating and those expected to operate during that time." The NRC concluded: "The crude cumulative probability of such an accident would be 45%." That disaster has not come . . . yet. "Luck" is the only reason it hasn't, says David Lochbaum of the Union of Concerned Scientists. But the drive to revive nuclear power, the push to relapse, will, if it succeeds, help make inevitable that catastrophe—along with extending the damage of every aspect of the nuclear power chain, from mining to milling to transportation to fuel enrichment and fabrication to reactor operation and the "routine" emissions of radioactivity and then atomic waste management in perpetuity.

And, new—but not really new—is the specter of nuclear plants as terrorist targets. In 1980, a landmark book by Bennett Ramberg was published, *Nuclear Power Plants as Weapons for the Enemy: An Unrecognized Military Peril.* Despite the "multiplication of nuclear power plants," it begins, "little public consideration has been given to their vulnerability in time of war."

Dr. Ramberg, now research director of the Los Angeles-based Committee to Bridge the Gap, said in a post-9/11 presentation at the National Press Club: "I presented my findings to the Nuclear Regulatory Commission raising questions about the vulnerability of American reactors to terrorist action. The commission dismissed my concerns." Indeed, in a rule-making in 1982, an Atomic Safety and Licensing Board of the NRC, in considering an operating license for the Shearon Harris nuclear power plant in North Carolina, dismissed a contention by an intervenor, Wells Eddleman, that the plant's safety analysis was deficient because it did not consider the "consequences of terrorists commandeering a very large airplane . . . and diving it into the containment." The NRC board declared: "Reactors could not be effectively protected against such attacks without turning them into virtually impregnable fortresses at much higher cost . . . The applicants are not required to design against such things as artillery bombardments, missiles with nuclear warheads, or kamikaze dives by large airplanes."

Meanwhile, new since 1982 is the full arrival of safe, clean, renewable energy technologies. The need is for broad-scale implementation. Wind power, solar energy, hydrogen fuel technologies including fuel cells, among other renewable energy technologies, are more than ready after years of dramatic advances. Coupled with energy efficiency, they can be tapped and widely utilized—and render nuclear power completely unnecessary.

As NIRS, Public Citizen's Critical Mass Energy and Environment Program, Greenpeace USA, Safe Energy Communication Council, and the Global Resource Action Center for the Environment said of the National Energy Policy: "The Bush/Cheney administration is recklessly promoting the building of new nuclear plants to address an energy crisis that in large part is being manufactured by the energy corporations that will benefit from building new power plants . . . We believe that instead of promoting dangerous and dirty forms of energy, the United States should be a world leader in promoting renewable energy and energy efficiency. Let us not sell our children's future." Amen.

POSTSCRIPT

Is It Time to Revive Nuclear Power?

In the year 2000, there were 100 nuclear reactors in use in the United States and 352 in the developed world as a whole. There were only 15 in developing nations. Stephen Ansolabehere, et al., "The Future of Nuclear Power: An Interdisciplinary MIT Study" (MIT, 2003), recognizes that even a very large increase in the number of nuclear power plants—to 1000–1500—will not stop all releases of carbon dioxide. Christine Laurent, in "Beating Global Warming with Nuclear Power?" *UNESCO Courier* (February 2001), notes that "For several years, the nuclear energy industry has attempted to cloak itself in different ecological robes. Its credo: nuclear energy is a formidable asset in battle against global warming because it emits very small amounts of greenhouse gases. This stance, first presented in the late 1980s when the extent of the phenomenon was still the subject of controversy, is now at the heart of policy debates over how to avoid droughts, downpours and floods." Laurent adds that it makes more sense to focus on reducing carbon emissions by reducing energy consumption.

The Schwartz and Reiss article says flatly that "There's only one sane, practical alternative: nuclear power." Most writers who favor the nuclear solution are more restrained. As Richard A. Meserve says in a *Science* editorial ("Global Warming and Nuclear Power," *Science* [January 23, 2004]), "For those who are serious about confronting global warming, nuclear power should be seen as part of the solution. Although it is unlikely that many environmental groups will become enthusiastic proponents of nuclear power, the harsh reality is that any serious program to address global warming cannot afford to jettison any technology prematurely. . . . The stakes are large, and the scientific and educational community should seek to ensure that the public understands the critical link between nuclear power and climate change."

Alvin M. Weinberg, former director of the Oak Ridge National Laboratory, notes in "New Life for Nuclear Power," *Issues in Science and Technology* (Summer 2003), that to make a serious dent in carbon emission would require perhaps four times as many reactors as suggested in the MIT study. The accompanying safety and security problems would be challenging. If the challenges can be met, says John J. Taylor, retired vice president for nuclear power at the Electric Power Research Institute, in "The Nuclear Power Bargain," *Issues in Science and Technology* (Spring 2004), there are a great many potential benefits. There are also problems, foremost among them the question of how to dispose of nuclear waste. Deep burial (as at Yucca Mountain, Nevada) is stalled by political controversy; according to Matthew L. Wald, "A New Vision for Nuclear Waste," *Technology Review* (December 2004), a more practical solution may be centralized above-ground storage.

It is well worth stressing that Karl Grossman is by no means alone in his resistance to any expansion of the role of nuclear power. His essay is one among many available in print and on the Web that see chiefly danger in nuclear power. See "Fact and Fission," *The Economist* (July 19, 2003). Environmental groups such as Friends of the Earth are adamantly opposed, saying "Those who back nuclear over renewables and increased energy efficiency completely fail to acknowledge the deadly radioactive legacy nuclear power has created and continues to create" ("Nuclear Power Revival Plan Slammed," press release, April 18, 2004, http://www.foe-scotland.org.uk/press/pr20040408.html).

Paul Lorenzini, "A Second Look at Nuclear Power," *Issues in Science and Technology* (Spring 2005), argues that the goal must be energy "sufficiency for the foreseeable future with minimal environmental impact." Nuclear power can be part of the answer, but making it happen requires that we shed ideological biases. "It means ceasing to deceive ourselves about what might be possible."

ISSUE 6

Will Hydrogen Replace Fossil Fuels for Cars?

YES: Jeremy Rifkin, from "Hydrogen: Empowering the People," *The Nation* (December 23, 2002)

NO: Michael Behar, from "Warning: The Hydrogen Economy May Be More Distant Than It Appears," *Popular Science* (January 2005)

ISSUE SUMMARY

YES: Social activist Jeremy Rifkin asserts that fossil fuels are approaching the end of their usefulness and that hydrogen fuel holds the potential not only to replace them but also to reshape society.

NO: Michael Behar argues that the public has been misled about the prospects of the "hydrogen economy." We must overcome major technological, financial, and political obstacles before hydrogen can be a viable alternative to fossil fuels.

$\mathbf{T}$he 1973 "oil crisis" heightened awareness that the world—even if it was not yet running out of oil—was extraordinarily dependent on that fossil fuel (and therefore on supplier nations) for transportation, home heating, and electricity generation. Since the supply of oil and other fossil fuels was clearly finite, some people worried that there would come a time when demand could not be satisfied, and our dependence would leave us helpless. At the same time, we became acutely aware of the many unfortunate side effects of fossil fuels, notably air pollution.

The 1970s saw the modern environmental movement gain momentum. The first Earth Day was in 1970. Numerous government steps were taken to deal with air pollution, water pollution, and other environmental problems. In response to the oil crisis, a great deal of public money went into developing alternative energy supplies. The emphasis was on "renewable" energy, meaning conservation, wind, solar, and fuels such as hydrogen gas (which, when burned with pure oxygen, produces only water vapor as exhaust). However, when the crisis passed and oil supplies were once more ample (albeit it did cost more to fill a gasoline tank), most public funding for alternative-energy research and demonstration projects vanished. What work continued was at the hands of a few enthusiasts and those corporations that saw future opportunities. In 1991, Roger Billings, who had converted cars to run on hydrogen, developed the use of metal hydrides for hydrogen storage, founded corporations to develop and market hydrogen technology, and self-published *The Hydrogen World View* (a new edition appeared in 2000); his dream was a future when hydrogen would be the universal fuel, as widely employed for transportation and home heating (among other uses) as oil is today. That dream was not his alone. For instance, in 2001, the Worldwatch Institute published Seth Dunn's *Hydrogen Futures: Toward a Sustainable Energy System*. In 2002, MIT Press published Peter Hoffman's *Tomorrow's Energy: Hydrogen, Fuel Cells, and the Prospects for a Cleaner Planet*. On the corporate side, fossil fuel companies have long been major investors in alternative energy systems; in just the last few years, Shell, BP/Amoco, and ChevronTexaco have invested large amounts of money in renewables, hydrogen, photovoltaics, and fuel cells.

What drives the continuing interest in hydrogen and other alternative or renewable energy systems is the continuing problems associated with fossil fuels (and the discovery of new problems such as global warming), concern about dependence and potential political instability, and the growing realization that the availability of petroleum will peak in the near future. See Colin J. Campbell, "Depletion and Denial: The Final Years of Oil," *USA Today Magazine* (November 2000), Charles C. Mann, "Getting Over Oil," *Technology Review* (January–February 2002), and Robert L. Hirsch, Roger H. Bezdek, and Robert M. Wendling, "Peaking Oil Production: Sooner Rather than Later?" *Issues in Science and Technology* (Spring 2005).

Will that interest come to anything? There are, after all, a number of other ways to meet the need. Coal can be converted into oil and gasoline (though the air pollution and global warming problems remain). Cars can be made more efficient (and mileage efficiency is much greater than it was in the 1970s despite the popularity of SUVs). Cars can be designed to use natural gas or battery power; "hybrid" cars use combinations of gasoline and electricity and are proving more popular every year. See Brendan I. Koerner, "Rise of the Green Machine," *Wired* (April 2005).

The hydrogen enthusiasts remain. In the selections that follow, Jeremy Rifkin maintains that as oil supplies decline, hydrogen can fill the gap with many fewer side effects. In addition, because hydrogen can be produced by small-scale operations, it will take energy supplies out of the hands of major corporations and favor the development of a decentralized, environmentally benign economy. Michael Behar argues that the public has been misled about the prospects of the "hydrogen economy." It will come, but first we must overcome major technological, financial, and political obstacles.

Hydrogen: Empowering the People

While the fossil-fuel era enters its sunset years, a new energy regime is being born that has the potential to remake civilization along radically new lines—hydrogen. Hydrogen is the most basic and ubiquitous element in the universe. It never runs out and produces no harmful CO_2 emissions when burned; the only byproducts are heat and pure water. That is why it's been called "the forever fuel."

Hydrogen has the potential to end the world's reliance on oil. Switching to hydrogen and creating a decentralized power grid would also be the best assurance against terrorist attacks aimed at disrupting the national power grid and energy infrastructure. Moreover, hydrogen power will dramatically reduce carbon dioxide emissions and mitigate the effects of global warming. In the long run, the hydrogen-powered economy will fundamentally change the very nature of our market, political and social institutions, just as coal and steam power did at the beginning of the Industrial Revolution.

Hydrogen must be extracted from natural sources. Today, nearly half the hydrogen produced in the world is derived from natural gas via a steam-reforming process. The natural gas reacts with steam in a catalytic converter. The process strips away the hydrogen atoms, leaving carbon dioxide as the byproduct.

There is, however, another way to produce hydrogen without using fossil fuels in the process. Renewable sources of energy—wind, photovoltaic, hydro, geothermal and biomass—can be harnessed to produce electricity. The electricity, in turn, can be used, in a process called electrolysis, to split water into hydrogen and oxygen. The hydrogen can then be stored and used, when needed, in a fuel cell to generate electricity for power, heat and light.

Why generate electricity twice, first to produce electricity for the process of electrolysis and then to produce power, heat and light by way of a fuel cell? The reason is that electricity doesn't store. So, if the sun isn't shining or the wind isn't blowing or the water isn't flowing, electricity can't be generated and economic activity grinds to a halt. Hydrogen provides a way to store renewable sources of energy and insure an ongoing and continuous supply of power.

Hydrogen-powered fuel cells are just now being introduced into the market for home, office and industrial use. The major auto makers have spent more than $2 billion developing hydrogen-powered cars, buses and

Reprinted with permission from the December 23, 2002 issue of *The Nation* pp. 40–45. For subscription information, call 1-800-333-8536. Portions of each week's *Nation* magazine can be accessed at http://www.thenation.com.

trucks, and the first mass-produced vehicles are expected to be on the road in just a few years.

In a hydrogen economy the centralized, top-down flow of energy, controlled by global oil companies and utilities, would become obsolete. Instead, millions of end users would connect their fuel cells into local, regional and national hydrogen energy webs (HEWs), using the same design principles and smart technologies that made the World Wide Web possible. Automobiles with hydrogen cells would be power stations on wheels, each with a generating capacity of 20 kilowatts. Since the average car is parked most of the time, it can be plugged in, during nonuse hours, to the home, office or the main interactive electricity network. Thus, car owners could sell electricity back to the grid. If just 25 percent of all U.S. cars supplied energy to the grid, all the power plants in the country could be eliminated.

Once the HEW is set up, millions of local operators, generating electricity from fuel cells onsite, could produce more power more cheaply than can today's giant power plants. When the end users also become the producers of their energy, the only role remaining for existing electrical utilities is to become "virtual power plants" that manufacture and market fuel cells, bundle energy services and coordinate the flow of energy over the existing power grids.

To realize the promise of decentralized generation of energy, however, the energy grid will have to be redesigned. The problem with the existing power grid is that it was designed to insure a one-way flow of energy from a central source to all the end users. Before the HEW can be fully actualized, changes in the existing power grid will have to be made to facilitate both easy access to the web and a smooth flow of energy services over the web. Connecting thousands, and then millions, of fuel cells to main grids will require sophisticated dispatch and control mechanisms to route energy traffic during peak and nonpeak periods. A new technology developed by the Electric Power Research Institute called FACTS (flexible alternative current transmission system) gives transmission companies the capacity to "deliver measured quantities of power to specified areas of the grid."

Whether hydrogen becomes the people's energy depends, to a large extent, on how it is harnessed in the early stages of development. The global energy and utility companies will make every effort to control access to this new, decentralized energy network just as software, telecommunications and content companies like Microsoft and AOL Time Warner have attempted to control access to the World Wide Web. It is critical that public institutions and nonprofit organizations—local governments, cooperatives, community development corporations, credit unions and the like—become involved early on in establishing distributed-generation associations (DGAs) in every country. Again, the analogy to the World Wide Web is apt. In the new hydrogen energy era, millions of end users will generate their own "content" in the form of hydrogen and electricity. By organizing collectively to control the energy they produce—just as workers in the twentieth century organized into unions to control their labor power—end users can better dictate the terms with commercial suppliers of fuel cells for lease, purchase or other use arrangements and with virtual utility companies, which will manage the decentralized "smart" energy grids. Creating the appropriate partnership between commercial and noncommercial interests will be critical to establishing the legitimacy, effectiveness and long-term viability of the new energy regime.

I have been describing, thus far, the implementation of hydrogen power mainly in industrialized countries, but it could have an even greater impact on emerging nations. The per capita use of energy throughout the developing world is a mere one-fifteenth of the consumption enjoyed in the United States. The global average per capita energy use for all countries is only one-fifth the level of this country. Lack of access to energy, especially electricity, is a key factor in perpetuating poverty around the world. Conversely, access to energy means more economic opportunity. In South Africa, for example, for every 100 households electrified, ten to twenty new businesses are created. Making the shift to a hydrogen energy regime— using renewable resources and technologies to produce the hydrogen—and creating distributed generation energy webs that can connect communities all over the world could lift billions of people out of poverty. As the price of fuel cells and accompanying appliances continues to plummet with innovations and economies of scale, they will become far more broadly available, as was the case with transistor radios, computers and cellular phones. The goal ought to be to provide stationary fuel cells for every neighborhood and village in the developing world.

Renewable energy technologies—wind, photovoltaic, hydro, biomass, etc.—can be installed in villages, enabling them to produce their own electricity and then use it to separate hydrogen from water and store it for subsequent use in fuel cells. In rural areas, where commercial power lines have not yet been extended because they are too expensive, stand-alone fuel cells can provide energy quickly and cheaply.

After enough fuel cells have been leased or purchased, and installed, mini energy grids can connect urban neighborhoods as well as rural villages into expanding energy networks. The HEW can be built organically and spread as the distributed generation becomes more widely used. The larger hydrogen fuel cells have the additional advantage of producing pure drinking water as a byproduct, an important consideration in village communities around the world where access to clean water is often a critical concern.

Were all individuals and communities in the world to become the producers of their own energy, the result would be a dramatic shift in the configuration of power: no longer from the top down but from the bottom up. Local peoples would be less subject to the will of far-off centers of power. Communities would be able to produce many of their own goods and services and consume the fruits of their own labor locally. But, because they would also be connected via the worldwide communications and energy webs, they would be able to share their unique commercial skills, products and services with other communities around the planet. This kind of economic self-sufficiency becomes the starting point for global commercial interdependence, and is a far different economic reality from that of colonial regimes of the past, in which local peoples were made subservient to and dependent on powerful forces from the outside. By redistributing power broadly to everyone, it is possible to establish the conditions for a truly equitable sharing of the earth's bounty. This is the essence of reglobalization from the bottom up.

Two great forces have dominated human affairs over the course of the past two centuries. The American Revolution unleashed a new human aspiration to universalize the radical notion of political democracy. That force continues to gain momentum and will likely spread to the Middle East, China and every corner of the earth before the current century is half over.

A second force was unleashed on the eve of the American Revolution when James Watt patented his steam engine, inaugurating the beginning of the fossil-fuel era and an industrial way of life that fundamentally changed the way we work.

The problem is that these two powerful forces have been at odds with each other from the very beginning, making for a deep contradiction in the way we live our lives. While in the political arena we covet greater participation and equal representation, our economic life has been characterized by ever greater concentration of power in ever fewer institutional hands. In large part that is because of the very nature of the fossil-fuel energy regime that we rely on to maintain an industrialized society. Unevenly distributed, difficult to extract, costly to transport, complicated to refine and multifaceted in the forms in which they are used, fossil fuels, from the very beginning, required a highly centralized command-and-control structure to finance exploration and production, and coordinate the flow of energy to end users. The highly centralized fossil-fuel infrastructure inevitably gave rise to commercial enterprises organized along similar lines. Recall that small cottage industries gave way to large-scale factory production in the late nineteenth and early twentieth centuries to take advantage of the capital-intensive costs and economies of scale that went hand in hand with steam power, and later oil and electrification. In the discussion of the emergence of industrial capitalism, little attention has been paid to the fact that the energy regime that emerged determined, to a great extent, the nature of the commercial forms that took shape.

Now, on the cusp of the hydrogen era, we have at least the "possibility" of making energy available in every community of the world—hydrogen exists everywhere on earth—empowering the whole of the human race. By creating an energy regime that is decentralized and potentially universally accessible to everyone, we establish the technological framework for creating a more participatory and sustainable economic life—one that is compatible with the principle of democratic participation in our political life. Making the commercial and political arenas seamless, however, will require a human struggle of truly epic proportions in the coming decades. What is in doubt is not the technological know-how to make it happen but, rather, the collective human will, determination and resolve to transform the great hope of hydrogen into a democratic reality.

 **NO**

Warning: The Hydrogen Economy May Be More Distant Than It Appears

In the presidential campaign of 2004, Bush and Kerry managed to find one piece of common ground: Both spoke glowingly of a future powered by fuel cells. Hydrogen would free us from our dependence on fossil fuels and would dramatically curb emissions of air pollutants, including carbon dioxide, the gas chiefly blamed for global warming. The entire worldwide energy market would evolve into a "hydrogen economy" based on clean, abundant power. Auto manufacturers and environmentalists alike happily rode the bandwagon, pointing to hydrogen as the next big thing in U.S. energy policy. Yet the truth is that we aren't much closer to a commercially viable hydrogen-powered car than we are to cold fusion or a cure for cancer. This hardly surprises engineers, fuel cell manufacturers and policymakers, who have known all along that the technology has been hyped, perhaps to its detriment, and that the public has been misled about what Howard Coffman, editor of *fuelcell-info.com*, describes as the "undeniable realities of the hydrogen economy." These experts are confident that the hydrogen economy will arrive—someday. But first, they say, we have to overcome daunting technological, financial and political roadblocks. Herewith, our checklist of misconceptions and doubts about hydrogen and the exalted fuel cell.

1. Hydrogen Is an Abundant Fuel

True, hydrogen is the most common element in the universe; it's so plentiful that the sun consumes 600 million tons of it every second. But unlike oil, vast reservoirs of hydrogen don't exist here on Earth. Instead, hydrogen atoms are bound up in molecules with other elements, and we must expend energy to extract the hydrogen so it can be used in fuel cells. We'll never get more energy out of hydrogen than we put into it.

"Hydrogen is a currency, not a primary energy source," explains Geoffrey Ballard, the father of the modern-day fuel cell and co-founder of Ballard Power

Systems, the world's leading fuel-cell developer. "It's a means of getting energy from where you created it to where you need it."

2. Hydrogen Fuel Cells Will End Global Warming

Unlike internal combustion engines, hydrogen fuel cells do not emit carbon dioxide. But extracting hydrogen from natural gas, today's primary source, does. And wresting hydrogen from water through electrolysis takes tremendous amounts of energy. If that energy comes from power plants burning fossil fuels, the end product may be clean hydrogen, but the process used to obtain it is still dirty.

Once hydrogen is extracted, it must be compressed and transported, presumably by machinery and vehicles that in the early stages of a hydrogen economy will be running on fossil fuels. The result: even more CO_2. In fact, driving a fuel cell car with hydrogen extracted from natural gas or water could produce a net increase of CO_2 in the atmosphere. "People say that hydrogen cars would be pollution-free," observes University of Calgary engineering professor David Keith. "Light-bulbs are pollution-free, but power plants are not."

In the short term, nuclear power may be the easiest way to produce hydrogen without pumping more carbon dioxide into the atmosphere. Electricity from a nuclear plant would electrolyze water—splitting H_2O into hydrogen and oxygen. Ballard champions the idea, calling nuclear power "extremely important, unless we see some other major breakthrough that none of us has envisioned."

Critics counter that nuclear power creates long-term waste problems and isn't economically competitive. An exhaustive industry analysis entitled "The Future of Nuclear Power," written last year by 10 professors from the Massachusetts Institute of Technology and Harvard University, concludes that "hydrogen produced by electrolysis of water depends on low-cost nuclear power." As long as electricity from nuclear power costs more than electricity from other sources, using that energy to make hydrogen doesn't add up.

3. The Hydrogen Economy Can Run on Renewable Energy

Perform electrolysis with renewable energy, such as solar or wind power, and you eliminate the pollution issues associated with fossil fuels and nuclear power. Trouble is, renewable sources can provide only a small fraction of the energy that will be required for a full-fledged hydrogen economy.

From 1998 to 2003, the generating capacity of wind power increased 28 percent in the U.S. to 6,374 megawatts, enough for roughly 1.6 million homes. The wind industry expects to meet 6 percent of the country's electricity needs by 2020. But economist Andrew Oswald of the University of

Warwick in England calculates that converting every vehicle in the U.S. to hydrogen power would require the electricity output of a million wind turbines—enough to cover half of California. Solar panels would likewise require huge swaths of land.

Water is another limiting factor for hydrogen production, especially in the sunny regions most suitable for solar power. According to a study done by the World Resources Institute, a Washington, D.C.-based nonprofit organization, fueling a hydrogen economy with electrolysis would require 4.2 trillion gallons of water annually—roughly the amount that flows over Niagara Falls every three months. Overall, U.S. water consumption would increase by about 10 percent.

4. Hydrogen Gas Leaks Are Nothing to Worry About

Hydrogen gas is odorless and colorless, and it burns almost invisibly. A tiny fire may go undetected at a leaky fuel pump until your pant leg goes up in flames. And it doesn't take much to set compressed hydrogen gas alight. "A cellphone or a lightning storm puts out enough static discharge to ignite hydrogen," claims Joseph Romm, author of *The Hype about Hydrogen: Fact and Fiction in the Race to Save the Climate* and founder of the Center for Energy and Climate Solutions in Arlington, Virginia.

A fender bender is unlikely to spark an explosion, because carbon-fiber-reinforced hydrogen tanks are virtually indestructible. But that doesn't eliminate the danger of leaks elsewhere in what will eventually be a huge network of refineries, pipelines and fueling stations. "The obvious pitfall is that hydrogen is a gas, and most of our existing petrochemical sources are liquids," says Robert Uhrig, professor emeritus of nuclear engineering at the University of Tennessee and former vice president of Florida Power & Light. "The infrastructure required to support high-pressure gas or cryogenic liquid hydrogen is much more complicated. Hydrogen is one of those things that people have great difficulty confining. It tends to go through the finest of holes."

To calculate the effects a leaky infrastructure might have on our atmosphere, a team of researchers from the California Institute of Technology and the Jet Propulsion Laboratory in Pasadena, California, looked at statistics for accidental industrial hydrogen and natural gas leakage—estimated at 10 to 20 percent of total volume—and then predicted how much leakage might occur in an economy in which everything runs on hydrogen. Result: The amount of hydrogen in the atmosphere would be four to eight times as high as it is today.

The Caltech study "grossly overstated" hydrogen leakage, says Assistant Secretary David Garman of the Department of Energy's Office of Energy Efficiency and Renewable Energy. But whatever its volume, hydrogen added to the atmosphere will combine with oxygen to form water vapor, creating noctilucent clouds—those high, wispy tendrils you see at dawn and dusk. The increased cloud cover could accelerate global warming.

5. Cars Are the Natural First Application For Hydrogen Fuel Cells

"An economically sane, cost-effective attack on the climate problem wouldn't start with cars," David Keith says. Cars and light trucks contribute roughly 20 percent of the carbon dioxide emitted in the U.S., while power plants burning fossil fuels are responsible for more than 40 percent of CO_2 emissions. Fuel cells designed for vehicles must cope with harsh conditions and severe limitations on size and weight.

A better solution to global warming might be to hold off building hydrogen cars, and instead harness fuel cells to generate electricity for homes and businesses. Plug Power, UTC, FuelCell Energy and Ballard Power Systems already market stationary fuel-cell generators. Plug Power alone has 161 systems in the U.S., including the first fuel-cell-powered McDonald's. Collectively, however, the four companies have a peak generating capacity of about 69 megawatts, less than 0.01 percent of the total 944,000 megawatts of U.S. generating capacity.

6. The U.S. Is Committed to Hydrogen, Pouring Billions Into R&D

Consider this: President George W. Bush promised to spend $1.2 billion on hydrogen. Yet he allotted $1.5 billion to promote "healthy marriages." The monthly tab for the war in Iraq is $3.9 billion—a total of $121 billion through last September. In 2004 the Department of Energy spent more on nuclear and fossil fuel research than on hydrogen.

The federal government's FreedomCAR program, which funds hydrogen R&D in conjunction with the big three American carmakers, requires that the companies demonstrate a hydrogen-powered car by 2008—but not that they sell one.

"If you are serious about [hydrogen], you have to commit a whole lot more money," contends Guenter Conzelmann, deputy director of the Center for Energy, Environmental and Economic Systems Analysis at Argonne National Laboratory near Chicago. Conzelmann develops computer models to help the energy industry make predictions about the cost of implementing new technology. His estimate for building a hydrogen economy: more than $500 billion, and that's if 60 percent of Americans continue to drive cars with internal combustion engines.

Shell, ExxonMobil and other oil companies are unwilling to invest in production, distribution, fueling facilities and storage if there are just a handful of hydrogen cars on the road. Nor will automakers foot the bill and churn out thousands of hydrogen cars if drivers have nowhere to fill them up. Peter Devlin, head of the Department of Energy's hydrogen-production research group, says, "Our industry partners have told us that unless a fourth to a third of all refueling stations in the U.S. offer hydrogen, they won't be willing to take a chance on fuel cells."

To create hydrogen fueling stations, California governor Arnold Schwarzenegger, who drives a Hummer, has championed the Hydrogen Highway Project. His plan is to erect 150 to 200 stations—at a cost of at least $500,000 each—along the state's major highways by the end of the decade. So that's one state. Now what about the other 100,775 filling stations in the rest of the U.S.? Retrofitting just 25 percent of those with hydrogen fueling systems would cost more than $13 billion.

7. If Iceland Can Do It, So Can We

Iceland's first hydrogen fueling station is already operating on the outskirts of Reykjavík. The hydrogen, which powers a small fleet of fuel cell buses, is produced onsite from electrolyzed tap water. Meanwhile the recently formed Icelandic New Energy—a consortium that includes automakers, Royal Dutch/ Shell and the Icelandic power company Norsk Hydro—is planning to convert the rest of the island nation to a hydrogen system.

Impressive, yes. But 72 percent of Iceland's electricity comes from geothermal and hydroelectric power. With so much readily available clean energy, Iceland can electrolyze water with electricity directly from the national power grid. This type of setup is impossible in the U.S., where only about 15 percent of grid electricity comes from geothermal and hydroelectric sources, while 71 percent is generated by burning fossil fuels.

Another issue is the sheer scale of the system. It could take as few as 16 hydrogen fueling stations to enable Icelanders to drive fuel cell cars anywhere in the country. At close to 90 times the size of Iceland, the U.S. would require a minimum of 1,440 fueling stations. This assumes that stations would be strategically placed to collectively cover the entire U.S. with no overlap and that everyone knows where to find the pumps.

8. Mass Production Will Make Hydrogen Cars Affordable

Simply mass-producing fuel cell cars won't necessarily slash costs. According to Patrick Davis, the former leader of the Department of Energy's fuel cell research team, "If you project today's fuel cell technologies into high-volume production—about 500,000 vehicles a year—the cost is still up to six times too high."

Raj Choudhury, operations manager for the General Motors fuel cell program, claims that GM will have a commercial fuel cell vehicle ready by 2010. Others are doubtful. Ballard says that first there needs to be a "fundamental engineering rethink" of the proton exchange membrane (PEM) fuel cell, the type being developed for automobiles, which still cannot compete with the industry standard for internal combustion engines—a life span of 15 years, or about 170,000 driving miles. Because of membrane deterioration, today's PEM fuel cells typically fail during their first 2,000 hours of operation.

Ballard insists that his original PEM design was merely a prototype. "Ten years ago I said it was the height of engineering arrogance to think that the architecture and geometry we chose to demonstrate the fuel cell in automobiles would be the best architecture and geometry for a commercial automobile," he remarks. "Very few people paid attention to that statement. The truth is that the present geometry isn't getting the price down to where it is commercial. It isn't even entering into the envelope that will allow economies of scale to drive the price down."

In the short term, conventional gasoline-burning vehicles will be replaced by gas-electric hybrids, or by vehicles that burn clean diesel, natural gas, methanol or ethanol. Only later will hydrogen cars make sense, economically and environmentally. "Most analysts think it will take several decades for hydrogen to make a large impact, assuming hydrogen technologies reach their goals," notes Joan Ogden, an associate professor of environmental science and policy at the University of California at Davis and one of the world's leading researchers of hydrogen energy.

9. Fuel Cell Cars Can Drive Hundreds of Miles on a Single Tank of Hydrogen

A gallon of gasoline contains about 2,600 times the energy of a gallon of hydrogen. If engineers want hydrogen cars to travel at least 300 miles between fill-ups—the automotive-industry benchmark—they'll have to compress hydrogen gas to extremely high pressures: up to 10,000 pounds per square inch.

Even at that pressure, cars would need huge fuel tanks. "High-pressure hydrogen would take up four times the volume of gasoline," says JoAnn Milliken, chief engineer of the Department of Energy's Office of Hydrogen, Fuel Cells and Infrastructure Technologies.

Liquid hydrogen works a bit better. GM's liquid-fueled HydroGen3 goes 250 miles on a tank roughly double the size of that in a standard sedan. But the car must be driven every day to keep the liquid hydrogen chilled to –253 degrees Celsius—just 20 degrees above absolute zero and well below the surface temperature of Pluto—or it boils off. "If your car sits at the airport for a week, you'll have an empty tank when you get back," Milliken says.

?. If Not Hydrogen, Then *What?*

The near-future prospects for a hydrogen economy are dim, concludes *The Hydrogen Economy: Opportunities, Costs, Barriers, and R&D Needs*, a major government-sponsored study published last February by the National Research Council. Representatives from ExxonMobil, Ford, DuPont, the Natural Resources Defense Council and other stakeholders contributed to the report, which urges lawmakers to legislate tougher tailpipe-emission standards and to earmark additional R&D funding for renewable energy and alternative fuels. It foresees "major hurdles on the path to achieving the vision of the hydrogen economy" and recommends that the Department of Energy "keep a balanced portfolio of R&D efforts and continue to explore supply-and-demand alternatives that do not depend on hydrogen."

Of course, for each instance where the study points out how hydrogen falls short, there are scores of advocates armed with data to show how it can succeed. Physicist Amory Lovins, who heads the Rocky Mountain Institute, a think tank in Colorado, fastidiously rebuts the most common critiques of hydrogen with an armada of facts and figures in his widely circulated white paper "Twenty Hydrogen Myths." But although he's a booster of hydrogen, Lovins is notably pragmatic. "A lot of silly things have been written both for and against hydrogen," he says. "Some sense of reality is lacking on both sides." He believes that whether the hydrogen economy arrives at the end of this decade or closer to midcentury, interim technologies will play a signal role in the transition.

The most promising of these technologies is the gas-electric hybrid vehicle, which uses both an internal combustion engine and an electric motor, switching seamlessly between the two to optimize gas mileage and engine efficiency. U.S. sales of hybrid cars have been growing steadily, and the 2005 model year saw the arrival of the first hybrid SUVs—the Ford Escape, Toyota Highlander and Lexus RX400h.

Researchers sponsored by the FreedomCAR program are also investigating ultralight materials—plastics, fiberglass, titanium, magnesium, carbon fiber—and developing lighter engines made from aluminum and ceramic materials. These new materials could help reduce vehicle power demands, bridging the cost gap between fossil fuels and fuel cells.

Most experts agree that there is no silver bullet. Instead the key is developing a portfolio of energy-efficient technologies that can help liberate us from fossil fuels and ease global warming. "If we had a wider and more diverse set of energy sources, we'd be more robust, more stable," says Jonathan Pershing, director of the Climate, Energy and Pollution Program at the World Resources Institute. "The more legs your chair rests on, the less likely it is to tip over."

Waiting for hydrogen to save us isn't an option. "If we fail to act during this decade to reduce greenhouse gas emissions, historians will condemn us," Romm writes in *The Hype about Hydrogen*. "And they will most likely be living in a world with a much hotter and harsher climate than ours, one that has undergone an irreversible change for the worse."

POSTSCRIPT

Will Hydrogen Replace Fossil Fuels for Cars?

Hydrogen as a fuel offers definite benefits. As Joan M. Ogden notes in "Hydrogen: The Fuel of the Future?" *Physics Today* (April 2002), the technology is available and compared to the alternatives, it "offers the greatest potential environmental and energy-supply benefits." To put hydrogen to use, however, will require massive investments in facilities for generating, storing, and transporting the gas, as well as manufacturing hydrogen-burning engines and fuel cells. Currently, large amounts of hydrogen can easily be generated by "reforming" natural gas or other hydrocarbons. Hydrolysis—splitting hydrogen from water molecules with electricity—is also possible, and in the future this may use electricity from renewable sources such as wind or from nuclear power. The basic technologies are available right now. See Thammy Evans, Peter Light, and Ty Cashman, "Hydrogen—A Little PR," *Whole Earth* (Winter 2001). Daniel Sperling notes in "Updating Automotive Research," *Issues in Science and Technology* (Spring 2002), that "Fuel cells and hydrogen show huge promise. They may indeed prove to be the Holy Grail, eventually taking vehicles out of the environmental equation," but making that happen will require research, government assistance in building a hydrogen distribution system, and incentives for both industry and car buyers. First steps along these lines are already visible in a few places; see Bill Keenan, "Hydrogen: Waiting for the Revolution," *Across the Board* (May/June 2004), and Annie Birdsong, "California Drives the Future of the Automobile," *World Watch* (March/April 2005). M. Z. Jacobson, W. G. Colella, and D. M. Golden, "Cleaning the Air and Improving Health with Hydrogen Fuel-Cell Vehicles," *Science* (June 24, 2005), conclude that if all onroad vehicles are replaced with fuel-cell vehicles using hydrogen generated by wind power, air pollution and human health impacts will both be reduced and overall costs will be less than for gasoline.

Is the hydrogen economy—if it happens—likely to be as decentralized as Jeremy Rifkin envisions? It's possible, as John A. Turner makes clear in "Sustainable Hydrogen Production," Science (August 13, 2004), but Henry Payne and Diane Katz, "Gas and Gasbags . . . or, the Open Road and Its Enemies," *National Review* (March 25, 2002), contend that a major obstacle to hydrogen is market mechanisms that will keep fossil fuels in use for years to come, local hydrogen production is unlikely, and adequate supplies will require that society invest heavily in nuclear power. Jim Motavalli, "Hijacking Hydrogen," *E Magazine* (January–February 2003), worries that the fossil fuel and nuclear industries will dominate the hydrogen future. The former wish to use "reforming" to generate hydrogen from coal, and the latter see hydrolysis as creating demand for nuclear power. Nuclear power, he says, is particularly favored by the U.S. government's 2001 National Energy Policy.

In January 2003, President George W. Bush proposed $1.2 billion in funding for making hydrogen-powered cars an on-the-road reality. Gregg Easterbrook, "Why Bush's H-Car Is Just Hot Air," *New Republic* (February 24, 2003), thinks it would make much more sense to address fuel-economy standards; Bush should "leave futurism to the futurists." Peter Schwartz and Doug Randall, "How Hydrogen Can Save America," *Wired* (April 2003), commend Bush's proposal but say the proposed funding is not enough. We need, they say, "an Apollo-scale commitment to hydrogen power. The fate of the republic depends on it." Toward that end, they list five steps essential to making the hydrogen future real.

1. Develop fuel tanks that can store hydrogen safely and in adequate quantity.
2. Encourage mass production of fuel cell vehicles.
3. Convert the fueling infrastructure to hydrogen.
4. Increase hydrogen production.
5. Mount a PR campaign.

The difficulty of the task is underlined by Robert F. Service in "The Hydrogen Backlash," *Science* (August 13, 2004) (the lead article in a special section titled "Toward a Hydrogen Economy").

But are fossil fuels as scarce as industry critics and hydrogen enthusiasts say? They are certainly finite, but it has become apparent that not all fossil fuels are included in most accountings of available supply. A major omission is methane hydrate, a form of natural gas locked into cage-like arrangements of water molecules and found as masses of white ice-like material on the seabed. There appear to be vast quantities of methane hydrate on the bottom of the world's seas. If they can be recovered—and there are major difficulties in doing so—they may provide huge amounts of additional fossil fuels. Once liberated, their methane may be burned directly or "reformed" to generate hydrogen, making the nuclear approach less necessary. However, the methane still poses global warming risks. Indeed, if methane hydrate deposits ever gave up their methane naturally, they could change world climate abruptly (just such releases may have been responsible for past global climate warmings). See Erwin Suess, Gerhard Bohrmann, Jens Greinert, and Erwin Lausch, "Flammable Ice," *Scientific American* (November 1999).

On the Internet . . .

Facing the Future: People and the Planet

Facing the Future strives to educate people about critical global issues, including population growth, poverty, overconsumption, and environmental destruction.

http://www.facingthefuture.org/

Cell Phones and Cancer

At this site, John E. Moulder, professor of radiation oncology, radiology, and pharmacology/toxicology at the Medical College of Wisconsin, answers frequently asked questions about the relationship between cell phones and cancer. The site also links to two related FAQ sites—the relationship between power lines and cancer, and the relationship between static electromagnetic fields and cancer.

http://www.mcw.edu/gcrc/cop/cell-
phone-health-FAQ/toc.html

Malaria Foundation International

The Malaria Foundation International seeks "to facilitate the development and implementation of solutions to the health, economic and social problems caused by malaria."

http://www.malaria.org/

The Foresight Nanotech Institute

The Foresight Nanotech Institute works closely with governments, environmental groups, the policy community, professional associations, and civic sector organizations to improve education on and public policy on nanotechnology.

http://www.foresight.org/

Risk Assessment: What It Is, What It Can (and Can't) Do

The Hampshire Research Institute maintains this site to explain the nature of environmental risk.

http://www.hampshire.org/risk01.htm

National Institute of Environmental Health Sciences

The National Institute of Environmental Health Sciences studies the health risks of numerous environmental factors, many of which are associated with the use of technology.

http://www.niehs.nih.gov

PART 3

Human Health and Welfare

*M*any *people are concerned about new technological and scientific discoveries because they fear their potential impacts on human health and welfare. In the past, fears have been expressed concerning nuclear bombs and power plants, irradiated food, the internal combustion engine, medications such as thalidomide and diethylstilberstrol, vaccines, pesticides and other chemicals, and more. Not too long ago, people worried that the population explosion would harm both the environment and human well-being. Today the trend appears to be toward a population "implosion," and human well-being remains of concerns. On the technology front, people worry about the possible health risks of cell phones and nanotechnology, among other things. It is worth stressing that risks may be real (as they are with insecticides such as DDT), but there may be a trade-off for genuine health benefits.*

- Do Falling Birth Rates Pose a Threat to Human Welfare?

- Is There Sufficient Scientific Evidence to Conclude that Cell Phones Cause Cancer?

- Should DDT Be Banned Worldwide?

- Should Potential Risks Slow the Development of Nanotechnology?

ISSUE 7

Do Falling Birth Rates Pose a Threat to Human Welfare?

YES: Michael Meyer, from "Birth Dearth," *Newsweek* (September 27, 2004)

NO: David Nicholson-Lord, from "The Fewer the Better," *New Statesman* (November 8, 2004)

ISSUE SUMMARY

YES: Michael Meyer argues that when world population begins to decline after about 2050, economies will no longer continue to grow, government benefits will decline, young people will have to support an elderly population, and despite some environmental benefits, quality of life will suffer.

NO: David Nicholson-Lord argues that the economic problems of population decline all have straightforward solutions. A less-crowded world will not suffer from the environmental ills attendant on over-crowding and will, overall, be a roomier, gentler, less materialistic place to live, with cleaner air and water.

In 1798 the British economist Thomas Malthus published his *Essay on the Principle of Population.* In it, he pointed with alarm at the way the human population grew geometrically (a hockey-stick curve of increase) and at how agricultural productivity grew only arithmetically (a straight-line increase). It was obvious, he said, that the population must inevitably outstrip its food supply and experience famine. Contrary to the conventional wisdom of the time, population growth was not necessarily a good thing. Indeed, it led inexorably to catastrophe. For many years, Malthus was something of a laughingstock. The doom he forecast kept receding into the future as new lands were opened to agriculture, new agricultural technologies appeared, new ways of preserving food limited the waste of spoilage, and the birth rate dropped in the industrialized nations (the "demographic transition"). The food supply kept ahead of population growth and seemed likely—to most observers—to continue to do so. Malthus's ideas were dismissed as irrelevant fantasies.

Yet overall population kept growing. In Malthus's time, there were about 1 billion human beings on Earth. By 1950—when Warren S. Thompson worried that civilization would be endangered by the rapid growth of Asian and Latin American populations during the next five decades (see "Population," *Scientific American* [February 1950])—there were a little over 2.5 billion. In 1999 the tally passed 6 billion. By 2025 it will be over 8 billion. Statistics like these, which are presented in *World Resources 2002–2004: Decisions for the Earth, Balance, Voice, and Power* (World Resources Institute, 2003) (http://governance.wri.org/pubs_description.cfm?PubID=3764), a biennial report of the World Resources Institute in collaboration with the United Nations Environment and Development Programmes are positively frightening. The Worldwatch Institute's yearly *State of the World* reports (W. W. Norton) are no less so. By 2050 the UN expects the world population to be about 9 billion (see *World Population Prospects: The 2004 Revision Population Database*; http://esa.un.org/unpp/; United Nations, 2005). While global agricultural production has also increased, it has not kept up with rising demand, and—because of the loss of topsoil to erosion, the exhaustion of aquifers for irrigation water, and the high price of energy for making fertilizer (among other things)—the prospect of improvement seems exceedingly slim to many observers.

Two centuries never saw Malthus' forecasts of doom come to pass. Population continued to grow, and environmentalists pointed with alarm at a great many problems that resulted from human use of the world's resources (air and water pollution, erosion, loss of soil fertility and ground water, loss of species, and a great deal more). "Cornucopian" economists such as the late Julian Simon, insisted that the more people there are on Earth, the more people there are to solve problems and that humans can find ways around all possible resource shortages. See Simon's essay, "Life on Earth Is Getting Better, Not Worse," *The Futurist* (August 1983).

Was Malthus wrong? Both environmental scientists and many economists now say that if population continues to grow, problems are inevitable. But earlier predictions of a world population of 10 or 12 billion by 2050 are no longer looking very likely. The UN's population statistics show a slowing of growth, to be followed by an actual decline in population.

Some people worry that such a decline will not be good for human welfare. Michael Meyer argues that a shrinking population will mean that the economic growth that has meant constantly increasing standards of living must come to an end, government programs (from war to benefits for the poor and elderly) will no longer be affordable, young people will have to support an elderly population, and despite some environmental benefits, quality of life will suffer. David Nicholson-Lord argues that the economic problems of population decline all have straightforward solutions. A less crowded world will not suffer from the environmental ills attendant on overcrowding and will, overall, be a roomier, gentler, less materialistic place to live, with cleaner air and water.

Michael Meyer

 **YES**

Birth Dearth

Everyone knows there are too many people in the world. Whether we live in Lahore or Los Angeles, Shanghai or Sao Paulo, our lives are daily proof. We endure traffic gridlock, urban sprawl and environmental depredation. The evening news brings variations on Ramallah or Darfur—images of Third World famine, poverty, pestilence, war, global competition for jobs and increasingly scarce natural resources.

Just last week the United Nations warned that many of the world's cities are becoming hopelessly overcrowded. Lagos alone will grow from 6.5 million people in 1995 to 16 million by 2015, a miasma of slums and decay where a fifth of all children will die before they are 5. At a conference in London, the U.N. Population Fund weighed in with a similarly bleak report: unless something dramatically changes, the world's 50 poorest countries will triple in size by 2050, to 1.7 billion people.

Yet this is not the full story. To the contrary, in fact. Across the globe, people are having fewer and fewer children. Fertility rates have dropped by half since 1972, from six children per woman to 2.9. And demographers say they're still falling, faster than ever. The world's population will continue to grow—from today's 6.4 billion to around 9 billion in 2050. But after that, it will go sharply into decline. Indeed, a phenomenon that we're destined to learn much more about—depopulation—has already begun in a number of countries. Welcome to the New Demography. It will change everything about our world, from the absolute size and power of nations to global economic growth to the quality of our lives.

This revolutionary transformation will be led not so much by developed nations as by the developing ones. Most of us are familiar with demographic trends in Europe, where birthrates have been declining for years. To reproduce itself, a society's women must each bear 2.1 children. Europe's fertility rates fall far short of that, according to the 2002 U.N. population report. France and Ireland, at 1.8, top Europe's childbearing charts. Italy and Spain, at 1.2, bring up the rear. In between are countries such as Germany, whose fertility rate of 1.4 is exactly Europe's average. What does that mean? If the U.N. figures are right, Germany could shed nearly a fifth of its 82.5 million people over the next 40 years—roughly the equivalent of all of east Germany, a loss of population not seen in Europe since the Thirty Years' War.

And so it is across the Continent. Bulgaria will shrink by 38 percent, Romania by 27 percent, Estonia by 25 percent. "Parts of Eastern Europe, already sparsely populated, will just empty out," predicts Reiner Klingholz, director of the Berlin Institute for Population and Development. Russia is already losing close to 750,000 people yearly. (President Vladimir Putin calls it a "national crisis.") So is Western Europe, and that figure could grow to as much as 3 million a year by midcentury, if not more.

The surprise is how closely the less-developed world is following the same trajectory. In Asia it's well known that Japan will soon tip into population loss, if it hasn't already. With a fertility rate of 1.3 children per woman, the country stands to shed a quarter of its 127 million people over the next four decades, according to U.N. projections. But while the graying of Japan (average age: 42.3 years) has long been a staple of news headlines, what to make of China, whose fertility rate has declined from 5.8 in 1970 to 1.8 today, according to the U.N.? Chinese census data put the figure even lower, at 1.3. Coupled with increasing life spans, that means China's population will age as quickly in one generation as Europe's has over the past 100 years, reports the Center for Strategic and International Studies in Washington. With an expected median age of 44 in 2015, China will be older on average than the United States. By 2019 or soon after, its population will peak at 1.5 billion, then enter a steep decline. By midcentury, China could well lose 20 to 30 percent of its population every generation.

The picture is similar elsewhere in Asia, where birthrates are declining even in the absence of such stringent birth-control programs as China's. Indeed, it's happening despite often generous official incentives to procreate. The industrialized nations of Singapore, Hong Kong, Taiwan and South Korea all report subreplacement fertility, says Nicholas Eberstadt, a demographer at the American Enterprise Institute in Washington. To this list can be added Thailand, Burma, Australia and Sri Lanka, along with Cuba and many Caribbean nations, as well as Uruguay and Brazil. Mexico is aging so rapidly that within several decades it will not only stop growing but will have an older population than that of the United States. So much for the cliche of those Mexican youths swarming across the Rio Grande? "If these figures are accurate," says Eberstadt, "just about half of the world's population lives in subreplacement countries."

There are notable exceptions. In Europe, Albania and the outlier province of Kosovo are reproducing energetically. So are pockets of Asia: Mongolia, Pakistan and the Philippines. The United Nations projects that the Middle East will double in population over the next 20 years, growing from 326 million today to 649 million by 2050. Saudi Arabia has one of the highest fertility rates in the world, 5.7, after Palestinian territories at 5.9 and Yemen at 7.2. Yet there are surprises here, too. Tunisia has tipped below replacement. Lebanon and Iran are at the threshold. And though overall the region's population continues to grow, the increase is due mainly to lower infant mortality; fertility rates themselves are falling faster than in developed countries, indicating that over the coming decades the Middle East will age far more rapidly than other regions of the world. Birthrates in Africa remain high, and despite the AIDS epidemic its population is projected to keep growing. So is that of the United States.

We'll return to American exceptionalism, and what that might portend. But first, let's explore the causes of the birth dearth, as outlined in a pair of new books on the subject. "Never in the last 650 years, since the time of the Black Plague, have birth and fertility rates fallen so far, so fast, so low, for so long, in so many places," writes the sociologist Ben Wattenberg in "Fewer: How the New Demography of Depopulation Will Shape Our Future." Why? Wattenberg suggests that a variety of once independent trends have conjoined to produce a demographic tsunami. As the United Nations reported last week, people everywhere are leaving the countryside and moving to cities, which will be home to more than half the world's people by 2007. Once there, having a child becomes a cost rather than an asset. From 1970 to 2000, Nigeria's urban population climbed from 14 to 44 percent. South Korea went from 28 to 84 percent. So-called megacities, from Lagos to Mexico City, have exploded seemingly overnight. Birth rates have fallen in inverse correlation.

Other factors are at work. Increasing female literacy and enrollment in schools have tended to decrease fertility, as have divorce, abortion and the worldwide trend toward later marriage. Contraceptive use has risen dramatically over the past decade; according to U.N. data, 62 percent of married or "in union" women of reproductive age are now using some form of nonnatural birth control. In countries such as India, now the capital of global HIV, disease has become a factor. In Russia, the culprits include alcoholism, poor public health and industrial pollution that has whacked male sperm counts. Wealth discourages childbearing, as seen long ago in Europe and now in Asia. As Wattenberg puts it, "Capitalism is the best contraception."

The potential consequences of the population implosion are enormous. Consider the global economy, as Phillip Longman describes it in another recent book, "The Empty Cradle: How Falling Birthrates Threaten World Prosperity and What to Do About It." A population expert at the New America Foundation in Washington, he sees danger for global prosperity. Whether it's real estate or consumer spending, economic growth and population have always been closely linked. "There are people who cling to the hope that you can have a vibrant economy without a growing population, but mainstream economists are pessimistic," says Longman. You have only to look at Japan or Europe for a whiff of what the future might bring, he adds. In Italy, demographers forecast a 40 percent decline in the working-age population over the next four decades—accompanied by a commensurate drop in growth across the Continent, according to the European Commission. What happens when Europe's cohort of baby boomers begins to retire around 2020? Recent strikes and demonstrations in Germany, Italy, France and Austria over the most modest pension reforms are only the beginning of what promises to become a major sociological battle between Europe's older and younger generations.

That will be only a skirmish compared with the conflict brewing in China. There market reforms have removed the cradle-to-grave benefits of the planned economy, while the Communist Party hasn't constructed an adequate social safety net to take their place. Less than one quarter of the population is covered by retirement pensions, according to CSIS. That puts the burden of elder care almost entirely on what is now a generation of only children. The one-child policy has led to the so-called 4-2-1 problem, in which each child will be potentially responsible for caring for two parents and four grandparents.

Incomes in China aren't rising fast enough to offset this burden. In some rural villages, so many young people have fled to the cities that there may be nobody left to look after the elders. And the aging population could soon start to dull China's competitive edge, which depends on a seemingly endless supply of cheap labor. After 2015, this labor pool will begin to dry up, says economist Hu Angang. China will have little choice but to adopt a very Western-sounding solution, he says: it will have to raise the education level of its work force and make it more productive. Whether it can is an open question. Either way, this much is certain: among Asia's emerging economic powers, China will be the first to grow old before it gets rich.

Equally deep dislocations are becoming apparent in Japan. Akihiko Matsutani, an economist and author of a recent best seller, "The Economy of a Shrinking Population," predicts that by 2009 Japan's economy will enter an era of "negative growth." By 2030, national income will have shrunk by 15 percent. Speculating about the future is always dicey, but economists pose troubling questions. Take the legendarily high savings that have long buoyed the Japanese economy and financed borrowing worldwide, especially by the United States. As an aging Japan draws down those assets in retirement, will U.S. and global interest rates rise? At home, will Japanese businesses find themselves competing for increasingly scarce investment capital? And just what will they be investing in, as the country's consumers grow older, and demand for the latest in hot new products cools off? What of the effect on national infrastructure? With less tax revenue in state coffers, Matsutani predicts, governments will increasingly be forced to skimp on or delay repairs to the nation's roads, bridges, rail lines and the like. "Life will become less convenient," he says. Spanking-clean Tokyo might come to look more like New York City in the 1970s, when many urban dwellers decamped for the suburbs (taking their taxes with them) and city fathers could no longer afford the municipal upkeep. Can Japanese cope? "They will have to," says Matsutani. "There's no alternative."

Demographic change magnifies all of a country's problems, social as well as economic. An overburdened welfare state? Aging makes it collapse. Tensions over immigration? Differing birthrates intensify anxieties, just as the need for imported labor rises—perhaps the critical issue for the Europe of tomorrow. A poor education system, with too many kids left behind? Better fix it, because a shrinking work force requires higher productivity and greater flexibility, reflected in a new need for continuing job training, career switches and the health care needed to keep workers working into old age.

In an ideal world, perhaps, the growing gulf between the world's wealthy but shrinking countries and its poor, growing ones would create an opportunity. Labor would flow from the overpopulated, resource-poor south to the depopulating north, where jobs would continue to be plentiful. Capital and remittance income from the rich nations would flow along the reverse path, benefiting all. Will it happen? Perhaps, but that presupposes considerable labor mobility. Considering the resistance Europeans display toward large-scale immigration

from North Africa, or Japan's almost zero-immigration policy, it's hard to be optimistic. Yes, attitudes are changing. Only a decade ago, for instance, Europeans
also spoke of zero immigration. Today they recognize the need and, in bits and
pieces, are beginning to plan for it. But will it happen on the scale required?

A more probable scenario may be an intensification of existing tensions
between peoples determined to preserve their beleaguered national identities on
the one hand, and immigrant groups on the other seeking to escape overcrowding and lack of opportunity at home. For countries such as the Philippines—still
growing, and whose educated work force looks likely to break out of low-
status jobs as nannies and gardeners and move up the global professional
ladder—this may be less of a problem. It will be vastly more serious for the
tens of millions of Arab youths who make up a majority of the population in
the Middle East and North Africa, at least half of whom are unemployed.

America is the wild card in this global equation. While Europe and much
of Asia shrinks, the United States' indigenous population looks likely to stay
relatively constant, with fertility rates hovering almost precisely at replacement levels. Add in heavy immigration, and you quickly see that America is
the only modern nation that will continue to grow. Over the next 45 years the
United States will gain 100 million people, Wattenberg estimates, while Europe
loses roughly as many.

This does not mean that Americans will escape the coming demographic
whammy. They, too, face the problems of an aging work force and its burdens.
(The cost of Medicare and Social Security will rise from 4.3 percent of GDP in
2000 to 11.5 percent in 2030 and 21 percent in 2050, according to the Congressional Budget Office.) They, too, face the prospect of increasing ethnic tensions, as a flat white population and a dwindling black one become gradually
smaller minorities in a growing multicultural sea. And in our interdependent
era, the troubles of America's major trading partners—Europe and Japan—will
quickly become its own. To cite one example, what becomes of the vaunted
"China market," invested in so heavily by U.S. companies, if by 2050 China
loses an estimated 35 percent of its workers and the aged consume an ever-
greater share of income?

America's demographic "unipolarity" has profound security implications
as well. Washington worries about terrorism and failing states. Yet the chaos
of today's fragmented world is likely to prove small in comparison to
what could come. For U.S. leaders, Longman in "The Empty Cradle" sketches
an unsettling prospect. Though the United States may have few military competitors, the technologies by which it projects geopolitical power—from laser-
guided missiles and stealth bombers to a huge military infrastructure—may
gradually become too expensive for a country facing massively rising social
entitlements in an era of slowing global economic growth. If the war on terrorism turns out to be the "generational struggle" that national-security adviser
Condoleezza Rice says it is, Longman concludes, then the United States might
have difficulty paying for it.

None of this is writ, of course. Enlightened governments could help hold
the line. France and the Netherlands have instituted family-friendly policies
that help women combine work and motherhood, ranging from tax credits

for kids to subsidized day care. Scandinavian countries have kept birthrates up with generous provisions for parental leave, health care and part-time employment. Still, similar programs offered by the shrinking city-state of Singapore—including a state-run dating service—have done little to reverse the birth dearth. Remember, too, that such prognoses have been wrong in the past. At the cusp of the postwar baby boom, demographers predicted a sharp fall in fertility and a global birth dearth. Yet even if this generation of seers turns out to be right, as seems likely, not all is bad. Environmentally, a smaller world is almost certainly a better world, whether in terms of cleaner air or, say, the return of wolves and rare flora to abandoned stretches of the East German countryside. And while people are living longer, they are also living healthier—at least in the developed world. That means they can (and probably should) work more years before retirement.

Yes, a younger generation will have to shoulder the burden of paying for their elders. But there will be compensations. As populations shrink, says economist Matsutani, national incomes may drop—but not necessarily per capita incomes. And in this realm of uncertainty, one mundane thing is probably sure: real-estate prices will fall. That will hurt seniors whose nest eggs are tied up in their homes, but it will be a boon to youngsters of the future. Who knows? Maybe the added space and cheap living will inspire them to, well, do whatever it takes to make more babies. Thus the cycle of life will restore its balance. . . .

David Nicholson-Lord  **NO**

The Fewer the Better

This is a story of two Britains and two futures. In the first Britain, the work culture dominates; the talk is of economic growth and dynamism and competing with the rest of the world. Labour is young, cheap and biddable, and driven by the urge to "succeed"—to make it in material and career terms, with the consumer goods and lifestyles to match. In the cities of this 24/7 society, population densities rise: so do crime, violence and antisocial behaviour. Outside the cities, urbanisation spreads, along with noise, congestion, the creep of human clutter and development. Unspoilt places are increasingly hard to find. Pollution gets steadily worse.

The second Britain is a quieter place. The age profile is older, the values less strident and materialistic. People work longer—they are not pensioned off in their fifties—but they save more and spend less, at least on ephemera and gadgets. They drink much less, too, and don't get involved in fights. Work is important but so are hobbies, family and community life. Cities are more spacious, roads emptier, the countryside more rural. The air and water are cleaner and there is hope of getting the weather back to normal because the planet is no longer warming so rapidly.

Which future would we prefer? The first—let us call it "UK plc"—with its economic engine revving at full speed? Or the second, where quality of life matters more: not so much a plc as a community enterprise, with the emphasis on community rather than enterprise? Most people would plump for the second. Yet we seem to be heading for the first.

What we do not admit is that the difference between the two futures is largely one of human numbers. Population is a subject we don't like to mention. In September Michael Howard, the Conservative leader, pointed out that, over the next 30 years, Britain's population would grow by 5.6 million—an increase of nearly 10 percent on the current 59 million. Immigration, running at an average net inflow of 158,000 a year in the past five years, accounts for 85 percent of this increase. Because population is forecast to rise, the government plans an extra 3.8 million houses in England over the next 20 years. But that plan is based on net immigration of 65,000 a year. If it continues at 158,000 a year, we will need 4.85 million new homes.

Howard went on to quote, with approval, the conclusions of the government's Community Cohesion Panel, which said in July that people "need sufficient time to come to terms with and accommodate incoming groups, regardless of their ethnic origin. The 'pace of change' . . . is simply too great . . . at present."

Alarmist? Electioneering? Playing the race card? In so far as these parts of Howard's speech were reported at all, that was how the left-liberal media interpreted them. Yet his figures understate the contribution of immigration to housing forecasts, because they ignore the changes in fertility and household formation resulting from a younger population. According to the Optimum Population Trust, a continuation of the 2001–2003 growth rate of 0.4 percent would result in a UK population of 71 million in 2050 and 100 million by the end of the century.

The implications of this bear examination. Given a population of "only" 65–66 million by mid-century, for example, we would need an extra nine or ten million houses by 2050—more than twice the numbers Howard was talking about, and an increase of nearly 50 percent on the current English housing stock. Should this worry us? Clearly many people think so; the government's housing plans have been a source of controversy ever since they were published. Examine this controversy in greater depth, and you will find a developing awareness of what ecologists call "carrying capacity": the balance (or lack of it) between a physical environment and the numbers it can support.

About all this, the environmental lobby is now silent. The last time such issues were deemed fit for public debate was in 1973, when a government population panel said Britain must accept "that its population cannot go on increasing indefinitely". The progressive-minded believe, on the one hand, in liberal multiculturalism and, on the other, in sustainability. They cannot resolve the conflict. The field has thus been abandoned to the political right.

The demographic facts are undeniable, however. Before the start of the current immigration surge in the 1990s, Britain's population, like that of many other developed countries, was heading for decline—as early as 2013, according to some forecasts. British women are having 1.7 children each, on average, above Germany (1.4) and Japan (1.3) but below the replacement level of 2.1. If this had been allowed to continue, with no immigration, we would be down to 30 million by 2120.

What would it be like to live in a country where population halved in the space of three or four generations? Environmentally, the case for population decline is unanswerable—less pollution, less strain on natural systems, greater national self-sufficiency, a reduction in fossil-fuel emissions, the freeing up of land for other species and higher-order human uses, such as wilderness. Psychologically, what the economist Fred Hirsch called "positional goods"—a view, an unspoilt beach, a piece of heritage—would be freer of the crowds and queues that now, for most people, mar them. Applied to social and economic life, this might reduce the awful sense of competitiveness that is a relatively recent feature of cultural life, for jobs, places at school or university, or entry to prized social institutions or niches.

Given the close association between crowding, densities, congestion and stress, and the greater distances available between people, we would also probably see less casual public aggression: less of the "rage" that emerged in the late 1980s. And, because young people are more likely to commit crimes, the ageing of society that would result from population decline would reinforce these trends. A Britain of 30 million people would almost certainly be a kindlier, more easygoing, more socially concerned place—exactly the sort of Britain that many readers of the *New Statesman* would like to see.

⋅⚙⋅

Most of the argument so far, however, has focused on the perils of decline: economic and social stagnation, the decrease in the support ratio (of workers to pensioners), emerging labour shortages and so on. Given that all of these "problems" are either illusory, fantastical or soluble it is instructive to ask why they obsess us. Why were the Tories, for example, thinking until recently about encouraging people to have babies and why does the government still envisage no upper limit on immigration? There are two answers. First, population growth is such a feature of the past two centuries—although not of preceding ages—that it has become synonymous in our minds with progress. Second, economic growth is how politicians and economists measure national success. And having more people is the quickest and easiest way to boost gross domestic product.

Much is made, therefore, of the impact of immigration on economic growth. Yet the growth comes almost entirely from additions to the national headcount. The increased wealth per person may be as little as 0.1 percent a year, according to US research.

More important is what happens when "immigrants" become "natives". This is the central fallacy of the demographic "timebomb" argument. Immigrants eventually become pensioners, and pensioners keep living longer. The only way to preserve a support ratio regarded as optimal is thus to have permanently high levels of immigration—and a population permanently, indeed infinitely, growing. David Coleman, professor of demography at Oxford University, has calculated that to keep the support ratio between pensioners and those of working age at roughly current levels would require a UK population in 2100 of approximately 300 million and rising. He calls it "the incredible in pursuit of the implausible".

And what about the world as a whole? How are developing countries, presumably expected to provide the young immigrants to the UK and other western countries, supposed to support their own old people?

New figures from the US Population Reference Bureau suggest a world population of roughly 9.3 billion in 2050, against 6.4 billion now. Studies such as the WWF's *Living Planet Report* say that by that time, humanity's footprint will be up to 220 percent of the earth's biological capacity. We would need, in other words, another couple of planets to survive. But if we manage to control global population (and it looks increasingly likely that we can) numbers will start to decline, possibly around 2070. What is the world supposed to do then? Import extra-planetary aliens to maintain the support ratio?

Even within Britain, it is hard to make a case for labour shortages when unemployment is three times the number of vacancies and economic inactivity, notably among the over-fifties, is at an all-time high. It is also hard, morally at least, to argue that we should deliberately cream off the skilled and educated workers of poorer countries—little different from people-trafficking, according to a National Health Service overseas recruiter addressing this year's Royal College of Nursing conference—or that we should bring people in because there is nobody else to sweep our streets and clean our toilets.

꧁◈꧂

The solutions to the "problems" of population decline, in fact, lie safely within the range of realistic policy options. They include: people saving more and consuming less; governments investing more in preventative health measures, to lengthen illness-free old age; better labour productivity; a higher retirement age; drawing the economically inactive back into economic activity (with penalties for ageism); and restructuring hard-to-fill jobs to make them more attractive. Population decline creates a (relative) shortage of workers and therefore shifts power from capital to labour and raises pay rates generally, as happened after the Black Death. Isn't the left supposed to be in favour of such an outcome and against the use of immigrants to create a US-style low-wage economy?

Yet the argument is not primarily about economics. Those who advocate increases in immigration and population do so largely on the grounds that they are good for GDP. They forget, as most economists do, that they are often bad for the environment and society. Economic growth, after all, is ethically undiscriminating: the wages earned from clearing up the effects of a car crash or a pollution mishap count towards GDP in the same way as those earned from making a loaf of bread. All over the world, Britain included, population growth is generating an extraordinary range of negative effects, from climate change and resource exhaustion to the destruction of species and habitats and the poisoning of the biosphere. Deliberately boosting Britain's population, either through large-scale net immigration or by telling people to have more babies, will ultimately make it a much worse place to live in.

How big should Britain's population be? That depends which sums you do—but some calculations from the Optimum Population Trust suggest 20 million or fewer.

Before you throw up your hands in disbelief at this idea, consider the view of a liberal from another generation, John Stuart Mill, who in his *Principles of Political Economy* (1848) acknowledged the economic potential for a "great increase in population" but confessed he could see little reason for desiring it. "The density of population necessary to enable mankind to obtain . . . all the advantages both of co-operation and of social intercourse," he wrote, "has, in all the most populous countries, been attained." In 1848, the world contained just over a billion people and the population of Britain was 21 million.

POSTSCRIPT

Do Falling Birth Rates Pose a Threat to Human Welfare?

Resources and population come together in the concept of "carrying capacity," defined very simply as the size of the population that the environment can support, or "carry," indefinitely, through both good years and bad. It is not the size of the population that can prosper in good times alone, for such a large population must suffer catastrophically when droughts, floods, or blights arrive or the climate warms or cools. It is a long-term concept, where "long term" means not decades or generations, nor even centuries, but millennia or more. See Mark Nathan Cohen, "Carrying Capacity," *Free Inquiry* (August/September 2004).

What is Earth's carrying capacity for human beings? It is surely impossible to set a precise figure on the number of human beings the world can support for the long run. As Joel E. Cohen discusses in *How Many People Can the Earth Support?* (W. W. Norton, 1996), estimates of Earth's carrying capacity range from under a billion to over a trillion. The precise number depends on our choices of diet, standard of living, level of technology, willingness to share with others at home and abroad, and desire for an intact physical, chemical, and biological environment, as well as on whether or not our morality permits restraint in reproduction and our political or religious ideology permits educating and empowering women. The key, Cohen stresses, is human choice, and the choices are ones we must make within the next 50 years. Phoebe Hall, "Carrying Capacity," *E Magazine* (March/April 2003), notes that even countries with large land areas and small populations, such as Australia and Canada, can be overpopulated in terms of resource availability. The critical resource appears to be food supply; see Russell Hopfenberg, "Human Carrying Capacity Is Determined by Food Availability," *Population & Environment* (November 2003).

Andrew R. B. Ferguson, in "Perceiving the Population Bomb," *World Watch* (July/August 2001), sets the maximum sustainable human population at about 2 billion. Sandra Postel, in the Worldwatch Institute's *State of the World 1994* (W. W. Norton, 1994), says, "As a result of our population size, consumption patterns, and technology choices, we have surpassed the planet's carrying capacity. This is plainly evident by the extent to which we are damaging and depleting natural capital" (including land and water).

If population growth is now declining and world population will actually begin to decline during this century, there is clear hope. But the question of carrying capacity remains. Most estimates of carrying capacity put it at well below the current world population size, and it will take a long time for global population to fall far enough to reach such levels. We seem to be moving in the right direction, but it remains an open question whether our numbers will decline far enough soon enough (i.e., before environmental problems become critical). On the other hand, Jeroen Van den Bergh and Piet Rietveld, "Reconsidering the Limits to World Population: Meta-Analysis and Meta-Prediction," *Bioscience* (March 2004), set their best estimate of human global carrying capacity at 7.7 billion, which is distinctly reassuring.

ISSUE 8

Is There Sufficient Scientific Research to Conclude That Cell Phones Cause Cancer?

YES: George Carlo and Martin Schram, from *Cell Phones: Invisible Hazards in the Wireless Age: An Insider's Alarming Discoveries About Cancer and Genetic Damage* (Carroll & Graf, 2001)

NO: United Kingdom's National Radiation Protection Board, from *Mobile Phones and Health 2004: Report by the Board of NRPB* (National Radiation Protection Board, Britain), http://www.hpa.org.uk/radiation/publications/documents_of_nrpb/abstracts/absd15-5.htm (Doc NRPB 15(5), 2004)

ISSUE SUMMARY

YES: Public health scientist George Carlo and journalist Martin Schram argue that there is a definite risk that the electromagnetic radiation generated by cell phone antennae can cause cancer and other health problems.

NO: The National Radiation Protection Board (now the Radiation Protection Division, http://www.hpa.org.uk/radiation/, of the United Kingdom's Health Protection Agency) argues that there is no clear indication of adverse health effects, including cancer, from the use of mobile phones, but precautions are nevertheless in order.

It seems inevitable that new technologies will alarm people. For example, in the late 1800s, when electricity was new, people feared the new wires that were strung overhead. See Joseph P. Sullivan, "Fearing Electricity: Overhead Wire Panic in New York City," *IEEE Technology and Society Magazine* (Fall 1995). More recently, electromagnetic fields (EMFs) have drawn attention. Now cell phones and other forms of wireless communications technology are the focus of controversy.

EMFs are emitted by any device that uses electricity. They weaken rapidly as one gets farther from the source, but they can be remarkably strong close to the source. Users of electric blankets (before the blankets were redesigned to minimize EMFs) and personal computers are thus subject to high exposures. Since EMF strength also depends on how much electricity is flowing through the source, people who live near power lines, especially high-tension, long-distance transmission lines, are also open to high EMF exposure.

Are EMFs dangerous? There have been numerous reports suggesting a link between EMF exposure and cancer, but inconsistency has been the curse of research in this area. In 1992 the Committee on Interagency Radiation Research and Policy Coordination, an arm of the White House's Office of Science and Technology Policy, released *Health Effects of Low Frequency Electric and Magnetic Fields,* a report that concluded, "There is no convincing [published] evidence . . . to support the contention that exposures to extremely low frequency electric and magnetic fields generated by sources such as household appliances, video terminals, and local powerlines are demonstrable health hazards." In 1996 Jon Palfreman, in "Apocalypse Not," *Technology Review* (April 1996), summarized the controversy and the evidence against any connection between cancer and EMFs. And in "Residential Exposure to Magnetic Fields and Acute Lymphoblastic Leukemia in Children," *The New England Journal of Medicine* (July 3, 1997), Martha S. Linet et al. report that they failed to find any support for such a connection.

Since cell phones are electrical devices, they emit EMFs. But they—or their antennae—also emit electromagnetic radiation in the form of radio signals. And after a few cell phone users developed brain cancer and sued the phone makers, people began to worry. See Gordon Bass, "Is Your Cell Phone Killing You?" *PC Computing* (December 1999). Now more lawsuits are being filed, and the research reports are coming in. Indeed, in 1999 Professor John Moulder and his colleagues published a review of the evidence in "Cell Phones and Cancer: What Is the Evidence for a Connection?" *Radiation Research* (May 1999). In it, they concluded, "Overall, the existing evidence for a causal relationship between RF radiation from cell phones and cancer is found to be weak to nonexistent." Tamar Nordenberg, "Cell Phones and Brain Cancer: No Clear Connection," *FDA Consumer* (November–December 2000), reported no real signs that cell phones caused cancer but noted that the evidence was sufficient to justify continuing research.

In the following selections, George Carlo and Martin Schram argue that there is a definite risk that the electromagnetic radiation generated by cell phone antennae can cause cancer and other health problems. Furthermore, wireless Internet devices also emit such radiation and may pose similar risks. The National Radiation Protection Board (now the Radiation Protection Division of the United Kingdom's Health Protection Agency) argues that the widespread adoption of mobile phones has not been accompanied by any clear increase in adverse health effects, including cancer, but the technology is still young, there has not been enough time for epidemiological studies of users, especially in subgroups of users, and there have been some suggestive laboratory studies. There are no clear indications of risk, but precautions are nevertheless in order.

 **YES**

Cell Phones: Invisible Hazards in the Wireless Age

Follow-the-Science: Piecing Together the Cancer Puzzle

Scientific findings are like pieces of a puzzle. Individually, they may not seem to show anything clearly. But by trying to fit the pieces together, it is possible to see if they form a big, coherent picture.

In the puzzle of cell phone radiation research, the pieces of scientific evidence we have now do fit together. Although many pieces are still missing, those that are in place indicate a big picture of cancer and health risk. The picture is alarming, because even if the risk eventually proves to be small, it will still be real—and that means millions of people around the world will develop cancer or other health problems due to using mobile phones.

Even more alarming, however, is that many in the industry, who are paid by the industry—and some who are paid by the public to oversee and regulate the industry—have persisted in talking publicly as if they cannot see the picture that is taking shape even as they speak.

In the study of public health, there is a well-known template that researchers use to put together individual scientific findings—like the pieces of a puzzle—to see if they show evidence of a public-health hazard. This template, known as the Koch-Henle Postulates, is a means of determining whether the findings indicate a true cause-and-effect process, from biological plausibility to exposure and dose-response. The postulates are:

1. If there is a biological explanation for the association derived from separate experiments that is consistent with what is known about the development of the disease, then the association is more likely to be causal. Scientists term this *biological plausibility.*
2. If several studies of people are showing the same finding while employing different methods and different investigators, the association that is being seen is more likely to be cause and effect, or causal. Scientists term this *consistency.*

3. If it is clear that the exposure precedes the development of the disease, then the association is more likely to be causal. Scientists term this *temporality*.
4. If the increase in risk is significant—more than a doubling in the risk or an increase that is statistically significant—the association is more likely to be causal. Scientists term this *significance*.
5. If the more severe the level of exposure, the higher the risk for the disease or the biological effect that is being studied, the association is more likely to be causal. Scientists term this *dose–response upward*.
6. If the absence of exposure corresponds to the absence of the disease, the more likely the association is to be causal. Scientists term this *dose–response downward*.
7. If there are similar findings in human, animal, and *in vitro* studies—in other words, if the same conclusions can be drawn from all—the more likely the association that is seen is causal. Scientists term this *concordance*.

Researchers use the Koch-Henle Postulates as a checklist. The greater the number of postulates that are met, the greater the likelihood that a hazard exists. For some of the more commonly recognized carcinogens, it has taken decades for the hazards to be judged as valid. For example, in the case of cigarette smoking, it took two decades of study and more than 100 years of consumer use to gather enough information that could be judged against the Koch-Henle standards to demonstrate the need for the U.S. Surgeon General's warning label on cigarette packs.

In the case of cellular telephones, consumers are fortunate that the health-hazard picture can be seen much sooner than that. Each of the red-flag findings about cell phone radiation provides a vital piece of information that fits into the overall cancer puzzle. A number of the other earlier studies, which on their own were inconclusive or seemed uninterpretable, now appear to fit into the puzzle as well. They clarify a troubling picture of cancer and health risk that is just now becoming clear.

Here is how the scientific pieces fit into the larger cancer puzzle:

Human blood studies These studies—by Drs. Ray Tice and Graham Hook, and most recently [corroborated by] Dr. Joseph Roti Roti—show genetic damage in the form of micronuclei in blood cells exposed to cell phone radiation. They provide evidence of the Koch-Henle postulate of *biological plausibility* for the development of the tumors following exposure to radio waves. Without some type of genetic damage, it is unlikely that radio waves would be able to cause cancer. Every direct mechanism that has been identified in the development of cancer involves genetic damage; the linkage is so strong that if an absence of genetic damage had been proven in these studies, scientists would have considered that to be reason enough to conclude that cancer is not caused by cell phones. (Indeed, that is what scientists were justified in saying prior to 1999.) Scientific literature has repeatedly confirmed that brain cancer is clearly linked to chromosome damage; brain tumors have consistently been shown to have a variety of chromosomal abnormalities. The studies by Tice, Hook, and Roti Roti consistently showed chromosomal damage in blood exposed to wireless phone radio waves.

Breakdown in the blood brain barrier   The findings of genetic damage by Tice, Hook, and Roti Roti now give new meaning and importance to Dr. Leif Salford's 1994 studies that showed a breakdown in the blood brain barrier of rats when they were exposed to radio waves. The blood brain barrier findings now fit into the overall cancer picture by providing a two-step explanation for how cancer could be caused by cell phone radiation. (The blood brain barrier filters the blood by not allowing dangerous chemicals to reach sensitive brain tissue.)

Step One: A breakdown in the blood brain barrier filter would provide an avenue for chemical carcinogens in the bloodstream (from tobacco, pesticides, or air pollution, for example) to leak into the brain and reach sensitive brain tissue that would otherwise be protected. Those chemicals, upon reaching sensitive brain tissue, could break the DNA in the brain or cause other harm to reach those cells.

Step Two: While a number of studies showed that cell phone radiation by itself does not appear to break DNA, the micronuclei findings of Tice, Hook, and Roti Roti suggest that DNA repair mechanisms in brain cells could be impaired by mobile phone radiation. (One reason micronuclei occur is that there has been a breakdown in the cell's ability to repair itself.) If the brain cells become unable to repair themselves, the process of chemically induced carcinogenesis—the creation of tumors—could begin.

This is further evidence of the Koch-Henle postulate of *biological plausibility* for cell phone radiation involvement in the development of brain cancer.

Studies of tumors in people who use cell phones   There have been four studies of tumors in people who use cellular phones—Dr. Ken Rothman's study of deaths among cell phone users, Joshua Muscat's two studies of brain cancer and acoustic neuroma, and Dr. Lennart Hardell's study of brain tumors. All four epidemiological studies, done by different investigators who used different methods, show some evidence of an increased risk of tumors associated with the use of cellular phones. This is evidence of the Koch-Henle postulate of *consistency.*

All four epidemiological studies provide some assurance in the methods used by the investigators that the people studied had used cellular telephones before they were clinically diagnosed as having tumors. This is evidence of the Koch-Henle postulate of *temporality.*

All four epidemiological studies showed increases in risk of developing brain tumors. Muscat's study of cell phone users showed a doubling of the risk of developing neuro-epithelial tumors. (The result was statistically significant.) Hardell's study showed that among cell phone users, tumors were twice as likely to occur in areas of the brain at the side where the user normally held the phone. (This result was also statistically significant.) Rothman's study showed that users of handheld cell phones have more than twice the risk of dying from brain cancer than do car phone users—whose antennas are mounted on the body of the car, far removed from the users' heads. (That finding was not statistically significant.) Muscat's study of acoustic neuroma indicates that cell phone users have a 50-percent increase in risk of developing tumors of the auditory nerve. (This finding was statistically significant only when correlated with the years of cell phone usage by the patient.) These findings are evidence of the Koch-Henle postulate of *significance.*

Studies of cell phone radiation dosage and response   In Dr. Michael Repacholi's study of mice, the risk of lymphoma increased significantly with the number of months that mice were exposed to the radio waves.

In the work by Tice, Hook, and Roti Roti, the risks of genetic damage as measured by the formation of micronuclei increased as the amount of radiation increased.

In the three epidemiological studies—two by Muscat and one by Hardell—that were able to estimate radiation exposure to specific parts of the brain, the risk of tumors was greater in the areas of the brain near where the cell phone was held.

These findings are all evidence of the Koch-Henle postulate known as *dose–response upward.* (In cell phones, minutes of phone usage are not a reliable indication of dosage, because the distance of the telephone from a base station during the call and any physical barriers to the signal are the most important factors in the amount of radiation the phone antenna emits during the call.)

The Hardell epidemiological study showed that patients with tumors in areas of the brain that could not be reached by radiation from a cell phone antenna were likely not to have been cell phone users. Similarly, in Muscat's study, when all brain-tumor patients were included in his analysis—those with tumors that were outside the range of radiation from the cellular phone antenna and those whose tumors were within that range—there was no increase in the risk of brain cancer. This is evidence of the Koch-Henle postulate that is called *dose–response downward*—which simply means that if there is no chance that cell phone radiation dosage could have been received, chances are the tumor was caused by something else.

Agreement of findings from in vitro and in vivo studies   The   test-tube studies by Tice and Hook; the mouse study by Repacholi; and the four epidemiological studies by Rothman, Muscat, and Hardell are all in agreement in that they suggest an increase in the risk of cancer among people who use mobile phones. This is evidence of the Koch-Henle postulate of *concordance.*

. . . And the Largest Piece of the Puzzle
As the officials of the government, officials of the industry, and just plain unofficial people try to fit together jigsaw pieces to see whether mobile phones indeed pose a cancer risk, the cancer experts themselves have provided what is by far the biggest and most revealing piece of the puzzle.

Writing in the U.S. government's own *Journal of the National Cancer Institute*, and other prestigious professional publications, these experts have made it clear that, if there are findings that micronuclei develop in blood cells exposed to mobile phone radiation, that is in itself evidence of a cancer risk. The risk is so persuasive, the experts have written, that preventative treatment should be given in order to best protect those people whose levels of micronuclei have increased.

The Big Picture

The pieces of the cell phone puzzle do indeed fit together to form the beginnings of a picture that researchers, regulators, and mobile phone users can all see for themselves. Many pieces are still missing. But enough pieces are already in place to see that there are legitimate reasons to be concerned about the health of people who use wireless phones.

Most alarming to public health scientists should be the fact that all seven of the Koch-Henle postulates have been met within the first decade of widespread mobile phone usage.

The big picture is becoming disturbingly clear: There is a definite risk that the radiation plume that emanates from a cell phone antenna can cause cancer and other health problems. It is a risk that affects hundreds of millions of people around the world. It is a risk that must be seen and understood by all who use cell phones so they can take all the appropriate and available steps to protect themselves—and especially to protect young children whose skulls are still growing and who are the most vulnerable to the risks of radiation.

Safety First: Health Recommendations

As the big picture becomes clear and we see that radiation from mobile phones poses a real cancer and health risk, it also becomes clear that there are basic recommendations that now demand the urgent attention of all who use, make, research, or regulate cell phones.

Mobile telephones are a fact of life and a fixture in the lifestyles of more than half a billion people around the world. That only makes it all the more vital that we understand and follow the recommendations by which all who use mobile phones can minimize their health risk, and especially can protect our children. Here are some basic suggests for mobile phone users, manufacturers, and science and medical researchers.

Recommendations for Consumers

To avoid radiation exposure and minimize health risks when using wireless phones:

1. The best advice is to keep the antenna away from your body by using a phone with a headset or earpiece. Another option is a phone with speakerphone capability.

2. If you must use your phone without a headset, be sure the antenna is fully extended during the phone's use. Radiation plumes are emitted mainly from the mid-length portion of the antenna; when the antenna is recessed inside the phone, the entire phone functions as the antenna—and the radiation is emitted from the entire phone into a much wider area of your head, jaw, and hand.

3. Children under the age of ten should not use wireless devices of any type; for children over the age of ten, pagers are preferable to wireless phones because pagers are not put up to the head and they can be used away from the body.

4. When the signal strength is low, do not use your phone. The reason: The lower the signal strength, the harder the instrument has to work to carry the call—and the greater the radiation that is emitted from the antenna.

5. Emerging studies, and common sense, make clear that handheld phones should not be used while driving a vehicle.

A Few Words of Caution for Consumers

The public is bombarded with waves of claims that are made at times by individuals who are well-meaning but not well-informed—and at other times by special interests who really want to sell a product. For example, there is no scientific basis for recommendations that have been made by some groups to limit phone use as a means of minimizing the risk of health effects. It is not possible to determine scientifically the difference in radiation exposure from one ten-minute call and ten one-minute calls. The total number of minutes is the same, but the pattern and amount of radiation could be very different. Also, the amount of radiation emitted by a mobile phone depends on the distance of the phone from a base station; the further the distance, the harder the phone has to work and the greater the radiation. Finally, the greatest amount of radiation emitted by a phone is during dialing and ringing. People who keep their phones on their belts or in their pockets should move the phones away from their bodies when the phones are ringing. (The amounts of radiation in a single call can vary by factors of ten to 100 depending on all of these variables.)

Consumers also need to be cautious about unverified claims that seem to have scientific backing. For example: The media recently carried an account published in Britain's *Which?* magazine that said a group called the Consumers' Association (with which the magazine is affiliated) had shown in tests that some cell phone headsets actually cause more radiation to go to the brain than the phones themselves. But the claim is unsubstantiated by any scientific evidence, and has been refuted by a number of studies by recognized researchers using established scientific methods. The only conclusion that can be drawn from existing scientific evidence is that headsets are the best option for mobile phone users to minimize exposure to wireless phone radiation.

Also, a number of devices on the market claim to eliminate the effects of antenna radiation and are being marketed as alternatives to using headsets or speakerphones. These products need to be tested to see if they will really protect consumers—a caution expressed by Great Britain's Stewart Commission. They recommended that their government set in place "a national system which enables independent testing of shielding devices and hands-free kits . . . which enable clear information to be given about the effectiveness of such devices. A kite mark or equivalent should be introduced to demonstrate conformity with the testing standard." In the United States, the FDA has been silent on the matter.

Recommendations for the Mobile Phone Industry

To enhance consumer protection:

1. Phones should be redesigned to minimize radiation exposure to consumers—antennas that extend out at an angle, away from the head, or that carry the radiation outward should be developed.
2. Headsets and other accessories that minimize radiation exposure should be redesigned so they are more durable and can be conveniently used.
3. Consumers should be given complete information about health risks and solutions through brochures, product inserts, and Internet postings so they can make their own decisions about how much of the risk inherent to mobile telephone use they wish to assume.
4. Emerging and advancing phone technologies need to be premarket tested for biological effects so dangerous products do not make it to the market.
5. Post-market surveillance is necessary for all phone users—surveys of analog and digital phone users to see if they experience any adverse health effects, and databases should be maintained where people can report any health effects they have experienced due to their phones.

Recommendations for Scientific, Medical, and Public Health Officials

To help consumers:

1. Science, medicine, and government must move immediately and aggressively with the goal of minimizing the impact of radio waves on adults, children, and pregnant women.
2. One federal agency must be designated as the lead agency for protecting people who use wireless communications devices, rather than having the responsibility remain undefined and shared among multiple agencies including the FDA, FCC, EPA, and others.
3. A genuine safety standard needs to be established to serve as the basis for future regulatory decisions. Since the specific absorption rate alone does not measure biological effects on humans, it does not serve the safety needs of consumers. . . .

Recommendations for Industry and Government Concerning the Wireless Internet

We need to recognize and learn from the mistakes we made when cellular phones were first introduced. The phones were sold to the public before there had been any premarket testing to determine whether they were safe or posed a potential health risk. Because the cell phones were not tested initially, by the time they were on the market, efforts to research the problem became intertwined with the forces of politics and profit. Consumer protection was not the highest priority.

As we enter the age of the wireless Internet, no one can say for sure whether or not the radio waves of the these new wireless products will prove harmless or harmful. But this much is known: The concern about mobile phones focuses on the near-field radiation that extends in a 2-to-3-inch plume from an antenna, and the radiation from the many wireless laptop and handheld computer products is just about the same. It would seem that these latter products should be safer because users don't hold their laptops and handheld computers against their heads. But no one has researched what the effect will be of a roomful of wireless products all being used simultaneously, with radio waves invisibly crisscrossing the space that is occupied by people. Will these passive occupants run a risk similar to nonsmokers in a room filled with smokers, who end up affected by passive smoke?

Thus, it is important that these new products must be formally testing under official regulatory control that includes specific premarket screening guidelines. There must also be post-market surveys of people who use the wireless Internet to see if health problems emerge that were not found in the premarket testing.

Mobile Phones and Health 2004

Executive Summary

Background

1. There are currently about 50 million mobile phones in use in the UK compared with around 25 million in 2000 and 4.5 million in 1995. These are supported by about 40,000 base stations in the UK network. The majority of these base stations operate under the Global System for Mobile Communications (GSM).

2. In less than ten years since the first GSM network was commercially launched as the second generation of mobile phones, it has become the world's leading and fastest growing telecommunications system. It is in use by more than one-sixth of the world's population and it has been estimated that at the end of January 2004 there were 1 billion GSM subscribers across more than 200 countries. The growth of GSM continues unabated with more than 160 million new customers in the last 12 months.

3. The revolution in communications continues world-wide. The third generation of mobile phones, 3G, is now being marketed in the UK and in many other countries and it is to be expected that further developments will become available in due course. In addition, there are many other telecommunications and related systems in use, all of which result in exposure of the population to radiofrequency (RF) fields.

4. The UK government has given strong encouragement to the development of mobile phone technology. Operators have been given support for the installation of the cellular networks and government has seen this as an important area for UK-based firms to establish themselves as world leaders. There have also been extensive developments in security-related equipment that utilise radiocommunications systems.

Public Health Concerns

5. The extensive use of mobile phones suggests that users do not in general judge them to present a significant health hazard. Rather they have welcomed the technology and brought it into use in their

From *DOC NRPB* 15(5) 1–116(2004), 2004, pp. #1–25, 31–37, 40–44, 55–32, 64–66, 69–71, 84–89. Copyright © 2004 by HPA/CRCE. Reprinted by permission. References omitted.

everyday lives. Nevertheless, since their introduction, there have been persisting concerns about the possible impact of mobile phone technologies on health.

6. This was appreciated by the UK government, which in 1999 took the early initiative of setting up the Independent Expert Group on Mobile Phones (IEGMP) to review the situation. Its report, *Mobile Phones and Health* (the Stewart Report), was published in May 2000. It stated:

    "The balance of evidence to date suggests that exposures to RF radiation below NRPB and ICNIRP (International Commission on Non-Ionizing Radiation Protection) guidelines do not cause adverse health effects to the general population."

    "There is now scientific evidence, however, which suggests that there may be biological effects occurring at exposures below these guidelines."

    "We conclude therefore that it is not possible at present to say that exposure to RF radiation, even at levels below national guidelines, is totally without potential adverse health effects, and that the gaps in knowledge are sufficient to justify a precautionary approach."

    "We recommend that a precautionary approach to the use of mobile phone technologies be adopted until much more detailed and scientifically robust information on any health effects becomes available."

7. The Board notes that a central recommendation in the Stewart Report was that a precautionary approach to the use of mobile phone technologies be adopted until much more detailed and scientifically robust information on any health effects becomes available.

8. The Stewart Report was welcomed by government, the general public and by industry. Various subsequent reports from across the world have supported the main thrust of its general conclusions.

9. Since then, the widespread development in the use of mobile phones world-wide has not been accompanied by associated, clearly established increases in adverse health effects. Within the UK, there is a lack of hard information showing that the mobile phone systems in use are damaging to health. It is important to emphasise this crucial point.

10. Nevertheless, the following issues have to be taken into consideration.

11. First, the widespread use of mobile phone technologies is still fairly recent and technologies are continuing to develop at a pace which is outstripping analyses of any potential impact on health (see paragraphs 55–57, 84 and 85).

12. Second, there are data which suggest that RF fields can interfere with biological systems.

13. Third, because the use of mobile phone technologies is a fairly recent phenomenon, it has not yet been possible to carry out necessary long-term epidemiological studies and evaluate the findings. However, an increase in the risk of acoustic neuromas has recently been reported in people in Sweden with more than ten years' use of mobile phones. This study has been able to obtain long-term follow-up data and highlights the need for extended follow-up studies on phone users, as has been noted in a number of reviews. Epidemiological studies, because of a lack of sensitivity, may miss any effects in small subsets of the general populations studied. This is a reason why the Board welcomes the large international cohort study proposed for

support by the Mobile Telecommunications and Health Research (MTHR) programme (see paragraph 89). A recent German study has also suggested concerns.

14. Fourth, a recent paper has suggested possible effects on brain function resulting from the use of 3G phones, although the study has some limitations and needs replication. The Stewart Report had previously identified the need for research on brain function.

15. Fifth, populations are not homogeneous and people can vary in their susceptibility to environmental and other challenges. There are well-established examples in the literature of the genetic predisposition of some groups that could influence sensitivity to disease. This remains an outstanding issue in relation to RF exposure and one on which more information is needed. A number of people also report symptoms they ascribe to electromagnetic hypersensitivity arising from exposure to a range of electromagnetic fields (EMFs) encountered in everyday life. There is concern by an increasing number of individuals, although relatively small in relation to the total UK population, that they are adversely affected by exposure to RF fields from mobile phones (see also paragraphs 58–64).

16. Sixth, IEGMP considered that children might be more vulnerable to any effects arising from the use of mobile phones because of their developing nervous system, the greater absorption of energy in the tissues of the head and a longer lifetime of exposure. Data on the impact on children have not yet been forthcoming. The potential for undertaking studies to examine any possible effects on children, however, are limited for ethical reasons.

17. Seventh, there are ongoing concerns in the UK about the use of Terrestrial Trunked Radio (TETRA) by the police and the nature of the signals emitted as well as about exposures to RF from other telecommunications technologies.

18. Eighth, there remain particular concerns in the UK about the impact of base stations on health, including well-being. Despite current evidence which shows that exposures of individuals are likely to be only a small fraction of those from phones, they may impact adversely on well-being. The large numbers of additional base stations which will be necessary to effectively roll out the 3G and other new networks are likely to exacerbate the potential impact. People can also be concerned about effects on property values when base stations are built near their homes.

19. The Board believes that the main conclusions reached in the Stewart Report in 2000 still apply today and that a precautionary approach to the use of mobile phone technologies should continue to be adopted.

Progress Made in Addressing Public Health Concerns

20. The recommendation in the Stewart Report to adopt a precautionary approach was immediately accepted by government. It also endorsed many of the other recommendations in the Report.

21. The Stewart Report made a number of other recommendations that were designed to provide more information about the operation of mobile phones and base stations and to address public concerns about this technology. This sought to allow individuals, local

communities and local authorities to make informed choices about how the technology should be developed.

22. The responses to the recommendations in the Stewart Report are reviewed in the report by the Board and issues where further progress is needed have been identified. The key findings are summarised below.

Tightening of Exposure Guidelines

23. A recommendation in the Stewart Report was that, as a precautionary approach, the ICNIRP guidelines for public exposure be adopted for use in the UK for mobile phone frequencies. It was felt that this would bring the UK into line with other countries in the European Union. These guidelines have now been adopted by government for application across the UK and provide for a five-fold reduction in exposure guidelines for members of the public compared with the recommended values for people whose work brings them into contact with sources of RF fields.

24. The Board welcomes the introduction by government of tighter exposure guidelines for the general public.

Base Stations

25. A wide variety of types of base stations make up the UK network. Macrocells provide the main framework of the system. Where there are areas of high demand, as in busy streets and shopping areas, microcells are used to infill the network and help to prevent 'lost' calls. Picocells may be installed in buildings or other enclosed areas to improve signal strength and to infill the network in areas of high demand for calls. . . .

31. The Board recommends that monitoring of potential exposures from 3G base stations should be concomitant with the rollout of the network.

Mobile Phones and SAR Values

32. In September 2001 the European Committee for Electrical Standardisation (CENELEC) published a standard testing procedure for the measurement of specific energy absorption rate (SAR) from mobile phones. Information on all phones marketed in the UK, using this standard testing procedure, is now available.

33. However, it is still difficult for people to readily and easily acquire the necessary information so that comparisons of different phones can be made.

34. The Board welcomes the provision of information on the SAR from phones by all manufacturers using a standard testing procedure. This is an important contribution to providing information to the public about the potential for exposure and informs consumer choice. It recommends that comparative information on the SAR from phones is readily available to the consumer. The inclusion of comparative data on the SAR from phones in its promotional literature by at least one retailer is a welcome development. The public also need to be able to understand the merits and limitations of published SAR values.

Planning Guidance on Base Station Locations

35. IEGMP was concerned that anxiety about the presence of local base stations and resulting exposure to RF fields could affect peoples' health, including well-being. IEGMP also heard at open meetings that information about base station developments was frequently not provided to the local community.

36. A number of recommendations were made in the Stewart Report to improve the transparency of the local planning process and to improve the planning procedure. A specific recommendation was that permitted development rights for the erection of masts under 15 m should be revoked and that the siting of all new base stations should be subject to the normal planning process.

37. Following publication of the Stewart Report reviews of the planning process were put in place throughout the UK. Revised guidance that was issued aimed to provide for more discussions between operators and local authorities on the development of all proposals for telecommunications equipment and to minimise visual intrusion. . . .

40. The Board notes that whilst there has been a plethora of documents about planning issues for base stations, public concerns have not abated.

41. The Board supports the government view that whilst planning is necessarily a local issue, the assessment of evidence related to possible health concerns associated with exposures to RF fields from base stations is best dealt with nationally.

42. Accepting that, the Board believes that it is timely for there to be set in place a much clearer and more readily understandable template of protocols and procedures to be followed by local authorities and phone operators across the UK. It is clear that at present the application of guidance is very variable and that the extent to which the underpinning facts are presented can also be variable. It recommends that there should be an independent review of the extent to which implementation of good practice guidelines by operators and local authorities is being carried out.

43. The Board considers that it is important that 'best practice' in relation to network development operates consistently across the country and that how planning applications are dealt with should be an open and transparent process.

44. The Board welcomes the ODPM *Code of Best Practice on Mobile Phone Network Development,* that incorporates the 'ten commitments on best siting practice'. . . .

Developing Technologies

55. A variety of additional technologies are now being progressively developed and implemented in the field of telecommunications. New technologies include third-generation (3G) mobile telephony, wireless local area networks (WLANs), Bluetooth and ultra-wideband (UWB) technology, and radio-frequency identification (RFID) devices.

56. The Board considers that it is important to understand the signal characteristics and field strengths arising from new telecommunications systems and related technologies, to assess the RF exposure of

people, and to understand the potential biological effects on the human body.

57. The Board also believes it important to ensure that the exposure of people from all new and existing systems complies with ICNIRP guidelines.

Sensitive Groups

58. Populations as a whole are not genetically homogeneous and people can vary in their susceptibility to environmental hazards. There could also be a dependency on age. The issue of individual sensitivity remains an outstanding one in relation to RF exposure and one on which more information is needed.

59. IEGMP considered that children might be more vulnerable to any effects arising from the use of mobile phones. The potential for undertaking studies to examine any possible effects on children are, however, limited for ethical reasons. It was recommended in the Stewart Report that the use of mobile phones by children should be minimised and this was supported by the Departments of Health. Text messaging has considerable advantages as the phone is in use for only a short time, when the phone transmits the message, compared with voice communication.

60. The Board concludes that, in the absence of new scientific evidence, the recommendation in the Stewart Report on limiting the use of mobile phones by children remains appropriate as a precautionary measure.

61. The Board also welcomes an initiative by the World Health Organization in its EMF programme to focus attention on research relevant to the potential sensitivity of children.

62. Additionally, there is concern by an increasing number of individuals, although relatively small in relation to the total UK population, that they are adversely affected by exposure either to EMFs in general or specifically to RF fields from mobile phones. A European Commission group of experts termed the syndrome 'electromagnetic hypersensitivity'. Similar concerns have been raised in the past in relation to exposure to agricultural chemicals and other materials. . . .

64. The Board considers that the issue of electromagnetic hypersensitivity needs to be carefully examined in the UK. It supports the strengthening of work designed to understand the reasons for the reported electromagnetic hypersensitivity of some members of the public.

Occupational Exposure

65. Levels of exposure to RF fields can be higher through occupational exposure than for members of the public and sometimes approach guideline levels.

66. The Board welcomes the establishment of a register of occupationally exposed people at the Institute of Occupational Health, Birmingham. This should facilitate the determination of whether, occupationally, there are health effects from exposure to RF fields not observed in the general public. . . .

Mobile Phones and Driving

69. The Stewart Report demonstrated that there is good experimental evidence that the use of mobile phones whilst driving has a detrimental effect on drivers' responsiveness. This translates into a substantial increased risk of an accident. The evidence suggested that the negative effects of phone use while driving were similar whether the phone was hand-held or hands-free.
70. The Board welcomes the intention of government to increase the penalty for the offence of using a hand-held mobile phone while driving by making it endorsable with three penalty points and an increased fine of £60.
71. The Board notes that the UK legislation on the use of phones in motor vehicles, making it illegal to use any hand-held phone, is tailored to the practicality of enforcement. The evidence remains, however, that the use of mobile phones in moving vehicles, both hand-held and hands-free, can significantly increase the risk of an accident. . . .

Health-Related Research

84. Outstanding health-related concerns can be addressed by epidemiological (human health) studies, experimental investigations with animals, and the use of cell-based techniques. Dosimetric studies are important for understanding the exposure of people from various sources and human volunteer studies can investigate short-term interactions of RF fields, for example, with brain function. In the area of telecommunications, however, technological change is rapid and it is a challenge to carry out comprehensive research and to determine the possibility of any health effects.
85. Research into any health effects of exposure to RF fields is still in a developmental phase. There are analogies with work on the consequences of exposure to EMFs from power lines. In the early 1980s, the epidemiological studies on exposure to extremely low frequency (ELF) EMFs lacked methods to directly assess exposure of individuals and instead surrogates for exposure were frequently used. Subsequently portable measurement equipment became available in the late 1980s/early 1990s and the quality of studies providing exposure-response information, for both occupational and domestic exposures, rapidly improved. Studies on RF exposure were in a similar position in the 1990s to those on ELF EMFs in the early 1980s. In recent years, however, considerable effort has gone into developing RF-related studies that combine high quality dosimetry with well-designed studies in experimental biology and epidemiology. Inevitably it will be some time before the present generation of studies comes to fruition. The MTHR programme in the UK has been at the forefront of this advance in RF-related research.
86. The MTHR programme was launched in February 2001 with an initial budget of £7.36 million funded by government and industry on a 50 : 50 basis. To date around 30 projects have been funded through MTHR with additional support from the Home Office, the Department

of Trade and Industry, and industry. It presently has a budget of £8.8 million, all of which has now been allocated to the ongoing research programme. The RF-related research in the UK is complementary to further research being carried out world-wide, much of it co-ordinated through the WHO EMF programme.

87. The Board considers that the MTHR programme, which was first announced in December 2000, has set the standard for independent, high quality, health-related research on RF exposure.

88. The Board further recommends that government and industry should provide support for a continuation of the programme.

89. The Board particularly supports the need for further research, in the following areas:

(a) an international cohort study of mobile phone users aimed at pooling and sharing experimental design, findings and expertise internationally,

(b) an expanded programme of research on TETRA signals and biological effects,

(c) effects of RF exposure on children,

(d) investigation of public concerns about mobile phone technology,

(e) electromagnetic hypersensitivity and its possible impact on health, including well-being, associated with mobile phone technology,

(f) studies of RF effects on direct and established measures of human brain function and investigations of possible mechanisms involved,

(g) complementary dosimetry studies focused on ascertaining the exposure of people to RF fields.

In developing the MTHR and other research programmes, care needs to be taken to prevent unnecessary duplication of studies whilst at the same time seeking to replicate significant findings.

POSTSCRIPT

Is There Sufficient Scientific Research to Conclude That Cell Phones Cause Cancer?

Is the cell phone cancer scare nothing more than media hype, as Sid Deutsch called the EMF cancer scare in "Electromagnetic Field Cancer Scares," *Skeptical Inquirer* (Winter 1994)? Or do cell phones pose a genuine hazard? L. Hardell, et al., reported in "Cellular and Cordless Telephones and the Risk for Brain Tumours," *European Journal of Cancer Prevention* (August 2002), that long-term users of older, analog phones were more likely to suffer brain tumors. U.S. District Judge Catherine Blake, presiding over the most famous phone-cancer lawsuit, was not swayed. She declared that the claimant had provided "no sufficiently reliable and relevant scientific evidence" and said she intended to dismiss the case (Mark Parascandola, "Judge Rejects Cancer Data in Maryland Cell Phone Suit," *Science*, October 11, 2002). Robert Clark, "Clean Bill of Health for Cell Phones," *America's Network* (April 1, 2004), reports that "A survey by the Danish Institute of Cancer Epidemiology . . . says there is no short-term danger of developing brain tumors." A Swedish study found no breast cancer link to electromagnetic fields; see Janet Raloff, "Study Can't Tie EMFs to Cancer," *Science News* (February 26, 2005), and U. M. Forssen, et al., "Occupational Magnetic Fields and Female Breast Cancer: A Case-Control Study using Swedish Population Registers and New Exposure Data," *American Journal of Epidemiology* (vol. 161, no. 3, 2005).

Skeptics insist that the threat is real. However, if it is real, this is not yet clear beyond a doubt. Unfortunately, society cannot always wait for certainty. In connection with EMFs, Gordon L. Hester, in "Electric and Magnetic Fields: Managing an Uncertain Risk," *Environment* (January/February 1992), asserts that just the possibility of a health hazard is sufficient to justify more research into the problem. The guiding principle, says Hester, is "'prudent avoidance,' which was originally intended to mean that people should avoid fields 'when this can be done with modest amounts of money and trouble.'" The same guideline surely applies to cell phone radiation.

Is it possible to prove that cell phones do *not* cause cancer? Unfortunately, no, because small, sporadic effects might not be detected even in massive studies. Thus, for some people, the jury will forever be out.

What should society do in the face of weak, uncertain, and even contradictory data? Can we afford to conclude that there is no hazard? Or must we ban or redesign a useful technology with no justification other than our fear that there might be a real hazard? Many scientists and politicians argue that even if there is no genuine medical risk, there is a genuine impact in terms of public anxiety. See Gary Stix, "Closing the Book," *Scientific American* (March 1998). It is therefore appropriate, they say, to fund further research and to take whatever relatively inexpensive steps to minimize exposure are possible. Failure to do so increases public anxiety and distrust of government and science.

Some of those "relatively inexpensive steps" are pretty simple. As Carlo and Schram note, they include repositioning cell phone antennae and using headsets. As Tamar Nordenberg, "Cell Phones and Brain Cancer: No Clear Connection," *FDA Consumer* (November–December 2000), says, quoting Professor John Moulder, using a cell phone while driving is much more hazardous even than using a conventional high-radiation cell phone. By 2003, cell phones were being broadly indicted as hazards on the highway. See "Cell Phones Distract Drivers, Hands Down," *Science News* (February 8, 2003), and "New Studies Define Cell Phone Hazards," *Consumer Reports* (May 2003). The basic problem is that using a cell phone increases the mental workload on the driver, according to Roland Matthews, Stephen Legg, and Samuel Charlton, "The Effect of Cell Phone Type on Drivers' Subjective Workload During Concurrent Driving and Conversing," *Accident Analysis & Prevention* (July, 2003); they too recommend using a hands-free phone. As a result of such studies, several states have already banned handheld phones while driving, with initial good effect; see Anne T. McCartt, Elisa R. Braver, and Lori L. Geary, "Drivers' Use of Handheld Cell Phones Before and After New York State's Cell Phone Law," *Preventive Medicine* (May 2003). Unfortunately, the initial good results have not lasted. Anne T. McCartt and Lori L. Geary, "Longer Term Effects of New York State's Law on Drivers' Handheld Cell Phone Use," *Injury Prevention* (February 2004), suggest that publicity campaigns and vigorous enforcement of anti-use laws will be necessary. See also "Motorists' Cell Phone Use Rising: NHTSA," *Safety & Health* (May 2005).

ISSUE 9

Should DDT Be Banned Worldwide?

YES: Anne Platt McGinn, from "Malaria, Mosquitoes, and DDT,"
World Watch (May/June 2002)

NO: Alexander Gourevitch, from "Better Living through
Chemistry," *Washington Monthly* (March 2003)

ISSUE SUMMARY

YES: Anne Platt McGinn, a senior researcher at the Worldwatch
Institute, argues that although DDT is still used to fight malaria,
there are other, more effective and less environmentally harmful
methods. She maintains that DDT should be banned or reserved
for emergency use.

NO: Alexander Gourevitch, an *American Prospect* writing fellow,
argues that, properly used, DDT is not as dangerous as its reputation insists it is, and it remains the cheapest and most effective way
to combat malaria.

The story of DDT is a crucial element of the story of environmentalism. The
chemical was first synthesized in 1874. Its insecticidal properties were first
noticed by Paul Mueller, and it was very quickly realized that this implied the
chemical could save human lives. It had long been known that in wars, more
soldiers died because of disease than because of enemy fire. During World War I,
some 5 million lives were lost to typhus, a disease carried by body lice. DDT was
first deployed during World War II to halt a typhus epidemic in Naples, Italy.
Dramatic success soon meant that DDT was used routinely as a dust for soldiers
and civilians. During and after the war, it was also successfully deployed against
the mosquitoes that carry malaria and other diseases. In the United States, cases
of malaria fell from 120,000 in 1934 to 72 in 1960. Yellow fever cases dropped
from 100,000 in 1878 to none. In 1948, Mueller received the Nobel Prize for
Medicine and Physiology because DDT had saved so many civilian lives. Roger
Bate, director of Africa Fighting Malaria, argues in "A Case of the DDTs,"
National Review (May 14, 2001), that DDT remains the cheapest and most effective way to combat malaria and that it should remain available for use.

DDT was by no means the first pesticide. But its predecessors were such
things as arsenic, strychnine, cyanide, copper sulfate, and nicotine, all of

which marked toxicity to humans that they gave rise to a host of murder mysteries such as the play "Arsenic and Old Lace." DDT was not only more effective as an insecticide; it was also less hazardous to users (not to mention potential murder victims). It is thus not surprising that DDT was seen as a beneficial substance, and was soon applied routinely to agricultural crops and used to control mosquito populations in American suburbs ("Rachel Carson's Silent Spring," a PBS American Experience video, includes footage of children at a picnic being engulfed in a cloud of DDT). However, insects quickly became resistant to the insecticide (in any population of insects, some will be more resistant than others; when the insecticide kills the more vulnerable members of the population, the resistant ones are left to breed and multiply; this is an example of natural selection). In *Silent Spring* (1961), Rachel Carson documented that DDT was concentrated in the food chain and affected the reproduction of predators such as hawks and eagles. In 1972, the U.S. Environmental Protection Agency banned almost all DDT uses (it could still be used to protect public health). Other developed countries soon banned it as well, but developing nations, especially in the tropics, saw it as an essential tool for fighting diseases such as malaria.

DDT is by no means the only pesticide or organic toxin with environmental effects. On May 24, 2001, the United States joined 90 other nations in signing the Stockholm Convention on Persistent Organic Pollutants (POPs). This treaty aims to eliminate from use the entire class of chemicals to which DDT belongs, beginning with the "dirty dozen," pesticides DDT, aldrin, dieldrin, endrin, chlordane, heptachlor, mirex, toxaphene, and the industrial chemicals polychlorinated biphenyls (PCBs), hexachlorobenzene (HCB), dioxins, and furans. Since then, 59 countries, not including the United States and the European Union, have formally ratified the treaty, which took effect in May 2004. Fiona Proffitt, "U.N. Convention Targets Dirty Dozen Chemicals," *Science* (May 21, 2004), notes that "About 25 countries will be allowed to continue using DDT against malaria-spreading mosquitoes until a viable alternative is found."

In the following selections, Worldwatch researcher Anne Platt McGinn grants that malaria remains a serious problem in the developing nations of the tropics, especially in Africa. DDT is still used to fight malaria in these nations, but because of resistance, it is far less effective than it used to be and environmental effects are serious concerns. She argues that alternative measures such as mosquito nets impregnated with pyrethrin insecticides are more effective and less environmentally harmful. DDT should be banned or reserved for emergency use. In the second selection, Alexander Gourevitch argues that, properly used, DDT is not as dangerous as its reputation insists it is; it remains the cheapest and most effective way to combat malaria, and environmentalist opposition to its use in Africa threatens the lives of millions.

Anne Platt McGinn  **YES**

Malaria, Mosquitoes, and DDT

This year, like every other year within the past couple of decades, uncountable trillions of mosquitoes will inject malaria parasites into human blood streams billions of times. Some 300 to 500 million full-blown cases of malaria will result, and between 1 and 3 million people will die, most of them pregnant women and children. That's the official figure, anyway, but it's likely to be a substantial underestimate, since most malaria deaths are not formally registered, and many are likely to have escaped the estimators. Very roughly, the malaria death toll rivals that of AIDS, which now kills about 3 million people annually.

But unlike AIDS, malaria is a low-priority killer. Despite the deaths, and the fact that roughly 2.5 billion people (40 percent of the world's population) are at risk of contracting the disease, malaria is a relatively low public health priority on the international scene. Malaria rarely makes the news. And international funding for malaria research currently comes to a mere $150 million annually. Just by way of comparison, that's only about 5 percent of the $2.8 billion that the U.S. government alone is considering for AIDS research in fiscal year 2003.

The low priority assigned to malaria would be at least easier to understand, though no less mistaken, if the threat were static. Unfortunately it is not. It is true that the geographic range of the disease has contracted substantially since the mid-20th century, but over the past couple of decades, malaria has been gathering strength. Virtually all areas where the disease is endemic have seen drug-resistant strains of the parasites emerge—a development that is almost certainly boosting death rates. In countries as various as Armenia, Afghanistan, and Sierra Leone, the lack or deterioration of basic infrastructure has created a wealth of new breeding sites for the mosquitoes that spread the disease. The rapidly expanding slums of many tropical cities also lack such infrastructure; poor sanitation and crowding have primed these places as well for outbreaks—even though malaria has up to now been regarded as predominantly a rural disease.

What has current policy to offer in the face of these threats? The medical arsenal is limited; there are only about a dozen antimalarial drugs commonly in use, and there is significant malaria resistance to most of them. In the absence of a reliable way to kill the parasites, policy has tended to focus

From Anne Platt McGinn, "Malaria, Mosquitoes, and DDT," *World Watch*, vol. 15, no. 3 (May/June 2002). Copyright © 2002 by The Worldwatch Institute. Reprinted by permission. http://www.worldwatch.org.

on killing the mosquitoes that bear them. And that has led to an abundant use of synthetic pesticides, including one of the oldest and most dangerous: dichlorodiphenyl trichloroethane, or DDT.

DDT is no longer used or manufactured in most of the world, but because it does not break down readily, it is still one of the most commonly detected pesticides in the milk of nursing mothers. DDT is also one of the "dirty dozen" chemicals included in the 2001 Stockholm Convention on Persistent Organic Pollutants [POPs]. The signatories to the "POPs Treaty" essentially agreed to ban all uses of DDT except as a last resort against disease-bearing mosquitoes. Unfortunately, however, DDT is still a routine option in 19 countries, most of them in Africa. (Only 11 of these countries have thus far signed the treaty.) Among the signatory countries, 31—slightly fewer than one-third—have given notice that they are reserving the right to use DDT against malaria. On the face of it, such use may seem unavoidable, but there are good reasons for thinking that progress against the disease is compatible with *reductions* in DDT use.

Malaria is caused by four protozoan parasite species in the genus *Plasmodium*. These parasites are spread exclusively by certain mosquitoes in the genus *Anopheles*. An infection begins when a parasite-laden female mosquito settles onto someone's skin and pierces a capillary to take her blood meal. The parasite, in a form called the *sporozoite,* moves with the mosquito's saliva into the human bloodstream. About 10 percent of the mosquito's lode of sporozoites is likely to be injected during a meal, leaving plenty for the next bite. Unless the victim has some immunity to malaria—normally as a result of previous exposure—most sporozoites are likely to evade the body's immune system and make their way to the liver, a process that takes less than an hour. There they invade the liver cells and multiply asexually for about two weeks. By this time, the original several dozen sporozoites have become millions of *merozoites*—the form the parasite takes when it emerges from the liver and moves back into the blood to invade the body's red blood cells. Within the red blood cells, the merozoites go through another cycle of asexual reproduction, after which the cells burst and release millions of additional merozoites, which invade yet more red blood cells. The high fever and chills associated with malaria are the result of this stage, which tends to occur in pulses. If enough red blood cells are destroyed in one of these pulses, the result is convulsions, difficulty in breathing, coma, and death.

As the parasite multiplies inside the red blood cells, it produces not just more merozoites, but also *gametocytes,* which are capable of sexual reproduction. This occurs when the parasite moves back into the mosquitoes; even as they inject sporozoites, biting mosquitoes may ingest gametocytes if they are feeding on a person who is already infected. The gametocytes reproduce in the insect's gut and the resulting eggs move into the gut cells. Eventually, more sporozoites emerge from the gut and penetrate the mosquito's salivary glands, where they await a chance to enter another human bloodstream, to begin the cycle again.

Of the roughly 380 mosquito species in the genus *Anopheles*, about 60 are able to transmit malaria to people. These malaria vectors are widespread throughout the tropics and warm temperate zones, and they are very efficient at spreading the disease. Malaria is highly contagious, as is apparent from a measurement that epidemiologists call the "basic reproduction number," or BRN. The BRN indicates, on average, how many new cases a single infected person is likely to cause. For example, among the nonvectored diseases (those in which the pathogen travels directly from person to person without an intermediary like a mosquito), measles is one of the most contagious. The BRN for measles is 12 to 14, meaning that someone with measles is likely to infect 12 to 14 other people. (Luckily, there's an inherent limit in this process: as a pathogen spreads through any particular area, it will encounter fewer and fewer susceptible people who aren't already sick, and the outbreak will eventually subside.) HIV/AIDS is on the other end of the scale: it's deadly, but it burns through a population slowly. Its BRN is just above 1, the minimum necessary for the pathogen's survival. With malaria, the BRN varies considerably, depending on such factors as which mosquito species are present in an area and what the temperatures are. (Warmer is worse, since the parasites mature more quickly.) But malaria can have a BRN in excess of 100: over an adult life that may last about a week, a single, malaria-laden mosquito could conceivably infect more than 100 people.

Seven Years, Seven Months

"Malaria" comes from the Italian "mal'aria." For centuries, European physicians had attributed the disease to "bad air." Apart from a tradition of associating bad air with swamps—a useful prejudice, given the amount of mosquito habitat in swamps—early medicine was largely ineffective against the disease. It wasn't until 1897 that the British physician Ronald Ross proved that mosquitoes carry malaria.

The practical implications of Ross's discovery did not go unnoticed. For example, the U.S. administration of Theodore Roosevelt recognized malaria and yellow fever (another mosquito-vectored disease) as perhaps the most serious obstacles to the construction of the Panama Canal. This was hardly a surprising conclusion, since the earlier and unsuccessful French attempt to build the canal—an effort that predated Ross's discovery—is thought to have lost between 10,000 and 20,000 workers to disease. So the American workers draped their water supplies and living quarters with mosquito netting, attempted to fill in or drain swamps, installed sewers, poured oil into standing water, and conducted mosquito-swatting campaigns. And it worked: the incidence of malaria declined. In 1906, 80 percent of the workers had the disease; by 1913, a year before the Canal was completed, only 7 percent did. Malaria could be suppressed, it seemed, with a great deal of mosquito netting, and by eliminating as much mosquito habitat as possible. But the labor involved in that effort could be enormous.

That is why DDT proved so appealing. In 1939, the Swiss chemist Paul Müller discovered that this chemical was a potent pesticide. DDT was first used during World War II, as a delousing agent. Later on, areas in southern Europe, North Africa, and Asia were fogged with DDT, to clear malaria-laden mosquitoes from the paths of invading Allied troops. DDT was cheap and it seemed to be harmless to anything other than insects. It was also long-lasting: most other insecticides lost their potency in a few days, but in the early years of its use, the effects of a single dose of DDT could last for up to six months. In 1948, Müller won a Nobel Prize for his work and DDT was hailed as a chemical miracle.

A decade later, DDT had inspired another kind of war—a general assault on malaria. The "Global Malaria Eradication Program," launched in 1955, became one of the first major undertakings of the newly created World Health Organization [WHO]. Some 65 nations enlisted in the cause. Funding for DDT factories was donated to poor countries and production of the insecticide climbed.

The malaria eradication strategy was not to kill every single mosquito, but to suppress their populations and shorten the lifespans of any survivors, so that the parasite would not have time to develop within them. If the mosquitoes could be kept down long enough, the parasites would eventually disappear from the human population. In any particular area, the process was expected to take three years—time enough for all infected people either to recover or die. After that, a resurgence of mosquitoes would be merely an annoyance, rather than a threat. And initially, the strategy seemed to be working. It proved especially effective on islands—relatively small areas insulated from reinfestation. Taiwan, Jamaica, and Sardinia were soon declared malaria-free and have remained so to this day. By 1961, arguably the year at which the program had peak momentum, malaria had been eliminated or dramatically reduced in 37 countries.

One year later, Rachel Carson published *Silent Spring*, her landmark study of the ecological damage caused by the widespread use of DDT and other pesticides. Like other organochlorine pesticides, DDT bioaccumulates. It's fat soluble, so when an animal ingests it—by browsing contaminated vegetation, for example—the chemical tends to concentrate in its fat, instead of being excreted. When another animal eats that animal, it is likely to absorb the prey's burden of DDT. This process leads to an increasing concentration of DDT in the higher links of the food chain. And since DDT has a high chronic toxicity—that is, long-term exposure is likely to cause various physiological abnormalities—this bioaccumulation has profound implications for both ecological and human health.

With the miseries of malaria in full view, the managers of the eradication campaign didn't worry much about the toxicity of DDT, but they were greatly concerned about another aspect of the pesticide's effects: resistance. Continual exposure to an insecticide tends to "breed" insect populations that are at least partially immune to the poison. Resistance to DDT had been reported as early as 1946. The campaign managers knew that in mosquitoes, regular exposure to DDT tended to produce widespread resistance in four to seven years. Since it took three years to clear malaria from a human population, that didn't leave a lot of leeway for the eradication effort. As it turned out, the logistics simply couldn't be made to work in large, heavily infested areas with high human populations, poor housing and roads, and generally minimal infrastructure. In 1969, the campaign was abandoned. Today, DDT resistance is widespread in *Anopheles,* as is resistance to many more recent pesticides.

Undoubtedly, the campaign saved millions of lives, and it did clear malaria from some areas. But its broadest legacy has been of much more dubious value. It engendered the idea of DDT as a first resort against mosquitoes and it established the unstable dynamic of DDT resistance in *Anopheles* populations. In mosquitoes, the genetic mechanism that confers resistance to DDT does not usually come at any great competitive "cost"—that is, when no DDT is being sprayed, the resistant mosquitoes may do just about as well as nonresistant mosquitoes. So once a population acquires resistance, the trait is not likely to disappear even if DDT isn't used for years. If DDT is reapplied to such a population, widespread resistance will reappear very rapidly. The rule of thumb among entomologists is that you may get seven years of resistance-free use the first time around, but you only get about seven months the second time. Even that limited respite, however, is enough to make the chemical an attractive option as an emergency measure—or to keep it in the arsenals of bureaucracies committed to its use.

Malaria Taxes

In December 2000, the POPs Treaty negotiators convened in Johannesburg, South Africa, even though, by an unfortunate coincidence, South Africa had suffered a potentially embarrassing setback earlier that year in its own POPs policies. In 1996, South Africa had switched its mosquito control programs from DDT to a less persistent group of pesticides known as pyrethroids. The move seemed solid and supportable at the time, since years of DDT use had greatly reduced *Anopheles* populations and largely eliminated one of the most troublesome local vectors, the appropriately named *A. funestus* ("funestus" means deadly). South Africa seemed to have beaten the DDT habit: the chemical had been used to achieve a worthwhile objective; it had then been discarded. And the plan worked—until a year before the POPs summit, when malaria infections rose to 61,000 cases, a level not seen in decades. *A. funestus* reappeared as well, in KwaZulu-Natal, and in a form resistant to pyrethroids. In early 2000, DDT was reintroduced, in an indoor spraying program. (This is now a standard way of using DDT for mosquito control; the pesticide is usually applied only to walls, where mosquitoes alight to rest.) By the middle of the year, the number of infections had dropped by half.

Initially, the spraying program was criticized, but what reasonable alternative was there? This is said to be the African predicament, and yet the South African situation is hardly representative of sub-Saharan Africa as a whole.

Malaria is considered endemic in 105 countries throughout the tropics and warm temperate zones, but by far the worst region for the disease is sub-Saharan Africa. The deadliest of the four parasite species, *Plasmodium falciparum,* is widespread throughout this region, as is one of the world's most effective malaria vectors, *Anopheles gambiae*. Nearly half the population of sub-Saharan Africa is at risk of infection, and in much of eastern and central Africa, and pockets of west Africa, it would be difficult to find anyone who has not been exposed to the parasites. Some 90 percent of the world's malaria infections and deaths occur in sub-Saharan Africa, and the disease now accounts for 30 percent of African childhood mortality. It is true that malaria is a grave problem in many parts of the world, but the African experience is misery on a very different order of magnitude. The average Tanzanian suffers more infective bites each *night* than the average Thai or Vietnamese does in a year.

As a broad social burden, malaria is thought to cost Africa between $3 billion and $12 billion annually. According to one economic analysis, if the disease had been eradicated in 1965, Africa's GDP would now be 35 percent higher than it currently is. Africa was also the gaping hole in the global eradication program: the WHO planners thought there was little they could do on the continent and limited efforts to Ethiopia, Zimbabwe, and South Africa, where eradication was thought to be feasible.

But even though the campaign largely passed Africa by, DDT has not. Many African countries have used DDT for mosquito control in indoor spraying programs, but the primary use of DDT on the continent has been as an agricultural insecticide. Consequently, in parts of west Africa especially, DDT resistance is now widespread in *A. gambiae*. But even if *A. gambiae* were not resistant, a full-bore campaign to suppress it would probably accomplish little, because this mosquito is so efficient at transmitting malaria. Unlike most *Anopheles* species, *A. gambiae* specializes in human blood, so even a small population would keep the disease in circulation. One way to get a sense for this problem is to consider the "transmission index"—the threshold number of mosquito bites necessary to perpetuate the disease. In Africa, the index overall is 1 bite per person per month. That's all that's necessary to keep malaria in circulation. In India, by comparison, the TI is 10 bites per person per month.

And yet Africa is not a lost cause—it's simply that the key to progress does not lie in the general suppression of mosquito populations. Instead of spraying, the most promising African programs rely primarily on "bednets"—mosquito netting that is treated with an insecticide, usually a pyrethroid, and that is suspended over a person's bed. Bednets can't eliminate malaria, but they can "deflect" much of the burden. Because *Anopheles* species generally feed in the evening and at night, a bednet can radically reduce the number of infective bites a person receives. Such a person would probably still be infected from time to time, but would usually be able to lead a normal life.

In effect, therefore, bednets can substantially reduce the disease. Trials in the use of bednets for children have shown a decline in malaria-induced mortality by 25 to 40 percent. Infection levels and the incidence of severe anemia also declined. In Kenya, a recent study has shown that pregnant women who use bednets tend to give birth to healthier babies. In parts of Chad, Mali, Burkina Faso, and Senegal, bednets are becoming standard household items. In the tiny west African nation of The Gambia, somewhere between 50 and 80 percent of the population has bednets.

Bednets are hardly a panacea. They have to be used properly and retreated with insecticide occasionally. And there is still the problem of insecticide resistance, although the nets themselves are hardly likely to be the main cause of it. (Pyrethroids are used extensively in agriculture as well.) Nevertheless, bednets can help transform malaria from a chronic disaster to a manageable public health problem—something a healthcare system can cope with.

So it's unfortunate that in much of central and southern Africa, the nets are a rarity. It's even more unfortunate that, in 28 African countries, they're taxed or subject to import tariffs. Most of the people in these countries would have trouble paying for a net even without the tax. This problem was addressed in the May 2000 "Abuja Declaration," a summit agreement on infectious diseases signed by 44 African countries. The Declaration included a pledge to do away with "malaria taxes." At last count, 13 countries have actually acted on the pledge, although in some cases only by reducing rather than eliminating the taxes. Since the Declaration was signed, an estimated 2 to 5 million Africans have died from malaria.

This failure to follow through with the Abuja Declaration casts the interest in DDT in a rather poor light. Of the 31 POPs treaty signatories that have reserved the right to use DDT, 21 are in Africa. Of those 21, 10 are apparently still taxing or imposing tariffs on bednets. (Among the African countries that have *not* signed the POPs treaty, some are almost certainly both using DDT and taxing bednets, but the exact number is difficult to ascertain because the status of DDT use is not always clear.) It is true that a case can be made for the use of DDT in situations like the one in South Africa in 1999—an infrequent flare-up in a context that lends itself to control. But the routine use of DDT against malaria is an exercise in toxic futility, especially when it's pursued at the expense of a superior and far more benign technology.

Learning to Live with the Mosquitoes

A group of French researchers recently announced some very encouraging results for a new anti-malarial drug known as G25. The drug was given to infected aotus monkeys, and it appears to have cleared the parasites from their systems. Although extensive testing will be necessary before it is known whether the drug can be safely given to people, these results have raised the hope of a cure for the disease.

Of course, it would be wonderful if G25, or some other new drug, lives up to that promise. But even in the absence of a cure, there are opportunities for progress that may one day make the current incidence of malaria look like some dark age horror. Many of these opportunities have been incorporated into an initiative that began in 1998, called the Roll Back Malaria (RBM) campaign, a collaborative effort between WHO, the World Bank, UNICEF, and the UNDP [United Nations Development Programme]. In contrast to the earlier WHO eradication program, RBM grew out of joint efforts between WHO and various African governments specifically to address African malaria. RBM focuses on household- and community-level intervention and it emphasizes apparently modest changes that could yield major progress. Below are four "operating principles" that are, in one way or another, implicit in RBM or likely to reinforce its progress.

1. Do away with all taxes and tariffs on bednets, on pesticides intended for treating bednets, and on antimalarial drugs. Failure to act on this front certainly undercuts claims for the necessity of DDT; it may also undercut claims for antimalaria foreign aid.

2. Emphasize appropriate technologies. Where, for example, the need for mud to replaster walls is creating lots of pothole sized cavities near houses—cavities that fill with water and then with mosquito larvae—it makes more sense to help people improve their housing maintenance than it does to set up a program for squirting pesticide into every pothole. To be "appropriate," a technology has to be both affordable and culturally acceptable. Improving home maintenance should pass this test; so should bednets. And of course there are many other possibilities. In Kenya, for example, a research institution called the International Center for Insect Physiology and Ecology has identified at least a dozen native east African plants that repel *Anopheles gambiae* in lab tests. Some of these plants could be important additions to household gardens.

3. Use existing networks whenever possible, instead of building new ones. In Tanzania, for example, an established healthcare program (UNICEF's Integrated Management of Childhood Illness Program) now dispenses antimalarial drugs—and instruction on how to use them. The UNICEF program was already operating, so it was simple and cheap to add the malaria component. Reported instances of severe malaria and anemia in infants have declined, apparently as a result. In Zambia, the government is planning to use health and prenatal clinics as the network for a coupon system that subsidizes bednets for the poor. Qualifying patients would pick up coupons at the clinics and redeem them at stores for the nets.

4. Assume that sound policy will involve action on many fronts. Malaria is not just a health problem—it's a social problem, an economic problem, an environmental problem, an agricultural problem, an urban planning problem. Health officials alone cannot possibly just make it go away. When the disease flares up, there is a strong and understandable temptation to strap on the spray equipment and douse the mosquitoes. But if this approach actually worked, we wouldn't be in this situation today. Arguably the biggest opportunity for progress against the disease lies, not in our capacity for chemical innovation, but in our capacity for *organizational innovation*—in our ability to build an awareness of the threat across a broad range of policy activities. For example, when government officials are considering loans to irrigation projects, they should be asking: has the potential for malaria been addressed? When foreign donors are designing antipoverty programs, they should be asking: do people need bednets? Routine inquiries of this sort could go a vast distance to reducing the disease.

Where is the DDT in all of this? There isn't any, and that's the point. We now have half a century of evidence that routine use of DDT simply will not prevail against the mosquitoes. Most countries have already absorbed this lesson, and banned the chemical or relegated it to emergency only status. Now the RBM campaign and associated efforts are showing that the frequency and intensity of those emergencies can be reduced through systematic attention to the chronic aspects of the disease. There is less and less justification for DDT, and the futility of using it as a matter of routine is becoming increasingly apparent: in order to control a disease, why should we poison our soils, our waters, and ourselves?

Alexander Gourevitch

Better Living Through Chemistry

By most measures, Uganda is one of the success stories of African development. Under President Yoweri Museveni, a former guerrilla and darling of the international donor community, Uganda has achieved GDP [gross domestic product] growth of 6 percent per year, gradually expanding political freedoms, and a measure of peace. In a continent beset by poverty and political disorder, Uganda has slowly become a model for how to get things right. Even the AIDS epidemic, which infected an estimated 20 percent of Uganda's population a decade ago, seems to be under control.

But a more old-fashioned plague has come back to haunt Uganda: malaria. The mosquito-borne illness costs Uganda more than $347 million a year. Today, up to 40 percent of the country's outpatient care goes to people thus infected. Total infections are so numerous that the government doesn't even try to track them; but last year, 80,000 people died of the disease, half of them children under the age of five.

So last December [2202], at a convention of regional health ministers held in Kampala, Jim Muhwezi, an army officer and member of parliament who today serves as Uganda's minister of health, announced the launch of a new campaign against the epidemic, using Dichloro-diphenyl-trichloroethane, or DDT. To Muhwezi, DDT—a pesticide widely proscribed in Europe and banned in the United States since 1972—was a cheap, effective weapon against malaria for a poor country with minimal public health resources. And in South Africa, the recent reintroduction of DDT spraying had reduced malaria rates by 75 percent over two years. "Instead of sitting back and watching our people die of malaria and lose in economic terms," he proclaimed, "an all-out war against the disease must be waged."

But Muhwezi encountered opposition almost immediately. After his announcement, Andrew Sisson, a USAID official attending the Kampala convention, told one session that in the United States DDT had been found to "cause environmental problems," according to Muhwezi. A member of Uganda's parliament warned Muhwezi that Europe and the United States might ban imports of Uganda's fish and agricultural exports, a fear shared by local environmentalists, according to the *Nairobi East African*, Kenya's leading daily. Since USAID prefers to fund bednets as a solution to Uganda's mosquito problem, Muhwezi is unsure if he'll be able to obtain international assistance to fund a DDT-based malarial eradication project. "We hope they'll come along. But if they don't, we'll do it alone."

Until recently, one might have considered Uganda's to be a tragic but unavoidable tradeoff—deprive many of an uncontaminated natural environment, or save few from malaria. In much of the world, after all, the popular conception of DDT is of a dangerous and toxic chemical that pollutes water and poisons the food chain; in the United States, DDT is remembered as the pesticide that helped put bald eagles on the endangered species list. But a growing body of scientific evidence suggests that the popular conception is wrong. Older studies on the effects of DDT have been called into question, and newer ones militate against the notion that DDT is inherently dangerous. For the kind of use Muhwezi has in mind, in fact, DDT may not be dangerous at all.

The stakes are high. Uganda is but one of many African countries suffering from malaria epidemics. Africa already accounts for 90 percent of the 2 million deaths and 300 million infections around the world each year, and it costs the continent 1.3 percent in annual growth per year, according to the economist Jeffrey Sachs. Mosquitoes are increasingly resistant to the main insecticide put into use to replace DDT; and the parasite that causes the disease has, in recent years, become increasingly resistant to the cheapest and most common medical treatment, a drug called chloroquine. Yet most international aid agencies, development agencies, and lending institutions have moved away from funding spraying projects in general, and DDT use specifically. Without assistance, African governments cannot afford spraying programs, leaving them bereft of a safe, effective, and cheap defense. Which means that aid agencies and governments opposed to DDT use may end up costing Africa millions of needless deaths.

Bad Medicine?

DDT first came to the United States after the late 1930s, when Dr. Paul Muller, a chemist with the Swiss firm J.R. Geigy, found that minuscule amounts of DDT killed just about every insect he could find. Slow to break down, a single application of DDT remained toxic for up to a year, which made spraying programs much easier to administer, especially in remote locations. It was cheap to produce, easy to ship, and did not require the extensive safety gear of other insecticides. And remarkably, even when mosquitoes developed resistance to the toxicity of DDT, it still acted as a repellent and irritant, driving nocturnal mosquitoes out of homes before they had a chance to bite. (This mechanism was discovered later—originally, it was just toxicity and safety that attracted people to DDT.)

Impressed, the U.S. military deployed DDT in 1942 to fight a third front against diseases like malaria, dengue, and typhus, which until then had seriously impaired U.S. fighting forces, especially in Italy and the Pacific Theater. Army personnel sprayed soldiers, dusted beachheads, and even deloused concentration camp survivors with DDT. After the war, DDT came into use for commercial and public health purposes. Farmers used DDT to protect cash crops like cotton, corn, and apples from a wide variety of agricultural pests. Around the same time, the U.S. government launched an ambitious DDT-centered malaria eradication project which by the early '60s had virtually eliminated malaria from Southern Europe, the Caribbean, and parts of East and South Asia. (In India, for example, annual deaths went from 800,000 to zero.) At the time, DDT was thought to be such an effective and useful substance that in 1948, Muller received a Nobel Prize in medicine. "To only a few chemicals does man owe as great a debt as to DDT," declared the National Academy of Sciences in a report in 1970. "In little more than two decades, DDT has prevented 500 million human deaths, due to malaria."

But by then, the tide had begun to turn against DDT. During the 1960s, reports began to emerge of increasing resistance to the drug among insects, probably sparked by its widespread use in agriculture. At the same time, case-detection followed by medical treatment began to emerge as the new model for malaria control. (By 1979, the World Health Organization [WHO] had formally endorsed this approach over that of preemptive insecticide spraying.) Most important, however, was the publication of Rachel Carson's book *Silent Spring* in 1962.

Carson's book was a lyrical broadside against synthetic chemicals in general, but against DDT in particular. She noted that as DDT seeped into the ground and ran off into streams, worms and fish stored it in their fatty tissues. Over time, songbirds like the robin and other prized avians, including bald eagles and peregrine falcons, ingested enough contaminated prey that they died of DDT poisoning. If they didn't die outright, Carson warned, studies also showed that DDT prevented reproduction by thinning eggshells. Carson also trumpeted studies of rats which suggested DDT was a liver carcinogen, and gathered anecdotal evidence of harm in human beings, like a farmer whose bone marrow wasted away after repeatedly inhaling a mixture of DDT and benzene hexachloride he used to spray his fields.

Silent Spring practically launched the modern environmental movement. The Environmental Defense Fund cut its teeth in national politics raising public alarm over—and bringing lawsuits against—DDT use, which in turn pushed the recently created Environmental Protection Agency [EPA] to hold a series of hearings on DDT. The critics were so successful that, although the administrative judge presiding over the hearings concluded that "DDT is not a carcinogenic hazard to man . . . DDT is not a mutagenic or teratogenic hazard to man," the EPA banned it anyway in 1972. (Chemical companies, of course, were more than happy to supply the less practical, more expensive alternatives.) The U.S. ban was a turning point; soon after, anti-DDT sentiment went global. Environmental organizations campaigned against its use abroad, wealthy countries began to restrict funding for DDT projects, and the World Health Organization shifted away from promoting it for public health uses. By 2000, a group of environmental activists, led by the World Wildlife Fund, was promoting a U.N. "persistent organic pollutants" treaty known as the Stockholm Convention, which would have banned DDT worldwide for all uses. Only at the last minute was an exemption added for public health use.

Reconsidering a Rogue Agent

But over the years, mainstream scientific opinion has absolved DDT of many of its supposed sins. Indeed, the Stockholm Convention partially backfired because it brought to light a slew of studies and literature reviews which contradicted the conventional wisdom on DDT. Like nearly any chemical, DDT is harmful in high enough doses. But when it comes to the kinds of uses once permitted in the United States and abroad, there's simply no solid scientific evidence that exposure to DDT causes cancer or is otherwise harmful to human beings.

Not a single study linking DDT exposure to human toxicity has ever been replicated. In 1993, Mary Wolff, an associate professor at Mount Sinai Medical Center, published a small study linking DDT exposure to breast cancer. But numerous follow-up studies with human subjects—including one large five-study review comparing 1,400 women with breast cancer to an equivalent number of controls—found no evidence for the link. David Hunter, an epidemiologist at Harvard University who ran one of the follow-up studies, says of the breast cancer connection, "the studies have really put that idea to rest." Similarly, various studies have contradicted initial concerns that DDT might cause myeloma, hepatic cancer, or non-Hodgkins lymphoma.

Other reports over the years postulating human toxicity in DDT exposure turned out to be cases of correlation without causation. In its heyday, for instance, DDT was mixed with a variety of dangerous chemicals, sometimes petroleum derivatives. In every anecdote of death or human harm by DDT that Carson related, the chemical had been dissolved in some other, highly toxic, substance, such as fuel oil, petroleum distillate, benzene hexachloride, or methylated naphthalenes. Such "mixtures with other chemicals or solvents," a 2000 review article in the medical journal *The Lancet* noted, were responsible for many of the reported deaths from DDT and for other problems like dermatitis. But even these dangers do not extend to public health use, where DDT is dissolved in water and sprayed as a thin film.

That's not to say that DDT is harmless. Matthew Longnecker studied American women who had lived during the period of high DDT use and suggested that high levels of DDT in the bloodstream of pregnant women might cause pre-term delivery and low birthweight, for instance. But public health use doses—two grams per square meter of wall sprayed indoors at most every six months—aren't likely to produce those concentrations. Since DDT is not absorbed through the skin, spraying DDT in houses is unlikely to expose pregnant women—or any one else—to amounts great enough to pose a danger. And scant evidence suggests DDT gets into the environment in significant amounts when sprayed indoors. According to a WHO report in 2000, "The targeted application of insecticides to indoor walls . . . greatly reduces dispersion of the chemicals into the environment. For this reason, the environmental risks from such targeted measures [are] considered minimal."

Agricultural use, on the other hand, is very different, amounting to literally tons of the chemical sprayed outdoors every few weeks. But almost nobody who supports using DDT to combat malaria wants to see it come back into use as an agricultural pesticide. The ideal pesticide is one that will stay on the crop but break down and virtually disappear by the time of harvest. DDT, on the other hand, is persistent and takes a long time to break down—which is why it tends to accumulate in the environment over time. "Even though there's no evidence right now that it's harmful to human beings, there's no sense in taking the risk of using it when other pesticides, better-suited for agricultural use, are available," says Donald Roberts, an expert on tropical health at the Uniformed Services University of the Health Sciences in Bethesda, Md. DDT is also so cheap that, when it was legal, farmers often used it well in excess of the officially prescribed amounts.

Yet environmental activists resist distinguishing between the agricultural and public health uses of DDT. Richard Liroff, a spokesman for the World Wildlife Fund, says, "We hang most of our argument" against DDT spraying on studies like Longnecker's. But the clear benefits of DDT use would seem to outweigh the potential dangers. Malaria, after all, also causes low birthweight in newborns (and mental retardation in infants). And while DDT may prove to have as-yet-unknown side effects, malaria has a well-known, direct effect: It kills millions of people a year.

Environmental Mea Culpa

But although prevailing scientific opinion favors the use of DDT in anti-malarial campaigns, international aid agencies still take their cues from environmental groups. Roll Back Malaria (RBM), a WHO-sponsored consortium of aid agencies, international institutions, and NGOs [nongovernmental organizations], has a 40-page action plan for reducing countries' reliance on DDT, with the goal of eventually eliminating its use for public health purposes. And the international donors who fund most anti-malaria campaigns usually follow RBM's technical guidelines. "Bottom line is, [RBM] favors the ultimate elimination of DDT from the malaria toolbox," says Dr. John Paul Clark, a former RBM adviser with expertise in DDT, although he concedes that "there are a number of countries that are not economically or epidemiologically ready to make that switch at this time."

While few organizations have a *de jure* ban on DDT projects, very few have actually put money behind them. No international aid agency will fund DDT use. The World Bank is currently funding a malaria control project in Eritrea on the condition that the country not use DDT. The recently formed Global Environmental Facility has donated money to projects in both Africa and South America, likewise with the intent of weaning recipient nations off DDT. In an emailed statement, USAID's malaria team informed me that its "activities are focused to reduce reliance on the pesticide DDT." They are "emphasizing prevention, medical intervention, and mosquito nets dipped in pyrethroid." Richard Tren, head of a group called Africa Fighting Malaria, says that the international aid agencies of Sweden, the United Kingdom, Norway, Japan, and Germany have all told him they would not fund DDT projects, nor will UNICEF. And lacking the resources to develop domestic programs on their own, most African countries bend to the requirements of these international funders. (South Africa is one of the few African countries wealthy enough to fund its own program.)

Those alternatives that aid agencies will fund are either less effective, more expensive, harder to administer, or inadequate on their own. "Eco-friendly" approaches like mosquito repellent trees or mosquito-larvae-eating fish have been tried in East Africa, where the malaria epidemic is particularly bad, but with little success. The pesticide pyrethroid was originally developed as a biodegradable DDT alternative, but mosquito resistance throughout Africa is rendering it increasingly useless. Other substitute pesticides, like carbamates and organophosphates, have turned out to be no more safe or effective than DDT, and most lack DDT's ability to repel mosquitoes even after they build up resistance to it. DDT is at least four times less expensive than the cheapest alternative—even though it is only still produced by one factory in India—and requires less frequent spraying. Both are significant advantages in poor African countries with minimal infrastructure, where every dollar not spent bringing malaria under control can be used for other public health priorities, such as supplying clean water. "DDT is long-acting, the alternatives are not," says Donald Roberts. "DDT is cheap, the alternatives are not. End of story."

Amir Attaran, a former WHO expert on malaria, once supported funding alternative pesticides, but South Africa's experience changed his mind. "If South Africa can't get by without DDT, it's pretty much as if to say that nobody can," says Attaran. "They really tried to phase this stuff out, and had the budget to afford the alternatives . . . They tried and failed." (South Africa had switched from DDT to pyrethroid in the mid-1990s, but switched back in 2000 when the mosquitoes became resistant to the pyrethroid, causing malaria cases to skyrocket). There has also been a move to use insecticide treated bednets, particularly in East Africa, but few believe that bednets alone can address the problem. "All large-scale programs that have been successful have been based on insecticide control," notes Brian Sharp, Director of the Malaria Research Program for South Africa's Medical Research Council and director of their spraying program. "I don't believe we should discriminate against [bednets or DDT] . . . One has to practice integrated vector control . . . [But] DDT is an important tool in this fight."

It is difficult to get a clear answer from aid agencies why they won't fund DDT. They may be hesitant because they receive contradictory guidance: National DDT bans conflict with WHO guidelines saying it's safe and effective, which in turn conflict with Roll Back Malaria's blueprint for phasing out DDT. Nobody seems to want to stick his or her neck out to clarify things. Most importantly, already-underfunded Western aid agencies are concerned about a backlash if they did fund DDT, since doing so might well provoke the lingering fear of DDT among the citizens of wealthier countries. Several experts told me that they are specifically afraid of tangling with the environmental lobby. When Attaran circulated a letter two years ago protesting a total ban on DDT, the head of Roll Back Malaria excoriated him for undermining RBM's relations with environmental groups. Attaran, formerly a lawyer for the Sierra Club, thinks the environmentalists should correct the misperceptions they have perpetuated. They should do what "the pharmaceutical [companies] did on access to AIDS medicine in Africa. They did a mea culpa. The environmentalists need to do the same thing."

"It Shouldn't Be This Hard"

That's not to say that all anti-malaria aid dollars should go to DDT. It makes sense to balance between funding available measures and investing in new ones. Presently, however, too little money goes to DDT at a time when few effective tools are available. Local conditions will determine the best course of action; in some places, DDT may be less effective than others, and funding should be adequate and open enough for countries to experiment with what's right for them. Brian Sharp, for instance, argues that money could go to a rotational spraying program, under which DDT would be rotated with other insecticides to prevent the development of resistance among mosquitoes and extending the effectiveness of non-DDT alternatives. Yet opposition to DDT has undercut even that compromise.

An environmentalist mea culpa would be a start, but in the United States, at least, nothing short of congressional hearings or an executive order from the Bush administration is likely to spur USAID to change its ways. The most direct approach would be a reconsideration of the EPA ban on DDT, with an explicit mandate to use some of the foreign aid budget for DDT spraying should countries ask for it. USAID's current goals for Uganda are for at least 60 percent of the country's population to have access to drugs and bednets; Jim Muhwezi, for one, would like USAID to set its goals higher. But it's not easy to get them to listen, especially with poor African countries trying to curry favor with aid agencies. Indeed, neighboring Tanzania has stayed away from DDT because, among other things, it is too "controversial," according to Alex Mwita, the program manager for Tanzania's National Malaria Control Programme. "You have to remove the myths that people have in their minds that it is not a good chemical." It shouldn't be this hard. African governments know what they need to do to control malaria—they just need the money. Like Mwita, Brian Sharp says he's waiting for the West to get over its "misguided opposition to DDT." So is Africa.

POSTSCRIPT

Should DDT Be Banned Worldwide?

Gourevitch comes close to accusing environmentalists of condemning DDT more on the basis of politics or ideology than of science. Angela Logomasini comes even closer in "Chemical Warfare: Ideological Environmentalism's Quixotic Campaign Against Synthetic Chemicals," in Ronald Bailey, ed., *Global Warming and Other Eco-Myths: How the Environmental Movement Uses False Science to Scare Us to Death* (Prima Publishing, 2002). Her admission that public health demands have softened some environmentalists' resistance to the use of DDT points to a basic truth about environmental debates. Over and over again, they come down to what we should do first: Should we meet human needs whether or not species die and air and water are contaminated? Or should we protect species, air, water, and other aspects of the environment even if some human needs must go unmet? Even if those human needs are the lives of children? This opposition is very clear in the debate over DDT. The human needs are clear, for insect-borne diseases have killed and continue to kill a great many people. Yet the environmental needs are also clear; the title of Rachel Carson's *Silent Spring* says it all. The question is one of choosing priorities and balancing risks. See John Danley, "Balancing Risks: Mosquitoes, Malaria, Morality, and DDT" (*Business & Society Review [1974]*, Spring 2002). See also Jon Cohen, "Mothers' Malaria Appears to Enhance Spread of AIDS Virus," *Science* (November 21, 2003).

Malaria can be treated with drugs, but the parasite has developed resistance to standard medications such as chloroquine. A new medication based on a Chinese plant extract (from Artemisia, or sweet wormwood or Qinghao) has shown promise but is in far too short supply; see Martin Enserink, "Source of New Hope Against Malaria In in Short Supply," *Science* (January 7, 2005). Mosquitoes can be controlled in various ways: Swamps can be drained (which carries its own environmental price), and other breeding opportunities can be eliminated. Fish can be introduced to eat mosquito larvae. Bednets can keep the mosquitoes away from people. But these (and other) alternatives do not mean that there does not remain a place for chemical pesticides. In "Pesticides and Public Health: Integrated Methods of Mosquito Management," *Emerging Infectious Diseases* (January–February 2001), Robert I. Rose, an arthropod biotechnologist with the Animal and Plant Health Inspection Service of the U.S. Department of Agriculture, says, "Pesticides have a role in public health as part of sustainable integrated mosquito management. Other components of such management include surveillance, source reduction or prevention, biological control, repellents, traps, and pesticide-resistance management." "The most effective programs today rely on a range of tools," says Anne Platt McGinn in "Combating Malaria," *State of the World 2003* (W. W. Norton, 2003).

As Gourevitch notes, some countries see DDT as essential. See "Outlaw-ing of DDT Proves Deadly," *USA Today* (October 2004). For more on Uganda, see Katherine Elizabeth Renz, Chris Keyser, Lisa Katayama, and Sara Knight, "Double-Edged DDT," *Earth Island Journal* (Spring 2005). Indonesia makes its case in "Bring Back DDT," *Far Eastern Economic Review* (March 4, 2004). Tina Rosenberg speaks for all in "What the World Needs Now Is DDT," *New York Times Magazine* (April 11, 2004).

Researchers have long sought a vaccine against malaria, but the parasite has demonstrated a persistent talent for evading all attempts to arm the immune system against it. The difficulties are covered by A. P. Waters, et al., "Malaria Vaccines: Back to the Future?" *Science* (January 28, 2005). Early in 2003, a new vaccine for humans was looking good; see David Lawrence, "Combination Malaria Vaccine Shows Early Promise in Human Trials," *Lancet* (May 2003). A newer approach is to develop genetically engineered (trans-genic) mosquitoes that either cannot support the malaria parasite or cannot infect humans with it; see Jane Bradbury, "Transgenic Mosquitoes Bring Malarial Control Closer" (*Lancet*, May 25, 2002).

It is worth stressing that malaria is only one of several mosquito-borne diseases that pose threats to public health. Two others are yellow fever and dengue. A new arrival in the United States is West Nile virus, which mosqui-toes can transfer from birds to humans. However, West Nile virus is far less fatal than malaria, yellow fever, or dengue fever. Pesticides are already being used in the United States to kill the mosquitoes that carry West Nile virus, and health effects are being seen; see Grace Ziem, "Pesticide Spraying and Health Effects," *Environmental Health Perspectives* (March 2005). Fortunately, a vaccine is in development. See Dwight G. Smith, "A New Disease in the New World," *The World & I* (February 2002), and Michelle Mueller, "The Buzz on West Nile Virus," *Current Health 2* (April/May 2002).

It is also worth stressing that global warming (see Issue 4) means climate changes that may increase the geographic range of disease-carrying mosqui-toes. Many climate researchers are concerned that malaria, yellow fever, and other now mostly tropical and subtropical diseases may return to temperate-zone nations and even spread into areas where they have never been known. See P. R. Hunter, "Climate Change and Waterborne and Vector-Borne Diseases," *Journal of Applied Microbiology* (May 2003 supplement).

ISSUE 10

Should Potential Risks Slow the Development of Nanotechnology?

YES: Peter Montague, from "Welcome to NanoWorld: Nanotechnology and the Precautionary Principle Imperative," *Multinational Monitor* (September 2004)

NO: Mike Treder, from "Molecular Nanotech: Benefits and Risks," *The Futurist* (January–February 2004)

ISSUE SUMMARY

YES: Peter Montague, executive director of the Environmental Research Foundation, argues that although nanotechnology is already sparking "a new industrial revolution," its potential hazards are also prompting demands for a go-slow precautionary approach.

NO: Mike Treder, executive director of the Center for Responsible Nanotechnology, argues that the task at hand is to realize the benefits of nanotechnology while averting the dangers but that attempts to control all risks may lead to abusive restrictions and wind up exacerbating the hazards.

The concept of nanotechnology dates back to 1959, when the late physicist Richard Feynman discussed in an American Physical Society talk ("There's Plenty of Room at the Bottom," *Engineering and Science* [February 1960]) the possibility of building machines the size of viruses. As described by K. Eric Drexler in his 1986 book *Engines of Creation*, such machines would be able to manipulate and position single atoms and molecules. For a time, enthusiasts talked of the devices as self-reproducing robots that needed only suitable programming to manufacture practically anything from dirt, air, and water, or to disassemble anything into its component atoms. Consumer goods—from steaks to cars—would be essentially free! Furthermore, nanomachines would repair wounds, destroy cancer, and scrub the cholesterol from our arteries. It sounded like magic, and it stirred debate over the possibility that out-of-control nanobeasties might turn everything into grey goo. Bill Joy, "Why the Future Doesn't Need Us," *Wired* (April 2000), argues that the hazards of nanotechnology, robotics, and genetic engineering are so serious that they threaten to make humans an endangered species; research into these areas should be halted immediately.

Enthusiasts such as the Foresight Institute (founded by Eric Drexler) remain optimistic. However, progress has been slow, and tiny manufacturing and disassembly robots now seem unlikely; Ken Donaldson and Vicki Stone, "Nanoscience Fact versus Fiction," *Communications of the ACM* (November 2004), say that the grey goo scenario "is a scientific fantasy, more in the tradition of *King Kong* than the realms of scientific plausibility." The National Heart, Lung, and Blood Institute published a report in 2003 (Denis B. Buxton, et al., "Recommendations of the National Heart, Lung, and Blood Institute Nanotechnology Working Group," *Circulation*, vol. 108, pp. 2737–2742) that called the medical prospects encouraging and called for increased research effort and funding. Chuck Lenatti, in "Nanotech's First Blockbusters?" *Technology Review* (March 2004), reports that the effort to learn how to make tiny things is having some practical payoffs already. No one is building tiny robots of any kind, but some companies are making tiny components (such as "nanowires") from which they hope to build marketable photovoltaic cells, LEDs, flexible circuitry, electronic devices, and so on. See, for instance, "Nanotechnology, Fuel Cells, and the Future," *Global Environmental Change Report* (June 2005).

How long will it take to go from the first primitive nanomachines able to build very simple things to the tiny robots that can make or unmake virtually anything? Most people have thought that if the step is possible at all, it will take decades. But in summer 2003, the Center for Responsible Nanotechnology concluded that instead it could be a matter of weeks, because even simple nanomanufacturing, combined with computer-aided design and manufacturing techniques, would enable extraordinarily rapid progress. This prospect, despite admittedly enticing potential benefits, alarms some people. Peter Montague, executive director of the Environmental Research Foundation, argues that although nanotechnology is already sparking "a new industrial revolution," its potential hazards are also prompting demands for a go-slow precautionary approach. Mike Treder, executive director of the Center for Responsible Nanotechnology, argues that the task at hand is to realize the benefits of nanotechnology while averting the dangers but that attempts to control all risks may lead to abusive restrictions and wind up exacerbating the hazards.

Peter Montague

Welcome to NanoWorld: Nanotechnology and the Precautionary Principle Imperative

Nanotechnology—or nanotech, for short—is a new approach to industrial production, based on the manipulation of things so small that they are invisible to the naked eye and even to most microscopes.

Nanotech is named for the nanometer, a unit of measure, a billionth of a meter, one one-thousandth of a micrometer. The Oxford English Dictionary defines nanotechnology as "the branch of technology that deals with dimensions and tolerances of less than 100 nanometers, especially the manipulation of individual atoms and molecules." Nanotech deals in the realm where a typical grain of sand is huge (a million nanometers in diameter). A human hair is 200,000 nanometers thick. A red blood cell spans 10,000 nanometers. A virus measures 100 nanometers across, and the smallest atom (hydrogen) spans 0.1 nanometers.

In the realm below 50 nanometers, the normal laws of physics no longer apply, quantum physics kicks in and materials take on surprising new properties. Something that was red may now be green; metals may become translucent and thus invisible; something that could not conduct electricity may now pass a current; nonmagnetic materials may become magnetized; insoluble substances may dissolve. Knowing the properties of a substance in bulk tells you nothing about its properties at the nano scale, so all nano materials' characteristics—including hazardous traits—must be learned anew by direct experiment.

Nanotechnologists foresee a second industrial revolution sweeping the world during our lifetimes as individual atoms are assembled together into thousands of useful new products. Few deny that new products may entail new hazards, but most nanotechnologists say existing regulations are adequate for controlling any hazards that may arise. In the United States, nanotech is not now subject to any special regulations and nano products need not even be labeled. Furthermore, no one has developed a consistent nomenclature for nano materials, so rigorous discussion of nanotech among regulators and policymakers is not yet possible. Without consistent nomenclature, standardized safety testing lies in the future.

No one denies that nanotech will produce real benefits, but, based on the history of nuclear power, biotechnology and the chemical industry, skeptics are calling for a precautionary approach. The resulting clash of philosophies—"Better safe than sorry" versus "Nothing ventured, nothing gained" or even in some cases "Damn the torpedoes, full speed ahead!"—may offer a major test of the Precautionary Principle as a new way of managing innovation.

"World Peace, Universal Prosperity"

The pressure for rapid development of nanotech is enormous. The surprising properties of materials at the nano scale have opened up a new universe of industrial applications and entrepreneurial dreams. Largely unnoticed, hundreds of products containing nano-sized particles have already reached the market—metal surfaces and paints so slick they clean themselves when it rains; organic light-emitting diodes for computer screens, digital cameras and cell phones; sub-miniature data storage devices (aiming to hold the Library of Congress in a computer the size of a sugar cube); specialty lubricants; long-mileage vehicle tires; nanoreinforced plastics for stronger automobile fenders; light-weight military armor; anti-reflective and scratch-resistant sun glasses; super-slippery ski wax; powerful tennis rackets and long-lasting tennis balls; inkjet photographic paper intended to hold an image for 100 years; high-contrast MRI scanners for medical diagnosis; efficient drug and vaccine delivery systems; vitamins in a spray; invisible sunscreen ointments containing nano particles of titanium or zinc; anti-wrinkle cosmetic creams; and so on.

And this is just the beginning. Nanotech wasn't possible until the invention in the 1980s and early 1990s of ways to arrange individual atoms under software control. Nano particles, nanotubes and carbon nano crystals called Bucky Balls (after Buckminster Fuller) are now being manufactured in ton quantities for industrial use. Currently technologists are working feverishly to coax nature's most successful nano factory, the living cell, to grow useful new nano assemblies. It is no exaggeration to say that the field of nanotech is gripped by something approaching a gold rush mentality. Worldwide, governments are spending an estimated $3 billion per year on nanotech research, and the private sector is thought to be spending at least that much. The U.S. government alone will spend at least $3.7 billion on nano R&D during the next four years. The global market for nano products is expected to reach $1 trillion in 10 years or less. Any day of the week you can check in at <http://nanotech-now.com> and catch a glimpse of the gold rush in action.

But for some prominent proponents of nanotech, this is about more than money—it is about reinventing the entire world, including humans, as they now exist. According to the U.S. National Science Foundation, nanotechnology is the foundation stone of NBIC—a revolutionary convergence of nanotech, biotech (manipulation of genes), info tech (computers), and cogno tech (brain function). In a report sponsored by the National Science Foundation and the Department of Commerce, the technologists and politicians who are promoting this revolution say it is "essential to the future of humanity" because it holds the promise of "world peace, universal prosperity, and evolution to a higher level of compassion and accomplishment." They say it may be "a watershed in history to rank with the invention of agriculture and the Industrial Revolution." The ultimate aim of this revolution has been an explicit human goal for at least 400 years—the "conquest of nature" and the enhancement of human capabilities.

Whatever else it may offer, the nanotech revolution entails a radical new approach to industrial production with the potential to change every existing industry, plus create new ones. Typical manufacturing today—even construction of the tiniest computer circuit—relies on "top-down" techniques, machining or etching products out of blocks of raw material. For example, a common technique for making a transistor begins with a chunk of silicon, which is etched to remove unwanted material, leaving behind a sculpted circuit. This "top-down" method of construction creates the desired product plus waste residues.

In contrast, nanotech makes possible "bottom-up" construction in which atoms are arranged under software control—or in ideal cases they will self-assemble, just as living cells self-assemble—into the desired configuration with nothing left over, no waste. Instead of cutting trees into lumber to make a table, why not just "grow" a table? Thus nanotech seems to offer the possibility of waste-free manufacturing and therefore a cleaner environment. Furthermore, nanotech may help remediate past pollution. U.S. Environmental Protection Agency (EPA) is funding research on releasing nano particles into the environment to detoxify mountains of toxic waste remaining from the 20th century's experiment with petroleum-based chemistry.

Insuring a Nanotech Future

Nevertheless, without denying plausible benefits, critics want nanotech's potential problems brought into the open:

- Unless nanotechnology is shared generously, it may create a "nano divide" similar to the "digital divide" that exists now between those with ready access to computers and those without.
- Humans given enhanced mental or physical capabilities may gain great advantage over normal people. On the other hand, some people may be coerced to accept dubious or unwanted enhancements.
- Inequalities within and between nations may be exacerbated if individuals and corporations gain monopoly control of nanotech by patenting the building blocks of the universe—a precedent set in 1964 when Glenn T. Seaborg was issued a patent on an element he discovered and named Americium.

In the longer term, some leading technologists like Ray Kurzweil, inventor of the first reading machine for the blind, and Bill Joy, one of the founders of Sun Microsystems, fear that nanotech will give individuals—inadvertently or intentionally—destructive potential greater than the power of atomic weapons. As Joy wrote in 2000, "I think it is no exaggeration to say we are on the cusp of the further perfection of extreme evil, an evil whose possibility spreads well beyond that which weapons of mass destruction bequeathed to the nation-states, on to a surprising and terrible empowerment of extreme individuals."

Others, such as the insurance industry, have more mundane concerns about nanotech—chiefly, the potential health and environmental hazards of tiny particles. In May of this year, Swiss Re, the world's second-largest reinsurance firm, issued a report calling for the Precautionary Principle to guide nanotech development. Swiss Re itemized a host of potential problems that it says need to be resolved before nanotech products are fully deployed, including these:

- One of the new properties of nano-sized particles is their extreme mobility. They have "almost unrestricted access to the human body," Swiss Re points out, because they can enter the blood stream through the lungs and possibly through the skin, and seem to enter the brain directly via olfactory nerves. Once in the blood stream, nano particles can "move practically unhindered through the entire body," unlike larger particles that are trapped and removed by various protective mechanisms.
- If they become airborne, nano particles can float for very long periods because—unlike larger particles—they do not readily settle onto surfaces. In water, nano particles spread unhindered and pass through most available filters. So, for example, current drinking water filters will not effectively remove nano particles. Even in soil, nano particles may move in unexpected ways, perhaps penetrating the roots of plants and thus entering the food chains of humans and animals.
- One of the most useful features of nano particles is their huge surface area. The smaller the particle, the larger its surface in relation to its mass. A gram of nano particles has a surface area of a thousand square meters. Their large surfaces give nano particles some of their most desirable characteristics. For example, drug-coated nano particles may one day transport pharmaceuticals directly to specific sites within the human body. Unfortunately, their large surface also means that nano particles may collect and transport pollutants. Furthermore, their large surface means nano particles are highly reactive in a chemical sense. As Swiss Re noted, "As size decreases and reactivity increases, harmful effects may be intensified, and normally harmless substances may assume hazardous characteristics."

Nano particles may harm living tissue, such as lungs, in at least two ways—through normal effects of chemical reactivity, or by damaging phagocytes, which are scavenger cells that normally remove foreign substances. Phagocytes can become "overloaded" by nano particles and cease functioning.

Worse, overloaded phagocytes retreat into deeper layers and so become unavailable to protect against foreign invaders. Successive particles are then able to do their full reactive damage, and other invaders, such as bacteria, may penetrate unhindered.

The surface reactivity of nano particles gives rise to "free radicals," which are atoms containing an "unsatisfactory" number of electrons (either too few or too many for stability). Free radicals swap electrons with nearby atoms, creating further instabilities and setting off a cascade of effects. Free radicals give rise to inflammation and tissue damage, and may initiate serious harm, such as growth of tumors. On the other hand, some free radicals are beneficial, destroying invaders. So the role of nano particles in producing free radicals remains to be clarified.

- Nano particles would normally tend to clump together, forming larger, less dangerous particles—but nanotechnologists take pains to prevent clumping by adding special coatings. As a result, nano particles in many commercial products, sprays and powders remain reactive and highly mobile.
- Whether nano particles can pass through the skin into the blood stream is the subject of intense debate. Different experiments have yielded conflicting results, presumably because test protocols have not been standardized. Some believe that nano particles may slip between the layers of outer skin and penetrate through to the blood below. Others believe that hair follicles offer a direct route for nano particles to penetrate from skin to blood. No one knows for sure. Despite this knowledge gap, sun screens, skin lotions and baby products containing nano particles are already on the market. Clearly this is a problem for insurance firms providing liability coverage. Swiss Re says, "Considering the wide variety of products already on the market, the need for a solution is urgent."
- Ingested nano particles can be absorbed through "Peyer's plaques," part of the immune system lining the intestines. From there, nano particles can enter the blood stream, be transported throughout the body, "and behave in ways that may be detrimental to the organism," Swiss Re notes. While in the blood stream, nano particles have been observed entering the blood cells themselves.
- Once in the body, nano particles can enter the heart, bone marrow, ovaries, muscles, brain, liver, spleen and lymph nodes. During pregnancy, nano particles would likely cross the placenta and enter the fetus. The specific effects in any given organ would depend upon the surface chemistry of particular particles, which in turn would be determined by their size and surface coating. "It is likely that in the course of its entire evolution, humankind has never been exposed to such a wide variety of substances that can penetrate the human body apparently unhindered," Swiss Re says.
- The brain is one of the best-protected of all human organs. A guardian "blood-brain barrier" prevents most substances in the blood from entering the brain (alcohol and caffeine being two well-known exceptions). However, nano particles have repeatedly been shown to pass into the brain, where their effects are unknown. Will they accumulate and, if so, to what effect?

- Nano particles may disrupt the immune system, cause allergic reactions, interfere with essential signals sent between neighboring cells, or disrupt exchanges between enzymes, Swiss Re says. Some of these characteristics may be harnessed for benefit—for example, in experiments a carbon nano crystal has been able to disrupt one of the processes that allows the AIDS virus to multiply.
- Nano particles in disposable products will eventually enter the environment. In the environment, nano particles represent an entirely new class of pollutants with which scientists (and nature) have no experience. Swiss Re speculates that, "Via the water cycle, nano particles could spread rapidly all over the globe, possibly also promoting the transport of pollutants." Swiss Re asks, "What would happen if certain nanoparticles did exert a harmful influence on the environment? Would it be possible to withdraw them from circulation? Would there be any way of removing nanoparticles from the water, earth, or air?"
- Turning to workplace hazards, Swiss Re asks whether nano particles will become the next asbestos. To protect workers, effective face masks are "not a very realistic prospect at present, since the requisite design would render normal breathing impossible." New designs may be possible but remain unproven.

Precaution on a Super-Small Scale

Swiss Re notes that, in the past, the drive toward rapid technological innovation has "prevented the introduction of the Precautionary Principle in relation to new technologies for more than 20 years." But now, "in view of the dangers to society that could arise out of the establishment of nanotechnology, and given the uncertainty currently prevailing in scientific circles, the Precautionary Principle should be applied whatever the difficulties," Swiss Re asserts. "The Precautionary Principle demands the proactive introduction of protective measures in the face of possible risks, which science at present—in the absence of knowledge—can neither confirm nor reject."

What would precaution look like in a rapidly developing field like nanotech? The British Royal Society and the Royal Academy of Engineering issued a nanotech report in July 2004 recommending a series of precautionary actions, with the following chain of reasoning:

- "The evidence we have reviewed suggests that some manufactured nanoparticles and nanotubes are likely to be more toxic per unit mass than particles of the same chemicals at larger size and will therefore present a greater hazard."
- "There is virtually no evidence available to allow the potential environmental impacts of nanoparticles and nanotubes to be evaluated."
- Therefore, "the release of nanoparticles to the environment [should be] minimized until these uncertainties are reduced."
- And, "until there is evidence to the contrary, factories and research laboratories should treat manufactured nanoparticles and nanotubes as if they were hazardous and seek to reduce them as far as possible from waste streams."

These recommendations reverse the traditional approach to industrial materials, which have historically been assumed benign until shown otherwise.

The Royal Society puts the burden of producing information about safety on industry, not on the public: "A wide range of uses for nanotubes and nanoparticles is envisaged that will fix them within products. . . . We believe that the onus should be on industry to assess . . . releases [of nano particles from products] throughout a product's lifetime (including at the end-of-life and to make that information available to the regulator." From such a recommendation, it is a very short step to the European Union's precautionary proposal for industrial chemicals, called REACH (Registration, Evaluation and Authorization of Chemicals), which is often summarized as, "No data, no market."

The Royal Society recommended that the use of zinc oxide nano particles and iron oxide nano particles in cosmetics should "await a safety assessment"—in other words a moratorium on these products is recommended. Likewise, "the release of free manufactured nanoparticles into the environment for [pollution] remediation (which has been piloted in the USA) should be prohibited until there is sufficient information to allow the potential risks to be evaluated as well as the benefits."

The Precautionary Principle is sometimes called the foresight principle. Importantly, the Royal Society's report fully embraces foresight for nanotechnology (and all other new technologies):

"Our study has identified important issues that need to be addressed with some urgency" and so it is "essential" for government to "establish a group that brings together representatives of a wide range of stakeholders to look at new and emerging technologies and identify at the earliest possible stage areas where potential health, safety, environmental, social, ethical and regulatory issues may arise and advise about how these might be addressed." The group must provide "an early warning of areas where regulation may be inadequate for specific applications of these technologies."

And, finally, "The work of this group should be made public so that all stakeholders can be encouraged to engage with the emerging issues."

Thus nanotech is sparking not only a new industrial revolution but demands for a reversal of traditional approaches to managing innovation and a turn toward precautionary action.

Whether the momentum gathering behind the precautionary approach can redirect the charge behind nanotech—a confluence of government and technophile advocates in alliance with an emerging industrial lobby—remains uncertain.

NO

Mike Treder

Molecular Nanotech: Benefits and Risks

The future shock of rapid change and technology run amok described by Alvin Toffler in his 1970 best seller has perhaps been less debilitating for most people than predicted, but even Toffler could not have envisioned the tidal wave of change that will hit us when *nanofactories* make the scene.

Imagine a world with billions of desktop-size, portable, nonpolluting, cheap machines that can manufacture almost anything—from clothing to furniture to electronics, and much more—in just a few hours. Today, such devices do not exist. But in the years ahead, this advanced form of nanotechnology could create the next Industrial Revolution—or the world's worst nightmare.

The technology described in this article is *molecular nanotechnology* (MNT). This is a big step beyond most of today's nanotech research, which deals with exploring and exploiting the properties of materials at the nanoscale. Industry has begun using the term *nanotechnology* to cover almost any technology significantly smaller than microtechnology, such as those involving nanoparticles or nanomaterials. This broad field will produce important and useful results, but their societal effects—both positive and negative—will be modest compared with later stages of the technology.

MNT, by contrast, is about constructing shapes, machines, and products at the atomic level—putting them together molecule by molecule. With parts only a few nanometers wide, it may become possible to build a supercomputer smaller than a grain of sand, a weapon smaller than a mosquito, or a self-contained nanofactory that sits on your kitchen counter.

"Picture an automated factory, full of conveyor belts, computers, and swinging robot arms," writes scientist and engineer K. Eric Drexler, who first brought nanotechnology to public attention with his 1986 book *Engines of Creation*. "Now imagine something like that factory, but a million times smaller and working a million times faster, with parts and workpieces of molecular size."

Unlike any machine ever built, the nanofactory will be assembled from the bottom up, constructed of specifically designed and placed molecules.

Originally published in the January/February 2004 issue of THE FUTURIST. Used with permission from the World Future Society, 7910 Woodmont Avenue, Suite 450, Bethesda, Maryland 20814. Telephone: 301/656-8274; Fax: 301/951-0394; http://www.wfs.org.

Drexler says, "Nanotechnology isn't primarily about miniaturizing machines, but about extending precise control of molecular structures to larger and larger scales. Nanotechnology is about making precise things *big*."

Virtually every previous technological improvement has been accomplished by making things smaller and more precise. But as the scales at which we work get smaller and smaller, we approach limits imposed by physics. The smallest unit of matter we can build with is the atom, or combinations of atoms known as molecules. The earthshaking insight of molecular nanotechnology is that, when we reach this scale, we can reverse direction and begin building *up*, making products by placing individual atoms and molecules exactly where we want them.

Ever since Richard Feynman enunciated MNT's basic concepts in 1959, and especially since Drexler began detailing its amazing possibilities in the 1980s, proposals for building products in various ways have been put forth. Some of these have been fanciful and many have been impractical. At this point, it appears that the idea of a nanofactory is the safest and most useful method of building general-purpose products by molecular manufacturing.

Inside a Nanofactory

The inner architecture of a nanofactory will be a stunning achievement, outside the realm of anything previously accomplished. Nanofactories will make use of a vast number of moving parts, each designed and precisely constructed to do a specific job. Some of these parts will be visible to the human eye. Most will be microscopic or even nanoscale, smaller than a human cell. An important feature of a nanofactory is that all of its parts will be fixed in place. This is significant because it greatly simplifies development of the device. Engineers won't have to figure out how to tell each little nanobot in a swarm where to go and how to get there, and none of the parts can get lost or go wild.

Perhaps the easiest way to envision the inner workings of a nanofactory is to picture a large city, with all the streets laid out on a grid. Imagine that in this city everyone works together to build gigantic products—ocean liners, for instance. To build something that big, you have to start with small parts and put them together. In this imaginary city, all the workers stand along the streets and pass the parts along to each other. The smallest parts are assembled on the narrowest side streets, and then handed up to the end of the block. Other small parts from other side streets are joined together to make medium-sized parts, which are joined together to make large parts. At the end, the largest parts converge in one place, where they are joined together to make the finished product. A nanofactory performs in this way, with multiple assembly lines operating simultaneously and steadily feeding into each other.

The first and hardest step in building a nanofactory is building an *assembler*, a tiny device that can combine individual molecules into useful shapes. An early plan for molecular manufacturing imagined lots of free-floating assemblers working together to build a single massive product, molecule by molecule. A more efficient approach is to fasten down the assemblers in orderly arrays of chemical fabricators, instruct each fabricator to create a tiny piece of the product, and then fasten the pieces together, passing them along to the next level within the nanofactory.

A human-scale nanofactory will consist of trillions of fabricators, and it could only be built by another nanofactory. But at the beginning, an assembler could build a very small nanofactory, with just a few fabricators. A smaller nanofactory could build a bigger one, and so on. According to the best estimates we have today, a fabricator could make its own mass in just a few hours. So a small nanofactory could make another one twice as big in just a few days—maybe less than a day. Do that about 60 times, and you have a tabletop model.

By the time the first working assembler is ready, the blueprint for a basic nanofactory may already be prepared. But until we have an assembler, we can't make a nanofactory.

Building an assembler is one of the ambitious research projects of Zyvex, a Texas firm that bills itself as "the first molecular nanotechnology company." Zyvex has gathered many leading minds in physics, chemistry, mechanical engineering, and computer programming to focus on the long-range goal of molecular assembler manufacturing technology. Along the way, the company has developed some of the world's most precise tools for manipulating and testing materials and structures at the nanoscale. Numerous other projects at research universities and in corporations around the world are contributing valuable knowledge to the field.

How far are we from having a working assembler? A 1999 media report on nanotech said, "Estimates vary. From five to 10 years, according to Zyvex, or from eight to 15 years, according to the research community."

And how long will it take from building a single assembler to having a fully functional nanofactory? The report continues, "After that, it could be decades before we'll be able to manufacture finished consumer goods." This reflects the common wisdom, but it's wrong. Very wrong.

The Center for Responsible Nanotechnology (CRN), a non-profit think tank co-founded by this author, published a detailed study in summer 2003 of the work required to progress from a single assembler to a full-fledged nanofactory that can create a wide variety of low-cost products. The startling conclusion of this report is that the span of time could be measured in weeks—probably less than two months. And what will the first nanofactory build? Another one, and another one.

Each nanofactory will be able to duplicate itself in as little as a few hours, or perhaps a half a week at most. Even using the most conservative estimate, in a couple of months you could have a million nanofactories, and a few months after that, a billion. Less than a year after the first basic assembler is completed, every household in the world conceivably could have its own nanofactory.

Creativity Unleashed

Before a tidal wave strikes, another dramatic event—usually an earthquake or major landslide—must occur to trigger it. The first generation of products to come out of nanofactories—inexpensive but high quality clothing, furniture, electronics, household appliances, bicycles, tools, building supplies, and more—may be like that: a powerful landslide of change, but only a portent of the gigantic wave that is to follow.

Most of these early products will probably be similar to what are current at the time nanofactories begin production. Because they are built by MNT, with every atom precisely placed, they will be better in every way—stronger, lighter, cheaper—but they still will be built on existing models.

The world-changing shock wave will hit when we realize that we no longer need be restricted to existing models—not when a supercomputer smaller than a grain of sand can be integrated into any product, and not when people everywhere—young, old, male, female, technical, nontechnical, practical, artistic, and whimsical—will have the opportunity to be designers.

MNT product design will be eased by CAD (computer-aided design) programs so simple that a child can do it—and that's no exaggeration. New product prototypes can be created, tested, and refined in a matter of hours instead of months and without the expense of traditional production facilities. No special expertise is needed beyond the skill for using CAD programs—only imagination, curiosity, and the desire to create.

Within months, conceivably, even the most up-to-date appliances, machines, communication media, and other electronics will be outmoded. Imagine embedding "smart" gadgetry into everything you own or might want to have. Demand for these new products will be intense. The cost of manufacturing them may be almost negligible.

To maximize the latent innovation potential in nanofactory proliferation, and to help prevent illicit, unwise, or malicious product design and manufacture, CRN recommends that designers work (and play) with modular *nanoblocks* of various compositions and purposes to create a wide variety of products, from consumer goods and educational tools to building supplies and even new modes of transportation. When combined with automated verification of design safety and protection of intellectual property, this should open up huge new areas for originality and improvement while maintaining safety and commercial viability.

Working with nanoblocks, designers can create to their hearts' content. The combination of user-friendly CAD and rapid prototyping will result in a spectacular synergy, enabling unprecedented levels of innovation and development. Among the many remarkable benefits accruing to humanity from nanofactory proliferation will be this unleashing of millions of eager new minds, allowed for the first time to freely explore and express their brilliant creative energy.

It becomes impossible to predict what might be devised then. The smart components and easy design systems of the nanotech revolution will rewrite the rules.

Benefits and Dangers

This all adds up to change that is sudden and shocking and could be extremely disruptive.

On the plus side, MNT could solve many of the world's problems. Simple products like plumbing, water filters, and mosquito nets—made cheaply on the spot—would greatly reduce the spread of infectious diseases. The efficient, cheap construction of strong and lightweight structures, electrical equipment, and power storage devices will allow the use of solar thermal power as a primary and abundant energy source.

Many areas of the world could not support a twentieth-century manufacturing infrastructure, with its attendant costs, difficulties, and environmental impacts, but MNT should be self-contained and clean. A single packing crate or suitcase could contain all the equipment required for a village-scale industrial revolution.

Computers and display devices will become stunningly inexpensive and could be made widely available. Much social unrest can be traced directly to material poverty, ill health, and ignorance. Nanofactories could greatly reduce these problems.

On the other hand, all this sudden change—the equivalent of a century's development packed into a few years—has the potential to disrupt many aspects of society and politics.

When a consumer purchases a manufactured product today, he is paying for its design, raw materials, the labor and capital of manufacturing, transportation, storage, marketing, and sales. Additional money—usally a fairly low percentage—goes to the owners of each of these businesses, and eventually to the employed workers. If nanofactories can produce a wide variety of products when and where they are wanted, most of this additional effort will become superfluous. This raises many questions about the nature of a post-MNT economy: Who will own the technology for molecular manufacturing? Will it be heavily restricted, or widely available? Will products become cheaper? Will major corporations disappear? Will new monopolies arise? Will most people retire—or be unemployed? What will it do to the gap between rich and poor?

It seems clear that molecular manufacturing could severely disrupt the present economic structure, greatly reducing the value of many material and human resources, including much of our current infrastructure. Despite utopian postcapitalist hopes, it is unclear whether a workable replacement system could appear in time to prevent the human consequences of massive job displacement.

MNT manufacturing will allow the cheap creation of incredibly powerful devices and products. Stronger materials will allow the creation of much larger machines, capable of excavating or otherwise destroying large areas of the planet at a greatly accelerated pace. It is too early to tell whether there will be economic incentive to do this. However, given the large number of activities and purposes that would damage the environment if taken to extremes, and the ease of taking them to extremes with molecular manufacturing, it seems likely that this problem is worth worrying about.

Some forms of damage can result from an aggregate of individual actions, each almost harmless by itself. For example, the extreme compactness of nanomanufactured machinery may lead to the use of very small products, which can easily turn into nanolitter that will be hard to clean up and may cause health problems. Collection of solar energy on a sufficiently large scale—by corporations, municipalities, and individuals—could modify the planet's albedo and directly affect the environment. In addition, if we are not careful, the flexibility and compactness of molecular manufacturing may allow the creation of free-floating, foraging self-replicators—a "gray goo" that could do serious damage to the biosphere by replicating out of control.

Molecular manufacturing raises the possibility of horrifically effective weapons. As an example, the smallest insect is about 200 microns; this creates a plausible size estimate for a nanotech-built antipersonnel weapon capable of seeking and injecting toxin into unprotected humans. The human lethal dose of botulism toxin is about 100 nanograms, or about 1/100 the volume of the weapon. As many as 50 billion toxin-carrying devices—theoretically enough to kill every human on earth—could be packed into a single suitcase. Guns of all sizes would be far more powerful, and their bullets could be self-guided. Aerospace hardware would be far lighter and offer higher performance; built with minimal or no metal, such craft would be much harder to spot on radar.

The awesome power of MNT may cause two or more competing nations to enter into an unstable arms race. Increased uncertainty of the capabilities of an adversary, less time to respond to an attack, and better targeted destruction of the enemy's resources during an attack all make nanotech arms races less stable than a nuclear arms race. Also, unless nanotech is tightly controlled on an international level, the number of nanotech nations in the world could be much higher than the number of nuclear nations, increasing the chance of a regional conflict expanding globally.

Criminals and terrorists with stronger, more powerful, and more compact devices could do serious damage to society. Chemical and biological weapons could become much deadlier and easier to conceal. Many other types of terrifying devices are possible, including several varieties of remote assassination weapons that would be difficult to detect or avoid. If such devices were available from a black market or a home factory, it would be nearly impossible to detect them before they were used; a random search capable of spotting them would be a clear violation of current human rights standards in most civilized countries.

Surveillance devices could be made microscopically small, low-priced, and very numerous—leading to questions of pervasive invasions of privacy, from illicit selling of sexual or other images to ubiquitous covert government or industrial spying. Attempts to control all these risks may lead to abusive restrictions, or create a black market that would be very risky and almost impossible to stop, because small nanofactories will be very easy to smuggle and fully dangerous.

Searching for Solutions

If you knew that in one year's time you would be forced to walk a tightrope without a net hundreds of feet above a rocky canyon, how soon would you begin practicing? The analogy applies to nanofactory technology. Because we know it is possible—maybe even probable—that everything we've reviewed here could happen within a decade, how soon should we start to prepare?

A report issued by the University of Toronto Joint Centre for Bioethics in February 2003 calls for serious consideration of the ethical, environmental, economic, legal, and social implications of nanotechnology. Report co-author Peter Singer says, "Open public discussion of the benefits and risks of this new technology is urgently needed."

There's no doubt that such discussion is warranted and urgent. But beyond talking about ethics, immediate research into the need, design, and building of an effective global administration structure is crucial. Unwise regulation is a serious hazard. Simple solutions won't work.

"A patchwork of extremist solutions to the wide-ranging risks of advanced nanotechnology is a grave danger," says Chris Phoenix, research director for the Center for Responsible Nanotechnology. "All areas of society stand to be affected by molecular manufacturing, and unless comprehensive international plans are developed, the multiplicity of cures could be worse than the disease. The threat of harm would almost certainly be increased, while many extraordinary benefits could go unrealized."

We have much to gain, and much to lose. The advantages promised by MNT are real, and they could be ours soon. Living conditions worldwide could be dramatically improved, and human suffering greatly diminished. But everything comes at a cost. The price for safe introduction of the miracles of nanofactory technology is thorough, conscientious preparation.

Several organizations are stepping up to this challenge. For example:

- The Foresight Institute has drafted a set of molecular nanotechnology guidelines for researchers and developers. These are mostly aimed at restricting the development of MNT to responsible parties and preventing the production of free-ranging self-replicating nanobots.
- The Millennium Project of the American Council for the United Nations University is exploring various scenarios for safe and socially conscious implementation of molecular manufacturing and other emerging technologies. These scenarios depict the world in 2050, based on various policy choices we might make between now and then.
- The Center for Responsible Nanotechnology is studying all the issues involved—political, economic, military, humanitarian, technological, and environmental—and developing well-grounded, complete, and workable proposals for effective administration and safe use of advanced nanotechnology. Current results of CRN's research lead to the conclusion that establishing a single international program to develop molecular manufacturing technology may be the safest course. The leading nations of the world would have to agree to join— or at least not to oppose—this effort, and a mechanism to detect and deter competing programs would have to be devised.

It will take all this and more. The brightest minds and clearest thinkers, the most energetic activists and committed organizers, the smartest scientists, most dedicated ethicists, and most creative social planners desperately will be needed.

Will it be easy to realize the benefits of nanofactory technology while averting the dangers? Of course it will not. Is it even possible? It had better be. Our future is very uncertain, and it's very near. Much nearer than we might have thought. Let's get started.

POSTSCRIPT

Should Potential Risks Slow the Development of Nanotechnology?

Nanotechnology sounds like the most wild-eyed of science-fiction dreams, and it has become a frequent guest-star in modern science fiction novels. But it seems reasonable to say that nanotechnology will not remain science fiction for very long. Nanotechnologists are not yet close to building the first nanofactories, but nanotechnology is gaining significant attention from government, industry, and investors. Its momentum is growing, as suggested by two recent book titles: Douglas Mulhall's *Our Molecular Future: How Nanotechnology, Robotics, Genetics and Artificial Intelligence Will Transform Our World* (Prometheus, 2002) and Mark A. Ratner's and Daniel Ratner's *Nanotechnology: A Gentle Introduction to the Next Big Idea* (Prentice Hall, 2002). The Bush administration has asked Congress for $1 billion for nanotechnology R&D, but critics are concerned that the money is going to those who are committed to the technology, not to those who wish to protect the public; see Neil Munro and Bara Vaida, "Who's Minding the Nanos?" *National Journal* (June 26, 2004), and Melissa A. Bailey and Rachel G. Lattimore, "Nanotechnology: Now Is the Time to Assess Risks," *Occupational Hazards* (September 2004).

In December 2004, the European Commission published "Towards a European Strategy for Nanotechnology" (http://europa.eu.int/comm/research/industrial_technologies/pdf/nanotechnology_communication_en.pdf), which called for a number of steps designed both to stimulate the development of nanotechnology in Europe and to "integrate societal considerations into the R&D process at an early stage; address any potential public health, safety, environmental and consumer risks upfront by generating the data needed for risk assessment, integrating risk assessment into every step of the life cycle of nanotechnology-based products, and adapting existing methodologies and, as necessary, developing novel ones; [and] complement the above actions with appropriate cooperation and initiatives at international level."

In July 2004, the Royal Society and Royal Academy of Engineering published "Nanoscience and Nanotechnologies: Opportunities and Uncertainties," recommending tighter UK and European regulations and public dialog. In February 2005, the UK government published a lengthy response to the report (http://www.ost.gov.uk/policy/issues/nanotech_final.pdf) that agreed on the need for research and regulation but failed to promise additional money.

Anthony Seaton and Kenneth Donaldson, in "Nanoscience, Nanotoxicology, and the Need to Think Small," *Lancet* (March 12, 2005), comment on the potential health risks of nanomaterials. Rory O'Neill, "Dangers Come in

Small Particles," *Hazards* (July–September 2004), warns that the industry holds the potential for "tomorrow's occupational health calamity." People such as Bill Joy are sounding even more dramatic cautionary notes, but others, such as John Seely Brown and Paul Duguid, "A Response to Bill Joy and the Doom-and-Gloom Technofuturists," *The Industry Standard* (April 13, 2000), are more optimistic. Joy, say Brown and Duguid, far too blithely assumes that very large obstacles in the development of nanotechnology will be overcome in short order. He focuses on hype and oversimplifications (and indeed, the "grey goo" problem is no longer taken seriously at all). He also ignores the role of society, which has shown itself quite capable of controlling the development of technologies in the past. On the other hand, society may not have adequate information in time to make an informed decision on whether to let nanotechnology proceed, perhaps especially considering the speed with which nanotechnology is likely to develop after the first simple assemblers are built. Fariborz Ghadar and Heather Spindler, in "Nanotechnology: Small Revolution," *Industrial Management* (May/June 2005), note that "While scientists and the federal government recognize the potential benefits of nanotechnology and it will not be possible to say that all nanotech applications are safe or are dangerous, it will be important to listen and address public concerns. And although much more data will be available in 10 years that will facilitate the decision, society will be forced to make a decision before then in the absence of complete data. And the adoption of nanotechnologies will be a very diverse and complex problem."

On the Internet . . .

National Aeronautics and Space Administration

At this site, you can find out the latest information on the International Space Shuttle, space exploration, and other space-related news.

http://www.nasa.gov

Mars Exploration

This NASA Web site provides a host of links related to Mars exploration and colonization.

http://nssdc.gsfc.nasa.gov/planetary/
mars_colonize_terraform.html

SETI Institute

The SETI Institute serves as a home for scientific research in the general field of life in the universe, with an emphasis on the search for extraterrestrial intelligence (SETI).

http://www.seti.org

SETI League

The SETI League, Inc., is dedicated to the electromagnetic (radio) search for extra-terrestrial intelligence.

http://seti1.setileague.org

Asteroid and Comet Impact Hazards

This site provides a list of upcoming close approaches to Earth.

http://impact.arc.nasa.gov/index.html

Near Earth Objects

The Near Earth Object Dynamic Site (NEODyS) provides information on all near earth asteroids (NEAs). Each NEA has its own dynamically generated home page. Note the Risk Page, which presents information on the likelihood of impacts with Earth.

http://131.114.72.13/cgi-bin/neodys/neoibo

PART 4

Space

*M*any interesting controversies arise in connection with technologies that are so new that they often sound more like science fiction than fact. Some examples are technologies that allow the exploration of outer space, the search for extraterrestrial intelligence, and genetic engineering. Such advances offer capabilities undreamed of in earlier ages, and they raise genuine, important questions about what it is to be a human being, the limits on human freedom in a technological age, and the place of humanity in the broader universe. They also raise questions of how we should respond: Should we accept the new devices and abilities offered by scientists and engineers? Or should we reject them? Should we use them to make human life safer and more secure? Or should we remain at the mercy of the heavens?

• Should We Expand Efforts to Find Near-Earth Objects?

• Is the Search for Extraterrestrial Life Doomed to Fail?

• Do Humans Belong in Space?

ISSUE 11

Should We Expand Efforts to Find Near-Earth Objects?

YES: Joseph Burns, from *Statement (for the National Research Council) before House Committee on Science* (October 3, 2002)

NO: Edward Weiler, from *Statement before House Committee on Science* (October 3, 2002)

ISSUE SUMMARY

YES: Professor of Engineering and Astronomy Joseph Burns contests that the hazards posed to life on Earth by near-Earth objects (NEOs) are great enough to justify increased efforts to detect and catalog NEOs. Scientific benefits may also be expected.

NO: Edward Weiler asserts that NASA's present efforts to detect the larger and more hazardous NEOs are adequate. It is premature to expand the program.

T homas Jefferson once said that he would rather think scientists were crazy than believe that rocks could fall from the sky. Since then, we have recognized that rocks do indeed fall from the sky. Most are quite small and do no more than make pretty streaks across the sky as they burn up in the atmosphere; they are known as meteors. Some—known as meteorites—are large enough to reach the ground and even to do damage. Every once in a while, the news reports one that crashed through a car or house roof. Very rarely, a meteorite is big enough to make a crater in the Earth's surface, much like the ones that mark the face of the Moon. An example is Meteor Crater in Arizona, almost a mile across, created some 50,000 years ago by a meteorite 150 feet in diameter. (The Meteor Crater Web site, http://www.meteorcrater.com/, includes an animation of the impact.) A more impressive impact is the one that occurred 65 million years ago; the scar has been found at Chicxulub, Mexico: The results included the extinction of the dinosaurs (as well as a great many other species). Chicxulub-scale events are very rare; a hundred million years may pass between them. Meteor Crater–scale events may occur every thousand years, releasing as much energy as a 100-megaton nuclear bomb and destroying an area the size of a city. And it has been calculated that a human being is more likely to die as the result of such an event than in an airplane crash.

It's not just Hollywood sci-fi, *Deep Impact* and *Armageddon*. Some people think we really should be worried. We should be doing our best to identify meteoroids (as they are called before they become meteors or meteorites) in space, plot their trajectories, tell when they are coming our way, and even develop ways of deflecting them before they cause enormous loss of life. In 1984, Thomas Gehrels, a University of Arizona astronomer, initiated the Spacewatch project, which aimed to identify space rocks that cross Earth's orbit. In the early 1990s, NASA workshops considered the hazards of these rocks. NASA now funds the international Spaceguard Survey, which finds about 25 new near-Earth Asteroids every month, and has identified more than 600 over 1 kilometer in diameter (1000 meters; 1.6 km equals 1 mile); none seem likely to strike Earth in the next century. See Peter Tyson, "Comet Busters," *Technology Review* (February/March 1995), Duncan Steel, *Target Earth: How Rogue Asteroids and Doomsday Comets Threaten our Planet* (Reader's Digest Association, 2000), and David Morrison, "Target Earth," *Astronomy* (February 2002). However, the news periodically issues alarming reports; in 2004, an asteroid 130 feet across looked for awhile like it would hit Earth in 2029 with the equivalent of a 10,000 megaton nuclear bomb, but improved data downgraded the warning to "near-miss"; see Govert Schilling, "The Sky Is Falling!" *Science Now* (February 7, 2005), and Guy Gugliotta, "Science's Doomsday Team vs. The Asteroids," *Washington Post* (April 9, 2005). Without the downgrade in the warning, we would have faced the serious question of whether we could devise effective methods for warding off disaster by 2029; see Russell L. Schweickart, Edward T. Lu, Piet Hut, and Clark R. Chapman, "The Asteroid Tugboat," *Scientific American* (November 2003).

Professor of engineering and astronomy Joseph Burns argues that the hazards posed to life on Earth by near-Earth objects (NEOs) are large. NEOs less than 300 meters (about 1,000 feet) in diameter can cause enormous numbers of deaths, and there is about a 1 percent chance of such a disaster in every century. Increased efforts to detect and catalog NEOs are justified. The same efforts would increase scientific knowledge of the solar system. Edward Weiler argues that only larger objects, over 1 kilometer in diameter, pose truly serious, global risks. NASA's present efforts have focused on those objects and are adequate. It is premature to expand the program before public discussion settles the question of where to set the cutoff point between NEOs "big enough" and "too small" to worry about.

 **YES**

The Threat of Near-Earth Asteroids, October 2002

Statement of Joseph Burns (for the National Research Council)

. . . [T]he Astronomy and Astrophysics community has a long history of creating, through the National Research Council (NRC), decadal surveys of their field. These surveys lay out the community's research goals for the next decade, identify key questions that need to be answered, and propose new facilities with which to conduct this fundamental research.

In April 2001, NASA Associate Administrator for Space Science Edward Weiler asked the NRC to conduct a similar survey for planetary exploration. Our report, New Frontiers in the Solar System, is the result of that activity. The Solar System Exploration Survey was conducted by an ad hoc committee of the Space Studies Board (SSB), overseen by COMPLEX. This committee was comprised of some 50 scientists, drawn from a diverse set of institutions, research areas, and backgrounds; it also received input from more than 300 colleagues. The SSE Survey had four subpanels which focused on issues pertaining to different types of solar system bodies (Inner Planets, Giant Planets, Large Satellites, and Primitive Bodies) and received direct input from COMPLEX on Mars issues and from the Committee on the Origins and Evolution of Life on issues pertaining to Astrobiology.

New Frontiers in the Solar System (the Executive Summary is appended to this statement) recommends a scientific and exploration strategy for NASA's Office of Space Science that will both enable dramatic new discoveries in this decade and position the agency to continue to make such discoveries well into the future. Your invitation indicated that I should focus on the conclusions that the SSE Survey reached in the area of Near-Earth Objects (NEOs).

Near-Earth Objects

The SSE Survey's charge from NASA included a request to summarize the extent of our current understanding of the solar system. This task was delegated to the subpanels, which in the particular case of NEOs was handled by the Primitive Bodies Panel.

From a Statement before the House Committee on Science, October 3, 2002.

Scientifically, the history of impacts on the Earth is vital for understanding how the planet evolved and how life arose. For example, it has been suggested that a majority of the water on this planet was delivered by comet impacts. A better known example of the role of impacts is the Cretaceous-Tertiary event that led to global mass extinctions, including that of the dinosaurs. Another case is the 20 megaton (MT) equivalent-energy explosion that devastated 2000 square-kilometers of pine forest in the Siberian tundra in 1908. The SSE Survey identifies the exploration of the terrestrial space environment with regards to potential hazards as a new goal for the nation's solar system exploration enterprise.

Current surveys have identified an estimated 50 percent of NEOs that have a diameter of 1 kilometer or greater and approximately 10–15 percent of objects between 0.5 and 1 km. The vast majority of these latter objects have yet to be discovered, but a statistical analysis indicates a 1% probability of impact by a 300-m body in the next century. Such an object would deliver 1000 MT of energy, cause regional devastation, and (assuming an average of 10 people per square-kilometer on Earth) result in 100,000 fatalities. The damage caused by an impact near a city or into a coastal ocean would be orders of magnitude higher. As of a year ago, 340 objects larger than a kilometer had been catalogued as Potentially Hazardous Asteroids. In addition, the number of undiscovered comets with impact potential is large and unknown.

The Primitive Bodies panel went on to state: "Important scientific goals are associated with the NEO populations, including their origin, fragmentation and dynamical histories, and compositions and differentiation. These and other scientific issues are also vital to the mitigation of the impact hazard (emphasis added), as methods of deflection of objects potentially on course for an impact with Earth are explored. Information especially relevant to hazard mitigation includes knowledge of the internal structures of near-Earth asteroids and comets, their degree of fracture and the presence of large core pieces, the fractal dimensions of their structures, and their degree of cohesion or friction."

While almost all of the SSE Survey's recommendations involved NASA flight missions, the Primitive Bodies subpanel recommended that ground-based telescopes be used to do a majority of the study of NEOs, supplemented by airborne and orbital telescopes.

A survey for NEOs demands an exacting observational strategy. To locate NEOs as small as 300 m requires a survey down to 24th magnitude (16 million times fainter than the feeblest stars that are visible to the naked eye). If images are to be taken every 10 sec to allow the sky to be studied often, the necessary capability is almost 100 times better than that of existing survey telescopes. NEOs spend only a fraction of each orbit in Earth's neighborhood, where they are most easily seen. Repeated observations over a decade would be required to explore the full volume of space populated by these objects. Such a survey would identify several hundred NEOs per night and obtain astrometric (positional) measurements on the much larger (and growing) number of NEOs that it had already discovered. Precise astrometry is needed to determine the orbital parameters of the NEOs and to assign a hazard assessment to each object. Astrometry at monthly intervals would ensure against losing track of these fast-moving objects in the months and years after discovery.

Large-Aperture Synoptic Survey Telescope In its most recent decadal survey, the Astronomy and Astrophysics community selected the proposed Large-aperture Synoptic Survey Telescope (LSST) as their third major ground-based priority. In addition, our SSE Survey chose LSST to be its top-ranked ground-based facility. Telescopes like HST and Keck peer at selected, very localized regions of the sky or study individual sources with high sensitivity. However, another type of telescope is needed to survey the entire sky relatively quickly, so that periodic maps can be constructed that will reveal not only the positions of target sources, but their time variability as well. The Large-aperture Synoptic Survey Telescope is a 6.5-m-effective-diameter, very wide field (~3 deg) telescope that will produce a digital map of the visible sky every week. For this type of survey observation, the LSST will be a hundred times more powerful than the Keck telescopes, the world's largest at present. Not only will LSST carry out an optical survey of the sky far deeper than any previous survey, but also—just as importantly—it will also add the new dimension of time and thereby open up a new realm of discovery. By surveying the sky each month for over a decade, LSST would revolutionize our understanding of various topics in astronomy concerning objects whose brightnesses vary on time scales of days to years. NEOs, which drift across a largely unchanging sky, are easily identified. The LSST could locate 90 percent of all near-Earth objects down to 300 m in size, enable computations of their orbits, and permit assessment of their threat to Earth. In addition, this facility could be used to discover and track objects in the Kuiper Belt, a largely unexplored, primordial component of our solar system. It would discover and monitor a wide variety of variable objects, such as the optical afterglows of gamma-ray bursts. In addition, it would find approximately 100,000 supernovae per year, and be useful for many other cosmological observations.

The detectors of choice for the temporal monitoring tasks would be thinned charge-coupled devices (CCDs); the requisite extrapolation from existing systems should constitute only a small technological risk. An infrared capability of a comparably wide field would be considerably more challenging but could evolve as the second phase of the telescope's operation. Instrumentation for LSST would be an ideal way to involve independent observatories with this basically public facility.

NASA/NSF Cooperation

Historically, the National Science Foundation (NSF) has built and operated ground-based telescopes, whereas NASA has done the same for space-based observatories. Although the Astronomy and Astrophysics Survey was noncommittal on who should build the LSST, the SSE Survey included a recommendation that NASA share equally with NSF in the telescope's construction and operations costs.

Such an arrangement has precedent. The SSE Survey noted that "NASA continues to play a major role in supporting the use of Earth-based optical telescopes for planetary studies. It funds the complete operations of the IRTF (InfraRed Telescope Facility), a 3-m diameter telescope located on Hawaii's Mauna Kea. In return for access to 50 percent of the observing time for non-solar-system observations, the NSF supports the development of IRTF's instrumentation. This telescope has provided vital data in support of flight missions and will continue to do so. As another example, NASA currently buys one-sixth of the observing time on the privately operated Keck 10-m telescopes. This time was purchased to test interferometric techniques in support of future spaceflight missions such as SIM (Space Interferometry Mission) and TPF (Terrestrial Planet Finder)."

The solar system exploration community is concerned that the NSF is often unwilling to fund solar system research. This is particularly unfortunate given NSF's charter to support the best science and its leadership role in other aspects of ground-based astronomy.

The shared responsibility between NASA and the NSF that we recommend is also endorsed by the more general findings last year of the NRC's Committee on the Organization and Management of Research in Astronomy and Astrophysics (COMRAA), chaired by Norman Augustine. COMRAA's report recommended that NASA continue to "support critical ground-based facilities and scientifically enabling precursor and follow-up observations that are essential to the success of space missions." COMRAA also noted that in 1980 the NSF provided most of the research grants in astronomy and astrophysics, but today NASA is the major supporter of such research.

The roles of the agencies also affect the ability of scientists to conduct a census of Near-Earth Objects. The SSE Survey commented that:

> "interestingly enough, NASA has no systematic survey-capability to discover the population distribution of the solar-system bodies. To do this, NASA relies on research grants to individual observers who must gain access to their own facilities. The large NEOs are being efficiently discovered using small telescopes for which NASA provides instrumentation funding, but all the other solar system populations—e.g., comets, Centaurs, satellites of the outer planets, and Kuiper Belt Objects—are being characterized almost entirely using non-NASA facilities. This is a major deficiency . . ."

The construction of the LSST would provide a central, federally sponsored location for such research.

LSST Costs and Survey Below 300 Meters The costs of the LSST are projected by the 2001 Astronomy and Astrophysics Survey as being $83 million for capital construction and $42 million for data processing and distribution for 5 years of operation, for a total cost of $125 million. Routine operating costs, including a technical and support staff of 20 people, are estimated at approximately $3 million per year. The LSST will be able to routinely discover and characterize NEOs down to 300 m in diameter. Increasing the sensitivity of the survey to 100 m would mean increasing the sensitivity of the telescope by a factor of ten. This may represent a "beyond the state-of-the-art" challenge to telescope builder, and certainly a much larger telescope—3 times the LSST and probably 10 to 100 times the cost unless innovative designs are found. The number of discovered objects would correspondingly increase substantially; this large data set may challenge current capabilities.

Concluding Thoughts By way of summary, let me place the LSST into the context of a robust scientific program. Systematically building an inventory of the Near-Earth Objects is crucial to an improved understanding of Earth's environment, especially to the prediction of future hazards posed to our species. It is also a necessary first step towards a rational program of NASA's exploration of these bodies with spacecraft: many of the most interesting targets may remain, as yet, undiscovered. The ability to create and play a "motion picture" of the night sky will also provide new insights in a wide variety of disciplines from cosmology to astrophysics to solar system exploration. A suitable analog might be the deepened knowledge that is obtained from dynamic movies of swirling clouds and weather patterns, as compared to an occasional static photo.

The immense volume of data from the LSST would provide a reservoir of information for numerous graduate students and researchers, as well as established scientists. Further, LSST will support flight missions—for example, identifying possible fly-by targets for a spacecraft mission to explore the Kuiper Belt. All in all, the SSE Survey committee believes that broad areas of planetary science, particularly NEO studies, would benefit very substantially from the construction of the LSST for a relatively small investment. . . .

The Threat of Near-Earth Asteroids, October 2002

Statement of Edward Weiler

NASA's NEO Program makes ground-based observations with the goal of identifying 90 percent of those NEOs that are 1 km or larger and characterizing a sample of them. This is a ten-year program, which began in 1998 and should be completed in 2008. (It should be noted that NASA had begun searching for NEOs many years before this program officially started.)

The threshold size for an asteroid striking the Earth to produce a global catastrophe is 1 km in diameter. NASA has an active program to detect such objects that could potentially strike the Earth and to identify their orbits. The best current estimates are that the total population of NEOs with diameters larger than 1 km is about 1000. The 1-km diameter limit for an NEO was set after extensive discussions within the scientific community to determine the size of an object that would likely threaten civilization. This community consensus is codified in the Spaceguard Report and in the Shoemaker Report. For comparison, the object that likely caused the extinction of the dinosaurs was in the 5–10 km range. The current survey of NEOs in that range is considered complete.

Status: NASA's NEO Search Program

As of the end of September, NASA has detected 619 NEOs with diameters larger than 1 km. We are currently discovering about 100 per year. At the present time, we have six groups which are funded by NASA's Near Earth Objects program to conduct this type of research. These groups, selected though peer review, have ten telescopes among them searching for NEOs. One of these groups just completed (and another one is about to complete) major upgrades to its facility; therefore, we expect this pace of discovery to continue, if not increase. In some cases, the search programs are not able to obtain the number of observations required to determine the orbit elements of certain objects to sufficient accuracy to fully characterize the orbital parameters. These objects require additional astrometric observations, commonly called "follow-up observations." We have also funded four investigations to obtain

From a Statement before the House Committee on Science, October 3, 2002.

astrometric follow-up observations of those objects that cannot be easily followed by the primary search programs.

Now, how well are we doing? I am happy to report that we are doing quite well; in fact, we are even a bit ahead of schedule.

There have been various reports to the effect that NASA would not reach its metric—90 percent of all the NEOs with diameters larger than 1 km—until many years after the end of 2008. However, these analyses have been based on the performance of individual search efforts, and they have tended not to use the current performance of the NEO search effort as a whole. As with most things, experience increases proficiency; therefore, we expect the rate of detection to increase. Even if we were to stay at our current rate, however, we are more than halfway to our goal of 90 percent by the end of 2008.

That does not mean we will grow complacent; we intend to continue to vigorously pursue detection of NEOs. In fact, we anticipate even better results due to technological developments such as better detector arrays, migration of existing search efforts to larger telescopes, and additional telescopes dedicated to the search program. In short, we are working to achieve both our goal and our metric and expect to be successful at both. One unanticipated result of the NEO search will be a list of over 1,000 potential candidates for future space science missions.

NASA's Future Role with Respect to NEOs

Next I would like to turn to another question. What should NASA's role be in the future? NASA is a space agency. While we are proud of our success in implementing the Congress's direction to us with regard to the search for NEOs, we do not feel that we should play a role in any follow-on search and cataloging effort unless that effort needs to be specifically space-based in nature. There are other agencies with far more expertise in ground-based observations that would be more suitable candidates to lead that portion of a future NEO endeavor.

NASA does, however, continue to have a large role to play in the scientific space exploration of asteroids. The frequent access to space for small missions offered by NASA's Discovery Program has benefited the study of asteroids and comets as no other program to date. The first in-depth study of an NEO, Eros, was performed by the NEAR-Shoemaker mission. The body of data returned by NEAR-Shoemaker was so large, and the quality of the data so high, that NEAR's database will require years of analysis. Just this year, we initiated funding for the first 17 investigations of that data. NEAR-Shoemaker's exploration of Eros will be followed by detailed exploration of two other asteroids, Vesta and Ceres, by the upcoming DAWN mission, currently scheduled to launch in 2006. There is no reason to expect that science-driven exploration of the asteroids, and of course NEOs, will not continue through the Discovery program. We believe that the critical measurements required for developing potential mitigation efforts are substantially the same as those required to achieve the pure scientific goals identified for these objects. We must be able to understand and characterize these objects before any mitigation efforts are even considered.

In addition to NEAR and DAWN, NASA has several other missions dedicated to studying comets and asteroids, such as Deep Impact and Stardust. Our total investment in understanding these bodies, both in the past and in our current FY 2003 budget run-out, is approximately $1.6 billion. That does not even take into account those spacecraft that have provided "bonus" information, such as Galileo, which found a moon orbiting asteroid Ida, and Deep Space 1, a technology demonstration mission that performed a close-up fly-by of comet Borelly. NASA deeply regrets not having the potential discoveries from the recently failed CONTOUR mission, which was to have studied Comets Encke and Schwassmann-Wachmann 3.

NASA's bold new technology initiatives, the In-Space Propulsion (ISP) Initiative and the Nuclear Systems Initiative (NSI), together offer new opportunities to enable capable new missions to NEOs early in the next decade. Improvements in solar-electric propulsion and development of solar sails are examples of new capabilities that might allow a spacecraft like NEAR-Shoemaker to visit many NEOs during a single mission rather than just one (and at the cost of a Discovery mission). If we are ever faced with the requirement to modify the motion of an NEO over time to ensure that the object will not come close to the Earth, nuclear propulsion may very well be the answer. The Nuclear Systems Initiative could address two elements in understanding the potential hazards of NEOs by: (1) providing technologies that could significantly increase our ability to identify and track NEOs, and (2) to possibly—in the future—provide sufficient power to move an Earth-intersecting object. The NSI could enable power and propulsion for an extended survey (in one mission) of multiple NEOs to determine their composition, which is a critical factor in understanding how to mitigate the risk of an Earth-intersecting object. In the future, the technologies under development by the NSI could provide us with the means to redirect the path of an Earth-intersecting asteroid, once we understand the orbital mechanics of these objects sufficiently to understand how to do this. These programs are being developed to serve a wide range of needs across NASA, but they will most certainly prove beneficial for space missions that help us to better understand and characterize NEOs.

What Should the Nation Be Doing beyond the Current Goal?

I feel that it is premature to consider an extension of our current national program to include a complete search for smaller-sized NEOs. There are several reasons for this belief. The first is that we need to have a better understanding of the true size of the population down to at least 100 m. How will we get the improved data we need on this population? We will obtain the necessary data from the existing NASA search effort for NEOs. The search program now finds about two NEOs with diameters less than 1 km for every large one (diameter greater than 1 km) that we find. In addition, we are supporting a search program which is optimized to detect smaller NEOs. We expect by the end of this decade to have a much better picture of the true size of the population, and hence, what will be required to detect all of them.

The second issue is how such a search could be most efficiently and cost-effectively implemented. Two groups that wish to build large survey systems have argued that the search goal should be extended to 300 m. NASA has at least two concerns with this proposition. First, we do not possess a non-advocate trade study to tell us how best to do such a search. For example, one issue to be addressed is whether it would be better to build one large 8-m class telescope or 2 4-m search telescopes. At these sizes, is a space-based system an option? Second, why 300m? The present limiting diameter of 1 km was the product of a broad public discussion. When we have another broad public discussion, the answer could be: "Leave the present limiting diameter as it stands." Or, perhaps the result of broad national debate on this issue would be: "Catalog the population down to 100 m." We at NASA don't know the answers to these questions, and we believe that further commitments to extend the search are simply premature at this point.

Within the Office of Space Science, the Solar System Exploration Division Director has appointed a small Science Definition Team (SDT) to consider the technical issues related to extending the search for NEOs to smaller sizes. The goal of the SDT is to evaluate what is technologically possible today. The scope of the SDT does not include consideration of any change to our present NEO search goal.

Conclusion

NASA has made impressive strides in achieving its goal of cataloging 90 percent of all Near-Earth Objects with diameters of more than 1 km and characterizing a sample of them. We are currently ahead of schedule with respect to having this effort completed in the 2008 time frame. While NASA certainly agrees that because these objects pose a potential threat to the Earth, they should be studied and understood, we respectfully defend our position that any expansion of NASA's current NEO effort is premature. Before any further effort is undertaken, we would want input from the scientific community as to how this subject should be approached, and if indeed NASA is even the proper agency to lead this type of an undertaking. . . .

POSTSCRIPT

Should We Expand Efforts to Find Near-Earth Objects?

In the debate over the risks of NEO impacts on Earth, there are a few certainties: They have happened before, they will happen again, and they come in various sizes. Many past craters mark the Earth, even though many more have been erased by plate tectonics and erosion. See Timothy Ferris, "Killer Rocks from Outer Space," *Reader's Digest* (October 2002). Ivan Semeniuk, "Asteroid Impact," *Mercury* (November/December 2002), says that, "If there is one question that best sums up the current state of thinking about the impact hazard, it is this: At what size do we need to act? In the shooting gallery that is our solar system, everyone agrees we are the target of both cannonballs and BBs. The hard part is deciding where to draw the line that separates them. For practical reasons, that line is now set at 1 kilometer. Not only are objects of this diameter a global threat (no matter where they hit, we're all affected to some degree), they are also the easiest to spot. Under a mid-1990s congressional mandate, NASA currently funds search efforts to the tune of about $3.5 million per year... 'The existing commitment to 1 kilometer and larger is to retire the risk,' says Tom Morgan, who heads NASA's NEO group. 'By the end of this decade we'll be able to tell you if any of these objects presents a threat in the foreseeable future.'" However, as Richard A. Kerr notes, "The Small Ones Can Kill You, Too," *Science* (September 19, 2003).

And if one of these objects does present a threat? In September 2002, NASA held a workshop on *Scientific Requirements for Mitigation of Hazardous Comets and Asteroids*, which concluded "that the prime impediment to further advances in this field is the lack of any assigned responsibility to any national or international governmental organization to prepare for a disruptive collision and the absence of any authority to act in preparation for some future collision mitigation attempt" and urged that "NASA be assigned the responsibility to advance this field" and "a new and adequately funded program be instituted at NASA to create, through space missions and allied research, the specialized knowledge base needed to respond to a future threat of a collision from an asteroid or comet nucleus." The results of the workshop appeared as *Mitigation of Hazardous Impacts due to Asteroids and Comets* (Cambridge University Press, 2004).

The Organization for Economic Cooperation and Development (OECD) Global Science Forum held a "Workshop on Near Earth Objects: Risks, Policies and Actions" in January 2003. It too concluded that more work is needed. In May 2005, the House Science Committee approved a bill to establish and fund a NASA program to detect and assess near-Earth asteroids and comets down to 100 meters in diameter.

Given political will and funding, what could be done if a threat were identified? There have been numerous proposals, from launching nuclear missiles to pulverize approaching space rocks to sending astronauts (or robots) to install rocket engines and deflect the rocks onto safe paths (perhaps into the sun to forestall future hazards). Several alternatives are discussed in Russell L. Schweickart, Edward T. Lu, Piet Hut, and Clark R. Chapman, "The Asteroid Tugboat," *Scientific American* (November 2003). Some possibilities are mentioned by Leon Jaroff and Dan Cray, "Whew!" *Time* (March 23, 1998). All require a stronger space program than any nation now has. Lacking such a program, knowing that a major rock is on the way would surely be little comfort. However, given sufficient notice—on the order of decades—a space program could be mobilized to deal with the threat.

ISSUE 12

Is the Search for Extraterrestrial Life Doomed to Fail?

YES: Stephen Webb, from *Where Is Everybody? Fifty Solutions to the Fermi Paradox and the Problem of Extraterrestrial Life* (Copernicus Books, 2002)

NO: Seth Shostak, from "When Will We Detect the Extraterrestrials?" *Acta Astronautica* (August 2004)

ISSUE SUMMARY

YES: Physicist Stephen Webb argues that "the one gleaming, hard fact in the whole debate [is] that we have not been visited by" extraterrestrial intelligences. The only way to reconcile this fact with everything else we know is to conclude that we are the only intelligent species around.

NO: Radio astronomer and SETI researcher Seth Shostak is more optimistic. He argues that if the assumptions behind the search are well grounded, signals of extraterrestrial origin will be detected soon, perhaps within the next generation.

In the 1960s and early 1970s, the business of listening to the radio whispers of the stars and hoping to pick up signals emanating from some alien civilization was still new. Few scientists held visions equal to Frank Drake, one of the pioneers of the search for extraterrestrial intelligence (SETI) field. Drake and scientists like him utilize radio telescopes—large, dish-like radio receiver–antenna combinations—to scan radio frequencies (channels) for signal patterns that would indicate that the signal was transmitted by an intelligent being. In his early days, Drake worked with relatively small and weak telescopes out of listening posts that he had established in Green Bank, West Virginia, and Arecibo, Puerto Rico. See Carl Sagan and Frank Drake, "The Search for Extraterrestrial Intelligence," *Scientific American* (May 1975) and Frank Drake and Dava Sobel, *Is Anyone Out There? The Scientific Search for Extraterrestrial Intelligence* (Delacorte Press, 1992).

There have been more than 50 searches for extraterrestrial radio signals since 1960. The earliest ones were very limited. Later searches have been more ambitious, culminating in the 10-year program known as the High Resolution Microwave Survey (HRMS). The HRMS, which began on Columbus Day of 1992, uses several radio telescopes and massive computers to scan 15 million radio frequencies per second. New technologies and techniques continue to make the search more efficient. See Seth Shostak et al., "The Future of SETI," *Sky & Telescope* (April 2001), and Seth Shostak, "SETI's Prospects Are Bright," *Mercury* (September/October 2002).

At the outset, many people thought—and many still think—that SETI has about as much scientific relevance as searches for Loch Ness Monsters and Abominable Snowmen. However, to Drake and his colleagues, it seems inevitable that with so many stars in the sky, there must be other worlds with life upon them, and some of that life must be intelligent and have a suitable technology and the desire to search for alien life too.

Writing about SETI in the September–October 1991 issue of *The Humanist*, physicist Shawn Carlson compares visiting the National Shrine of the Immaculate Conception in Washington, D.C., to looking up at the stars and "wondering if, in all [the] vastness [of the starry sky], there is anybody out there looking in our direction. . . . [A]re there planets like ours peopled with creatures like us staring into their skies and wondering about the possibilities of life on other worlds, perhaps even trying to contact it?" That is, SETI arouses in its devotees an almost religious sense of mystery and awe, a craving for contact with the *other*. Success would open up a universe of possibilities, add immensely to human knowledge, and perhaps even provide solutions to problems that our interstellar neighbors have already defeated.

SETI also arouses strong objections, partly because it challenges human uniqueness. Many scientists have objected that life-bearing worlds such as Earth must be exceedingly rare because the conditions that make them suitable for life as we know it—composition and temperature—are so narrowly defined. Others have objected that there is no reason whatsoever to expect that evolution would produce intelligence more than once or that, if it did, the species would be similar enough to humans to allow communication. Still others say that even if intelligent life is common, technology may not be so common, or technology may occupy such a brief period in the life of an intelligent species that there is virtually no chance that it would coincide with Earth scientists' current search. Whatever their reasons, SETI detractors agree that listening for extraterrestrial signals is futile. Ben Zuckerman, "Why SETI Will Fail," *Mercury* (September/October 2002), argues that the simple fact that we have not been visited by extraterrestrials indicates that there are probably very few ET civilizations and SETI is therefore futile.

In the selections that follow, physicist Stephen Webb represents the objections of skeptical scientists, arguing that because we have not been visited by extraterrestrials, there are probably very few ET civilizations. In fact, he says, we are probably alone. Seth Shostak defends SETI and argues that if the assumptions behind the search are reasonable, the search will succeed, perhaps within the next generation.

YES

Stephen Webb

Where Is Everybody? Fifty Solutions to the Fermi Paradox and the Problem of Extraterrestrial Life

[Enrico] Fermi was at Los Alamos in the summer of 1950. One day, he was chatting to Edward Teller and Herbert York as they walked over to Fuller Lodge for lunch. . . . Emil Konopinski joined them . . . [and] there followed a serious discussion about whether flying saucers could exceed the speed of light. Fermi asked Teller what he thought the probability might be of obtaining evidence for superluminal travel by 1960. Fermi said that Teller's estimate of one-in-a-million was too low; Fermi thought it was more like one-in-ten.

The four of them sat down to lunch, and the discussion turned to more mundane topics. Then, in the middle of the conversation and out of the clear blue, Fermi asked: "Where *is* everybody?" His lunch partners Teller, York and Konopinski immediately understood that he was talking about extraterrestrial visitors. And since this was Fermi, perhaps they realized that it was a more troubling and profound question than it first appears. York recalls that Fermi made a series of rapid calculations and concluded that we should have been visited long ago and many times over. . . .

. . . So why do we not hear from some of them? In fact, why are they not already here? If some of the civilizations are extremely long-lived, then we might expect them to colonize the Galaxy—and have done so before multicellular life even developed on Earth. The Galaxy should be swarming with extraterrestrial civilizations. Yet we see no sign of them. We should already know of their existence, but we do not. Where is everybody? *Where are they?* This is the Fermi paradox. . . .

. . . [It] was a 1975 paper by Michael Hart in the *Quarterly Journal of the Royal Astronomical Society* that sparked an explosion of interest in the paradox. Hart demanded an explanation for one key fact: there are no intelligent beings from outer space on Earth at the present time. He argued that there are four categories of explanation for this fact. First, "physical explanations," which are based on some difficulty that makes space travel unfeasible. Second, "sociological explanations," which in essence suppose that extraterrestrials have chosen not to visit Earth. Third, "temporal explanations," which suggest that ETCs [extraterrestrial civilizations] have not had time to reach us. Fourth, there are explanations arguing that perhaps they *have* been on Earth, but we do not see them now. These categories were meant to exhaust the possibilities. Hart then forcefully showed how none of these four categories provide a convincing account of the key fact, which led him to offer his own explanation: *we are the first civilization in our Galaxy.*

Hart's paper led to a vigorous debate, much of it appearing in the pages of the *Quarterly Journal.* It was a debate that anyone could enter—one of the earliest contributions came from the House of Lords at Westminster! Perhaps the most controversial offering came from Frank Tipler, in a paper with the uncompromising title "Extraterrestrial Intelligent Beings Do Not Exist." Tipler reasoned that advanced ETCs could use self-replicating probes to explore or colonize the Galaxy cheaply and in a relatively short time. The abstract to Tipler's paper sums it up: "It is argued that if extraterrestrial intelligent beings exist, then their spaceships must already be present in our Solar System." Tipler contended that the SETI program had no chance of success, and was therefore a waste of time and money. His argument poured oil on the fires of the debate and led to a further round of argument. The coolest and best summary of the arguments came from David Brin, who called the paradox the "great silence."

In 1979, Ben Zuckerman and Michael Hart organized a conference to discuss the Fermi paradox. The proceedings were published in book form, and although the volume contains a variety of views it is difficult to read it without concluding that ETCs have the means, motive and opportunity to colonize the Galaxy. The means: interstellar travel seems to be possible, if not easy. The motive: Zuckerman showed how some ETCs would be forced into interstellar travel by the death of their star, and in any case it seems a wise idea for a species to expand into space to guard against the possibility of planetary disaster. The opportunity: the Galaxy is 13 billion years old, but colonization can take place over a period of only a few million years. Yet we do not see them. If this were a murder mystery, we would have a suspect but no body.

Not everyone was struck by the force of the argument. A recent book by the mathematician Amir Aczel makes the case for the probability of extraterrestrial life being 1. The physicist Lee Smolin wrote that "the argument for the non-existence of intelligent life is one of the most curious I have ever encountered; it seems a bit like a ten-year-old child deciding that sex is a myth because he has yet to encounter it." The late Stephen Jay Gould, referring to Tipler's contention that ETCs would deploy probe technology to colonize the Galaxy, wrote that "I must confess that I simply don't know how to react to such arguments. I have enough trouble predicting the plans and reactions of people closest to me. I am usually baffled by the thoughts and accomplishments of humans in different cultures. I'll be damned if I can state with certainty what some extraterrestrial source of intelligence might do." . . .

Nevertheless, surely Hart's key fact *does* require an explanation. We have been searching for ETCs for more than 40 years. And the continuing silence, despite intensive searches, is beginning to worry even some of the most enthusiastic proponents of SETI. We observe a natural universe when we could so easily observe an artificial universe. Why? Where *is* everybody? Fermi's question still demands an answer. . . .

⌒⟨◉⟩⌒

There is just one gleaming, hard fact in the whole debate: we have not been visited by ETCs, nor have we heard from them. So far, the Universe remains silent to us. . . .

. . . [With] just one piece of evidence to play with, our biases will come to the fore. My own biases, such as I can identify them, include optimism about our future. I like to think our scientific knowledge will continue to expand and our technology to improve; I like to think mankind will one day reach the stars—first by sending messages and then later, perhaps, by sending ships. I like to think something akin to the Galaxy-spanning civilization described by Asimov in his classic *Foundation* stories might one day come to pass. But these biases collide with the Fermi paradox: if *we* are going to colonize the Galaxy, why have *they* not already done so? They have had the means, the motive and the opportunity to establish colonies, yet they appear not to have done so. Why? . . .

[The] only position that is consistent with the observed absence of extra-terrestrials and that at the same time supports my prejudices—the only resolution of the Fermi paradox that makes sense to me—is that we are alone.

⌒⟨◉⟩⌒

If you look up at the sky on a clear moonless night and gaze with the naked eye at the myriads of stars and the vastness of space, it is difficult to believe we might be alone. We are too small and the Universe is too big for this to make sense. But appearances can be deceptive: even under ideal observing conditions you are unlikely to see more than about 3000 stars, and few of those would provide conditions hospitable to our form of life. The gut reaction we perhaps all feel when we look at the night sky—that there *must* be intelligent life somewhere out there—is not a good guide. We have to be guided by reason, not gut reaction, when discussing this matter. Well . . . reason tells us there are a few hundred billion stars in our Galaxy alone, and perhaps a hundred billion galaxies in the Universe. Just one sentient species when there is such an immense number of places life might get started? Come *on* . . . surely I cannot be serious?

When discussing some of the different types of paradox [earlier in the book], I noted Rapoport's observation that the shock of a paradox may compel us to discard an old (perhaps comfortable) conceptual framework. I believe the Fermi paradox provides a shock that forces us to examine the widespread notion that the vast number of planets in existence is sufficient to guarantee the existence of extraterrestrial intelligent life. In fact, we need not be too surprised. The Drake equation is a product of several terms. If one of those terms is zero, then the product of the Drake equation will be zero; if several of the terms are small, then the product of the Drake equation will be very small. We will be alone. . . .

It is usual at this point to pick some numbers favorable to one's position, plug them into the Drake equation, and then put forward the required result. I would prefer to present here a more pictorial approach.

❧❦❧

When I was a schoolboy, I was fascinated by the Sieve of Eratosthenes. Eratosthenes was a Greek astronomer and mathematician, famed for being head of the Library at Alexandria and for being the first to provide an accurate measurement of Earth's circumference. He also developed a technique—his "sieve"—for finding all prime numbers less than some given number N. Primes—numbers evenly divisible only by themselves and 1—are extremely important in mathematics; they are like atoms, from which we can compose all other numbers through multiplication. If you are given a number at random, it can be difficult to know whether it is composite or prime. The Sieve of Eratosthenes is a technique for sifting out the composite numbers and leaving only the prime numbers standing.

Suppose you are a Greek mathematician who wants to find all primes less than or equal to 100. First, you take a sheet of papyrus and write down the numbers from 1 to 100. The number 1 is special, so ignore it. The number 2 is prime so leave it; but go through the list and cross out all its multiples: 4, 6, 8, . . . 100. Repeat the process, using the next smallest remaining number, 3; leave it because it is prime, but cross out its multiples all the way up to 99. Continue until you reach the end of the list. Remarkably quickly, you find all the numbers up to 100 have been deleted—except for the 25 prime numbers, which are still standing. Even for a computer, the Sieve of Eratosthenes is the quickest way of finding all primes less than about 10^8.

As a schoolboy, I was intrigued by the way the Sieve caught more and more of the large numbers. The technique was inexorable: on large grids I found myself chopping down number after number. Since the distribution of primes thins out quickly the higher you count, there are long stretches where all the numbers have been crossed out—numbers that have failed to make it through the Sieve.

I picture something similar happening with the Fermi paradox. Imagine writing down a grid of numbers, from 1 to 1000,000,000,000, with each number representing an individual planet in the Galaxy. (I arrive at this number by multiplying the number of stars in the Galaxy, which is about 10^{11}, with an assumed average of 10 planets per star. In fact, the number of stars is probably greater than this, with some estimates suggesting that our Galaxy contains as many as 400 billion stars. On the other hand, the average number of planets per star is likely to be less than 10. So although a figure of 10^{12} planets is a rough guess, it may not be too wrong—and anyway, this hardly matters when all the other numbers in the problem are so vague.) We assign Earth the number 1, since the Earth is special: it is the only planet on which we *know* intelligent life exists. Now start applying a sieve—let us call it the Sieve of

Fermi. (The process I describe here is not meant to be the *only* way of working the numbers. You may prefer different numerical values for the quantities I describe, but the process shows why we should not be surprised if we discover that we are alone.)

⟨◦⟩

Step 1. [Earlier] we briefly discussed the notion of a galactic habitable zone (GHZ) in which a star must reside before it can give rise to a viable planetary system. A recent suggestion is that the GHZ contains only 20% of the stars in the Galaxy. So cross out those numbers corresponding to planets not orbiting a star in the GHZ: with 10 planets per star, $2 \quad 10^{10}$ planets remain. Now make a second application of the Sieve.

Step 2. The bright O and B stars die too quickly for life to evolve around them; the dull K and M stars are too miserly with their energy for life to prosper. For life *as we know it,* we need consider only stars like the Sun. . . . ([This] assumption may be an expression of chauvinism—or a failure of scientific imagination. But I think it is the best assumption we can make at this time.) Only about 5% of stars in our Galaxy are like the Sun; cross out numbers corresponding to planets not orbiting a Sun-like star, and 10^8 planets remain.

Step 3. Life as we know it requires a terrestrial planet to remain in the continuously habitable zone (CHZ) for billions of years. . . . My own guess is that only 1% of planets will be both suitable for life and remain in a CHZ for billions of years. You may think a different figure is in order here (and one could argue for higher or lower figures), but 1% seems reasonable to me. So cross out numbers corresponding to planets that do not remain in a CHZ: 10^6 planets remain.

Step 4. Of the million planets that orbit in the CHZ of a Sun-like star that is itself in the GHZ, how many are home to life? If you believe the genesis of life is exceptionally rare . . . , then the answer is: none. If you believe a special set of circumstances is required, such as life originating on a planet like Mars and then being transported via impact ejecta to an Earth-like planet . . . , then the answer is: not many. I prefer to believe that life is a probable occurrence: that if conditions are suitable, then there is a good chance of cells evolving. Let us say that the chance is 0.5. Cross out numbers corresponding to planets on which life does not arise, and 5×10^5 planets remain. Half a million planets with life!

Step 5. The Universe is a dangerous place. . . . On many planets, life may be snuffed out—or at least prevented from evolving into complex life-forms—by some disaster. My guess is that as many as 20% of planets may suffer such a fate. (This *is* just a guess, and it may be an overestimate.) So cross out numbers corresponding to planets on which disaster strikes: 10^5 planets remain.

Step 6. . . . Earth's system of plate tectonics was important in the development of life . . . and . . . the Moon [played] a role. . . . If both these factors are *necessary* for the evolution of complex life, then the number of planets with the sentient species we are searching for may be small. However, although I believe these phenomena *are* important in some ways, I have no feel for the numbers involved. So I will ignore these factors, and at this stage of the sifting process all the planets make it through: 10^5 planets still remain.

Step 7. Cross out numbers corresponding to planets where life never evolves beyond the prokaryotic grade. . . . The development of the modern eukaryotic cell took aeons on Earth, which perhaps indicates that this step is far from inevitable. No one knows what fraction of planets with prokaryotes will go on to host complex multicellular life-forms; my own estimate of one in ten may be *very* generous. We are left with 10^4 numbers—ten thousand planets possessing complex multicellular life. Does that mean the Galaxy contains ten thousand ETCs? Unfortunately not, because we must make several further applications of the Sieve before we arrive at the number of species *with whom we can communicate*. Let us combine all these into one last pass through the sifting process.

Step 8. Cross out numbers corresponding to planets on which advanced life-forms do not develop tool use and the ability to continuously improve their technology. . . . Cross out numbers corresponding to planets on which advanced life-forms do not develop the type of abstract high-level intelligence we are familiar with. . . . Finally, and to my mind crucially, cross out numbers corresponding to planets on which advanced life-forms do not develop complex, grammatical language. . . . How many planets remain? Of course, no one knows; it is impossible to assign accurate probabilities to these matters. My feeling is that many of these developments were far from inevitable. The feeling arises because, of the 50 billion speciation events in the history of our planet, only one led to language—and language is the key that enabled all our other achievements to take place. My own guess, then, is that none of the planets make it through this final sifting process.

After applying the Sieve of Fermi I believe that *all* grid numbers will be crossed out, except the number 1. Only Earth remains. We are alone.

⋯⊙⋯

I believe that the Fermi paradox tells us mankind is the only sapient, sentient species in the Galaxy. (We are probably also unique in our Local Group of galaxies, since many Local Group galaxies are unlikely to possess a GHZ. Perhaps we are even unique in the whole Universe—although the finite speed of light means ETCs could now exist in very distant galaxies without us yet being aware of them.) Yet the Galaxy need not be sterile. The picture I have is of a Galaxy in which simple life is not uncommon; complex, multicellular life is much rarer, but not vanishingly rare. There may be tens of thousands of exceptionally interesting biospheres out there in the Galaxy. But only *one* planet—Earth—has intelligent life-forms.

Such a picture is often criticized as violating the Principle of Mediocrity. The picture seems to suggest that Earth, and mankind, is special. Is this not the height of arrogance?

Paradoxically, at least to my mind, the expectation that other sentient species *must* be out there itself smacks of arrogance. Or rather, it achieves the tricky feat of being both self-important and self-effacing at the same time. At the core of this expectation is the belief that *human* adaptations, attributes such as creativity, and general intelligence, that we think important, are qualities to which other Earth organisms aspire and alien creatures may possess in even more abundance. Allow us a few more million years, so the logic seems to go, and we might evolve into the cognitively, technologically and spiritually superior beings that already exist out there. But the converse of this position is surely false. Give chimps another few million years, so the reasoning goes, and they too will be as intelligent and creative as us. But why should they be? Chimpanzees are good at being chimpanzees; dolphins are good at being dolphins; elephants are good at being elephants. . . . Rather than patronizing these species for not exhibiting *human* characteristics, we should respect them on their own terms for earning a living in a harsh world that cares not whether they live or die.

On the other hand it is undeniable that mankind *is* profoundly different from every other species on Earth. We alone have language, a high level of self-consciousness, and a moral sense. We *are* special. But surely our uniqueness could not have arisen by mere chance, by the blind and random groping of evolution, could it? Well, why not?

As Stephen Jay Gould pointed out in a delightful analogy, we can account for any growth in the complexity of living organisms through a drunkard's walk effect. Imagine a drunk leaning against a wall. A few meters to his right is a gutter. If the drunk takes random equal-sized steps to his left or to his right, then he *inevitably* ends up in the gutter. No force propels him to his right; he moves randomly, and at any time he is as likely to move to his left as to his right. But the wall eventually stops his leftward motion; over time, there is only one direction in which to move. Eventually, completely by chance, the drunk stumbles into the gutter. The same effect can explain any advance we might observe in the complexity of organisms. At one end we have a wall of minimum complexity that organisms can possess and still be alive. This wall is where life began, and where most life on Earth remains. Over time, evolution tinkers with more advanced organisms; when life itself was young, that was the only available possibility—evolution could not try out simpler designs, because its path was blocked by the wall of minimum complexity. Some of the new designs worked, in the sense that the organisms were adapted well enough in their immediate environments to survive long enough to reproduce. And so evolution staggered on, like a blind drunk, tentatively producing organisms of greater complexity. After almost 4 billion years of random tinkering, we end up with the living world we see today. But there was nothing *inevitable* about the process; the purpose of evolution was not to produce us. Play the tape of history again, and there is no reason to suppose *Homo sapiens*—or any equivalent sentient species—would play any role at all.

Many eminent scientists argue that Mind is in some way predestined in this Universe. That far from being the outcome of chance, Mind is an inevitable outcome of deep laws of self-complexity. They argue that, over aeons, organisms will inevitably self-complexify and form a "ladder of progress": prokaryote to eukaryote to plants to animals to intelligent species like us. It is a comforting idea, but I know of no definite evidence in its favor, and I believe the silence of the Universe argues against it.

The famous French biologist Jacques Monod wrote that "evolution is chance caught on the wing." Even more evocatively, he wrote that "Man at last knows he is alone in the unfeeling immensity of the Universe, out of which he has emerged only by chance." It is a melancholy thought. I can think of only one thing sadder: if the only animals with self-consciousness, the only species that can light up the Universe with acts of love and humor and compassion, were to extinguish themselves through acts of stupidity. If we survive, we have a Galaxy to explore and make our own. If we destroy ourselves, if we ruin Earth before we are ready to leave our home planet . . . well, it could be a long, long time before a creature from another species looks up at its planet's night sky and asks: "Where *is* everybody?"

NO

Seth Shostak

When Will We Detect the Extraterrestrials?

Abstract

It has been more than four decades since the first, modern SETI experiment. Many hundreds of star systems have been observed in the radio over wide bandwidth and with impressive sensitivity, and the entire sky has been surveyed in a more restricted mode several times. Optical SETI experiments are underway, and have already scrutinized several thousand nearby stars, looking for nanosecond light pulses.

Still, there is no confirmed signal detection. Given the anticipated improvement in both telescopes and digital electronics applied to SETI, what is the time scale for making such a discovery? In this paper we investigate the rate of stellar surveillance by targeted radio SETI experiments for the foreseeable future, and conclude that it is likely that—if the principal assumptions underlying modern SETI are reasonable—a detection will occur within a single generation.

Introduction

When will SETI succeed is a perennial question which does not, and some would say, cannot, engender reliable answers[*]. The search has a long history compared with historical exploration efforts, which were typically a decade or so in length—Columbus' four voyages extended over a dozen years, and Cook's reconnaissance of the South Pacific (three voyages) spanned eleven years. In contrast, the first SETI experiment was more than forty years ago (Project Ozma). As has been pointed out, the searches since 1960 have been quite intermittent, and amount to less than two years of continuous observation at sensitivities and spectral coverage comparable to today's experiments. Nonetheless, many SETI researchers are inclined to make the Copernican assumption that our temporal location in the search for signals is mediocre,

---

[*]To avoid the ambiguity which some researchers ascribe to the word "success" in SETI, we define it as the unambiguous detection of an artificial, extraterrestrial signal.

and that another few decades, or thereabouts, will be necessary for success. Others speak of SETI as a multi-generational project, and encourage a mindset sympathetic to the "long haul." It is the author's own experience that the most common response by scientists engaged in SETI, when queried as to how long success will take, is to answer with the approximate number of years until their own retirement.

Given the myriad uncertainties of the SETI enterprise, is there any reason to believe that a better prediction could be made, or are such "gut feelings" the best we can hope for? It is the purpose of this brief paper to offer a somewhat more quantitative estimate of when SETI might succeed, based on typical assumptions made by the SETI researchers themselves. Of course, these assumptions could be grossly in error, but the merit of this approach is that the timescales presented here are congruent with SETI's own postulates. To the extent that the arguments made for conducting today's SETI experiments are credible, then the sort of predictions presented here of when a signal might be found are similarly worthy of consideration.

Approach

As for any discovery enterprise, the time required to find a sought-for phenomenon depends on (a) the frequency with which it occurs, and (b) the speed of the reconnaissance. For SETI searches, the first is, crudely, the number of contemporaneous signal generators (transmitters, if you will), and the second is the rapidity with which our telescopes can survey the sky (or, for targeted search strategies, likely locations on the sky) using spectral coverage and sensitivity adequate to find one of these transmitters.

Since the inception of modern SETI, reckoning the number of celestial transmitters has been done using the Drake Equation. The equation computes N, the number of contemporaneous, galactic transmitting sites, as the product of the rate at which intelligent societies arise and the length of time they remain in the transmitting state. As noted, these computations are restricted to our own Galaxy, on the assumption that intelligence in other galaxies would not have the incentive to send signals (or provoke replies) that would be millions of years in transit. In addition, some note that intergalactic messaging, even from nearby nebulae, would require untenable power levels: hundreds to millions of times higher than required for communication over typical intragalactic distances. These arguments have not been considered overly persuasive however, since a number of searches for extragalactic transmitters have been made.

Of possibly greater consequence is the Drake Equation's assumption that searches should be directed to stellar systems capable of hosting Earth-like worlds. Interstellar travel is difficult but not impossible, and it's unclear whether truly advanced intelligences would remain exclusively, or even principally, confined to the solar system of their birth. If migration away from the home star is common to technological intelligence, then targeted SETI searches, which are the most sensitive, could miss the most advanced (and possibly the most easily detected) transmitters.

Number of Stars to Search

With these caveats in mind, we begin by taking a conservative position, and consider the number of (galactic) transmitters predicted by Drake's Equation. It is not the provenance of this paper to evaluate the individual terms of this equation; we are only interested in their product, N. A compilation of published estimates assembled by Dick yields a (logarithmic) average of N ~ 10^5 – 10^6. (We note that one of Dick's compiled estimates is N = 0.003, which, if correct, would mean that it is overwhelmingly likely that there is nothing and no one to find. Among the SETI research community, this is obviously a minority view.) Drake himself is more conservative, and suggests N ~ 10^4. In the discussion that follows, we adopt a range of values for N of 10^4 to 10^6.

With this range estimate for N, and assuming a disk galaxy with diameter of ~90,000 light-years and half-power disk thickness (locally) of ~1,000 light-years, we can conclude that the nearest transmitter is 200–1,000 light-years away.

How many suitable targets lie within this distance? There are ~10^{11} stars in the Galaxy. Traditionally, 5–10% of these have been considered preferred candidates for harboring intelligence: these comprise, roughly speaking, single F, G or K-type stars at least a few billion years old. The major groups excluded by this historical choice include multiple stars (approximately half of all stars) and M-dwarfs (about 90% of stars.) However, recent research has shown that both close double stars and those that are widely separated (tens of AU or more) could host planets in stable orbits. M-dwarfs are presently being reconsidered as SETI targets. It might soon be concluded that only short-lived, massive stars (types A and earlier) can be reliably excluded *ab initio* as SETI targets. Since these comprise only ~1% of all stars, this would mean that virtually the entire stellar complement of the Milky Way would qualify for SETI scrutiny.

However, foreseeable astronomical discoveries may once again narrow the range of interesting stars. The current search for extrasolar planets has shown that ~10% of solar-type stars have detectable worlds, but these are skewed in favor of stars that have higher metallicities. This suggests an obvious target selection criterion. In addition, new space-based interferometers (e.g., NASA's Terrestrial Planet Finder and ESA's Darwin) proposed for deployment in a decade's time will allow not only the direct imaging of Earth-sized worlds, but spectral analyses of their atmospheres. Such techniques could tell us not only which star systems host suitable planets, but could pinpoint worlds that evidence the spectral signatures of life. And, of course, it's still possible that a deeper investigation of the conditions of planets around M-dwarfs could serve to reliably eliminate this very numerous stellar class from consideration.

Consequently, and mindful of this expected progress in our understanding of extrasolar planets, we assume that: (1) for the present decade, all galactic stars remain qualified SETI targets. (2) In the following decade, half of all unobserved stars can be eliminated *a priori* from our SETI target lists, and (3) in the third decade, 90% of unobserved stars can be eliminated. This is, we propose, a conservative projection of progress in choosing which star systems to observe. Indeed, today's experiments often have more restrictive target lists than we are projecting for 2020 and beyond.

Rate of Target Scrutiny

Having estimated (a) the number of galactic transmitters, and (b) the fraction of star systems that need to be searched, we need only consider the rate at which the search is conducted in order to arrive at our goal: an estimate for when a signal will be found.

We first consider radio searches. Note that large swaths of the celestial sphere have been examined in so-called Sky Survey SETI experiments. The failure (so far) of these experiments to discover a signal, assuming such signals exist, could be due to (a) insufficient sensitivity (note that such sky surveys are typically at least an order-of-magnitude less sensitive than targeted searches, which means that the volume of sky sampled at any given sensitivity level is less by a factor of >60), (b) inadequate spectral coverage, or (c) an inability to monitor specific locations for more than a few seconds, with no facility for making immediate follow-up observations. This precludes detection of all but fully continuous signals.

Targeted searches moderate these shortcomings, but have the disadvantage of being a very slow reconnaissance. This is principally due to the fact that the large telescopes favored for SETI research are only intermittently available. The total number of star systems surveyed to date by the SETI Institute's premier radio search, Project Phoenix (which uses the Arecibo radio telescope), is ~500.

This slow pace of targeted radio searches is about to change. The Allen Telescope Array (ATA), a joint project of the SETI Institute and the University of California at Berkeley, will be a highly sophisticated radio antenna that can be used full-time to make SETI observations. It is anticipated that this instrument will be completed within the current decade. This immediately increases by an order of magnitude the amount of telescope time available for the Institute's targeted searches. In addition, an international consortium is planning the construction of an even larger telescope, the Square Kilometer Array (SKA). If built, this instrument could also be partially dedicated to SETI observations. For the purposes of this paper, we assume that this instrument will double the speed of SETI reconnaissance beginning in the (rather uncertain) year of 2015.

Project Phoenix surveys approximately 50–60 stellar systems annually. The ATA will not only have the benefit of ten times as much observing time as this effort, but will also incorporate multiple beams that allow the simultaneous observation of at least three star systems. In addition, efficiencies in follow-up and wider instantaneous spectral coverage will add at least another factor of 2–3 speed improvement. At a minimum, we can say that, once completed, the ATA will increase the rapidity with which nearby stars are checked for signals by at least two orders of magnitude. In its first year, it will observe considerably more stellar systems than the total investigated by Project Phoenix. We will (conservatively) assume this number to be 1,000 systems, applicable to the year 2006.

The ATA is conceived as an instrument whose capabilities can be expanded as the cost of digital computation continues to decline. According to Moore's Law, a fact-of-life in the field of computing hardware for three decades, the density of transistors on commercially available chips doubles every 18 months. In more practical terms, this means that the cost of computing is halved each 1-1/2 years. The speed (not necessarily the efficacy) of SETI experiments has historically followed this law. . . .

We can expect, therefore, that at least the speed of stellar scrutiny using the ATA will grow at this exponential rate, at least so long as Moore's Law continues to hold. How long might that be? Various pundits, including Moore himself, point to the fact that the further exploitation of silicon technology will likely hit a physical "wall" at which the dimensions of the transistors become nearly molecular in size. An additional (and perhaps more formidable) barrier to the continued reign of this law is the economic cost of new fabrication facilities and even of the chips themselves. On the other hand, foreseeing this technological barrier has stimulated research into optical and quantum computing, and these approaches are expected by many to not only sustain the pace of improvement, but perhaps to accelerate it.

For the purposes of this paper, we adopt widespread industry predictions that Moore's Law in its current form will continue to hold until 2015. Thereafter, we conservatively assume a decrease by half: doubling of computational power per dollar will take 36 months, rather than 18. The speed of SETI reconnaissance is postulated to follow this technological growth.

Having considered at some length the speed and expected improvements in radio SETI searches, we note that several optical SETI experiments are also underway. These look for short ($\leq 10^{-9}$ sec) bursts of photons that could be produced by, for example, a pulsed laser deliberately targeting our solar system. While optical SETI experiments are still relatively new, several thousand star systems have already been observed, and an instrument dedicated to an optical sky survey of the two-thirds of the sky visible from the northern hemisphere is currently under construction.

Despite these encouraging developments, we will not incorporate them into our estimate of when extraterrestrial intelligence will be found. This is because of the very real possibility that optical signals might be either highly intermittent or sent to only small numbers of targets. However, with not-unreasonable assumptions, optical SETI might succeed very soon. Consider a simple example: suppose that an extraterrestrial beacon is set up to serially target all $\sim 10^{11}$ galactic star systems, briefly illuminating their inner solar systems with a burst of nanosecond pulses once every 24 hours. (This brute-force approach would provide each star with a daily kilobit of data, which might be adequate to serve as a "pointer" to other information being served up by this transmitting society.) The observation time per beam for the planned Harvard-Princeton optical sky survey is ≥ 48 seconds, so that the chance of a detection for every sweep of the northern sky (estimated to take 150 days) is $\sim 3 \times 10^{-4}$ N, or >1 for all our estimates for N.

This sunny assessment assumes that all transmitters are detectable by the sky survey. In fact, optical searches for signals from star systems at great distance need to be sensitive in the infrared to defeat the attenuating effect of interstellar dust. Such systems are not yet operational, as they must be space-based. However, there is no technical reason to doubt that they could be deployed within a decade or two. On the other hand, very low transmitter duty cycles may dictate that an effective optical SETI search will require the use of multiple, or possibly all-sky, detectors. Given the newness of optical SETI, and the lack of a body of historical "assumptions" regarding optical signaling, we will not factor such searches into our estimate of when a SETI detection will be made. This is obviously a conservative approach, assuming that optical SETI has any chance at all to succeed.

When a Detection Will Take Place

We now have in hand the requisite parameters to estimate the likely date of a (radio) SETI detection. . . . [We can plot] the number of targeted star systems observed using the ATA with, eventually, the addition of the SKA. . . . [We can then calculate] the volume of space (specified by a maximum distance) in which we've observed all suitable target star systems [and date when we will have observed enough star systems to expect successful SETI. If $N = 10^6$, the date will be about 2015. If $N = 10^4$, the date will be about 2027.] . . .

We remark that this span of dates for a predicted SETI detection extends less than two dozen years forward. Although SETI searches are sometimes referred to as multigenerational projects, our estimate suggests that this isn't the case: success is within the foreseeable future. Among other things, this justifies the efforts being made to plan for a detection, as well as to consider society's likely reaction and what would be a suitable response (if any).

We have tried to make conservative assumptions in this presentation. In particular, a reconnaissance of extrasolar planets, which would chart out their size, orbit, and whether or not they evidence spectral biomarkers, will eventually tightly focus the interest of SETI researchers, reducing (substantially, one assumes) the number of suitable target systems. We have only made a crude correction for this highly likely development. We have also made no assumption that SETI observations, particularly those that reach beyond a few hundred light-years, will concentrate their attentions on the galactic plane, thereby increasing the efficiency of the search.

While we have reckoned on an exponential improvement in technology that governs SETI search speed over the next two-and-a-half decades, this extrapolation is based on four decades in which this has been demonstrably true. To be on the safe side, we have assumed a slowing of this growth beginning in 2015. Finally, we have taken no account of the likelihood that a detection will be made with radio sky surveys, or using optical SETI techniques.

On the other hand, there are many possible reasons why our assessment that a detection will be made within a generation might be wrong. We have not considered the luminosity function or duty cycle of extraterrestrial transmitters, but have instead assumed that the N transmitters estimated by the Drake Equation are all detectable by the ATA and SKA. We have not speculated on the possibility that the frequency coverage of our telescopes is inadequate, nor that the signal types to which they are sensitive are the wrong ones. And, indeed, we do not consider that physical laws of which we are still unaware might dictate a completely different approach to interstellar signaling. And, of course, our range of estimates for N are only considered opinion—and some of that opinion avers that *no* other contemporary, sentient galactic societies exist.

Nonetheless, we reiterate that the intention of this exercise is to improve upon existing "gut feeling" speculation as to when SETI might expect a detection. While there are a myriad uncertainties attendant upon our estimate that this will occur within two dozen years, we have made this prediction using the assumptions adopted by the SETI research community itself. This community builds equipment and uses strategies that it reckons are adequate to find an extraterrestrial signal. It does this based on more than four decades of thought as to how best to prove the presence of extraterrestrial sentience. If such analyses are well grounded, then such proof will not be long in coming.

POSTSCRIPT

Is the Search for Extraterrestrial Life Doomed to Fail?

If the universe is full of intelligent species, why haven't they shown up yet? As Stephen Webb notes, this is the Fermi Paradox. The idea is that at least some of those species should have been around for quite a long time, and they have had plenty of time to spread.

So why haven't they shown up? Are we in fact alone? Or first? Are the conditions that lead to life and intelligence rare? Are there aliens living in disguise amongst us? Or are we quarantined? Reservationed? Zooed? Or maybe there's nobody there at all—not even us! (Sure, that could be it—if we are just simulations in some cosmic computer.) In his book, Webb describes Fermi and his paradox in more detail and offers a variety of answers that have been suggested—most seriously, some a bit tongue-in-cheek—for why the search has not succeeded. His own opinion is on the pessimistic side.

The SETI community, however, remains convinced that their effort is worthwhile. *SETI 2020: A Roadmap for the Search for Extraterrestrial Intelligence* (SETI Press, SETI Institute, 2002) is the report of the Search for Extraterrestrial Intelligence (SETI) Science and Technology Working Group, which between 1997 and 1999 developed a plan for the SETI effort through 2020, which will center on multi-antenna arrays, improved multi-channel scanning, and initial efforts to look for infrared and optical signals. The book provides plentiful details, as well as a brief survey of SETI history, the science that backs up the idea that SETI is worth attempting, and the technology that makes SETI even remotely possible.

Naomi Lubick, "An Ear to the Stars," *Scientific American* (November 2002), describes the SETI career of Jill Tarter and discusses new technology being developed for the search. The Terrestrial Planet Finder is discussed by Ray Jayawardhana, "Searching for Alien Earths," *Astronomy* (June 2003). The continuing determination and optimism of the SETI community is described by Richard A. Kerr, "No Din of Alien Chatter in Our Neighborhood," *Science* (February 20, 2004). See also Seth Shostak, "Listening for a Whisper," *Astronomy* (September 2004).

What if SETI succeeds? Frank Drake noted in *Is Anyone Out There? The Scientific Search for Extraterrestrial Intelligence* (Delacorte Press, 1992) that positive results would have to be reported to everyone, at once, in order to prevent attempts to suppress or monopolize the discovery. Albert A. Harrison, "Confirmation of ETI: Initial Organizational Response," *Acta Astronautica* (August 2003), focuses on the need for a response to success but he is skeptical that an effective response is possible; he says, "Foresight and advance preparation are among the steps that organizations may take to prepare for contact, but conservative values, skepticism towards SETI, and competing organizational priorities make serious preparation unlikely." Should our response include sending an answer back to the source of whatever radio signals we detect? H. Paul Schuch, "The Search for Extraterrestrial Intelligence," *Futurist* (May/June 2003), suggests that there may be dangers in such a move. On the other hand, a few nonscientists have begun to consider the implications of successful contact. See, for instance, Thomas Hoffman, "Exomissiology: The Launching of Exotheology," *Dialog: A Journal of Theology* (Winter 2004).

Want to help? Look into the SETI@Home project (http://www.seticlassic.ssl.berkeley.edu). Data collected from radio telescopes are distributed to home computers (4.5 million at last count) for analysis by software that runs in the background. See David P. Anderson, Jeff Cobb, Eric Korpela, Matt Lebofsky, and Dan Werthimer, "SETI@Home," *Communications of the ACM* (November 2002). SETI@Home and other efforts have turned up a few "tantalizing signals"; T. Joseph W. Lazio and Robert Naeye discuss them in "Hello? Are You Still There?" *Mercury* (May/June 2003).

ISSUE 13

Do Humans Belong in Space?

YES: William Tucker, from "The Sober Realities of Manned Space Flight," *The American Enterprise* (December 2004)

NO: Steven Weinberg, from "The Wrong Stuff," *New York Review of Books* (April 8, 2004)

ISSUE SUMMARY

YES: Journalist William Tucker argues that the question is not whether we should pursue the mysteries of space, nor even whether we should send people into space, but whether we should spend vast amounts of money to do so.

NO: Physicist and Nobel laureate Steven Weinberg argues that nothing needs doing in space that cannot be done without human presence. Until we find something that does need humans on the scene, there is no particular reason to send humans—at great expense—into space.

T he dream of conquering space has a long history. The pioneers of rocketry—the Russian Konstantin Tsiolkovsky (1857–1935) and the American Robert H. Goddard (1882–1945)—both dreamed of exploring other worlds, although neither lived long enough to see the first artificial satellite, the Soviet *Sputnik*, go up in 1957. That success sparked a race between America and the Soviet Union to be the first to achieve each step in the progression of space exploration. The next steps were to put dogs (the Soviet Laika was the first), monkeys, chimps, and finally human beings into orbit. Communications, weather, and spy satellites were designed and launched. And on July 20, 1969, the U.S. Project Apollo program landed the first men on the moon.

There were a few more *Apollo* landings, but not many. The United States had achieved its main political goal of beating the Soviets to the moon and, in the minds of the government, demonstrating American superiority. Thereafter, the United States was content to send automated spacecraft (computer-operated robots) to observe Venus, Mars, and the rings of Saturn; to land on Mars and study its soil; and even to carry recordings of Earth's sights and sounds past the distant edge of the solar system, perhaps to be retrieved in the distant future by intelligent life from some other world. (Those recordings are attached to the

Voyager spacecraft, launched in 1977; published as a combination of CD, CD-ROM, and book, *Murmurs of Earth: The Voyager Interstellar Record,* it is now long out of print.) Humans have not left near-Earth orbit for two decades, even though space technology has continued to develop. The results of this development include communications satellites, space shuttles, space stations, and independent robotic explorers such as the *Mariners* and *Vikings* and—landing on Mars in January 2004—the rovers *Spirit* and *Opportunity* (http://marsrovers. jpl.nasa.gov/overview/). In the same month, President George W. Bush announced a bold plan to send humans to the moon and Mars, beginning as soon as 2015. See James A. Van Allen, "Is Human Spaceflight Obsolete?" *Issues in Science and Technology* (Summer 2004). Skeptics were quick to express themselves; see Andrew Lawler, "How Much Space for Science?" *Science* (January 30, 2004), and Robert L. Park, "Sending Astronauts to Mars: A Quaint, Costly, Needless Proposal," *Chronicle of Higher Education* (March 5, 2004).

Why has human space exploration gone no further to date? One reason is that robots are now extremely capable. Although some robot spacecraft have failed partially or completely, there have been many grand successes that have added enormously to humanity's knowledge of Earth and other planets. Another is money: Lifting robotic explorers into space is expensive, but lifting people into space—along with all the food, water, air, and other supplies necessary to keep them alive for the duration of a mission—is much more expensive. And there are many people in government and elsewhere who cry that there are many better ways to spend the money on Earth.

Still another reason for the reduction in human space travel seems to be the fear that astronauts will die in space. This point was emphasized by the explosion on takeoff of the space shuttle *Challenger* in January 1986, which killed seven astronauts and froze the entire shuttle program for over two and a half years, and reinforced by the breakup of *Columbia* on entry February 1, 2003. After the latter event, the public reaction included many calls for an end to such risky, expensive enterprises. See Jerry Grey, "*Columbia*—Aftermath of a Tragedy," *Aerospace America* (March 2003); John Byron, "Is Manned Space Flight Worth It?" *Proceedings* (of the U.S. Naval Institute) (March 2003) (and Richard H. Truly's response in the May issue); and "Manned or Unmanned into Space?" *USA Today* (February 26, 2003), among many others.

Journalist William Tucker argues that space travel will come eventually. The question is not whether we should pursue the mysteries of space, nor even whether we should send people into space, but whether we should spend vast amounts of money to do so. It may be better to wait for technological advance to bring the price down, or to leave it to the private sector. Physicist and Nobel laureate Steven Weinberg argues that nothing needs doing in space that cannot be done without human presence. Until we find something that does need humans on the scene, there is no particular reason to send humans—at great expense—into space. Indeed, the president's Mars initiative may prove to be no more than a ploy to look visionary and force later presidents to face financial realities.

William Tucker

 **YES**

The Sober Realities of
Manned Space Flight

President Bush's announcement of a 280-million-mile manned space flight to Mars caught everyone by surprise. Space enthusiasts, arguing for years that NASA had lost its way, were electrified. "We've been stuck in low Earth orbit for decades," said Louis Friedman, executive director of the Planetary Society. "The goal should be exploration." NASA, still recovering from the recent Space Shuttle catastrophe, was eager to rededicate itself. A quick NASA calculation, however, revealed that the Mars effort would cost nearly $500 billion over 30 years. With funding tight and trouble brewing in the Middle East, Congress decided to ignore the project. After very little debate, the proposal dropped from sight.

That's what happened in 1989 when the elder President Bush proposed a manned flight to Mars by 2019. In 2004, President Bush the younger returned to his father's unfinished business and called for his own revival of space exploration, which would have astronauts getting back to the moon in 2020 and on to Mars thereafter. Only a year before, NASA director Sean O'Keefe was calling such an idea a "Hail Mary pass" and urging the public to be satisfied with slow, steady exploration by robotic probes. But the spirit of adventure seemed to be reasserting itself.As the President put it at a memorial service for the *Columbia* astronauts last year, "This cause of exploration and discovery is not an option we chose. It is a desire written in the human heart."

The $500 billion price tag has been scaled down considerably. Building on existing research, NASA will begin with $12 billion in spending over the next five years. Among most space veterans, however, these initial estimates are treated as a joke. "The Space Shuttle was originally supposed to break even and fly every two weeks," reminds Greg Klerkx, whose book *Lost in Space* is a critique of NASA. "It ended up costing $500 million per launch, and flying four or five times a year. When President Ronald Reagan first proposed the International Space Station, it was scheduled to be finished in eight years and cost $9 billion. Now it's over $70 billion and still isn't scheduled for completion until 2010."

From *American Enterprise*, December 2004, pp. 28–35. Copyright © 2004 by American Enterprise Institute. Reprinted by permission.

This is the picture of a federal agency immune to the competitive influences of the private sector. "You see this little metal loop? It's called a carabineer," California space entrepreneur Rick Tumlinson told a Senate hearing right after the President's announcement in January. "You could go to any sporting goods shop and buy it for $20. Yet NASA pays over $1,000 for the same object because of its procurement methods. It's the 'not-invented-here' mentality and distrust of the private sector that makes the cost of these projects so astronomical."

So will the Mars expedition be different? "The obstacles in getting to Mars are going to be bureaucratic, not technological," says Howard McCurdy, a space program expert at American University. "The NASA that got to the moon in 1969 was a totally different animal from the NASA that got the job in 1961. The current NASA may have to undergo the same kind of transformation."

NASA has always been a mix of science and show business. "The moon expedition was basically an episode of the Cold War," says Dr. Eligar Sadeh, assistant professor at the Odegard School of Aerospace Sciences. "Planting the flag, putting footprints on the moon—that was done to prove we had a better system than the Soviet Union. Since then, NASA has never been able to refocus its mission."

Neil Armstrong's "One giant step for mankind" defined a generation. Yet few people remember that after 1972 the last three *Apollo* missions were canceled because the public was losing interest. There are only so many times you can hit a golf ball on the moon. "There's a need for heroics," says Supriya Chakrabarti, director of the Boston University Center for Space Physics. "It's hard for the public to get excited about astronomers looking at squiggly lines on their computer screens."

⋅◈⋅

Once the moon had been reached, Mars seemed the next obvious destination. Instead, President Nixon scaled back the program. At the time, NASA was absorbing an unsustainably large 4 percent of the federal budget. The next step became the Space Shuttle—a workhorse that seemed eminently practical at the time but has turned out to be an expensive, clumsy albatross. With the exception of a few spectacular missions such as the repair of the Hubble Space Telescope, "the plain fact is that the shuttle has very little to do other than ferrying cargo to the International Space Station," sighs Louis Friedman of the Planetary Society.

"I vividly remember President Ronald Reagan going down to Texas after the *Challenger* disaster and memorializing the astronauts as heroes going further and faster into the unknown," says Friedman. "Of course they were doing no such thing. They were simply launching a communications satellite and carrying on the teacher-in-space show for schoolchildren—both rather mundane tasks. But by once again evoking the exploration theme, Reagan saved the space program."

Each Space Shuttle (there are now three) must be virtually reconstructed after each flight. The process takes two months and 20,000 people. Some of the parts are so outdated that engineers troll eBay for replacements. "What we save on re-use, we throw away on maintenance of the aging fleet," says Alex Roland, professor of military history at Duke and former historian of NASA. The Shuttles are scheduled to be retired for good in 2010.

The Shuttle's main task, launching communications satellites, could be performed just as well by expendable launch rockets. Fearing the program would have little business if this were allowed, Congress mandated that all government satellites be carried aloft by a Shuttle. "This very nearly ended the production of launch vehicles in this country," says Klerkx. "The powerful Saturn rocket, which carried *Apollo* to the moon, was abandoned after 1970."

When the *Challenger* disaster canceled Shuttle flights for the next three years, our burgeoning communications industry was left high and dry. It turned instead to the European Space Agency and its Ariane rocket, which picked up the slack. It was many years before big U.S. contractors such as Boeing and Lockheed Martin regained market share. "It was a classic case of a trade protection that backfired," says Klerkx.

In their plodding way, the Russians have become the most reliable technicians for putting satellites into space. They have stuck with Soyuz, the dependable old missile-based platform that hasn't been modified much since the time of Yuri Gagarin. The Russians have become experts in permanent laboratories. Our Skylab lasted from 1973 to 1979. The Russians launched their Salyut experimental station in 1971, then followed with Mir in January 1986. Mir stayed aloft for 15 years, with one Russian cosmonaut clocking 748 days in space, more than all the Shuttle trips put together. When Mir began losing altitude in 2000, two American entrepreneurs paid the Russians $5 million for permission to try to salvage it. The space merchants funded one rescue mission but were unable to lift enough fuel to keep Mir in orbit. It rained down over the Fiji Islands in March 2001. "NASA did everything it could to frustrate the Americans' effort," says Klerkx. "It doesn't like private competitors in its domain."

✎❦✎

Today's International Space Station (ISS) was originally proposed as "Space Station Freedom" in 1984 by the Reagan administration. The orbiting outpost was conceived as an extraterrestrial mini-city along the lines suggested by Wernher von Braun—in a series of *Collier's* articles in the 1950s—and MIT visionary Gerard O'Neill in his 1977 book, *The High Frontier,* which suggested 20 million people could live in space. By 1992, however, after spending $11 billion, Space Station Freedom was still on the drawing board. Sensing a quagmire, the Clinton administration brought the Russians in on the project, both to tap their experience and to prevent newly unemployed Russian military scientists from peddling their expertise to rogue nations.

Although scaled down considerably, the freshly christened International Space Station was to include platforms for launching flights to the moon and Mars, and for housing dozens of astronauts carrying on experiments in drug manufacturing, protein crystallization, and molding perfect ball bearings. All this would help the ISS pay for itself, and in June 1993, the House authorized another $13 billion by one vote. But since the first stage was lifted into orbit by the Russians in 1995, costs have soared while ambitions faded. Assembly platforms for launching moon rockets have vanished.When completed, the ISS will hold six astronauts. The two in residence now spend 85 percent of their time on construction and maintenance. In essence, the U.S. is spending billions so that two astronauts can build a space shed.

The only experiments the astronauts are performing are on themselves, measuring the long-term effects of life in zero gravity. The news has not been good. Muscles atrophy quickly and—for reasons yet unknown—the human body does not manufacture bone tissue in space. Russian cosmonauts return from the ISS virtually helpless for the first few days. This doesn't bode well for sending astronauts on an 18-month journey to Mars. Artificial gravity could alleviate the problem, but it can't be tested on the Space Station since it requires a large revolving body like the Jupiter probe in Arthur Clark's *2001*.

Meanwhile, the ISS has sucked up funds from nearly every other NASA project. Russia has been unable to pay its share, so the U.S. quietly picks up the tab. "It's hard to pin down because of NASA's accounting, but it looks like we've spent about $80 billion thus far," says Dr. Sadeh, author of 2003's *Space Politics and Policy*. "By the time it's finished it will probably cost $150 billion." Yet the Bush plan calls for continued expansion, adding European and Japanese modules over the next few years. "Right now the argument for completing the ISS is that we have to fulfill our international obligations," adds Klerkx. "Otherwise it would probably be put in mothballs."

Ironically, while NASA's manned efforts have been of dubious value, its unmanned probes have been hugely successful. Many scientists are calling the last 30 years a "golden age of astronomy" thanks to their discoveries. The *Viking*, which mapped Mars in the 1970s; the *Voyager* trips to Jupiter, Saturn, Uranus, and Neptune in the late 1970s and early 1980s; the Galileo probe of the 1990s, which explored Jupiter's moons and discovered an apparent salty ocean beneath the icy crust of Europa; the Cassini-Huygens mission which this year reached Saturn and its moon Titan; the *Spirit* and *Opportunity* rovers investigating Mars at this moment—all have expanded our knowledge to a spectacular degree.

To be sure, there have been embarrassments. The Mars Polar Lander failed in 1999 because someone forgot to convert English measurements to metric. *Genesis*, which probed the sun's environment, recently crashed in the Utah desert when its parachute failed to open. And of course the Hubble Telescope turned out to be myopic—a manufacturing error 1/50th the width of a human hair left the original telescope out of focus.

But that was mostly repaired when Shuttle astronauts fitted it with a "contact lens," and NASA's "eye in the sky" has since returned a decade's worth of breathtaking images and fresh knowledge. Hubble has mapped the heavens, observed gravitational lenses that confirm Einstein's theory of general relativity, discovered galaxies that go back almost to the beginning of time, and made a convincing case for the "Dark Energy" that appears to be driving the expansion of the universe.

Yet a week after Bush's Mars proposal, O'Keefe announced that NASA would abandon Hubble. New safety precautions require that the Shuttle be able to dock at the International Space Station in case of any emergency. Since the telescope orbits far from the ISS, any mission bound for Hubble for one of its regularly required maintenance visits would be unable to reach the Space Station if it ran into trouble.

"Hubble's last gyroscopes are due to fail within the next three to four years," says Dr. Sadeh. "After that it can't be positioned for observations." Pressure from the scientific community and Congress has forced O'Keefe to explore robotic repair, but many remain skeptical. "I wouldn't be surprised if a couple of astronauts volunteer to risk one last mission," says Dr. Sadeh.

꿍

So NASA's manned programs had just about come to the end of the line when President Bush announced his plan to visit Mars. The message sent a jolt of electricity through the ranks of space enthusiasts, who have been pushing for the new goal for more than a decade. "This was long overdue," says Friedman.

But the Mars mission raises an immediate question—will a reinvigorated NASA finally open space exploration to competition and the private sector? Or will it simply use the Mars mandate to pile cost upon cost in the same old way? "When Sir Edmund Hillary first climbed Mount Everest, he had so many porters he needed ten more just to carry the money to pay the others," says McCurdy, who analyzes the space program in his book *Faster, Cheaper, Better*. "Now two people can climb Mount Everest by themselves. We need the same approach to Mars. You've got to pare down. Closing down the Space Station and the Shuttle would be a start."

Dozens of companies have been hot for chances to launch passengers and cargo into space. Visionaries have suggested that cash prizes could encourage the necessary innovation and competition. Tumlinson has proposed that NASA offer a prize of $50 million to any private company that can map the south pole of Mars, where a landing is likely to take place. "People don't remember that when Charles Lindberg crossed the Atlantic, he was competing for the $25,000 Orteig prize," he says.

In 1995 Greg Maryniak, a St. Louis trial lawyer, founded the Ansari X-Prize, offering $10 million to the first group to launch a passenger-carrying spaceship 100 kilometers above the Earth, return it to the ground, and launch it again within two weeks. On October 4, the Mojave Aerospace Ventures Team claimed the prize when pilot Brian Binnie took *SpaceShipOne* 368,000 feet above the Earth for the second time in a week. Almost simultaneously, British entrepreneur Richard Branson announced he would soon be carrying space tourists above the atmosphere for $200,000 a seat.

"The mission of NASA should be the same as the mission of the old National Advisory Commission for Aeronautics in the 1920s," says Klerkx. "NACA continued to do research but turned the building and flying of airplanes over to the private sector."

In 1990, an obscure engineer at Martin Marietta named Robert Zubrin caused a sensation by proposing Mars Direct, a way of getting to the Red Planet without stopping at either the ISS or the moon. Zubrin's plan would send a robotic Earth Return Vehicle two years ahead of time to mine the planet for the methane needed for the return trip.

"We're much better prepared to get to Mars now than we were to get to the moon in 1961," says Zubrin, who has since founded the Mars Society and written *The Case for Mars* (1996). "The whole mission could be accomplished in a decade, rather than 20 years, as NASA is proposing." Yet NASA's not-invented-here policy makes such outside suggestions unlikely.

One of the keys to NASA's plan is the development of a new system for generating electricity from nuclear radiation. In 2002, O'Keefe launched the Prometheus Project, a $1 billion effort to develop an improved nuclear propulsion system. Conventional reactors use radioactive heat to drive steam turbines, but such boilers are too heavy for space.

Another problem: Astronauts making the 560-million-mile round trip will be exposed to huge doses of cosmic radiation. The only protection is a shield made of the heaviest elements—which would weigh down the ship. All this raises an obvious question: Why send people to Mars at all? Couldn't we just rely on improved robotics? "The risk to human life is obviously great," says Friedman. "But the payoff for sending astronauts is huge. A human being exploring the geology of Mars could do in one day what a robot can do in a month."

꧁◉꧂

This leads to an even bigger question: Why go in the first place? Other than planting the flag and establishing our hegemony over the solar system, where is the lasting purpose in such an effort? Viewers from Manila to Moscow would be glued to their TV screens, and nations of the world might feel united (except for Islamic radicals, who would be scheming on how to blow the thing up). But the Olympics serve much the same purpose.

The justifications for human space exploration are generally stated as these: adventure and the stimulation of pushing into the unknown; making new worlds habitable for future generations; scientific discovery and unraveling the mystery of who we are.

These are no small things. European cultures were vastly invigorated during the Renaissance by the discovery of the New World. Columbus, Vasco de Gama, and Magellan became heroes who defined the West for centuries. Cultures that pioneer seem to thrive, while those that stop pioneering often fester and degenerate. "Human beings either look out or they look down," says Friedman.

Space enthusiasts have always been big fans of Frederick Jackson Turner's "Frontier Thesis," which says that the American character was formed by the constant exploration of new horizons. "Lots of people stayed home in Europe during the settling of the New World," says McCurdy. "Maybe there's been some selection in our genes."

Whether it is our destiny to colonize the solar system, however, is an entirely different matter. The moon is not a virgin continent waiting to be inhabited, but a barren oxygen-less desert that will have to be claimed inch by inch. At best, it will require the construction of huge, closed-in Earth-like environments that would have to be provisioned continuously. Space enthusiasts often suggest other planets could be "terraformed"—transformed into an Earth-like environment—in case humans have to escape if the Earth should be destroyed by an asteroid. This may make good science fiction but can hardly serve as a goal for NASA policy.

Finally, there is the matter of scientific investigation. The great question that hovers over all space exploration is the oldest philosophical quest: How did we get here? Are we alone? Are other planets inhabited? Is life a miraculous one-time occurrence or a normal process in the evolution of the universe? These great questions have puzzled humanity since Empedocles asked, "Why is there something instead of nothing?"

As Isaac Newton once said in describing his own scientific motivations, we are sitting on the seashore amused by a few pebbles while whole vast oceans of the unknown lie before us. No one would suggest we should not pursue these mysteries. The question is whether we have to squander vast amounts of money to do it.

Space travel will come eventually. It was more than a century before Columbus's discoveries led to any attempts to colonize the New World. Our timetable may not be all that different. Yet we should also be chastened by the example of sixteenth-century Spain, which bankrupted itself in pursuing the Age of Discovery.

Now as then, "privateering" may be a solution. It is certainly better than shoveling money at an entrenched bureaucracy.

NO

Steven Weinberg

The Wrong Stuff

Ever since NASA was founded, the greater part of its resources have gone into putting men and women into space. On January 14 of this year, President Bush announced a "New Vision for Space Exploration" that would further intensify NASA's concentration on manned space flight. The International Space Station, which has been under construction since 1998, would be completed by 2010; it would be kept in service until around 2016, with American activities on the station from now on focused on studies of the long-term effects of space travel on astronauts. The manned spacecraft called the space shuttle would continue flying until 2010, and be used chiefly to service the space station. The shuttle would then be replaced by a new manned spacecraft, to be developed and tested by 2008. Between 2015 and 2020 the new spacecraft would be used to send astronauts back to the moon, where they would live and work for increasing periods. We would then be ready for the next step—a human mission to Mars.

This would be expensive. The President gave no cost estimates, but John McCain, chairman of the Senate Commerce, Science, and Transportation Committee, has cited reports that the new initiative would cost between $170 billion and $600 billion. According to NASA briefing documents, the figure of $170 billion is intended to take NASA only up to 2020, and does not include the cost of the Mars mission itself. After the former President Bush announced a similar initiative in 1989, NASA estimated that the cost of sending astronauts to the moon and Mars would be either $471 billion or $541 billion in 1991 dollars, depending on the method of calculation. This is roughly $700 billion in today's dollars. Whatever cost may be estimated by NASA for the new initiative, we can expect cost overruns like those that have often accompanied big NASA programs. (In 1984 NASA estimated that it would cost $8 billion to put the International Space Station in place, not counting the cost of using it. I have seen figures for its cost so far ranging from $25 billion to $60 billion, and the station is far from finished.) Let's not haggle over a hundred billion dollars more or less—I'll estimate that the President's new initiative will cost nearly a trillion dollars.

Compare this with the $820 *million* cost of recently sending the robots *Spirit* and *Opportunity* to Mars, roughly one thousandth the cost of the President's initiative. The inclusion of people inevitably makes any space mission vastly more expensive. People need air and water and food. They have to be protected against cosmic rays, from which we on the ground are shielded by the Earth's atmosphere. On a voyage to Mars astronauts would be beyond the protective reach of the Earth's magnetic field, so they would also have to be shielded from the charged particles that are sent out by the sun during solar flares. Unlike robots, astronauts will want to return to Earth. Above all, the tragic loss of astronauts cannot be shrugged off like the loss of robots, so any casualties in the use of the new spacecraft would cause costly delays and alterations in the program, as happened after the disastrous accidents to the *Challenger* shuttle in 1986 and to the *Columbia* shuttle in February 2003.

The President's new initiative thus makes it necessary once more to take up a question that has been with us since the first space ventures: What is the value of sending human beings into space? There is a serious conflict here. Astronomers and other scientists are generally skeptical of the value of manned space flight, and often resent the way it interferes with scientific research. NASA administrators, astronauts, aerospace contractors, and politicians typically find manned space flight just wonderful. NASA's Office of Space Science has explained that "the fundamental goal of the President's Vision is to advance US scientific, security, and economic interests through a robust space exploration program." So let's look at how manned space flight advances these interests.

◦◦◉◦◦

Many Americans remember the fears for US national security that were widely felt when the Soviets launched the unmanned Sputnik satellite in October 1957. These fears were raised to new heights in 1961, when the Soviet cosmonauts Yuri Gagarin and then Gherman Titov went into space. Titov's spacecraft made seventeen orbits around the Earth, three of them passing for the first time over the United States. The American reaction is described by Tom Wolfe in *The Right Stuff*:

> Once again, all over the country, politicians and the press seemed profoundly alarmed, and the awful vision was presented; suppose the cosmonaut were armed with hydrogen bombs and flung them as he came over, like Thor flinging thunderbolts. . . . Toledo disappears off the face of the earth . . . Kansas City . . . Lubbock. . . .

As it turned out, the ability to send rockets into space did have tremendous military importance. Ballistic missiles that travel above the Earth's atmosphere all but replaced bombers as the vehicle of choice for carrying Soviet or American nuclear weapons to an adversary's territory. Even in the nonnuclear wars of today, artificial satellites in orbit around the Earth play an essential part in surveillance, communications, and navigation. But these missiles and satellites are all unmanned. One can't just drop bombs from satellites to the Earth's surface—once something is put in orbit above the Earth's atmosphere, it stays in orbit unless a rocket brings it down. As far as I know there never has been a moment from Titov's flight to the present when the ability to put people into space gave any country the slightest military advantage.

I say this despite the fact that some military satellites have been put into orbit by the space shuttle. This could be done just as well and much more cheaply by unmanned rockets. It had been hoped that the shuttle, because reusable, would reduce the cost of putting satellites in orbit. Instead, while it costs about $3,000 a pound to use unmanned rockets to put satellites in orbit, the cost of doing this with the shuttle is about $10,000 a pound. The physicist Robert Park has pointed out that at this rate, even if lead could be turned into gold in orbit, it would not pay to send it up on the shuttle. Park could have added that in this case NASA would probably send lead bricks up on the shuttle anyway, and cite the gold in press releases as proof of the shuttle's value. There doesn't seem to have been any reason for the use of the shuttle to take some military satellites into orbit other than that NASA has needed some way to justify the shuttle's existence. During the Carter administration, NASA explained to the deputy national security adviser that unless President Carter forced military satellite missions onto the space shuttle it would be the President who would be responsible for the end of the shuttle program, since the shuttle could never survive if it had to charge commercial users the real cost of space launches.

Similar remarks apply to the direct economic benefits of space travel. There is no doubt about the great value of artificial satellites in orbit around the Earth. Those that survey the Earth's surface give us information about weather, climate, and environmental change of all sorts, as well as warnings of military buildups and rocket launches. Satellites relay television programs and telephone conversations beyond the horizon. The Global Positioning System, which calculates the location of automobiles, ships, and planes, as well as missiles, relies on the timing of signals from satellites. But again, these are all unmanned satellites, and can be put into orbit most cheaply by unmanned rockets.

It is difficult to think of any direct economic benefit that can be gained by putting people into space. There has been a continuing effort to grow certain crystals in the nearly zero gravity on an orbiting satellite such as the International Space Station, or to make ultra-pure semiconductor films in the nearly perfect vacuum in the wake of the space station. Originally President Reagan approved the space station in the expectation that eventually it could be run at a profit. Nothing of economic value has come of this, and these programs have now apparently been wisely abandoned in the President's new plans for the space station. . . .

In his speech on January 14 President Bush emphasized that the space program produces "technological advances that have benefited all humanity." It is true that pursuing a demanding task like putting men on Mars can yield indirect benefits in the form of new technologies, but here too I think that unmanned missions are likely to be more productive. Trying to think of some future spinoff from space missions that would really benefit humanity, I find it hard to come up with anything more promising than the experience of designing robots that are needed for unmanned space missions. This experience can help us in building robots that can spare humans from dangerous or tedious jobs here on Earth. Surprises are always possible, but I don't see how anything of comparable value could come out of developing the specialized techniques needed to keep people alive on space missions.

❦

President Bush's presentation of his space initiative emphasized the scientific knowledge to be gained. Some readers of his speech may imagine astronauts on the shuttle or the space station peering through telescopes at planets or stars, or wandering about on the moon or Mars making discoveries about the history of the solar system. It doesn't work that way.

There is no question that observatories in space have led to a tremendous increase in astronomical knowledge. . . .

❦

Exciting research, of which NASA may justly feel proud. Research of this sort has made this a golden age for cosmology. But neither the Cosmic Microwave Background Explorer nor the Wilkinson Microwave Anisotropy Probe had any astronauts aboard. People were not needed. On the contrary, through their movements and body heat they would have fouled up these measurements, as well as greatly increasing the cost of these missions. The same is true of every one of the space observatories that have expanded our knowledge of the universe through observations of ultraviolet light, infrared light, X-rays, or gamma rays from above the Earth's atmosphere. Some of these observatories were taken into orbit by the shuttle, while others (including the Cosmic Microwave Background Explorer and the Wilkinson Microwave Anisotropy Probe) were carried up by unmanned rockets, as all of them could have been.

The Hubble Space Telescope is a special case. Like the other orbiting observatories, the Hubble operates under remote control, with no people traveling with it. But unlike these other observatories, the Hubble was not only launched by the shuttle, but has also been serviced several times by astronauts brought up to its orbit by the shuttle. The Hubble has made a great contribution to astronomy, one that goes way beyond taking gorgeous color photos of planets and nebulae. . . . The Hubble may have given NASA its best argument for the scientific value of manned space flight.

But like the other space observatories, the Hubble Space Telescope could have been carried into orbit by unmanned rockets. This would have spared astronauts the danger of shuttle flights, and it would have been much cheaper. Riccardo Giacconi, the former director of the Space Telescope Science Institute, has estimated that by using unmanned rockets instead of the space shuttle, we could have sent up seven Hubbles without increasing the total mission cost. It would then not have been necessary to service the Hubble; when design flaws were discovered or parts wore out, we could just have sent up another Hubble.

⋯⊙⋯

What about the scientific experiments done by astronauts on the space shuttle or the space station? Recently I asked to see the list of experiments that NASA assigned to the astronauts aboard the *Columbia* space shuttle on its last flight, which ended tragically when the shuttle exploded during re-entry. It is sad to report that it is not an impressive list of experiments. Roughly half had to do with the effect of the space environment on the astronauts. This at least is a kind of science that cannot be done without the presence of astronauts, but it has no point unless one plans to put people into space for long periods for some other reason.

Of the other half of the *Columbia's* experiments, a large fraction dealt with the growth of crystals and the flow of fluids in nearly zero gravity, old standbys of NASA that have neither illuminated any fundamental issues of science nor led to any practical applications. It is always dangerous for a scientist in one field to try to judge the value of work done by specialists in other fields, but I think I would have heard about it if anything really exciting was coming out of any of these experiments, and I haven't. Much of the "scientific" program assigned to astronauts on the space shuttle and the space station has the flavor of projects done for a high school science talent contest. Some of the work looks interesting, but it is hard to see why it has to be done by people. For instance, there was just one experiment on *Columbia* devoted to astronomy, a useful measurement of variations in the energy being emitted from the sun. The principal investigator tells me that the only intervention of the astronauts consisted of turning the apparatus on and then turning it off.

Looking into the future, we need to ask, what scientific work can be done by astronauts on Mars? They can walk around and look at the terrain, and carry out tests on rocks, looking for signs of water or life, but all that can be done by robots. They can bring back rock samples, as the Apollo astronauts did from the moon, but that too can be done by robots. Samples of rocks from the moon were also brought back to Earth by unmanned Soviet lunar missions. It is sometimes said that the great disadvantage of using robots in a mission to Mars is that they can only be controlled by people on Earth with a long wait (at least four minutes) for radio signals to travel each way between the Earth and Mars. That would indeed be a severe problem if the robots were being sent to Mars to play tennis with Martians, but not much is happening there now, and I don't see why robots can't be left to operate with only occasional intervention from Earth. Any marginal advantage that astronauts may have over robots in exploring Mars would be more than canceled by the great cost of manned missions. For the cost of putting a few people in a single location on Mars, we could have robots studying many different landscapes all over the planet.

⋯⊙⋯

Many scientists and some NASA administrators understand all this very well. I have frequently been told that it is necessary publicly to defend programs of manned space flight anyway, because the voters and their elected representatives only care about the drama of people in space. (Richard Garwin has reminded me of the old astronauts' proverb "No bucks without Buck Rogers.") It is hoped that while vast sums are being spent on manned space flight missions, a little money will be diverted to real science. I think that this attitude is self-defeating. Whenever NASA runs into trouble, it is science that is likely to be sacrificed first. After NASA had pushed the Apollo program to the point where people stopped watching lunar landings on television, it canceled Apollo 18 and 19, the missions that were to be specifically devoted to scientific research.

It is true that the administration now projects a 5 percent increase per year in NASA's funding for the next three years. So far, funding is being maintained for the next large space telescope, and is being increased for some other scientific programs, including robotic missions to the planets and their moons. But we can already see damage to programs that are not related to exploration of the solar system, and especially to research in cosmology. Studying the origin of the planets is interesting, but certainly not more so than studying the origin of the universe.

Two days after President Bush presented his new space initiative, NASA announced that the planned shuttle mission to service Hubble in 2006 would be canceled. This mission would have replaced gyroscopes and batteries that are needed to extend Hubble's life into the next decade, and it would have installed two new instruments (which have already been built, at a cost of $167 million) to extend Hubble's capacities. . . .

NASA's stated reason for terminating the Hubble while continuing work on the space station is that it is more dangerous for the shuttle to go up to Hubble than to the space station. Supposedly, if the astronauts on the shuttle find that damage has been done to the shuttle's protective tiles during launch, they could wait in the space station for a rescue, while this would not be possible during a mission to the Hubble. But there are many other dangers to astronauts that are the same whether the shuttle is going to the space station or the Hubble Space Telescope. Among these is an explosion during launch, like the one that destroyed the *Challenger* shuttle in 1986. . . .

I share the widespread suspicion that Hubble is being sacrificed to save funds for the President's initiative, and in particular in order to reserve all flights on the shuttle's limited schedule for the one purpose of taking astronauts to and from the space station.

⋅✦⋅

Perhaps because of its timing, the Hubble decision attracted great public attention, but there are other recent NASA decisions that have nothing to do with safety, and that therefore give clearer evidence of the willingness of NASA and the administration to sacrifice science to save money for manned space flight. In January 2003, after several years of scientists' making difficult decisions about their priorities, NASA announced a new initiative, called Beyond Einstein, to explore some of the more exotic phenomena predicted by Einstein's General Theory of Relativity. This includes a satellite (to be developed jointly with the Department of Energy) that would look at many more galaxies at great distances, in order to uncover the nature of the dark energy by finding whether its density has been changing as the universe expands. Equally important for cosmology, there would be another probe that would study the polarization of the cosmic microwave background to find indirect effects of gravitational waves from the early universe. (Gravitational waves bear the same relation to ordinary gravity that light waves bear to electric and magnetic fields—they are self-sustaining oscillations in the gravitational field, which propagate through empty space at the speed of light.)

Beyond Einstein also includes another satellite dedicated to searching for black holes, and two larger facilities. One is an array of X-ray telescopes called Constellation-X, which would observe matter falling into black holes. The other is called LISA, the Laser Interferometer Space Antenna. This "antenna" would consist of three unmanned spacecraft in orbit around the sun, separated from each other by about three million miles. Changes in the distances between the three spacecraft would be continually measured with a precision better than a millionth of an inch by combining laser beams passing between them. These exquisite measurements would be able to reveal the presence of gravitational waves passing through the solar system. LISA would have enough sensitivity to detect gravitational waves produced by stars being torn apart as they fall into black holes or by black holes merging with each other, events we can't see with ordinary telescopes. NASA has another particularly cost-effective program called Explorer, which has supported small and mid-sized observatories like the Cosmic Background Explorer and Wilkinson Microwave Anisotropy Probe.

Alas, NASA's Office of Space Science has now announced that the Beyond Einstein and Explorer programs "do not clearly support the goals of the President's Vision for space exploration," so their funding has been severely reduced. Funding for the three smaller Einstein missions has been put off for five years; LISA will be deferred for a year or more; Explorer will be reduced in scope for the next five years; and no proposals for new Explorer missions will be considered for one or two years. None of this damage is irreparable, but spending on the President's "New Vision" has barely begun. These deferrals, along with the end of Hubble servicing, are warnings that as the moon and Mars missions absorb more and more money, the golden age of cosmology is going to be terminated, in order to provide us with the spectacle of people going into space for no particular reason.

⋆◈⋆

When advocates of manned space flight run out of arguments for its contribution to "scientific, security, and economic interests," they invoke the spirit of exploration, and talk of the Oregon Trail (Bush I) or Lewis and Clark (Bush II). Like many others, I am not immune to the excitement of seeing astronauts walking on Mars or the moon. We have walked on Mars so often in our reading—with Dante and Beatrice, visiting the planet of martyrs and heroes; with Ray Bradbury's earthmen, finding ruins and revenants of a vanished Martian civilization; and more recently with Kim Stanley Robinson's pioneers, transforming Mars into a new home for humans. I hope that someday men and women will walk on the surface of Mars. But before then, there are two conditions that will need to be satisfied.

One condition is that there will have to be something for people to do on Mars which cannot be done by robots. If a few astronauts travel to Mars, plant a flag, look at some rocks, hit a few golf balls, and then come back, it will at first be a thrilling moment, but then, when nothing much comes of it, we will be left with a sour sense of disillusion, much as happened after the end of the Apollo missions. Perhaps after sending more robots to various sites on Mars something will be encountered that calls for direct study by humans. Until then, there is no point in people going there.

The other necessary condition is a reorientation of American thinking about government spending. There seems to be a general impression that government spending harms the economy by taking funds from the private sector, and therefore must always be kept to a minimum. Unlike what is usually called "big science"—orbiting telescopes, particle accelerators, genome projects—sending humans to the moon and Mars is so expensive that, as long as the public thinks of government spending as parasitic on the private economy, this program would interfere with adequate support for health care, homeland security, education, and other public goods, as it has already begun to interfere with spending on science.

My training is in physics, so I hesitate to make pronouncements about economics; but it seems obvious to me that for the government to spend a dollar on public goods affects total economic activity and employment in just about the same way as for government to cut taxes by a dollar that will then be spent on private goods. The chief difference is in the kind of goods produced by the economy—public or private. The question of what kind of goods we most need is not one of economic science but of value judgments, which anyone is competent to make. In my view the worst problem facing our society is not that there is a scarcity of private goods—food or clothing or SUVs or consumer electronics—but rather that there are sick people who cannot get health care, drug addicts who cannot get into rehabilitation programs, ports vulnerable to terrorist attack, insufficient resources to deal with Afghanistan and Iraq, and American children who are being left behind. As Justice Holmes said, "Taxes are what we pay for civilized society." But as long as the public is so averse to being taxed, there will be even less money either to ameliorate these societal problems or to do real scientific research if we spend hundreds of billions of dollars on sending people into space.

❧❦❧

In the foregoing, I have taken the President's space initiative seriously. That may be a mistake. Before the "New Vision" was announced, the administration was faced with the risk of political damage from a possible new fatal shuttle accident like the *Columbia* disaster less than a year earlier. That problem could be eased by canceling all shuttle flights before the 2004 presidential election, and allowing only enough flights after that to keep building the space station. The space station posed another problem: no one was excited any more by what had become the Great Orbital Turkey. While commitments to domestic contractors and international partners protected it from being immediately scrapped, its runaway costs needed to be cut. But just cutting back on the shuttle and the space station would be too negative, not at all in keeping with what might be expected from a President of Vision. So, back to the moon, and on to Mars! Most of the huge bills for these manned missions would come due after the President leaves office in 2005 or 2009, and the extra costs before then could be covered in part by cutting other things that no one in the White House is interested in anyway, like research on black holes and cosmology. After the end of the President's time in office, who cares? If future presidents are not willing to fund this initiative then it is they who will have to bear the stigma of limited vision. So, looking on the bright side, instead of spending nearly a trillion dollars on manned missions to the moon and Mars we may wind up spending only a fraction of that on nothing at all.

POSTSCRIPT

Do Humans Belong in Space?

As a result of the *Columbia* tragedy, the United States shuttle fleet is down to three: the *Endeavour, Atlantis*, and *Discovery*. Stephen L. Petuanch, "No More Shuttles, Please," *Discover* (May 2003), denounces the space shuttle program as too expensive and unsafe, but the next generation of shuttles is far from ready; see Bill Sweetman, "Space Shuttle: The Next Generation," *Popular Science* (May 2003), and Mark Alpert, "Rethinking the Shuttle," *Scientific American* (April 2003). There are also efforts to develop an affordable spacecraft capable of many safe trips to and from orbit. In October 2004, Bert Rutan's *SpaceShipOne* won the $10 million Ansari X prize by becoming the first private, reusable craft to reach space (though not orbit). See Kathy A. Svitil and Eric Levin, "*SpaceShipOne* Opens Private Rocket Era," *Discover* (January 2005), and Bert Rutan, "Rocket for the Rest of Us," *National Geographic* (April 2005). The next step is to reach orbit.

Do we need to send people into space? Won't robots do? The question is timely because in 1997—two decades after the two *Viking* landers extensively mapped and characterized the Red Planet—scientists returned to Mars with the *Pathfinder* lander and its accompanying *Sojourner* rover. The Mars *Global Surveyor* arrived in September to photograph the planet from orbit, inventory rock types, and map future landing sites. In January 2004, the rovers *Spirit* and *Opportunity* began their very successful survey of the Martian surface. It seems likely that as long as the robots continue to succeed in their missions, manned missions will continue to be put off because funding shortages will probably continue. Funding for space exploration remains low largely because problems on Earth (environmental and other) seem to need money more urgently than space exploration projects do. The prospects for manned space expeditions to the moon, Mars, or other worlds seem very dim, although Paul D. Spudis, "Harvest the Moon," *Astronomy* (June 2003), asserts that there are four good reasons for putting people at least on the Moon: "The first motivation to revisit the Moon is that its rocks hold the early history of our own planet and the solar system. Next, its unique environment and properties make it an ideal vantage point for observing the universe. The Moon is also a natural space station where we can learn how to live off-planet. And finally, it gives us an extraterrestrial filling station, with resources to use both locally and in near-Earth space." See also Paul D. Spudis, "The New Moon," *Scientific American* (December 2003). Nader Elhefnawy, "Beyond *Columbia*: Is There a Future for Humanity in Space?" *The Humanist* (September/October 2003), says that we cannot ignore the wealth of resources in space. Alex Ellery, "Humans versus Robots for Space Exploration and Development," *Space Policy* (May 2003), maintains that although "robotics and artificial intelligence are becoming more sophisticated, they will not be able to deal with 'thinking-on-one's-feet' tasks that require generalisations from past experience. . . . [T]here will be a critical role for humans in space for the foreseeable future." Mark Williams, "Toward a New Vision of Manned Spaceflight," *Technology Review* (January 2005), suggests that for prolonged spaceflight, however, humans are so vulnerable to radiation and other space hazards that they may have to be reengineered.

Center for Democracy & Technology

The Center for Democracy & Technology works to promote democratic values and constitutional liberties in the digital age.

http://www.cdt.org/

Electronic Frontier Foundation

The Electronic Frontier Foundation is concerned with protecting individual freedoms and rights such as privacy as new communications technologies emerge.

http://www.eff.org

Banned Books Week

The American Library Association's Banned Books Week Web site shows that the issue of censorship is by no means restricted to the Internet.

http://www.ala.org/ala/oif/bannedbooksweek/
bannedbooksweek.htm

Project Gutenberg

Project Gutenberg is an ongoing project to convert the classics of literature into digital format.

http://www.gutenberg.org/

Pew Internet & American Life Project

The Pew Internet & American Life Project explores the impact of the Internet on children, families, communities, the work place, schools, health care, and civic/political life.

http://www.pewinternet.org/

PART 5

The Computer Revolution

*F**ans of computers have long been sure that the electronic wonders offer untold benefits to society. When the first personal computers appeared in the early 1970s, they immediately brought unheard-of capabilities to their users. Ever since, those capabilities have been increasing. Today children command more sheer computing power than major corporations did in the 1950s and 1960s. Computer users are in direct contact with their fellow users around the world. Information is instantly available and infinitely malleable.*

Some observers wonder about the purported untold benefits of computers. Specifically, will such benefits be outweighed by threats to children (by free access to pornography), civil order (by free access to sites that advocate racism and violence), traditional institutions (will books, for example, become an endangered species?), or to human pride (a computer has already outplayed the human world chess champion)? Does all that time we spend online weaken our connections to our fellow human being? Is Privacy Vanishing?

- Does the Internet Strengthen Community?

- Does the Spread of Surveillance Technology Threaten Privacy?

- Will Screens Replace Pages?

ISSUE 14

Does the Internet Strengthen Community?

YES: John B. Horrigan, from "Online Communities: Networks that Nurture Long-Distance Relationships and Local Ties," *Pew Internet & American Life Project* (October 2001)

NO: Jonathon N. Cummings, Brian Butler, and Robert Kraut, from "The Quality of Online Social Relationships," *Communications of the ACM* (July 2002)

ISSUE SUMMARY

YES: John B. Horrigan asserts that when people go online, they both form relationships with distant others who share their interests and strengthen their involvement with their local communities.

NO: Jonathon N. Cummings, Brian Butler, and Robert Kraut maintain that online communication is less valuable for building strong social relationships than more traditional face-to-face and telephone communication.

It is a truism to say that technologies have social impact, and that that impact can be both far-reaching and unforeseen. Thus the Gutenberg printing press, whose first product was the Bible, wound up contributing to the Protestant Reformation, making public schools essential, creating the scientific and industrial revolutions, and spreading the idea of human rights and thus leading to the American, French, and other revolutions. It also quite shattered what used to be thought of as "community" when most people lived and died within a mile of their birthplace and took the shape of their lives from a single unquestionable religious or civil authority.

Whether these effects were for good or ill depends very much on whom you ask. Most citizens of the modern developed world—the products and beneficiaries of those changes—would surely say they were for good. Some are more skeptical.

When the Internet was new, its partisans promised that it would bring a new age of public participation in political decision-making and link together far-flung people to create a "global village" far more real than anything forecast for television by Marshall McLuhan. However, some people feared that it would be harmful to society. Clifford Stoll claimed the Internet would weaken commitment to and enjoyment of real friendships (*Silicon Snake Oil*, Doubleday, 1995). David Paletz wrote that "the new information technology . . . can inspire populism, but one based on ignorance; it can facilitate the expression of public opinion, but one inspired by demagoguery; it can engender community, but of ethnic, religious, and single-issue groups" ("Advanced Information Technology and Political Communication," *Social Science Computer Review*, Spring 1996). Sherry Turkle feared the Internet would lead to the destruction of meaningful community ("Virtuality and Its Discontents: Searching for Community in Cyberspace," *American Prospect*, Winter 1996). Robert Kraut et al. reported that new Internet users became less socially involved and more depressed ("Internet Paradox: A Social Technology that Reduces Social Involvement and Psychological Well-Being?" *American Psychologist*, 53[9], 1998). Andrew L. Shapiro admitted that the Internet's potential for fostering personal growth and social progress seemed limitless but worried that "customizing our lives to the hilt could undermine the strength and cohesion of local communities . . . shared experience is an indisputable essential ingredient" ("The Net that Binds," *Nation*, June 21, 1999). At least one critic criticizes the Internet because it fosters "voluntary" communities based on mutual interests and argues that "learning to make the best of circumstances one has not chosen is part of what it means to be a good citizen and a mature human being. We should not organize our lives around the fantasy that entrance and exit can always be cost-free: On-line groups can fulfill important emotional and utilitarian needs. But they must not be taken as comprehensive models of a future society" (William A. Galston, "Does the Internet Strengthen Community?" *National Civic Review*, October 2000).

Since then, the Internet has grown tremendously. By late 2004, an eighth of the world population (801 million people) had Internet access. The social impact of online communication is thus increasingly a matter of global concern. Does it strengthen society by helping people make and keep friends, form "virtual" communities stretching around the globe, and exchange information? Or does it weaken society by drawing people away from face-to-face interactions and local community groups, substituting weak friendships for strong ones, and interfering with the development of mature, good citizens?

John B. Horrigan, a senior researcher with the Pew Internet & American Life Project, reports the results of a survey showing that Internet users strengthen their connections to others, expand their social worlds, and increase their involvement with communities, both local and virtual, in a process called "glocalization." Jonathon N. Cummings, Brian Butler, and Robert Kraut maintain that online communication is less valuable for building strong social relationships than more traditional face-to-face and telephone communication. The overall effect depends on whether online communication replaces or supplements traditional communication.

John B. Horrigan

 **YES**

Online Communities: Networks that Nurture Long-Distance Relationships and Local Ties

Summary of Findings

The Vibrant Social Universe Online

In recent years, there has been concern about the social impact of the Internet on several levels. One major worry was that use of the Internet would prompt people to withdraw from social engagement and become isolated, depressed, and alienated. A related fear was that Internet users might abandon contact with their local communities as they discovered how easy it is to go online to communicate with those in other parts of the world and get information from every point on the planet.

We surveyed 1,697 Internet users in January and February [2001] to explore the breadth and depth of community online. Our findings suggest that the online world is a vibrant social universe where many Internet users enjoy serious and satisfying contact with online communities. These online groups are made up of those who share passions, beliefs, hobbies, or lifestyles. Tens of millions of Americans have joined communities after discovering them online. And many are using the Internet to join and participate in longstanding, traditional groups such as professional and trade associations. All in all, 84% of Internet users have at one time or another contacted an online group.

The pull of online communities in the aftermath of the September 11 attacks shows how Americans have integrated online communities into their lives. In the days following the attacks, 33% of American Internet users read or posted material in chat rooms, bulletin boards, or other online forums. Although many early posts reflected outrage at the events, online discussions soon migrated to grieving, discussion and debate on how to respond, and information queries about the suspects and those who sponsored them. With the dramatic displays of community spirit around the country following September 11, there are hopes that Americans' repulsion and shock [from] the attacks might have sparked a renewal of civic spirit in the United States. The existing vibrancy of online communities profiled in this report suggests that

Internet groups can play a supporting role in any enduring boon to community life in the aftermath of the attacks.

Our winter survey also showed that many Americans are using the Internet to intensify their connection to their local community. They employ email to plan church meetings, arrange neighborhood gatherings, and petition local politicians. They use the Web to find out about local merchants, get community news, and check out area fraternal organizations. Moreover, there is evidence that this kind of community engagement is particularly appealing to young adults.

Sociologist Barry Wellman argues that many new social arrangements are being formed through "glocalization"—the capacity of the Internet to expand users' social worlds to faraway people and simultaneously to bind them more deeply to the place where they live. This report illustrates how widely "glocalization" is occurring. The Internet helps many people find others who share their interests no matter how distant they are, and it also helps them increase their contact with groups and people they already know and it helps them feel more connected to them.

90 Million Americans Have Participated in Online Groups

- 84% of Internet users, or about 90 million Americans, say they have used the Internet to contact or get information from a group. We call them "Cyber Groupies."
- 79% of Cyber Groupies identify at least one particular group with which they stay in regular contact.
- 49% of Cyber Groupies say the Internet has helped them connect with groups or people who share their interests.
- Cyber Groupies try out different groups; the average Cyber Groupie has contacted four online groups at one time or another.

Use of the Internet often prompts Americans to join groups. More than half of Cyber Groupies (56%) say they joined an online group *after* they began communicating with it over the Internet. This includes those who joined traditional groups whose existence predated the Internet, such as professional or fraternal groups. In other words, Internet access is helping people join all kinds of communities, including those that are not exclusively virtual communities.

- 40% of Cyber Groupies say the Internet has helped them become more involved with groups to which they already belong.

28 Million Have Used the Internet to Deepen Their Ties to Their Local Communities

In addition to helping users participate in communities of interest that often have no geographical boundaries the Internet is a tool for those who are involved with local groups, particularly church groups.

- 26% of Internet users have employed the Internet to contact or get information about local groups. That comes to 28 million people.

Virtual Third Places

In the face of widespread worries that community activity is ebbing in the United States, these findings demonstrate that the Internet, while not necessarily turning the tide, has become an important new tool to connect people with shared interests globally and locally. In some ways, online communities have become *virtual third places* for people because they are different places from home and work. These places allow people either to hang out with others or more actively engage with professional associations, hobby groups, religious organizations, or sports leagues.

Online Communities Foster Chatter and Connection

These groups are lively online communities. People exchange emails, hash out issues, find out about group activities, and meet face-to-face as a result of online communities. Approximately 23 million Americans are *very* active in online communities, meaning that they email their principle online group several times a week.

- 60% of Cyber Groupies say they use email to communicate with the group; of these emailers 43% email the group several times a week.
- 33% of the 28 million Local Groupies who use email send email to their main local organization several times a week.

More Contact with Different People

Many Cyber Groupies and Local Groupies say that online communities have spurred connections to strangers and to people of different racial, ethnic, and economic backgrounds.

- 50% of Cyber Groupies say that participation in an online community has helped them get to know people they otherwise would not have met.
- 35% of Local Groupies say that participation in an online community has helped them get to know people they otherwise would not have met. This lower number relative to Cyber Groupies may be due to the fact that Local Groupies probably were acquainted already with members of the online group.
- 37% of Cyber Groupies say the Internet has helped them connect with people of different ages or generations.
- 27% of Cyber Groupies say the Internet has helped them connect with people from different racial, ethnic, or economic backgrounds.

The types of connections people establish depend on the kind of group to which they belong. Members of some cyber groups go to their groups to establish personal relationships, while others just want to keep up with group news and activities.

- Members of belief groups, ethnic online groups, and especially online groups oriented to lifestyle issues are most interested in using the Internet to establish personal relationships.

- Members of entertainment, professional, and sports online groups tend to use email in group activities less often than those who belong to other kinds. They focus their online activities on getting information about popular culture.
- Men tend to be drawn to online groups involving professional activities, politics, and sports.
- Women tend to be drawn to online medical support groups, local community associations that are online, and cyber groups relating to entertainment.

Joiners of Online Groups Differ from Those Who Belonged to the Group Prior to Participating in It via the Internet

There are differences between those who have used the Internet to join a group and those who use the Internet to participate in groups to which they already belong. Many who join online groups are relative newcomers to the Internet. They tend to be urban dwellers, young adults, and less well-educated than the typical Internet user. As a cohort they are more ethnically diverse than other Internet users, and more likely to be interested in online groups relating to fun activities.

The 56% of Cyber Groupies who joined a group after having first contacted it through the Internet have very different tastes in online groups than the "Long-timers" who belonged to the group before engaging with it online. Joiners of Cyber Groups identify hobby groups as the online community that they contact most, followed closely by trade or professional associations. A significant number of joiners also say they contact online fan groups of an entertainer or TV show. In contrast, Long-timers are most likely to say they are most closely in touch with trade or professional groups online.

At the local level, Long-timers are anchored in faith-based and community groups, while the joiners—who make up 20% of the Local Groupie population—show a greater tendency toward groups devoted to sports or with an explicitly social orientation.

Net Joiners of local groups are demographically diverse. They also tend to be highly experienced Internet users. This suggests that the Internet use is drawing new and different kinds of people to local groups. Once people have found local groups online and joined them, they report high levels of community involvement.

Civic Involvement by the Young

These differences among Joiners—particularly their relative youth, newness to the Internet, and racial diversity—suggests that the Internet may be drawing a segment of the population to community engagement who have not been very tied to civic activities. Political scientist Robert Putnam has argued that one major reason for the decline in civic engagement in the United States is the reluctance among younger people to participate in community groups. Our findings indicate that many young people are turning to the Internet as an outlet for community activity. Although young people tend to focus on online groups that involve hobbies, they also are much more likely than other users to report that the Internet has helped them become more involved orga-nizations in their community and connect with people of different genera-tions, economic backgrounds, and ethnic groups. In other words, the primary draw to online communities for young people appears to be hobby groups; however, a secondary outcome, as young people surf to other online commu-nities, is to connect many to groups that help foster civic engagement.

The Internet's Role in Local Engagement

At the local level, people use the Internet mainly as an information utility to find out about local merchants and community activities. The Internet's role in public deliberation is modest. Public access to the Internet is only moder-ately available throughout the United States.

- 41% Internet users say that they "often" or "sometimes" go online to seek out information about local stores or merchants.
- 35% of Internet users "often" or "sometimes" go online for news about their local community or to find out about community events.
- 30% go online "often" or "sometimes" for information about local government.
- 24% go online "often" or "sometimes" to get information about local schools.
- 13% of Internet users say that they "often" or "sometimes" email pub-lic officials. This low rate may be because only half of all Internet users say their town has a Web site, and few Internet users find the town's Web site very useful.
- 11% of Internet users say that they are aware of at least one local issue in which the Internet played a role in organizing citizens to communi-cate with public officials. However, this percentage doubles to 22% for Internet users who are active members of online communities.
- 51% percent of all Americans know of a place in their community where the Internet is publicly available. Overwhelmingly, these places are public libraries. African-Americans are the most likely to say that their community lacks public access to the Internet; 42% of African-Americans say their community does not have publicly available Internet terminals somewhere, compared with 29% of whites and 33% of Hispanics.

Main Report

Part 1: Background

When ARPANET, the Internet's precursor, came online in 1969, it did not have a foundational moment like the telephone's, where Alexander Graham Bell ordered his associate Thomas Watson: "Mr. Watson, come here, I want you." That sentence signaled an era of person-to-person communication over dis-tance. In contrast, ARPANET connected a community. In its earliest days, it was a community of computer researchers at major U.S. universities working on similar problems. Since then, the Internet's capability of allowing many-to-many communications has fostered communities of various sizes and sorts.

In this report, we assess the scope of online communities in the United States and the impact they are having on people's lives. We examine two kinds of communities—those that are primarily cyber-based with no inherently geographic aspect (i.e., online communities) and those in which people use the Internet to connect with groups based in the community in which they live (i.e., communities online). We call members of the former group "Cyber Groupies." We define people who belong to any group having to do with their community as "Local Groupies" and analyze how they use the Internet to stay in touch with local affairs.

Our survey suggests that going online to connect with a group is a central part of Americans' Internet experience. More people have used the Internet to contact an online group than have done extremely popular activities, such as getting news online, health information, or financial information. More people participate in online groups than have bought things online. Fully 84% of all Internet users have contacted an online group at one time or another. We call them Cyber Groupies and there are about 90 million of them. Some 79% of Cyber Groupies identify a particular group with which they remain in contact. Additionally, Cyber Groupies often surf to more than one online group; the average Cyber Groupie has gone to about four different online groups at one time or another. Finally, a quarter of Internet users (26%) say they have used email and the Web to contact or get information about groups and organizations in their communities. These Local Groupies number more than 28 million.

The demographics of the Cyber Groupie population are fairly close to the overall Internet population. Where differences do emerge, the pattern suggests that early adopters of the Internet are more likely to have contacted online groups. This means that Cyber Groupies are more likely to be men and to have college educations or better. Cyber Groupies also tend to be younger than non-groupies. This no doubt is linked to the fact that online groups play a minor role in the lives of people over the age of 55.

The broad appeal of online groups and the youthful tilt of the Cyber Groupie population—especially among those active in online groups and those who have recently joined them—suggests that the Internet is providing an important place for associational activity for some of the most enthusiastic online Americans. This is occurring in the context of widespread worry that Americans are less and less willing to get involved in community affairs and group activities. It is too soon to say that use of the Internet is reversing that trend. But the findings from this survey indicate that group activity is flourishing online and it is a place that attracts Internet users to new group activity.

Part 2: The Internet, Communities, and the Virtual "Third Place"

Social scientists cite any number of indicators to illustrate that Americans' level of civic engagement is on the decline. Membership in organizations whose health may be seen as an indicator of strong community involvement—such as the Parent-Teachers Association (PTA)—has declined steadily over the past several decades. The share of Americans voting in presidential elections has fallen since the 1960s, with voting rates in some local elections no higher than 10%. There has been some evidence of growth in certain kinds of organization called "tertiary associations," but that has not been encouraging to those who worry about the decline of community in America. Tertiary organizations have members spread throughout the country, rarely have local chapters, and usually ask members only for a membership check in exchange for an occasional newsletter. These organizations expect little of their members besides their financial contributions.

While concurring that community involvement is on the wane, many activists believe that the Internet might be able to reverse the trend. Since the early days of the Web, activists have argued that "community networks" could bind increasingly fragmented communities together and provide a voice for segments of society that have been traditionally ignored. Such electronic communities can lower the barriers to democratic participation. Advocates hope lower barriers, coupled with deliberate activities that bring all segments of a town or city into the planning process for building community networks, can help revive the community spirit in America. These advocates do not argue that it is inevitable that the Internet will create community involvement, but rather that the Internet presents an opportunity to build community at a time when the need is great.

Though often focused on the opportunities the Internet presents for a renaissance of local places, technology activists also recognize that virtual communities (i.e., online groups that connect people with common interests without any concern about distance) can play an important role in users' lives. One of the earliest proponents of virtual communities, Howard Rheingold, argues that "people anywhere . . . inevitably build virtual communities" as "informal public spaces disappear from our real lives." Rheingold holds out hope that virtual communities can revive democratic participation, in part by increasing the diversity of sources of information and by sparking public debate that is not mediated by large corporations or special interests.

The hopes for the Internet and community are tempered by the acknowledgement that it is a technology that has the potential to undermine community. As author Andrew Shapiro points out, the Internet's potential to give people more control also allows them to restrict the flow of information they receive. By giving people a choice to block out information that somehow does not "fit" with a community's beliefs or norms, the Internet could exacerbate existing trends toward community fragmentation. Nothing about this is inevitable, but Shapiro notes that the evidence on online communities suggests that some degree of face-to-face interaction is necessary for an online community to be sustainable. As Katie Hafner points out in her new account of the pioneering online community "The Well," this cyber group really gained vitality once members, most of whom lived in the San Francisco Bay Area, had met face-to-face.

The findings of the Pew Internet & American Life Project survey indicate that something positive is afoot with respect to the Internet and community life in the United States. People's use of the Internet to participate in organizations is not necessarily evidence of a revival of civic engagement, but it has clearly stimulated new associational activity. And, because they have been both physical and virtual, these group interactions are richer than those found in "tertiary associations." This type of activity might be likened to what sociologist Ray Oldenburg calls the "third place"—the corner bar, café, or bookstore where people hang out to talk about things that are going on in their lives and neighborhood.

Although Oldenburg very clearly has physical interaction in mind in talking about third places, the Internet has spurred in cyberspace the types of conversations that Oldenburg describes in third places. Our survey suggests that significant numbers of Cyber Groupies are enjoying new relationships because of their use of the Internet. One-quarter (27%) of Cyber Groupies say the Net has helped them connect with people of different economic and ethnic backgrounds and 37% say it has helped them connect with people of different generations. Whether through cyber groups or online groups grounded in local communities, the Internet's "virtual third places" appear to be building bridges among their participants. . . .

Jonathon N. Cummings,
Brian Butler, and Robert Kraut

 **NO**

The Quality of Online
Social Relationships

People use the Internet intensely for interpersonal communication, sending and receiving email, contacting friends and family via instant messaging services, visiting chat rooms, or subscribing to distribution lists, among other activities. The evidence is clear that interpersonal communication is an important use of the Internet, if not its *most* important use. For example, both self-report surveys and computer monitoring studies indicate that email is the most popular online application.

Claims regarding the Internet's usefulness for developing social relationships, however, remain controversial. Both personal testimonials and systematically collected data document the deep and meaningful social relationships people can cultivate online.

This evidence, however, conflicts with data comparing the value that people place on their online relationships with offline relationships and with data comparing social relationships among heavy and light Internet users. For example, Parks and Roberts surveyed users of multiplayer environments called MOOs. Ninety-three percent of the users had made friends online, but when asked to compare their online friendships with those offline, respondents rated offline ones higher. Respondents to Nie's national survey reported spending less time with friends and family since going online, with the decline greatest among the most frequent Internet users. And Kraut et al. presented longitudinal evidence to demonstrate that among new Internet users, online time diminished social involvement and psychological well being.

Understanding the impact of the Internet on human social relationships requires two types of evidence. First, we need to know how computer-mediated communication affects the quality of particular social interactions and relationships. Are the online ones better, the same, or worse than those sustained by other means? Second, we need to know how computer-mediated communication affects one's mix of social interactions and relationships. The impact of the Internet is likely to be very different if it supplements communication with existing friends and family, or if instead it substitutes for more traditional communication and social ties.

This article addresses the first question by explicitly comparing online and offline social interaction. We briefly summarize evidence from several

From *Communications of the ACM,* vol. 45, no. 7, July 2002, pp. 103–108. Copyright © 2002 by Communications of the ACM. Reprinted with permission.

empirical studies, all of which suggest that computer-mediated communication, and in particular email, is less valuable for building and sustaining close social relationships than face-to-face contact and telephone conversations. These studies include the following surveys:

- International bank employees who describe the value of particular communication sessions for work relationships;
- College students, using the same methodology, but focusing on personal relationships;
- A longitudinal study of new Internet users; and
- Examination of behavior on email-based listservs.

Comparing Communication over Different Media

One way to evaluate the usefulness of the Internet for developing and maintaining social ties is to ask people to compare particular communication sessions on relevant outcomes. One can then relate the outcomes to features of the communication session (for example, who it was with, the duration, and the modality over which it occurred). This technique has been used to uncover features of conversation that lead to the development of social relationships in face-to-face settings. We apply it to email, telephone, and face-to-face communication among bank employees and university students.

In our 1991 study, 979 employees of a multinational bank reported on their most recent communication conducted over different media. About 81% used email in their jobs, sending an average of 15 messages per week. Respondents evaluated the usefulness of communication episodes using criteria related to the success of work groups, including usefulness for getting work done and for developing or sustaining a work relationship, utilizing a 3-point scale, where 1 meant not very useful and 3 meant very useful. We report data on 5,205 communication episodes that occurred in person, by telephone, or by email. . . .

Respondents reported communication by email to be reliably worse than communication conducted face-to-face or by telephone, both for getting work done and for sustaining work relationships. However, the disadvantages of email were significantly greater for maintaining relationships than for getting work done. These differences among the media remain even when one statistically controls for relevant variables, including respondents' gender, age, job title, daily volume of communication, and experience with email.

One might object that this data comes from the early years of email, although employees in this firm had been using email since the mid-1970s. In addition, one might also object that personal relationships are not central to work activity, although many studies stress their importance for getting work done. To counter these objections, we replicated the original study in 1999 among students at an eastern university. These students used email extensively, estimating a mean of 11 messages per day, and were in a stage in life that stressed the importance of developing personal relationships. Some 39 students completed a diary, recording information about each of 259 communication episodes in which they had participated during a four-hour block—late afternoon to early evening. Students recorded their relationship with their communication partner (relative, friend, acquaintance, or other), its duration, the topic of conversation (schoolwork, personal, or other), and the modality over which it occurred. Respondents evaluated each communication for its usefulness in getting work done, exchanging information, and developing or maintaining a personal relationship. They made their evaluations on 5-point scale.

Like the banking study, students evaluated email communication sessions as an inferior means to maintaining personal relationships compared to those conducted in person ($p < 0.05$) and by telephone ($p < 0.05$), these latter being equal. The students, however, found email to be as good as the telephone and in-person communication for completing schoolwork ($p > 0.10$), and even better for the exchange of information ($p < 0.05$).

Students also estimated the frequency of communication over the different modalities and the strength of their relationship with each of the 148 partners. We created an index of relationship strength by averaging their answers to two questions: "How close do you feel to this person?" and "How often do you get favors or advice from this person" (alpha = 0.92). We used linear regression to predict the strength of the relationship from frequency of communication with that partner over the different modalities: email, in-person, and telephone. Frequency of communication across all three modalities was significantly related to the strength of relationship, both directly and once the partner's gender, nature of the relations, length of the relationship, and geographic distance between the parties were controlled statistically. However, communicating in person (Beta s = 0.36) and by telephone (Beta = 0.27) were both significantly better predictors of a strong relationship than was communication by email (Beta = 0.15).

Comparing Internet Versus NonInternet Social Partners

In these studies, respondents selected communication episodes and partners based on the recency of the communication session. This procedure has the advantage of sampling all potential conversations, but may over-represent social relationships not important to the respondents, but are frequent simply because the partners are nearby. Here, we compare the value of using computer-mediated and noncomputer-mediated communication to keep up with partners with whom the respondents have a substantial amount of communication. The data comes from the HomeNet project, a field trial that tracked Internet usage and communication behavior among a sample of 93 households in Pittsburgh during their first year or two online.

Participants answered a series of questions about two individuals with whom they had frequent communication. The first, whom we refer to as the "Internet partner," was the individual outside of their household to whom they sent the most email, as recorded in computer-generated usage logs collected as part of the project. Some 111 respondents answered questions about an Internet partner. The second, whom we refer to as the "nonInternet partner," was the person outside of their household with whom respondents claimed to have the most frequent communication in any modality. Some 125 respondents answered questions about a nonInternet partner. To allow for comparisons between relationships conducted by email and those conducted primarily over other modalities, we limit our analyses here to the 99 respondents who answered questions both about an Internet and a nonInternet partner, and for whom these partners were different individuals.

Respondents indicated each partner's gender and age, duration of acquaintance, role relation (for example, family, friend, co-worker), and geographic proximity (for example, neighborhood, city, state). Participants then rated their frequency of email, face-to-face, and telephone communication: (5-daily, 4-weekly, 3-monthly, 2-less often, 1-never). A 5-point scale indicated psychological closeness with the partner: "I feel very close," "I could freely confide in this person," "This person is important to me," and "I understand this person fully" (alpha = 0.90).

We were interested in three questions: Do people differ in the overall volume of communication they have with the people they keep up with using different modalities? Do they differ in how close they feel toward them? Is communication with a partner over different modalities predictive of differing degrees of psychological closeness?

The number of respondents' communication sessions per month, broken and summed over all modalities, indicate that participants communicated less frequently with their Internet partner (5.2 times/month) than their nonInternet partner (7.2 times/month, $p < 0.001$). . . . Although respondents communicated more by email with their Internet partner ($p < 0.001$), they communicated less using the other modalities ($p < 0.001$ for face-to-face and $p < 0.001$ for telephone). Respondents also reported feeling less close to their Internet partner than to their nonInternet partner ($p < 0.001$).

Using a least squares regression analysis, we predicted psychological closeness from frequency of communication for the nonInternet partner and Internet partner, controlling for sex, age, role relation, duration of acquaintance, and physical proximity. Most notably, frequency of communication was a critical predictor of psychological closeness with the nonInternet partner (Beta = 0.40), but not with the Internet partner (Beta = −0.08). The difference is statistically significant ($p < 0.001$). The weaker association of communication with closeness for the Internet sample is analogous to findings from the student sample.

Social relationships offline involve more communication than those developed online, and thus predicted psychological closeness. Given our cross-sectional data, we cannot tell if communication does not lead to closeness when people are communicating electronically, or if people are exchanging email with people to whom they do not feel close. In either case, they are not getting as much social benefit from email as they do from their other communication activity.

Online Social Groups

The research we described so far concentrates on dyadic relationships between individuals in their online and offline lives. Yet one of the prominent features of the Internet is the presence of larger social collectives, which researchers have called "electronic groups" or "communities." Even before the advent of the Web, the Internet provided an infrastructure for online group-level social behavior, through USENET and email-based distribution lists. In descriptions of social life on the Internet, these electronic or virtual communities are often described as groups where relationships form, and whose members provide each other with companionship, information, and social support.

While existing studies and stories of electronic groups provide insight into the types of social activity that can occur in electronic collectives, the anecdotal nature of this research leaves open the question of what typically happens. Are active, tightly knit electronic groups, in which people form personal relationships and develop a sense of belonging, the norm or are the cases reported in the literature interesting exceptions? To examine this question, we collected data from a sample of 204 Internet listservs. The data shows that, on average, listservs are much more like loosely knit, voluntary organizations than the tightly knit social communities highlighted in prior case studies.

The sample consisted of 204 unmanaged and unmoderated email-based listservs, drawn from a population of approximately 70,000 listservs. An initial random sample of 1,066 was stratified by topic type (work-related, personal, and mixed) to ensure it included a range of topics and member populations. Listservs were dropped from the initial sample if the list owner declined to participate in the study (21%); the listserv was defunct (16%); it had closed membership, generally as part of an organization, course, or task force (15%); or it could not provide membership data in an automated fashion. The final sample consisted of lists evenly divided among those oriented around professional, personal, and academic topics. Based on descriptions of the lists, we were able to classify them as purely electronic or as hybrid, combining both electronic and traditional communications, especially conventional face-to-face meetings. For example, a national list for youth hockey was judged as purely electronic, while the mailing list for a city-specific country dancers' group was judged as hybrid.

For a 130-day period we collected data on each listserv's membership and communication activity. During the observation period, membership was characterized in terms of size (number of members), growth (members entering as a percentage of initial size), loss (members leaving as a percentage of initial size), and net change in size (as a percentage of initial size). Communication activity was measured in terms of volume (number of messages per day) and interactivity (length of discussion threads). In addition, measures of member participation (percentage of members contributing messages and the concentration of message contributions among the active participants) were created for each listserv. . . .

Unlike traditional small groups, listservs have large, fluctuating memberships in which a small core of active participants generates relatively low levels of sporadic communication, whose messages rarely receive a response. Small groups, as described in the social psychological research literature, have between 3 and 15 members, with relatively low turnover. By comparison, the listservs were much larger (median of 64 members), with high churn (22% of original members dropping out annually and double this number joining). In contrast to highly interactive conversation involving almost all group members (typical of small groups), listservs exhibit little communication, with a full 33% exhibiting no communication during the 130-day observation period. Of those that did, the median listserv accrued 0.28 messages per day (or less than 0.0004 messages per subscriber per day). Over 50% of members contributed no messages over the 130-day observation period, and a small number generated most of the messages. Conversation was not interactive. On average, fewer than one message out of three received any response.

The hybrid groups differed little from the purely electronic groups. Though they were significantly smaller, probably reflecting the more limited geographic area from which they could attract members, both types of groups had similar high turnover, low volume of messages, low level of interactivity, and domination by a small proportion of their membership. Regardless of how the hybrid groups acted when they met face-to-face, online they acted like typical weak-tie collectives.

In terms of membership size and change, communication volume and structure, and participation levels, Internet listservs do not appear to be intimate social groups. These findings highlight a bias in prior research on online social activity. While the goal of describing the existence of true social behaviors in online environments has been well served by focusing on highly active and interactive examples of electronic collectives, these cases are not representative of what typically happens. For example, interactivity is a common theme in many descriptions of online social activity. However, our results imply that while interactivity can occur in these contexts, it is the exception, not the rule, when it occurs.

It was not the case that all listservs in this sample had impoverished social behavior, although this was the norm. Nor is it necessarily the case that all types of electronic collectives will look like listservs in terms of the quality of their social behavior. MUDs, MOOs, and Internet Relay Chat are highly interactive, at least among those who actively participate. As is the case with asynchronous media, however, research studying these phenomena has focused on interesting cases (that is, active ones). As a result, we know little about typical behavior in synchronic electronic collectives.

Clearly, there are cases of both synchronous and asynchronous electronic collectives that support the formation of substantial personal relationships and the development of group identity. On the other hand, these types of social activities seem unlikely to occur regularly in the typical listserv, where turnover is high and communication activities is low, noninteractive, and the result of contributions by a small percentage of the membership. This suggests that social places on the Internet where close personal relationships are formed and maintained are rare.

Conclusion

Using the Internet to build social relationships results in social interaction that is wanting, at least when it is explicitly compared to the standards of face-to-face and telephone communication, to social relationships that are primarily conducted offline, and to traditional small groups. We do not assert that online social interaction has little value. Surveys of the general public continually reveal that most people using the Internet value email and other forms of online social interaction. Even in the age of the Web and e-commerce, online social interaction is still the most important use of the Internet. However, in one-to-one comparisons, an email message is not as useful as a phone call or a face-to-face meeting for developing and sustaining social relationships. Listservs are not as valuable as small groups for establishing a sense of identity and belonging and for gaining social support. Relationships sustained primarily over the Internet are not as close as those sustained by other means.

Should these observations be a source of concern? To answer this question, we need additional information not yet available. Our data suggests the Internet is less effective than other means of forming and sustaining strong social relationships. The consequences of using the Internet for social relations, however, depend not only on the quality of the relationships sustained using it, but on opportunity costs as well. Do less-effective email messages substitute for or supplement telephone conversations and personal visits? Do weak social relationships formed online add to one's total stock of social relations or substitute for a more valuable partner? Does the time people spend reading listservs and participating in MUDs add to their social interaction, or substitute for time they would have spent in real-world groups? Only by examining people's full set of social behavior and examining their full inventory of social ties can we assess the net social impact of online social relationships.

POSTSCRIPT

Does the Internet Strengthen Community?

The debate over the social impact of the Internet is by no means over, although the opponents do tend to be less polarized today, perhaps because online communication clearly has benefits. For instance, in the first 48 hours after the September 11, 2001, destruction of the World Trade Towers in New York City, 4 million people used e-mail to check on friends and family (see Bruce Bower, "The Social Net," *Science News*, May 4, 2002). It has also become apparent that the initial effects of going online are not the same as later effects. Robert Kraut et al. reported that new Internet users became less socially involved and more depressed ("Internet Paradox: A Social Technology that Reduces Social Involvement and Psychological Well-Being?" *American Psychologist*, 53[9], 1998), but in a later study Robert Kraut, Sara Kiesler, Konka Boneva, Jonathon Cummings, Vicki Hegelson, and Anne Crawford conclude that the earlier negative effects largely dissipated with continued use of the Internet; they also note in a separate study of new computer and television purchasers that the outcome is clearly better for extraverts and those with more social support ("Internet Paradox Revisited," *Journal of Social Issues*, vol. 58, No. 1, 2002).

In February 2000, the Stanford Institute for the Quantitative Study of Society released a study by Norman Nie of Stanford and Lutz Erbring of the Free University of Berlin that found that "the more hours people use the Internet, the less time they spend in contact with real human beings," with a quarter of regular Internet users saying it has reduced their in-person or phone time "with friends and family or attending events outside the home." Since time online increases with the number of years one has had Internet access, Nie and Erbring see a potential problem in personal isolation and reduced community participation. James E. Katz, Ronald E. Rice, and Philip Aspden, on the other hand, used telephone surveys from 1995 to 2000 to conclude that Internet users typically have more social contacts and are more involved in their community and in politics ("The Internet, 1995–2000: Access, Civic Involvement, and Social Interaction," *American Behavioral Scientist*, November 2001). Janis Wolak, Kimberly J. Mitchell, and David Finkelhor, "Escaping or Connecting? Characteristics of Youth Who Form Close Online Relationships," *Journal of Adolescence* (February 2003), note that at least with younger people, "girls who had high levels of conflict with parents or were highly troubled were more likely than other girls to have close online relationships, as were boys who had low levels of communication with parents or were highly troubled, compared to other boys." Examining college students, Katie Bonebrake, "College Students' Internet Use, Relationship Formation, and Personality

Correlates," *CyberPsychology & Behavior* (December 2002), did not see such differences. Lee Rainie and John Horrigan, in "A Decade of Adoption: How the Internet Has Woven Itself into American Life," *Pew Internet & American Life Project* (http://www.pewinternet.org/PPF/r/148/report_display.asp) (January 25, 2005), note that "For the most part, the online world mirrors the offline world [and the] Web has become the 'new normal' in the American way of life." Donna L. Hoffman, Thomas P. Novak, and Alladi Venkatesh suggest that "normal" is too mild a term in "Has the Internet Become Indispensable?" *Communications of the ACM* (July 2004). Linda A. Jackson et al., "The Impact of Internet Use on the Other Side of the Digital Divide," *Communications of the ACM* (July 2004), suggest that it is still true that neither "normal" nor "indispensable" apply to the poor.

Paul DiMaggio, Eszter Hargittai, W. Russell Neuman, and John P. Robinson say that most of the research on the social impacts of the Internet is flawed, having been performed by nonacademic survey organizations and focused too much on individuals rather than the organizational structure of the Internet itself; more research by academic sociologists is needed. Still, they call the Internet "a potentially transformative technology" and note that it "tends to complement rather than displace existing media and patterns of behavior" (see "Social Implications of the Internet," *Annual Review of Sociology*, 2001).

ISSUE 15

Does the Spread of Surveillance Technology Threaten Privacy?

YES: Simon Cooper, from "Who's Spying on You?" *Popular Mechanics* (January 2005)

NO: Stuart Taylor, Jr., from "How Civil-Libertarian Hysteria May Endanger Us All," *National Journal* (February 22, 2003)

ISSUE SUMMARY

YES: Computer professional Simon Cooper argues that technology is enabling a massive increase in routine surveillance and the collection of personal data by both government and business with very few restrictions on how the data are used. Personal privacy is indeed threatened.

NO: Stuart Taylor, Jr., contends that those who object to surveillance—particularly government surveillance—have their priorities wrong. Curbing "government powers in the name of civil liberties [exacts] too high a price in terms of endangered lives."

T he Fourth Amendment to the U.S. Constitution established the right of private citizens to be secure against unreasonable searches and seizures. "Unreasonable" has come to mean "without a search warrant" for physical searches of homes and offices, and "without a court order" for interceptions of mail and wiretappings of phone conversations.

Private citizens who—for whatever reason—do not wish to have their communications with others shared with law enforcement and security agencies have long sought ways to preserve their privacy. They therefore welcomed changes in communications technology, from easily tappable copper wires to fiber optics, from analog (which mimics voice vibrations) to digital (which encodes them). But the U.S. Department of Justice sought legislation to require that the makers and providers of communications products and services ensure that their products remain tappable, and in September 1992, the Clinton Administration submitted to Congress the Digital Telephony Act, a piece of legislation designed to prevent advancing technology from limiting the government's ability legally to intercept communications. For a defense of this measure, see Dorothy Denning, "To Tap or Not to Tap," *Communications of the ACM* (March 1993).

Yet people fear the Internet because it makes a huge variety of information available to everyone with very little accountability. Even children can find sites dedicated to pornography, violence, and hate. Marketers can build detailed profiles. Fraud, identity theft, invasion of privacy, and terrorism have taken new forms. Criminals can use encryption (secret codes) to make their email messages and transmitted documents unreadable to anyone (such as law-enforcement personnel with the digital equivalent of wiretap warrants).

In response, the Department of Justice developed an Internet wiretapping system called Carnivore. It was a computer program designed to run on an Internet service provider's (ISP's) computers, sifting through the email messages and other Internet traffic of that ISP's clients, as well as all those messages that are relayed through that ISP's computers. Supposedly, Carnivore searched for activity only by certain persons (as specified by a court order) and ignored all other activity. In 2004, Carnivore was abandoned; the FBI now relies on commercial products for the same purposes. See Wilson P. Dizard, III, and Roseanne Gerin, "Case Management and Carnivore Both on Life Support at FBI," *Government Computer News* (http://appserv.gcn.com/24_2/executive-management/34878-1.html) (January 24, 2005). Before then, however, many people had been disturbed by Carnivore's invisibility; they saw a potential for abuse in its ability to search Internet traffic without a court order and to search for any keywords its operators desire. They would have been much happier if the objects of surveillance were told they were being watched or even if the objects of surveillance were able to monitor the surveillance itself. For a fertile discussion of the balance between surveillance and accountability, see David Brin, *The Transparent Society* (Perseus, 1999).

After September 11, 2001, the objections to Carnivore vanished almost entirely. The War on Terrorism had begun, and every tool that promised to help identify terrorists before or catch them after they committed their dreadful acts was seen as desirable. However, when the Department of Defense's Defense Advanced Research Projects Agency proposed a massive computer system capable of sifting through purchases, tax data, court records, and other information from government and commercial databases to seek suspicious patterns of behavior, the objections returned in force. Objections to the Total or Terrorism Information Awareness program, discussed by J. Michael Waller, "Fears Mount over 'Total' Spy System," *Insight on the News* (December 24, 2002), were vigorous enough that it soon died, but the basic issues did not vanish, and the technology of information collection continued to develop to the point where computer professional Simon Cooper can now argue that we are subject to massively increased routine surveillance and the collection of personal data by both government and business with very few restrictions on how the data are used. Personal privacy is seriously threatened. Stuart Taylor, Jr., contends that those who object to surveillance—particularly government surveillance—have their priorities wrong. Curbing "government powers in the name of civil liberties [exacts] too high a price in terms of endangered lives."

YES

Simon Cooper

Who's Spying on You?

James Turner had more than 400 miles and 8 hours on the road ahead of him as he set out from his home in New Haven, Conn., on a chilly October morning in 2000. Turner, a theater manager, was going to Portsmouth, Va., to check out a play he wanted to bring to his hometown stage. Half an hour into the trip, as Turner passed through the town of Westport, Conn., he pushed down on the accelerator. The needle on his rented Chrysler minivan nudged up to 70 miles per hour as he continued south on 1-95.

Eleven thousand miles above Turner, four NAVSTAR Global Positioning System (GPS) satellites were transmitting signals being picked up—and recorded—by a tiny receiver inside his vehicle. Later, as he traveled along the New Jersey Turnpike, the receiver clocked him at 83 mph.

Why were Turner and the minivan under such close scrutiny?

Turner rented the minivan from ACME Car Rentals, a New Haven firm that had installed GPS receivers in its fleet and contracted a Canadian company, AirIQ, to monitor them. ACME didn't want its cars exceeding 70 mph. If one did, the processor inside the car woke up and wirelessly connected to a remote computer, which sent ACME a report of each incident.

By the time Turner reached Virginia, his bank account had been debited an extra $450 by ACME—$150 for three speeding infractions—and his original $196 rental fee had ballooned to $646.

"I was completely blown away," says Turner. "Not only by the fines, but also by the invasion of my privacy. It's a scary situation, how they can watch you like that." Turner sued ACME and over the past four years the case has rumbled through the courts.

Along the way, it has helped spotlight a growing trend that many observers believe is permanently reshaping society.

There's a tradeoff to be made for enjoying the high-tech benefits of the 21st century. The latest technologies make life safer, more convenient, more fun. The price? Your anonymity. Every day, each of us leaves behind an indelible trail of electronic crumbs that other entities can pick up and follow.

In the digital age, innovations cut both ways. Cellphones let us talk virtually anywhere, but some new models can now betray our locations to within a few feet. DSL and cable modems let us roam the universe faster than ever, but leave us more vulnerable to hackers, hijackers and malicious spyware. Digital

From *Popular Mechanics*, January 2005, pp. 57–58, 60–61, 111–112. Copyright © 2005 by Simon Cooper. Reprinted by permission.

video recorders let us record and pause programs at will, but they also track what we watch and when we watch it. Even the automobile—the universal symbol of freedom—has become a surveillance center on wheels, with black box data recorders and on-board navigation systems tracking our every mile.

And in the most Orwellian tech development of all, a microchip that can be implanted in the human body—revealing anything about its host from medical history to security clearances—was approved for medical use in the States.

Bottom line: "It is impossible to exist in today's society without surrendering to almost constant monitoring of one kind or another," says Jay Stanley, a technology expert with the American Civil Liberties Union (ACLU).

Is this necessarily a bad thing? Proponents say data gathering enhances lives, enabling better services, less waste, cheaper prices and, perhaps most important, greater safety in a post-9/11 world. But opponents fear a loss of personal privacy and a creeping progression toward a kind of information eugenics—a bleak future where huge databases segregate America, determining who gets the best jobs, the best opportunities and even the best prices while shopping.

Both sides agree on one thing: The digital information stream generated by the average American is getting bigger every day. But who's collecting all this data? And what are they doing with it?

The GPS Invasion

Most of the technologies creating what some call the Fishbowl Society aren't cutting-edge. As Richard Hunter, author of *World Without Secrets,* notes, the technology "isn't necessarily new, but is newly *ubiquitous.*"

Take the GPS that nailed Turner. Conceived by the U.S. military in the 1960s, the Global Positioning System network took more than 20 years to come online. Yet, GPS tracking is on its way to becoming a $28 billion-a-year industry by 2008. GM's OnStar system, for example, places GPS in millions of cars. Those cars can be tracked at the behest of the police and government agencies.

Lately, GPS technology has expanded into a controversial new area: cellphones. Federal regulations require all cellphone networks to be enabled with an E911 system; this allows a cellphone's location to be isolated to within 100 meters using triangulation between three cellphone towers or as close as a few feet using a GPS chip. While E911 ostensibly sends location information only when someone dials 911, newer phones incorporate location-based services, and can constantly send precise location information back to the cellular provider.

"In essence, every cellphone in America is now a pocket tracking device," says Beth Givens of the Privacy Rights Clearinghouse, a consumer advocacy group in San Diego.

Watchdogs like Givens say E911 technology, though intended as a public service, is ripe for abuse. Some cases are already working their way through the courts. In August 2004 Ara Gabrielyan was arrested in Glendale, Calif., after allegedly duct taping a GPS-enabled phone under his ex-girl-friend's car to track her movements. "This is what I would call stalking of the 21st century," Lt. John Perkins of the Glendale Police Department told reporters. Gabrielyan, 32, pleaded innocent to stalking and making terrorist threats, and is awaiting trial on $500,000 bail.

According to police, Gabrielyan subscribed to one of the handful of new services that allow a cellphone's owner to track its movements over the Internet. Sites like ULocate and FollowUs show a phone's location and the speed at which it's moving, all superimposed on digital maps detailed to street level. Not surprisingly, these do-it-yourself tracking services have attracted plenty of critics. FollowUs, for example, was recently labeled one of the "most invasive companies" by the advocacy group Privacy International.

Still, there is no shortage of entrepreneurs trying to turn GPS tracking into a profitable business. AirIQ, the company used by ACME to monitor renters like James Turner, integrates five technologies—wireless communication, GPS tracking, digital mapping, computing intelligence and the Internet—to create "telematics," a high-tech, low-cost service used by some car rental firms, large distribution companies and commercial boat owners.

AirIQ CEO Don Simmonds even uses his system to enforce no-speeding rules on his three teenagers. "If one of my kids exceeds 80 mph for more than a minute, I get a message on my BlackBerry." His kids get a $25 fine and Simmonds gets peace of mind—and the ability to locate his kids in an instant.

While it's not known what Simmonds's children think of this system, it's quickly becoming apparent that rental car customers hate it. Currently, the industry's top guns, Hertz and Avis, say they use GPS solely for fleet monitoring. But some of the smaller players are using the technology for contract enforcement, with decidedly mixed results. In 2004, dozens of complaints were filed against San Francisco rental firm Payless when it used GPS tracking to prove drivers crossed state lines, something the rental contract's small print forbade. In November 2003, Canadian tourist Byungsoo Son was charged $1 for every mile he traveled outside California in a Payless car. His rental fee catapulted from $260 to an eye-opening $3400. The dispute was settled out of court.

As for Turner, in May 2004 a court ruled he'd been unfairly penalized, but rejected his claim for damages. Turner appealed. "This kind of tracking can't be ignored," he says.

State legislators agree. New "anti-GPS tracking" laws have been enacted in California and New York, banning rental firms from deploying what outgoing California Assembly member Ellen Corbett called the "Big Brother tactics" of using GPS technology to impose penalties for speeding or crossing state lines.

A Lie Detector in Your Car

You don't need to rent a car to be monitored. In 2004, black box data recorders were a standard feature in nearly 70 percent of cars manufactured; they're now installed in about 40 million cars in the United States. Tiny event data recorders (EDRs) live under the dash or seats and silently record what happens to the vehicle in the seconds surrounding a crash—speed, when the brakes are applied and so on. Like the black boxes in airliners, they become critical after serious accidents.

In a number of recent cases EDR data has been instrumental in prosecuting serious crimes. Walter Rhoads pleaded guilty to vehicular homicide in Pennsylvania in May 2002 after he was confronted with black box data from his Corvette showing he'd been traveling at 106 mph, and braked only 2 seconds before crashing into another car, killing its driver, William Stott. "The black box doesn't lie," said Stott's son after the case.

In 2003 the National Transportation Safety Board announced it wanted EDRs installed in all new vehicles. Only California currently requires owners to be notified if an EDR is on board. Despite their obvious benefits, the boxes have privacy advocates worried. Can lawyers demand access for use in civil lawsuits? And can info on your driving habits cause insurance premiums to rise—or be canceled?

Progressive, the country's third-largest auto insurer, recently started a pilot program that is being watched keenly by other insurers. Five thousand Minnesota drivers signed up to allow Ohio-based Progressive to install a tiny TripSense monitor in their cars to record their driving habits. Drivers the devices reveal as "low-risk" will be rewarded with policy discounts of up to 25 percent. These kinds of voluntary discount incentives are seen by privacy advocates as Trojan horses, designed to lure consumers into giving up personal data and to punish those who don't by imposing higher prices.

The Spy in AISLE 3

Mexico's attorney general, Rafael Macedo de la Concha, has seemingly little in common with a handful of nightcrawling regulars at a trendy bar in Barcelona, Spain. But under the skin, Mexico's top lawyer and some 50 VIPs at the Baja Beach Club share a common bond—they've been implanted with a microchip that uniquely identifies them when scanned.

The tiny in-body transmitter, called a VeriChip, is made by Florida-based Applied Digital Systems (ADS) and each is encoded with a unique 16-digit number. In Mexico it's used to restrict access to a room filled with top-secret documents; in Barcelona it's used to automate entry to the club and payment for drinks.

The VeriChip is the latest member of a tech family called Radio Frequency Identification (RFID). RFID tags are microchips (some as small as a grain of sand) that broadcast encoded information to special readers. They're now used for everything from electronic toll collection to tracking supplies in Iraq.

VeriChip's human-implant applications aside, RFID manufacturers believe retailing is the best use for the technology, eventually capable of cataloging purchases, activating cameras and special display monitors, and finally speeding customers through checkout—creating a true 21st century shopping experience. "With RFIDs, it's as though every item has its own license plate," says WalMart spokesman Gus Whitcomb.

But for many, stripping away the anonymity once guaranteed as part of the supermarket shopping experience is a disturbing prospect. Some consumers are worried about the potential for privacy invasion, fearing the minute analysis of shopping habits or even the possibility that RFID tags could be used to track people once they leave the store.

Such paranoia seemed to be validated last year when Katherine Albrecht, founder of Consumers Against Super-market Privacy Invasion and Numbering, received an anonymous tip about a strange-looking shelf being installed in a Wal-Mart in Brockton, Mass. Albrecht investigated and says she found a so-called "smart shelf" for razors, similar to one recently tested in England. The blades were rigged with RFID technology designed to trigger a camera when a customer picked up a pack and again when he paid at the checkout. Wal-Mart's Whitcomb says the shelf was a "field test" to see if in-store tagging "was possible at this stage. We learned it wasn't." The surreptitious test was quickly abandoned.

For now, the nation's top retailers say they are focusing on RFID technology strictly for backroom inventory control. In July 2003, Wal-Mart told its top 100 suppliers to start using RFID tagging on all shipments by early 2005. "If Wal-Mart can use RFIDs to improve sales by just 1 percent, they'll gain an extra $2.5 billion per year in revenue," says Mark Roberti, editor of *RFID Journal*.

Roberti dismisses fears of postshopping tracking: If RFID tracking becomes economically feasible, he says, "the chip will be in the packaging. It gets thrown away."

But of course this isn't the case with implantable RFIDs, which for many people raises the sci-fi specter of a tagged and tracked population. In October 2004, ADS won Food and Drug Administration approval to use its tiny Veri-Chips in humans for medical applications. Scott Silverman, the company's CEO, says concerns the VeriChip could be used for some kind of covert tracking program are unfounded. "If you are using a portable reader, it has to pass within 2 or 3 in. of the site of where the chip is implanted," he explains. Some say future advances in scanning technology, however, could potentially make long-range tracking possible.

Silverman, who was himself VeriChip tagged in 2002, says the chips would eliminate security issues over access to confidential information. "A swipe card or a password can be stolen," he says. "These can't." He sees the best application of the technology in medicine: The VeriChip's code can be linked to a patient's computerized medical records, potentially proving invaluable in emergencies. ADS is also in talks with the U.S. government over potential military applications.

Where It All Goes

Most Americans have files kept on them by private companies known as "data aggregators." In the past decade these firms have built huge databases by vacuuming up billions of records purchased from credit agencies, state governments, courts and, lately, some sources of digital tracking data. The amount compiled on each American keeps getting bigger, as does the number of customers eager to pay for that data. The biggest U.S. data aggregation firm is ChoicePoint, of Alpharetta, Ga., which earned nearly $800 million in 2003 mainly by selling information. The company boasts 19 billion files; they're available online to anyone with a credit card and PC. (Background checks require a subject's permission.)

But the fastest-growing demand for such aggregated data seems to come from the federal government. A recent study by the Electronic Privacy Information Center revealed that nine government agencies—including the FBI—have signed multimillion-dollar contracts with data aggregators.

"There's nothing wrong with government agencies having the same access to information your real estate broker can access," says Paul Rosenzweig, of the conservative think tank The Heritage Foundation. Rosenzweig notes the study of such data is becoming critical in the fight against terrorism, and believes many privacy advocates are misguided. Officials "are studying what good people's patterns look like to make it easier to spot bad patterns."

Swarm Intelligence Meets Function Creep

The nightmare scenario is one created by something called "swarm intelligence": the potential ability of automated programs to move from database to database, mining billions of bytes of data into a huge central electronic repository where every aspect of an individual's life—from birth date to what toothpaste he buys—could be collated, analyzed, and accessed by individuals and organizations for whom it was not originally intended.

"This scenario is already possible," says the ACLU's Jay Stanley. "All that's missing is the policy to implement it."

The possibility of swarm intelligence surfaced in 1999 with the announcement of the Department of Defense's Total Information Awareness (TIA) program, designed to comb through billions of records looking for suspicious behavior. TIA was scrapped by Congress in 2003 after a public outcry, but according to an interview given in August by TIA's former chief, John Poindexter, aspects of the program live on, buried in ultrasecret military "black budget" programs.

And TIA may not be alone. In May 2004 the General Accounting Office issued a report on the government's use of data mining, revealing 199 such operations.

The problem with all this data collection, say experts like Jim Harper, director of information policy studies for the Cato Institute, is that "databases have clear tendencies to grow and adopt new uses, uses that at some point may vary dramatically from their original purposes." It's known as "function creep."

Just ask Robert Rivera. In 1999, Rivera sued a Vons supermarket in Los Angeles after slipping on yogurt and shattering his knee. The then 59-year-old was a Vons's Club Card member; all of his purchases were recorded in a database. According to Rivera and his lawyer, during mediation they were told Vons had accessed Rivera's shopping records and concluded he bought "a lot" of liquor. Rivera claims he was told by a mediator that if he went to court, purchases would be used to show he was a heavy drinker. Rivera sued anyway and Vons settled. (Vons denied Rivera's claims.)

Rivera's allegation raises serious questions about a future dominated by the trade in information. Will insurance companies raise a policyholder's premium if shopping records indicate he often buys cigarettes? Will dates be canceled after home-based data mining reveals purchases of Prozac or Viagra? Will the Drug Enforcement Administration track loyalty-card purchases of Sudafed and plastic baggies to root out methamphetamine labs?

Possibly, says writer Richard Hunter. "There are significant implications for society regarding the vast amounts of data being aggregated, analyzed and made available. Because at the moment there are virtually no restrictions on what information can be shared."

Stuart Taylor, Jr.

 **NO**

How Civil-Libertarian Hysteria May Endanger Us All

Someday Americans may die because of Congress's decision earlier this month to cripple a Defense Department program designed to catch future Mohamed Attas before they strike. That's not a prediction. But it is a fear.

The program seeks to develop software to make intelligence-sharing more effective by making it instantaneous, the better to learn more about suspected terrorists and identify people who might be terrorists. It would link computerized government data-bases to one another and to some non-government databases to which investigators already have legal access. If feasible, it would also fish through billions of transactions for patterns of activities in which terrorists might engage.

But now these goals are all in jeopardy, because of a stunningly irresponsible congressional rush to hobble the Pentagon program in ways that are far from necessary to protect privacy. This is not to deny that, absent stringent safeguards and oversight, the ineptly named "Total Information Awareness" [TIA] program might present serious threats to privacy. It might, for example, subject thousands of innocent citizens and noncitizens alike to unwelcome scrutiny, and might even expose political dissenters to harassment by rogue officials.

But some curbs on potentially dangerous (and potentially life-saving) government powers in the name of civil liberties are not necessary to protect privacy and exact too high a price in terms of endangered lives. Congress's rush to strangle TIA in its infancy is such a case. It makes little more sense than would a flat ban on any and all wire-tapping of phones that might be used by U.S. citizens. Like TIA, wiretapping poses grave risks to privacy if not carefully restricted. So we restrict it. We don't ban it.

The problem with the near-ban on TIA—sponsored by Sens. Ron Wyden, D-Ore., and Charles Grassley, R-Iowa, and known as the Wyden amendment—is that rather than weighing the hoped-for security benefits against the feared privacy costs, and devising ways to minimize those costs, Congress was stampeded by civil-libertarian hysteria into adopting severe and unwarranted restrictions. The Bush administration shares the blame because the person it put in charge of TIA research is Adm. John M. Poindexter, whose record of lying to Congress about the Iran-Contra affair does not inspire trust.

"There are risks to TIA, but in the end I think the risks of not trying TIA are greater, and we should at least try to construct systems for [minimizing] abuse before we discard all potential benefits from technological innovation," says Paul Rosenzweig, a legal analyst at the Heritage Foundation who has co-authored a thoughtful 25-page analysis of the TIA program, including a list of muscular safeguards that Congress could adopt to protect privacy and prevent abuses. Instead of weighing such factors, Rosenzweig says, Congress has "deliberately and without much thought decided to discard the greatest advantage we have over our foes—our technological superiority."

The Wyden amendment seems reasonable enough at first blush. That may be why all 100 senators and the House conferees voted to attach it to the omnibus spending bill that cleared Congress on February 13. The amendment allows pure TIA *research* to continue, if the administration files a detailed report within 90 days or the president invokes national security needs. And the amendment's restrictions on TIA *deployment* have been sold as a tempo-rary move to allow time for congressional oversight.

But such measures, once adopted, are a good bet to become permanent in today's habitually gridlocked Congress, where determined minorities have great power to block any change in the status quo. And the Wyden amend-ment's impact is likely to be far broader than advertised. It flatly bars *any* deployment of TIA-derived technology, by any agency, with exceptions only for military operations outside the U.S. and "lawful foreign intelligence activi-ties conducted *wholly* [my emphasis] against non-United States persons" (defined to mean nonresident aliens).

The scope of the latter exception is ambiguous. But Rosenzweig fears that it will be read narrowly, and that the Wyden amendment will be read broadly—especially by officials fearful of congressional wrath—as barring virtu-ally *all* uses of TIA technology, even to search the government's own databases for suspected foreign terrorists. This is because virtually all large databases are "mixed": They contain information about U.S. citizens, resident aliens, and nonresident aliens alike.

In any event, the Wyden amendment quite clearly prohibits any use of TIA technology to pursue the unknown but apparently substantial number of U.S. citizens and resident aliens who may be loyal to Al Qaeda, such as sus-pected dirty-bomb plotter Jose Padilla and the six suspected Yemeni-American "sleepers" arrested in Lackawanna, N.Y., last year. As a technical matter, the FBI, the CIA, and the Department of Homeland Security remain free to develop and deploy similar technology on their own. But they will hesitate to risk charges of evading Congress's will. Not to mention the wastefulness of barring these agen-cies from building on the TIA technology already developed by the Pentagon.

How did TIA become such a dreaded symbol of Big Brotherism? Part of the reason was well-founded concern that unless strictly controlled, the more exotic uses of TIA, such as surveying billions of transactions involving hun-dreds of millions of people for patterns deemed indicative of possible terrorist activities, could subject huge numbers of innocent Americans to scrutiny as potential terrorists. But Rosenzweig and others who share these concerns, including officials of the TIA program itself, have already been crafting safeguards. Among them are software designs and legal rules that would block human agents from learning the identities of people whose transactions are being "data-mined" by TIA computers unless the agents can obtain judicial warrants by showing something analogous to the "probable cause" that the law requires to justify a wiretap.

It was largely misinformation and over-heated rhetoric from civil-libertarian zealots—on both the left and the right—that pushed the Wyden amendment through Congress. The misinformation included the false claim that Poindexter would preside over a domestic spying apparatus, and the false suggestion that TIA was poised to rummage through the most private of databases to compile dossiers on millions of Americans' credit card, banking, business, travel, educational, and medical records and e-mails.

To the contrary, Poindexter's job is limited to developing software. And even without the Wyden amendment, TIA would give investigators access only to databases and records—government and nongovernment—that they already have a right to access. Its most basic function would be simply to expedite the kinds of intelligence-sharing that might have thwarted the September 11 attacks, by linking the government's own databases with one another and with any legally accessible private databases. The goal is to enable investigators to amass in minutes clues that now could take weeks or months to collect.

Here's a hypothetical example (adapted from Rosenzweig's analysis) of how as-yet-non-existent TIA technology might help stop terrorists—and how the Wyden amendment might prevent that.

Say the government learns from a reliable informant that the precursor elements of Sarin gas have been smuggled into the United States by unidentified Qaeda operatives via flights from Germany during the month of February. Its first investigative step might be a TIA-based "query" of foreign databases that might help generate a list of possible terrorists. (But the Wyden amendment would bar a TIA-based query for the names of any who might be Americans. And it could be construed as putting entirely off-limits *any* "mixed database" that includes Americans.)

A second step might be a pattern-based query to U.S. government databases to produce a list of all passengers, or perhaps all nonresident aliens, entering the U.S. on flights from Germany during February. (But the Wyden amendment would bar a query for all passengers, and would again pose the mixed-database problem.)

A third query might seek to find which of these passengers' names are also in government databases of known or suspected terrorists. (But the Wyden amendment would pose the same obstacles.)

Fourth, with a list of subjects for further investigation based on these queries, TIA could be used—perhaps after obtaining a judicial warrant—to link to any legally accessible commercial databases to find out whether any of these subjects has bought canisters suitable for deployment of Sarin gas, or rented airplanes suitable for dispersing it, or stayed in the same motels as other subjects of investigation. And so on. (But for the Wyden amendment, that is.)

It is not yet clear whether it is even possible to develop technology powerful enough to do all of this. But it might be possible. Shouldn't we be racing to find out?

POSTSCRIPT

Does the Spread of Surveillance Technology Threaten Privacy?

The basic shape of the debate is simple: surveillance and data collection are useful. Government insists that private citizens do not have the right to act in such a way that they cannot be watched, supervised, and punished if government deems it necessary. The issue gained fresh importance in 2005, when the PATRIOT Act came up for renewal (see "'Trust Me' Just Doesn't Fly," *USA Today* [April 13, 2005]) and the federal 2006 budget for surveillance technology and manpower increased greatly (see `http://www.epic.org/privacy/budget/fy2006/`). Private businesses have very similar attitudes toward employees and even customers. The Electronic Frontier Foundation (EFF), the Electronic Privacy Information Center (EPIC), and numerous other groups and individuals insist equally strenuously that the right to privacy must come first.

Carnivore and the Total or Terrorism Information Awareness (TIA) program reflect many fears about the Net—that it is a place where evil lurks, where technically skilled criminals use their skills to fleece the unsuspecting public, where terrorists plot unseen, and where technology lends immunity to detection, apprehension, and prosecution. Law enforcement has long wished to compensate for the advantages enjoyed here by evil-doers. Carnivore was a milestone attempt to maintain the upper hand. Echelon, an international and until recently top-secret version of Carnivore that searches emails, faxes, and phone calls, is operated by the U.S.'s National Security Agency in partnership with Canada, Australia, New Zealand, and Britain. See Nat Hentoff, "1984 Is Here," *Free Inquiry* (Spring 2003), John Foley, "Data Debate," *InformationWeek* (May 19, 2003) and Wayne Madsen, "US Insight—The Secrets of DARPA's TIA: The US Government's Electronic Intelligence Snooping Machine," *Computer Fraud & Security* (May 2003). Nor is the issue solely American. Yves Poullet, "The Fight against Crime and/or the Protection of Privacy: A Thorny Debate!" *International Review of Law Computers & Technology* (July 2004), discusses the issue from the European standpoint and notes that "there is no worse danger than this cyber-surveillance, which hunts a man down in his most intimate space and raises within him a perpetual and haunting fear of exposure."

In case anyone should conclude that the only surveillance to worry about comes from government and business, "Move Over, Big Brother," *Economist* (December 4, 2004), outlines how surveillance technology—in the form of camera phones and digital cameras—is now available to everyone. People have attached GPS-enabled phones to cars to track spouses or stalk ex-spouses and used camera phones and digital cameras for industrial espionage and identity theft. They have also used them to record crimes in progress and help law enforcement do its job. The full impact on society, whether for good or bad, is not yet clear.

ISSUE 16

Will Screens Replace Pages?

YES: Steve Ditlea, from "The Real E-Books," *Technology Review* (July/August 2000)

NO: Stephen Sottong, from "E-Book Technology: Waiting for the 'False Pretender,'" *Information Technology & Libraries* (June 2001)

ISSUE SUMMARY

YES: Writer Steve Ditlea argues that computers can simplify publishing, improve access to readers, and enhance the reading experience and that e-books are becoming both practical and popular.

NO: Librarian Stephen Sottong argues that e-books are not cheap, readable, or durable enough to replace paper books and that they pose special problems for libraries.

When personal computers first came on the market in the 1970s, they were considered useful tools, but their memory was limited to only a few thousand bytes, hard drives were expensive add-ons, and the Internet was a distant dream (though something similar was already connecting university and government mainframe computers). By the 1980s some people had begun to realize that computer disks could hold as much information as a book, were smaller, took less postage to mail, and could be recycled. By this time Project Gutenberg, founded in 1971 by Michael Hart at the University of Illinois, had already been converting works of classic literature into digital form and making them available on disk for a number of years. By 1990 several small companies—including Soft Press, Serendipity Systems, and High Mesa Publishing—were trying to turn this insight into profitable businesses. All are now gone.

The approach failed partly because people seemed to find paper books more congenial for reading than computer screens. But then the Internet came along, and the early 1990s saw an explosion of activity exploiting this new ability to put information of all kinds—including poetry, fiction, and nonfiction of precisely the sort one used to find only on paper—onto "Web pages" that Internet users could access for free. Digital publishing boomed, and companies such as Fictionwise (http://www.fictionwise.com) and

Embiid Publishing (http://www.embiid.net) now sell their wares to be downloaded via the Internet. This is not the first time that the nature of publishing has changed. Five centuries ago the printing press greatly increased the availability of books, including Bibles, and contributed to the Protestant Reformation and the American and French Revolutions. See Rudi Volti, *Society and Technological Change*, 4th ed. (St. Martin's Press, 2001), chapter 11. The printing press also utterly destroyed the primacy of the scroll and delivered the first hard blow to literacy as a distinguishing characteristic of the social elite. There were, of course, protests aimed at the way this new technology was threatening handwritten text and undermining the social order.

Now major publishers are making books available in both paper and digital form, and e-books can be downloaded from online booksellers such as Barnes & Noble.com (http://www.barnesandnoble.com) and Amazon.com (http://www.amazon.com). At the same time, magazines and newspapers are insisting that contributors sign away electronic publishing rights (usually for no additional payment), while the same rights are becoming major negotiating points in book contracts. Reviews of e-books now appear in major magazines. And Bill Gates is trumpeting the virtues of e-books—he expects their sales to rival those of paper books within a decade—from the parapets of Microsoft. See Bill Gates and Lora Haberer, "E-Books," *Executive Excellence* (April 2001). But despite the excitement in some quarters, e-books are not yet threatening traditional paper books. See Karen Coyle, "E-Books: It's about Evolution, Not Revolution," *Library Journal* (Fall 2003), and Barbara Quint, "Digital Books: More Value-Added, Please," *Information Today* (January 2005).

In the following selections, Steve Ditlea argues that, at least so far, electronic publishing is no threat to conventional, paper publishing, but because computers can simplify publishing, improve access to readers, and enhance the reading experience, e-books are bound to become more and more familiar to readers. Stephen Sottong asserts that e-books are not cheap, readable, or durable enough to replace paper books. Nor is the technology mature or stable enough for libraries to trust for long-term storage. Libraries must be cautious about adopting the technology.

YES

Steve Ditlea

The Real E-Books

It took a contemporary master of macabre thrillers to awaken the media and public to the existence of e-books. [Recently], with great fanfare, Simon & Schuster brought out a novella by Stephen King called *Riding the Bullet*—the first work by a best-selling author released exclusively for electronic publication, to be read only on computerized screens, not paper. King's stunt made headlines and magazine covers, and the tsunami of demand for downloads of this e-book crashed Web sites and traditional publishing assumptions.

But the future of e-books may have less to do with Stephen King than with Eric Rowe and other less well-known authors. Rowe is a British potter who lives in the South of France, drawn there by the region's clays and minerals, which have been mined for stoneware since Roman times. To help ceramists in other areas unearth their own raw materials, he wrote *A Potter's Geology*. But he couldn't find a book publisher in England for his manuscript. This was just too specialized a topic for a publisher in any one country. Still, Rowe was certain that there would be interest in his book from potters everywhere.

Half a world away, in Medicine Hat, Alberta, Tony Hansen read about *A Potter's Geology* from a posting by Rowe in a ceramists' online discussion group. Hansen owns Digitalfire, a company specializing in software for calculations in ceramic chemistry. Hansen offered to publish Rowe's book electronically, selling the text on the Web as digital files in the Portable Document Format (PDF). PDF files are displayable on any Windows, DOS, Mac or Unix computer screen (and easily printed out) using the Acrobat reader software, downloadable free from Adobe Systems.

"I said I'd rather have my manuscript printed first," Rowe recalls. But Hansen won him over by pointing out that e-publication would produce immediate worldwide distribution. Now the book can be downloaded from the Web and viewed on any personal computer. Readers of the e-book can search the entire book and zoom in on high-resolution photos—even contact the author via an online hyperlink. The economics look good too: E-books require no printing, binding, inventory or shipping costs, allowing these savings to be passed on to the author in the form of higher royalties. *A Potter's Geology* has sold only a few dozen copies, but Rowe is optimistic:

From Steve Ditlea, "The Real E-Books," *Technology Review* (July/August 2000). Copyright © 2000 by Technology Review, Inc. Reprinted by permission of *Technology Review;* permission conveyed through Copyright Clearance Center, Inc.

"It won't be something that sells fast, but over a long time. It's not a subject that will go out of date. Even so, in digital format it's easy to update or improve."

Thanks to Digitalfire and other budding digital publishing enterprises, authors like Rowe are being empowered to write about esoteric, highly personal topics and still find a worldwide audience—transcending the antiquated economics of shipping ink on wood pulp and bypassing the gatekeepers to traditional publishing. Just a little searching on the Web finds a growing e-book industry: more than 150 e-book-only publishers, e-only bookstores, e-book trade publications online, even e-book best-seller lists. The new e-publishers are testing a variety of business models for digital book distribution, while opening the way for a broader range of authors and works to be published on old-fashioned bound paper.

The great wonder is that this hasn't happened any sooner. The first digital books date back to 1971 when Michael Hart was given a virtually unlimited account of computer time on the mainframe at the Materials Research Lab at the University of Illinois and decided that widely disseminating the contents of libraries was the greatest value computers could create. He typed in the text of the Declaration of Independence and so began Project Gutenberg, which now includes more than 2000 classic works online, all free. To date, these are all plain text files—lacking the typeset-quality formatting that makes books eminently readable, somewhat compromising the reading experience. "When we started," Hart recalls, "there was *only* uppercase—how about *that* for a compromise?" Because Project Gutenberg's books were no longer under copyright, the original e-books required no copy protection schemes. Hart explains: "We encourage everyone to repost our books in whatever formats they want. The most books to the most people—that's our only real goal."

In 1990, Voyager Co. introduced the first e-books meant to be read on personal computers. But these diskette-borne works, including *Jurassic Park* and *Alice in Wonderland*, were never offered by other publishers. Meanwhile, attempts to publish books on CD-ROM proved a dead end for all but encyclopedia and database publishers. The advent of the Web brought both opportunity and distraction for e-books. As the first universal publishing medium, the Web could make e-books easily accessible, with its Hypertext Markup Language (HTML) even retaining some print-style formatting. But HTML's orientation toward short documents was hardly optimized for book-length texts.

In the last year or so, the term "e-book" has been appropriated by companies selling portable gadgets whose sole purpose is to display electronic texts. . . . At the moment the number of these dedicated e-book readers—about 20,000—is dwarfed by the 6 million Palm Pilots and other Palm OS devices in use, making this versatile hardware the handheld reader of choice. "Single-purpose devices like handheld readers are never going to have as big an installed base as general-purpose ones," insists Mark Reichelt, CEO of Peanut Press, the Maynard, Mass., company that pioneered commercial e-book publishing on the Palm Pilot.

Rubber and Glue

The most general-purpose hardware boxes of all are personal computers. Yet despite hundreds of millions of PCs in use around the world, only a few hundred thousand of their users have downloaded e-books. The slow start is partly due to the perception that an e-book doesn't fully replicate the book-reading experience. More importantly, the download culture—first evident with browser plug-ins, then with software upgrades and MP3 music files—has only taken hold recently with the non-geek public.

Ads by Microsoft would have us believe that what the e-book world has been waiting for is the company's Reader program, which will be given away with every new copy of Windows. Microsoft Reader features ClearType software that evens out type edges on the screen. The reality is, however, that ClearType is warmed-over technology that failed to save handheld Windows CE devices from oblivion. To people accustomed to reading text on a computer for hours at a time, e-book screen clarity is a nonissue. Microsoft Reader also provides copy protection for authors and booksellers. But while e-books rights management may be important to intellectual property holders, it could be a futile quest. Any PC-based copy protection scheme can be cracked, as happened within two days of Stephen King's first e-publication.

With more than 100 million Acrobat readers already downloaded onto computers, PDF is the de facto standard for e-book publication. PDF was specifically designed for preserving professional-quality documents across computer platforms and printers. And PDF technology offers a ready solution for those reluctant to read off a screen; simply print out the files. To counter Microsoft Reader, Adobe has recently beefed up its offerings with e-commerce encryption software called PDF Merchant, allowing rights to an electronic copy of a book to be assigned to a single computer. In addition, Adobe has challenged Microsoft's ClearType with screen-enhancement routines of its own, which it calls CoolType; the competing technologies are similar enough in performance to make screen clarity even less of a concern. . . . PDF will face a worthy challenger in the e-book format battle, as a consortium of e-book hardware makers, traditional publishers, and Microsoft push the new Open eBook (OEB) standard.

The difference between OEB and PDF is like the child's rhyme that begins: "I'm rubber, you're glue." PDF is glue, locking in a book's formatting so it can be preserved intact across output devices; once created, it is not meant to be modified in any way. This can be a drawback if an author or publisher wants to access parts of the text for excerpting or reconfiguring for a customized e-book, or for sampling or sale in smaller increments than book length. OEB is rubber: It allows an e-book's content to be reformatted on the fly, using a markup language that is essentially an extension of HTML. OEB also makes it easy for dedicated reading devices to reformat text to fit their proprietary display configurations.

The first published spec for OEB addresses neither security nor e-commerce protocols, leaving it to individual vendors to come up with their own approaches. This omission raises the possibility that the proposed standard could splinter into a variety of incompatible implementations. Ultimately, both OEB *and* PDF could survive, with the rival formats used for different output stages of the same e-book—OEB in the intermediate stages of massaging editorial content, and PDF for final versions. (For all the flexibility of digital books, scholarship will probably demand that different editions of a work remain available in permanent form.)

Rewriting Business Models

E-books are shaking up publishing business models that have remained unchanged since the days of Dickens, much as MP3 compression technology has rocked the music industry. For the moment, even the most forward-looking print publishers are pricing their initial e-book offerings almost identically with paper editions, as if there were no difference in their underlying atoms versus bits economics. At St. Martin's Press, the first major publisher to simultaneously issue a hardcover and e-book edition of the same title (*Monica's Story* in March 1999), senior vice president for finance administration Steve Cohen explains: "Our prices on new titles are at the hardcover level because there's a high start-up cost for e-book editions." Kate Tentler, publisher of Simon & Schuster Online, was responsible for Web distribution of Stephen King's *Riding the Bullet* (priced at $2.50, the 66 pages of the e-novella averaged out to the retail per-page cost of a King hardcover novel). Says Tentler, "We think of an e-book as just another book."

As a few traditional publishers defensively convert to digital files for downloads, the independent e-publishing industry has seen countless business models bloom. On the same March day that the Stephen King brand name sold 400,000 paperless copies of *Riding the Bullet*, Frank Weyer received a grand total of two requests for his serialized e-mystery, *MIT Can Be Murder*, on his own site (e-bookpress.com). Despite such paltry numbers, efforts by Weyer and other e-book authors are already undermining the influence of blockbuster-minded agents and trend-driven book editors. Weyer, for example, had sent the manuscript for his first murder mystery to 10 literary agents, all of whom declined to submit it to book publishers. "They said the mystery field is difficult for a newcomer," Weyer recalls. "But how do you become a published mystery author if you can't get published?"

Self-publishing on paper, a solution for some, seemed prohibitive for this patent and trademark attorney and small-scale Internet entrepreneur (he holds exclusive right to sell Web domain names registered in the nation of Moldova—ending in .md—to doctors in California and New York). Rather than letting his manuscript molder in a drawer, Weyer decided to publish it via e-mail. The first four chapters of the whodunnit, inspired by the year he spent at MIT studying for a PhD in ocean engineering, were offered first to 3,000 MIT alumni, and then to 15,000 names on other university alumni lists. He released the rest of the 210-page book in 12 monthly installments. Some 1,400 readers have downloaded the entire e-novel.

Weyer's novel-by-subscription might seem like an innovation made possible by the digital era. In fact, it is a throwback to the early days of 19th-century book publishing, when books were sold by subscription before publication, to raise revenue to pay the printing costs up front. With no printing to worry about, the frictionless economy lets Weyer distribute his work for free. Now that he has successfully bypassed print publishers to get his words read, he has begun subscription-publishing the work of other writers. The first addition is *The Butcher's Cleaver*, a spy thriller by W. Patrick Lang. Soon Weyer plans to generate income by selling print-on-demand versions of both his and Lang's books. Nonetheless, he would like *MIT Can Be Murder* to be picked up by a mainstream publisher. "I just wanted to build word of mouth," he says of his e-book. "I would like to see it in as many forms as possible."

Giving away complete works to help an author build a following is still anathema to most traditional publishers, who must absorb the cost to produce, store and ship the physical books. But giving away paperless e-books is a no-brainer, following the time-tested freeware and shareware models in computer software. Independently published e-books may not be as polished or as slick as store-bought commercial offerings, but they can hold their own in user appreciation. And Frank Weyer's writing is certainly on par with that in much of today's mass-produced paperback fiction.

Traditional publishers' understandable fear that e-books may cannibalize sales of print editions seems to be overblown, at least judging from the experience of one of their more adventurous colleagues. [In] September [1999], veteran science-fiction publisher Jim Baen initiated what he calls eWebScriptions; for $10 a month, visitors to Baen.com may download quarter-of-a-book-sized installments of four titles about to appear in print. Even after receiving the full text in HTML, "more of our subscribers buy the finished book than don't buy it," says Baen. By March, the added promotion had already helped propel one of the earliest eWebScriptions titles, *Ashes of Victory* by David Weber, onto hardcover best-seller lists.

In addition to alternative marketing strategies, e-publishers can tap into income streams legally denied to traditional publishers. For instance, the U.S. Postal Service disallows low book-mailing rates for printed material that contains advertising. No such restriction inhibits the sales of ads for e-books. Bartleby.com, for example, offers free, ad-supported classics and reference works online. At BiblioBytes.com, books can be read on ad banner-sponsored Web pages, with some popular titles downloadable for a fee; authors get a cut of the ad revenue. Abroad, the alternatives are just as dramatic; in France, pioneer e-publisher Zero Hour is able to offer less-expensive editions of current books because digital files cannot be taxed as print books are.

Embracing the E

The power of e-books as a promotional medium has probably best been demonstrated by Melisse Shapiro, who writes under the nom de plume M.J. Rose. Her first novel, *Lip Service*, an erotically charged thriller, was rejected by a dozen book publishers for being too steamy for the chain bookstores. She opted to publish from her own Web site, offering digital downloads for $10 or photocopies of the manuscript for $20.

Even when the password for her e-book was stolen and posted online, resulting in 1,000 pirated downloads, she managed to receive 150 paid orders for e-books and 500 orders for photocopies. She invested in printing 3,000 copies to help create buzz; at one point, it was the 123rd best-selling title on Amazon.com. Following her online blitz, Doubleday Direct picked up *Lip Service* for its mail-order book clubs and soon after, Pocket Books signed up print rights in hardcover and paperback. Building on her success, Shapiro has become a leading advocate of e-books, with her frequent reports to Wired News online providing the most comprehensive ongoing coverage of e-publishing. "Everything in my life would be different if not for e-books," she says.

On the same day in March that Stephen King generated 400,000 orders, Leta Childers' comic romance e-novel, *The Best Laid Plans*, was downloaded 200 times from her publisher's Web site, DiskUspublishing.com. Childers is King's peer in one respect: Hers is the best-selling work released to date among digital-format-only publishers, according to the best-seller list compiled by eBook Connections. With some 20,000 copies of her e-book issued (at $3.50 for a downloaded copy, $6.50 on diskette), the rural South Dakota-based Childers has helped establish DiskUs Publishing of Albany, Ind., as one of the most successful digital-only publishers. In the still largely New York-based traditional publishing world, Childers says, "submission envelopes with Midwest return addresses are easy to ignore." Then in a familiar refrain for e-book authors, she adds: "I would love to be traditionally published."

DiskUs is a publisher in the traditional sense of having editors who help prepare manuscripts for publication. Other e-publishers disseminate authors' works for a fee, without exercising editorial control. Such "vanity presses" have long been the Rodney Dangerfields of publishing, but vanity e-publishers are proving attractive to mainstream book firms exploring new publishing paradigms. Following a recent investment by Random House, Xlibris.com now provides a no-fee, no-frills e-publishing package. Barnes & Noble is backing iUniverse.com, which offers new authors a basic $99 e-publishing service; it reserves free publication for authors submitting out-of-print works, a program originally developed with The Authors Guild.

For authors who've already been in print, one of the greatest benefits that e-books can offer is the resurrection of their old hard-to-find titles. As publishing companies have consolidated, worthy works have been relegated to the limbo of out-of-print. E-publishing provides an inexpensive way to restore the availability of these lapsed works. Among the most innovative of e-publishers, Alexandria Digital Literature has revived hundreds of out-of-print stories and poems, typically priced from 30 cents to $1.25. Buyers are asked to send in their ratings; when enough ratings accumulate, they can be compared to others' ratings and other reading recommendations are offered.

Also being revived are questions about traditional publishers' exclusivity over their authors' works. When Simon & Schuster made Stephen King's *Riding the Bullet* available through online booksellers and e-book hardware and software firms, one site was pointedly excluded: Fatbrain.com. Since last fall, Fatbrain has been posting works it brands as "eMatter": original fiction and nonfiction ranging from 10 to 100 pages (lengths that many people will be willing to print out). Subsequently designating the site for such pieces `MightyWords.com`, Fatbrain has targeted a segment of publishing that falls between magazines and books, where the modern economics of print have all but shut out a once-thriving sector of short stories and novellas. Simon & Schuster saw Fatbrain as a rival.

Fatbrain's brief history shows how quickly e-book business plans and branding can change. A mere six months after launching the eMatter trademark and drawing attention to the similarly named Web site, Fatbrain decided to let its trademark lapse. "MightyWords was a name that could ring through to our professional audience, while eMatter is a generic term for the range of electronic documents we are publishing," explains Judy Kirkpatrick, executive vice president and general manager of MightyWords. Already the eMatter 10- to-100-page category encompasses many of e-book publishing's early milestones, including King's *Riding the Bullet*. Simon & Schuster may not like it, but Fatbrain's publication of an eMatter essay by science fiction author Arthur C. Clarke was the inspiration for King to test the digital publishing waters. Also fitting the eMatter designation: Eric Rowe's 91-page *A Potter's Geology*.

King and Rowe have something else in common: an abiding belief in the importance of traditional books. King has been widely quoted as stating: "I don't think anything will replace the printed word and the bound book. Not in my lifetime, at least." For Rowe, too, it's not a question of digital books supplanting analog ones. "For some kinds of book," he says, "the aesthetic pleasure of having the object in the hand will be difficult to replace."

It should come as no surprise that proponents of e-books are not out to eliminate paper publishing. After all, most e-books attempt to replicate traditional books' content and appearance. For the most part, e-books can be printed out with only minimal loss of information (primarily broken hypertext links). And for all their seeming differences, print and electronic publishers are putting out similar content. Eventually, digital downloads seem destined to become just one more format for readers, one more step on the convenience/ cost continuum from hardcover to paperback to e-book.

At some point in the future, however, e-books and print are bound to diverge. Lurking amidst e-publishing today is the notion of multimedia books that seamlessly incorporate hypertext, sound and animation. A hypertext branching narrative in a novel or a history book, for instance, would be impossible to reproduce in a book.

A glimmer of tomorrow's multimedia books, or m-books, may be discerned in a dark-horse contender among e-publishing file formats called TK3. Introduced by Night Kitchen—a New York startup headed by Voyager Co. co-founder Bob Stein—TK3 is the basis for a sophisticated literary software environment. The Night Kitchen TK3 Reader offers the most booklike reading experience on a desktop or laptop computer screen—complete with highlighting, corner-folding bookmarks, even Post-it-like "stickie notes." And TK3's easy-to-use multimedia authoring tools are meant, according to Stein, "to empower a new generation of authors who want to express themselves in the new media." Using this hyperlink-sound-and-motion superset of traditional books to express themselves, such a new generation of authors would hasten Stein's prediction that "the locus of intellectual discourse will shift from the print medium to the electronic medium."

For now, the advent of e-books means not replacing print, but supplementing it—redefining publishing economics and opening the way for authors whose work has been kept from appearing between book covers. If e-books do nothing more, regardless of the success or lack thereof of new gadgetry to display them, this technology will have a profound effect on what we read and what we think.

Stephen Sottong

E-Book Technology: Waiting for the "False Pretender"

Technology is one of the foundations of today's library. Our catalogs have become databases while the venerable cards are shipped to the recycler or used as scratch paper. We process and deliver interlibrary loans via the Web along with an increasing number of journals and indexes. This transition forces libraries to make decisions about a plethora of new technologies on a daily basis. As an electronic engineer until 1993, I am especially interested in the relationship of technology to my new profession.

A model of the life cycle of a technology was proposed by Raymond Kurzweil in 1992. This model can help libraries determine whether a technology is appropriate to adopt. In this article, I will amplify Kurzweil's technology life cycle model and apply this improved model to determine the current state of e-books within Kurzweil's framework.

Background

Raymond Kurzweil, noted inventor and futurist, wrote "The Futurecast" column for *Library Journal* in the early 1990s. A three-part series in this column titled "The Future of Libraries" appeared from January through March of 1992. The first part of this series, "The Technology of the Book," listed seven stages in the life cycle of a technology:

1. Precursor
2. Invention
3. Development
4. Maturity
5. False Pretenders
6. Obsolescence
7. Antiquity

In the precursor stage, ideas about a new technology exist, but have not been implemented (e.g., DaVinci's helicopter). Invention gives the ideas concrete form. Development hones the technology into a practical form (e.g., automobile technology at the turn of the last century). Finally the technology reaches

From *Information Technology & Libraries,* June 2001. Copyright © 2001 by Stephen Sottong.

maturity and is practical and useful. Maturity can last for years, decades, or centuries depending on how well the technology meets the need for which it was invented.

As the mature technology ages, newer technologies arise to challenge it. If the newer technologies have some superior features but are not yet comparable in all facets, they may become false pretenders. Kurzweil defined this stage: "Here an upstart threatens to eclipse the older technology. Its enthusiasts prematurely predict victory. While providing some distinct benefits, the newer technology is found on reflection to be missing some key element of functionality or quality." The false pretenders may coexist with the mature technology, but they will not supplant the mature technology.

A newer technology can supplant the mature technology only when most or all of its features are comparable, and it has some improved feature to compensate the user for the trouble and expense of switching technologies. When a newer technology supplants a mature technology, the older mature technology enters obsolescence, in which it coexists with the newer technology for approximately 5 percent to 10 percent of its mature lifespan. Finally a supplanted technology reaches antiquity and ceases to be produced or used.

Kurzweil's stages provide a useful framework for evaluating current and proposed technology. Investment in the precursor, invention, and development stages of a technology is not worthwhile because of their instability and lack of features. A false pretender, on the other hand, may have a long lifespan and be worth some investment. For example, audio cassette technology is a false pretender that has remained popular for thirty years. The majority of library investments, however, will be in mature technologies with proven quality and functionality.

Criteria

Kurzweil did not provide criteria for determining which stage a particular technology had reached. After examining his examples in "The Future of Libraries" articles, I developed a set of eight criteria for determining how mature and newer technologies compare with each other.

With respect to the mature technology, the newer technology must have comparable:

1. quality
2. durability
3. initial cost
4. continuing cost
5. ease of use
6. features

In addition, the new technology must:

7. be standardized
8. have extra features

These criteria provide a nonarbitrary method for evaluating a technology. Kurzweil used audio technology as an example of his stages [and . . .] stated in 1992 that electronic books were at the false pretender stage. . . .

Quality

For both print books and e-books quality is determined by the display. The print book's display is far superior to either the Cathode Ray Tube (CRT) or Liquid Crystal Display (LCD) used for e-books. Display quality can be measured in terms of display resolution (in units of dots per inch—dpi) and contrast. Most books are printed at a resolution of 1,200 dpi. Commercially available video displays (whether CRT or LCD) have a maximum resolution of 100 dpi. The 1,200 dpi resolution of print is not twelve times the resolution video displays, but 144 times since a display is a two-dimensional surface and print is twelve times the resolution of a video display both horizontally and vertically. . . .

Kurzweil recognized display technology problems . . . but underestimated their magnitude and the time it would take to make improvements. He predicted that video display resolution would catch up to print in three years, but display resolution remains stalled at 100 dpi. As Jacobo Valdés (developer of Clearview, a competitor of ClearType) put it, "Screen resolution hasn't improved much over the past decade. It is still abysmal. Until it increases another 50 percent or so in each direction—which means about twice as many pixels per square inch—things will not get substantially better." Or as Bill Gates put it, "The computer screen is a terrible limitation versus reading the newspaper."

. . . IBM [has] announced a 200 dpi LCD display that has yet to go into production or have a price announcement . . . , and this display will still be only 1/36 the resolution of print. Entirely new electronic display technologies such as electronic ink, which is being developed by MIT and Xerox, are still a minimum of five years from being produced commercially.

In addition to resolution problems, contrast is greater for print than for CRT displays. Contrast is the ratio of maximum brightness to maximum darkness. For CRTs it can be as high as 100:1 and for LCDs 300:1; however, this is only a theoretical maximum. Any display device which emits light (CRT, backlit LCD, projectors, etc.) loses contrast with increased ambient light (hence our darkened electronic classrooms and movie theaters). For LCD, the contrast also decreases if the display is at an angle to the reader. Practical figures for the contrast of CRTs in normal light is 20:1 to 40:1 and for LCD it is approximately 100:1. Ink on paper has a contrast ratio of around 120:1 or three to six times greater than CRT displays and, since paper reflects light, the contrast does not deteriorate with ambient light. Most library patrons still use CRT displays and will continue to use them to read the e-books our libraries purchase. John Dvorak, a columnist for *PC Magazine,* said that for e-books to be practical, "The display needs to be at least 300 dots per inch with a contrast ratio of 40:1 to 50:1 and it must be readable in both the brightest sunlight and the most poorly lit office. Good luck."

The physical problems caused by computer use have been classified by the American Optometric Association as "Computer Vision Syndrome" or CVS. Symptoms of CVS include eyestrain, blurred vision, headaches, back and neck aches, dry eyes, distorted color vision, temporary myopia, double vision, after images, and increased sensitivity to light. A Harris poll called "computer related eyestrain" the number one office-related health complaint. Nearly 10 million people annually seek eye exams because of problems related to computer use, forty times the number of people afflicted with carpal tunnel syndrome and other repetitive stress injuries. Between 50 percent and 75 percent of PC users complain of eye problems associated with computer use. The National Institute of Health and Safety said that 88 percent of the 66 million people in the United States who work at computers for more than three hours a day suffer from eyestrain. All types of computer monitors (color or monochrome) produce these symptoms. Investigations at UC Berkeley indicate that the effects of CVS decrease productivity from 4 percent to 19 percent. The treatment cost for CVS approaches $2 billion annually.

Reading on computer displays is also inherently slower and less accurate. Proofreading experiments showed that reading speed is between 10 percent and 30 percent slower on a CRT and accuracy is 10 percent to 20 percent less. In one experiment, Gould et al. showed that an extremely bad copy of poor quality print deemed unacceptable by test participants could still be read as fast and as accurately as a CRT, even by experienced computer users.

This combination of physical stress and lower reading speed and accuracy is why the "paperless society" envisioned in the 1970s and 1980s never happened. Whenever readers encounter more than a few paragraphs of text, they print them out as an unconscious protection mechanism. Bill Gates acknowledged this in a speech at Harvard in 1996 where he said, "when you get a large document it's very typical to print it out on your local printer and then read it on paper. Many people do this because anything more than about four or five screensful is just easier to read that way." Walt Crawford estimated that, "people will print out anything longer than five hundred words or so." Kurzweil also recognized this: "Until the computer display truly rivals the qualities of paper, computers will increase the use of paper rather than replace it." E-books transfer the cost of printing from publishers to patrons without reducing library expenses and with *increased* environmental damage. Paul Curlander, chairman of printer maker Lexmark, predicted that office consumption of paper worldwide would increase from today's three trillion pages to eight trillion in 2010. . . .

Durability

The print book is a model of durability. It can be dropped from great heights, exposed to sand and food, and even fully immersed in water for brief periods without losing its information content. As a truly severe test, give a print book and an e-book reader to a six year old and see which one survives longer.

Even if the pages of a print book are ripped out, the information content still remains. Libraries recognize this and rebind books to return them to full usefulness. Print books degrade gradually; the content remains useful even when the pages are yellowed and the binding is worn. Electronic devices, by contrast, tend to fail catastrophically; a single transistor in one chip can turn the entire device and all contents into scrap.

From five-thousand-year-old papyrus scrolls to five-hundred-year-old Gutenberg Bibles, paper has demonstrated durability. Print on nonacid paper can last for five hundred years. No digital storage media are stable for longer than one hundred years and I have found none guaranteed longer than twenty-five years. This is less than the lifespan of acid paper which most libraries prefer not to collect.

Even if a digital medium and its data survive one hundred years, the hardware and software needed to read it will no longer be available. How many computers can read a 5 1/4" inch disk, the standard only a decade ago? The time before magnetic or optical media becomes obsolete is estimated by Van Bogart of National Media Laboratory (NML) to be "ten or twenty years (or less)." As Kodak says on its Web site, after bragging about the projected one-hundred-year lifespan of its CDs:

> The principal fact of life for all digital storage media is the rapid obsolescence of hardware and software. Users of CD technology should be reassured by the long physical life of CD discs, but they must not lose sight of the need to maintain a viable path for migration of data to new hardware and software platforms. Digital storage media impose a strict discipline that human-readable records do not: their rapid evolution creates a continual progression of technology that cannot safely be ignored for too long.

A more serious durability problem is the nature of the Internet, which is used as the primary means of distribution for most e-book systems. Internet companies and sites are notoriously short lived, as recent "dot-com" shakeouts have shown. The Kodak site still exists; however, the information on media durability quoted above was removed from NML's site after it was used in a *U.S. News & World Report* article, which Van Bogart said misrepresented NML's findings. The site itself is no longer open to the public. The only verifiable copies of the Van Bogart data are the print copies from the 1996 conference where he presented the data. A book in the hand is worth a database of books on a shut-down server.

Initial Cost

No hardware is required to read a print book. All e-books require an expensive reader, whether a $1,000 computer or a $200 SoftBookTM Reader. There is a social aspect to this initial cost: the poor cannot afford computers or e-book readers. Unless we wish to develop an elitist collection, libraries must lend the expensive e-book readers. If they are lost or damaged, the library will also have to assume the replacement expense. It would be unacceptable in most libraries (especially public libraries) either to charge a deposit or to hold poor patrons liable for massive damage expenses. This makes e-book readers a continuing expense for the library.

Continuing Cost

Electronic books are still as expensive or more expensive than their print counterparts. One of the paradoxes of any new technology is that to become inexpensive, a technology must be ubiquitous, but it will not become ubiquitous until it is inexpensive. To overcome this, most new technologies must be produced at a loss and marketed on a par or at a discount compared to their mature competition until they gain ubiquity. That e-book vendors are not doing this may say something about the lack of confidence they have in their product.

Some continuing costs are unique to each media. Print books have shelving and space costs for libraries. If delivered via the Web, e-books have continuing subscription costs and costs associated with the computers, servers, and networks used to access them. If e-books are stand-alone, then the books must either be periodically repurchased or transferred to new media as they age or their format becomes obsolete. Since these costs are long-term and e-books have only been around for a short time, it is not yet possible to compare them.

Ease of Use

While technologically savvy people find e-books easy to use, nothing matches the simplicity of a print book—just open it and read. There is no learning curve involved. In addition, print books can be annotated easily with a pencil or highlighter and, while such annotations are the bane of libraries, they usually do not damage the information content. Dedicated e-book readers have some moderately complicated mechanism for annotation, while computer-based e-books have either no mechanism or one which requires significant practice to master and greater time to perform.

Features

E-books have features comparable to print with the exception of skimming, browsing, and sharing content. A print book can be rapidly flipped through to find a certain text or illustration while the inherent slowness of computer displays, especially LCD displays, along with the inherent difficulty in reading displays makes this task impossible for e-books.

Most dedicated e-book readers tie the purchased book to a specific reader while e-books accessed over the Internet are usually tied to a specific set of IP addresses. This means the book cannot be loaned or given to another person without including the reader. "Paper seems ideally suited for sharing. . . . For the most part, paper provides an easy and inexpensive solution that is unlikely to be bettered by reading appliances."

Standardization

Most e-books use proprietary formats that cannot be read on different machines. This may change in the near future with the advent of the Open eBook standard (www.openebook.org); however, this standard could make current e-book readers obsolete.

Added Features

E-books have four added features: text searching, hyperlinking, greater data density, and rapid updating. Text searching provides the ability to find specific sections in an e-book; however, this has limited usefulness since one must search on the exact word or phrase used by the author. By contrast, human-created indexes, often omitted from e-books, index concepts rather than words and cross-reference commonly used alternate terms. Hyperlinking can make electronic indexes very friendly and allow rapid switching between related sections of the text. This feature is most useful in highly cross-referenced texts and not as useful in linear texts such as novels and longer, descriptive works. Increased data density means that many e-books can be stored in one reader, allowing a person, for example, to carry a small reference library in a limited space. Rapid updating can be accomplished via the Internet. This can keep reference works much more up-to-date than their print counterparts.

Conclusions

E-books fail six of the eight criteria. They are not comparable to print books. As Wildstrom put it, "They're too pricey, hard to read, and offer limited titles." The print book, as the *New York Times* stated in a 1994 editorial "is close to perfect: cheap, durable, portable, and complete unto itself." As Harold Bloom, noted educator and literary critic put it, "Imagine that for the last five hundred years we had nothing but e-books, and then there was some great technological advance that brought us the printed and bound book. We would all be ecstatic. We would be celebrating after the long horror of the e-book."

E-books are still very much in Kurzweil's development stage and not yet advanced enough to be a false pretender. The sales figures show this too; only twenty thousand to fifty thousand dedicated e-book readers have been sold, far fewer than the first day sales of the latest Harry Potter book or the contents of a small branch library. The recent success of Stephen King's e-book, *Riding the Bullet*, does not counter this, since it is estimated that only 1 percent of those who downloaded the book actually read it.

In spite of this, e-books may have a limited place in library collections where their special features outweigh their flaws. If searchability, linking, and currency are highly important and text is in short, discrete segments, e-books may be a useful solution. Such categories of books include:

- indexes
- encyclopedias
- almanacs
- gazetteers
- technical manuals
- handbooks (e.g., *PDR, Merck Index, CRC Handbook of Chemistry and Physics*)

As Gass put it, "Gazetteers, encyclopedias, and dictionaries are scholarly tools, but they are *consulted* rather than *read*" (emphasis mine). E-books do not work well with long segments of linear text such as novels, scholarly research works, most nonfiction, and text books. Even journals with lengthy articles do not lend themselves to electronic reading. These categories still comprise the majority of works in a library's collection.

Some librarians feel "they need to get on the e-book bandwagon now or risk being marginalized." Hage stated, "People want their library to be hip. They want their library to be willing to experiment when something new comes out," and pointed to library collections of VHS and Beta videocassettes as well as eight-track and audio cassettes. These arguments are predicated on the notion that libraries have always been on the cutting edge of technology, but this is not the case. Libraries may have collections of Beta tapes, but how many collected U-Matic videocassettes? We may have collected eight-tracks, but where are the collections of four-track cassettes or quadraphonic records? Libraries may have PCs in storage dating back to the IBM original, but how many of our libraries bought Altairs or IMSAIs? If the reader does not recognize U-Matic, quadraphonic, and Altair, this only emphasizes my point; these technologies were too preliminary and transient to be taken seriously for our collections. Libraries have seldom adopted the earliest, developmental stages of a technology. We are not true "early adopters" but "moderately early adopters." We wait until technologies sort themselves out and reach some level of standardization. This is all that I am suggesting for e-books. John V. Lombardi made a similar point during his speech to the 2000 ALA Annual Conference: "Being first to invent large-scale digital library projects is for those with money to lose, tolerant customers, and tenure. If it will take ten years to deliver value, let someone else invent it." Being the first to invest in a new technology is always expensive and generally unrewarding. The earliest libraries with online catalogs found themselves stuck with a huge investment in mainframe computers and custom software that provided limited, unreliable service for their patrons. Yet they could not afford to scrap these expensive systems and upgrade when smaller, cheaper, more reliable systems with greater functionality became available. Even choosing the most sophisticated new technology is not a guarantee of success as anyone with a Betamax video recorder or the OS/2 computer operating system will attest. Waiting for the market to settle lowers expenses, increases reliability, and reduces the chances that you will be left with rapidly outmoded technology.

Display technology is slowly improving and a standard format for e-books is in the works, but this still does not ensure the final adoption of e-book technology as the successor or even false pretender to the print book. Walt Crawford warns, "perhaps 80 percent of the time, the new technologies simply disappear or fade into specialized use." Other technologies now on the market such as print-on-demand will compete head-to-head with e-books. Print-on-demand stations can download a work from a vendor and provide a properly bound, paper book with all its inherent advantages in as little as five minutes. When the initial cost of this technology drops (as the cost of computer printers has dramatically done), it may be possible for libraries to provide patrons with print copies of any work and change the paradigm for collection development from "just in case" to "just in time."

Kurzweil's stages reassure us that we have no reason to hurry. Even if all of the technological problems with e-books were solved tomorrow and print books reached the stage of obsolescence, they would still be produced and remain useful for 5 percent to 10 percent of their mature lifespan. For print books, which have been produced for over five hundred years, that means we would have twenty-five to fifty years (one or two generations) to transition to the new technology.

If we begin more than limited collection of e-books, we risk alienating patrons who quickly will weary of the eyestrain caused by current e-books. We also risk wasting money on hardware and software that rapidly will become obsolete. As progress is made on e-book development, the eight criteria outlined here can be used to judge whether the technology is finally ready for widespread acceptance.

POSTSCRIPT

Will Screens Replace Pages?

Media theorist Paul Levinson, in *Wired, Analog, and Digital Writings* (`Pulpless.com`, 1999), tries "to disentangle the extent to which our attachment to books is based on real advantages in performance versus rosy nostalgia." Levinson concludes that digital texts have genuine advantages but that books have enough advantages of their own that they will remain with us for the foreseeable future. Wade Roush, in "A Genuine Button-Pusher," *Technology Review* (November/December 1999), asserts that "the electronic book is [already] beginning to give paper some serious competition." But in the July 6, 2002, *Washington Post,* Linton Weeks could title an article "E-Books Not Exactly Flying Off the Shelves." People who read prefer paper.

Yet Web-based e-books are now appearing, and e-reference material is already here; see Mick O'Leary, "Safari/ProQuest Team Boosts E-Book Prospects," *Information Today* (March 2003) and "netLibrary Rolls Out an Online Reference Collection," *Information Today* (May 2003). E-books are also being tested in many libraries; see for instance Marc Langston, "The California State University E-book Pilot Project: Implications for Cooperative Collection Development," *Library Collections, Acquisitions, & Technical Services* (Spring 2003). David A. Bell, "The Bookless Future," *New Republic* (May 2, 2005), glories in how much easier it is to do research with electronic resources. Andrew K. Pace, "Gimme that E-Book Religion," *Computers in Libraries* (May 2005), discusses Google's plans to digitize millions of books in major libraries and enable online searching through them all (see also Charles H. Ferguson, "What's Next for Google?" *Technology Review* [January 2005]) but expresses some reservations about the strings that may be attached to access.

To this we can add the impact of two new technologies, one that is already in play and one that is coming soon. The first is "print-on-demand" (POD) publishing. This process uses computer technology, high-quality laser printers, and automated binding equipment to print single copies of books that have been stored in electronic form. Some publishers have used this technology to make large numbers of out-of-print classics available, as well as to publish many books that large, conventional publishers think would not sell enough copies to be worth their effort. Print-on-demand publishing is suffering growing pains at present, but many observers think that its prospects are strong. See Jason Epstein, "The Future of Books," *Technology Review* (January 2005).

The second technology is "electronic paper," one version of which is paper with tiny plastic balls embedded in it. One half of each ball is black, and one half is white. Electronics allows the balls to be turned so the black or the white shows, which means that this paper can behave almost like a computer monitor. Ultimately, say some, e-books will look just like paper books, except that the text can be changed by displaying different files; indeed, a single "book" may be able to hold the equivalent of a library, just as can a laptop today. See Michael J. Miller, "The Next Step in Electronic Paper," *PC Magazine* (May 7, 2002), David Cameron, "Flexible Displays Gain Momentum," *Technology Review* (January 2002), and Marie Granmar and Adrian Cho, "Electronic Paper: A Revolution About to Unfold?" *Science* (May 6, 2005).

Perhaps the wave of the future is a combination of old and new that blurs the distinction between screen and page and expands the potential of the reading experience. Roxane Farmanfarmaian, in "Beyond E-Books: Glimpses of the Future," *Publishers Weekly* (January 1, 2001), quotes Rich Gold, director of Research on Experimental Documents (RED) at Xerox Parc in Palo Alto, California, as saying, "E-book readers, print-on-demand, these are just passing technologies, like the telex machine was, that do a lousy job of adding high tech to an old medium. What we can expect in the future is a slew of radically new media where the reader reads at all levels, and content and form deeply resonate."

Foundation for Biomedical Research

The Foundation for Biomedical Research promotes public understanding and support of the ethical use of animals in scientific and medical research.

http://www.fbresearch.org

Union of Concerned Scientists

The Union of Concerned Scientists is an independent nonprofit alliance of concerned citizens and scientists committed to building a cleaner, healthier environment and a safer world. Its Web site provides a great deal of information on many issues, including the use of genetic engineering in agriculture.

http://www.ucsusa.org

Center for Bioethics

The mission of the Center for Bioethics is to advance scholarly and public understanding of ethical, legal, social, and public policy issues in health care.

http://bioethics.net

National Human Genome Research Institute

The National Human Genome Research Institute directs the Human Genome Project for the National Institutes of Health (NIH).

http://www.genome.gov/

The U.S. Department of Energy Human Genome Project

This site offers a huge amount of information and links on genetics and cloning research.

http://www.ornl.gov/techresources/
Human_Genome/elsi/Cloning.html

PART 6

Ethics

*S*ociety's standards of right and wrong have been hammered out over millennia of trial, error, and (sometimes violent) debate. Accordingly, when science and technology offer society new choices to make and new things to do, debates are renewed over whether or not these choices and actions are ethically acceptable. Today there is vigorous debate over such topics as the use of animals in research, genetic engineering, and cloning.

- Is the Use of Animals in Research Justified?

- Should Genetically Modified Foods Be Banned?

- Is It Ethically Permissible to Clone Human Beings?

ISSUE 17

Is the Use of Animals
in Research Justified?

YES: John P. Gluck and Jordan Bell, from "Ethical Issues in the Use of Animals in Biomedical and Psychopharmacological Research," *Psychopharmacology* (May 28, 2003)

NO: Tom Regan, from "The Rights of Humans and Other Animals," *Ethics & Behavior* (vol. 7, no. 2, 1997)

ISSUE SUMMARY

YES: John P. Gluck and Jordan Bell argue that although the use of animals in research has been productive, the debate over the ethical justification of using animals in research lacks clarity. Nevertheless, there is strong agreement that researchers have an ethical obligation and duty to protect the welfare of the animals they use in their research.

NO: Philosopher Tom Regan argues that any attempt to define what it is about being human that gives all humans moral rights must also give animals moral rights, and that therefore we have no more right to use animals as research subjects than we have to use other humans.

Modern biologists and physicians know a great deal about how the human body works. Some of that knowledge has been gained by studying human cadavers and tissue samples acquired during surgery and through "experiments of nature" (strokes, for example, have taught a great deal about what the various parts of the brain do; extensive injuries from car accidents and wars have also been edifying). Some knowledge of human biology has also been gained from experiments on humans, such as when patients agree to let their surgeons and doctors try experimental treatments.

The key word here is *agree*. Today it is widely accepted that people have the right to consent or not to consent to whatever is done to them in the name of research or treatment. In fact, society has determined that research done on humans without their free and informed consent is a form of scientific misconduct. However, this standard does not apply to animals, experimentation on which has produced the most knowledge of the human body.

Although animals have been used in research for at least the last 2,000 years, during most of that time, physicians who thought they had a workable treatment for some illness commonly tried it on their patients before they had any idea whether or not it worked or was even safe. Many patients, of course, died during these untested treatments. In the mid-nineteenth century, the French physiologist Claude Bernard argued that it was sensible to try such treatments first on animals to avoid some human suffering and death. No one then questioned whether or not human lives were more valuable than animal lives. In the twentieth century, Elizabeth Baldwin, in "The Case for Animal Research in Psychology," *Journal of Social Issues* (vol. 49, no. 1, 1993), argued that animals are of immense value in medical, veterinary, and psychological research, and they do not have the same moral rights as humans. Our obligation, she maintains, is to treat them humanely.

Today geneticists generally study fruit flies, roundworms, and zebra fish. Physiologists study mammals, mostly mice and rats but also rabbits, cats, dogs, pigs, sheep, goats, monkeys, and chimpanzees. Experimental animals are often kept in confined quarters, cut open, infected with disease organisms, fed unhealthy diets, and injected with assorted chemicals. Sometimes the animals suffer. Sometimes the animals die. And sometimes they are healed, albeit often of diseases or injuries induced by the researchers in the first place.

Not surprisingly, some observers have reacted with extreme sympathy and have called for better treatment of animals used in research. This "animal welfare" movement has, in turn, spawned the more extreme "animal rights" movement, which asserts that animals—especially mammals—have rights as important and as deserving of regard as those of humans. Thus, to kill an animal, whether for research, food, or fur, is the moral equivalent of murder. See Steven M. Wise and Jane Goodall, *Rattling the Cage: Toward Legal Rights for Animals* (Perseus, 2000) and Roger Scruton and Andrew Tayler, "Do Animals Have Rights?" *The Ecologist* (March 2001).

This attitude has led to important reforms in the treatment of animals, to the development of several alternatives to using animals in research, and to a considerable reduction in the number of animals used in research. See Alan M. Goldberg and John M. Frazier, "Alternatives to Animals in Toxicity Testing," *Scientific American* (August 1989); Wade Roush, "Hunting for Animal Alternatives," *Science* (October 11, 1996); and Erik Stokstad, "Humane Science Finds Sharper and Kinder Tools," *Science* (November 5, 1999). However, it has also led to hysterical objections to in-class animal dissections, terrorist attacks on laboratories, the destruction of research records, and the theft of research materials (including animals).

In the following selections, John P. Gluck and Jordan Bell review the ethical justifications for using animals in research and argue that although the use of animals in research has been productive, the debate over the ethical justification of such use lacks clarity. Nevertheless, there is strong agreement that researchers have an ethical obligation and duty to protect the welfare of the animals they use in their research. Writing in a special issue of the journal *Ethics & Behavior,* philosopher Tom Regan argues that any attempt to define what it is about being human that gives all humans moral rights must also give animals moral rights, and that therefore we have no more right to use animals as research subjects than we have to use other humans.

John P. Gluck and
Jordan Bell

 **YES**

Ethical Issues in the Use of Animals in Biomedical and Psychopharmocological Research

Introduction

While there is certainly a long and productive history of using animals in biomedical and psychopharmocological research, the debate concerning its ethical justification continues to lack clarity. Given the continued degree of contention inherent in the debate, it has been increasingly recognized that as researchers, we need to improve our sophistication about the ethical issues in question and scientifically and ethically evaluate our use of animals. . . .

Do Animals Have Moral Standing?

To begin with, the notion of "standing" comes to us from law, where the issue is related to whether an individual has the status to bring forth some form of legal action. If Smith's neighbor Jones fails to properly trim her tree and it falls and crushes Smith's car and then Jones refuses to repair it, the question becomes whether Smith has standing to bring a legal action against Jones. In this case, Smith gets access to the legal system by virtue of the fact that she has the status of taxpayer, car owner, citizen, and has apparently suffered a direct loss because of her neighbor's negligence. In other words, standing in the legal sense permits access to the law and its mechanisms to evaluate and redress a claim. Extending from this example to the question about whether animals have *moral* standing requires us to determine what characteristics an entity must possess in order to achieve the status necessary to access the protections provided by the moral and ethical standards of a society. What are those characteristics that provide this access? It is here where ethical theorists have a variety of perspectives.

From *Psychopharmacology*, May 28, 2003, pp. 6–12. Copyright © 2003 by Springer-Verlag GmbH & Co.KG. Reprinted by permission. References omitted.

Utilitarian Ethical Theories

These theories turn on the notion that if an action is to be considered right it must be one that is drawn from the population of possible responses that produces the greatest amount of good for the collection of individuals affected by the act. The onus on the ethical decision-maker is to strive to maximize the amount of aggregate good (the principle of utility). To do this, the decision maker is required to calculate impartially the consequences of a given choice on all those affected. Therefore, in order to be counted as an entity that has moral standing a being must possess at least some rudimentary ability to experience a consequence. That is, it must have the ability to experience pain and pleasure, have preferences, or have a welfare that matters to it. As Jeremy Bentham (1748–1832) put it, an entity is not required to posses some high level of cognitive ability like thinking, intention or rationality but only the ability to suffer. That characteristic alone is sufficient to be considered relevant for ethical consideration. The possession of higher or more complex cognitive abilities do come into play as these abilities potentially increase the variety of ways that an individual may be pleased or harmed. Therefore, all sentient lives count, but not all lives necessarily have the same value because the overall value of a life increases as the richness (the ways that the entity can pleasured or harmed) of that life increases. The converse is also true. "If a being is not capable of suffering, or of enjoyment, there is nothing to take into account" morally. In a related approach, Raymond Frey, a strong advocate for the use of animals in research, agrees that if the value of a life parallels the emergence of capabilities such as intelligence, sentience, and self-direction, the value of that life also increases and deserves increasing levels of ethical consideration. Frey, however, wants us to recognize that there are some humans whose quality of life is below that of some animals [e.g. say between a human in a persistent vegetative state (PVS) with no living relatives or friends and a healthy chimpanzee living in a social group in west Africa]. Assume for a moment that from a physiological perspective both are appropriate subjects for a particular research project. In this unique case, according to Frey, the greater level of protection should go to the chimpanzee because its life is of a higher quality. In other words, Frey insists that the implications of the utilitarian perspective be carried out consistently regardless of species membership because he cannot see how species membership divorced from these capabilities can matter morally. To make species membership matter one must leave the domain of secular ethics and enter the realm of specific religious doctrine.

To summarize, this perspective does not disallow the use of animals in biomedical research in general, and psychopharmacological research in particular. Nor does it prevent the use of human. What is required, however, is a high level of justification based upon a realistic and good faith assessment of the benefits of the research and the harmful impact on research subjects. In a recent opinion piece in the June 13, 2002 issue of *Nature,* entitled "Distasteful But Necessary," this point is emphasized in a discussion about the use of primates in biomedical research. The piece explicitly calls for an evaluation of whether the benefits of drug toxicity tests that are currently carried out on nonhuman primates are ethically justified "bearing in mind that primates may have a greater capacity for suffering than other animals."

Kantian or Deontological Theories

Theories of this sort reject the consequentialist calculation method of evaluating the ethical acceptability of actions. What matters here instead is the evaluation of the acceptability of the moral rule on which an action is based, regardless of the consequences. Immanuel Kant's (1724–1804) notion of the "categorical imperative" requires that we act only in such a way that the maxim which grounds a particular action could be taken as a universal law, to be followed under all similar circumstances and times. So assume that I run out to pick up my newspaper early in the morning because I have an important need to know if the city council made a particular vote the previous evening. However, I discover that my paper is not there. Am I permitted to take my neighbors instead? Assume that I judge that the benefits to me, my business, and the financial welfare of my family far outstrip the costs to my neighbor, since I know that he rarely reads the paper in the first place. From a utilitarian perspective, I am in fact obligated to steal my neighbor's newspaper in this situation. For Kant, in order for me to justify taking the paper I must be willing to say that I would sanction the act of stealing whenever a person honestly believes that someone else's property would do them more good than the owner. In other formulations of the categorical imperative, more relevant to our current discussion about research participation. Kant states that morality requires that we treat human persons as "ends in themselves" and never merely as means to our ends. Kant based this position on the belief that only humans were persons capable of moral and ethical deliberation of the kind that could result in the discovery of moral law. Only humans could become part of moral communities where our treatment of one another could be argued debated and resolved. Only humans were autonomous "to give oneself the law" and therefore only humans rightfully have access to the protections afforded by ethical norms.

While Kant was quite clear in his writing that he believed that humans had no primary ethical responsibilities to animals, he did believe that we had secondary ethical responsibilities to them. In other words, Kant believed that the way we treat animals could become relevant to the way we treat humans and therefore morally important. If we treated "dumb" animals with cruelty, he felt that there was an increased probability that we would do the same to humans. In that way, and that way only, our treatment of animals was morally relevant.

In general, while pure Kantian perspectives about animals (i.e. no direct obligations) are quite rare, many other ethical perspectives have been influenced by Kant at least in that they require that an entity have demonstrated higher levels of cognitive ability to be considered to have moral standing. The list of characteristics stemming from these considerations includes consciousness, self-awareness, rationality, autonomy, and the ability to have second-order intentions (i.e. the ability to have intentions about one's intentions). The argument goes that characteristics such as these are required to make morality a possibility in the first place. Where we draw the line on the list of characteristics has significant implications. If we draw the line at the low end of complexity—say, basic consciousness—it would have the effect of ensuring that all intact humans have moral standing. It would also have the effect of covering many animals as well. On the other hand, if we draw the line higher, say at the level of having an awareness of self through time or second-order intentions, that would leave all or most animals out, except for perhaps the great apes, but would also leave some humans out as well (e.g. PVS patients, anencephalic infants). When Goodman and Check, in their review of the debate about the use of the so-called higher primates in research, point out that the very characteristics that make primates desirable research subjects also triggers questions about the ethical justification of the practice, they are emphasizing the influence of these types of considerations.

Arguments from Inherent Value and Rights

Perhaps the best exemplar of this thinking can be found in the work of Tom Regan. In his influential work "The case for animal rights," Regan proposes that as long as there is something it is like to be a particular organism, the ability to experience that "something" bestows inherent value to that being. This is what Regan refers to as being a "subject of a life," which bestows rights. The existence of those rights protects against intrusions by humans seeking to take hold of and use that life for their own purposes, no matter how well intentioned the planned use may be. The implication here is that unless a being specifically consents to participation in research, science and society are required to find alternatives ways of discovery. While these perspectives reflect important considerations, they offer no middle ground and are therefore not likely to move the discussion along to resolution.

Speciesism

Up to this point we have seen that being a member of a particular species has not yet been emphasized as relevant to the protection afforded by ethical norms. To base access on species membership alone has been referred to as speciesism by Peter Singer and is meant by him to be a derogatory characterization similar to sexism or racism. This is a difficult issue. Certainly, some important philosophers have argued that having a preference for one's own kind is understandable and is, to at least some extent, ethically acceptable. However, this move toward ethically favoring "our own" has serious downside potential. For example, if we let that argument stand without qualification, what is to prevent others from using this standard to make acceptable special treatment of their "own kind" over nongroup members this time based not on characteristics like species membership but on color, gender, race, or ethnicity? Clearly some uses of the "our own" argument are extremely problematic. In addition, Sapontzis points out that the history of ethics and moral philosophy has been one characterized not by a hardening of boundaries between protected groups, but by an ever widening of the circle of inclusion. As we have seen in our discussion of utilitarian and Kantian theories, each incorporates different decisional strategies that help to support an emphasis on the characteristic of impartiality. The problem ethically then is find the balance between acceptable partiality and impartiality.

As the discussion shows clearly, the tendency of ethicists has been to put a heavier emphasis on the relationship between cognitive and sentient characteristics and the level of deserved moral protection. This fact is of particular importance to pharmacological research as many of the traditional uses of animals are based upon the assumption that animals are capable of experiencing complex emotional and cognitive states such as helplessness, depression, anxiety, and perhaps even psychotic symptoms.

Clearly Pro-Use Perspectives

Adrian Morrison, a prominent neuroscientist and veterinarian, while admittedly not formally trained in moral philosophy, has become established as a respected authority for the ethical justification of pro-use positions. It is important to consider his influential perspectives. While acknowledging that researchers have strong obligations to care for animal welfare when we restrict their lives for our purposes, he is unambiguous about his support for the extensive use of animals in biomedical research. The ethical base of his arguments focus on the following four points:

1. Animal research has produced enormous benefit for the physically and mentally ill and is necessary for continued biomedical advance.
2. Our primary obligations are to our fellow humans.
3. All human beings are persons but animals are not persons.
4. Humans get to decide what animals are to be in relationship to us.

There are many strengths in Morrison's general arguments. For example, he effectively maintains the specter of disease and human suffering clearly before us. He highlights the many successes that have emerged from animal research, like the development of psychotropic medications. He reminds researchers of their obligations to laboratory animals and the relationship between good animal welfare and good science. He is also a poignant critic of Peter Singer's brand of utilitarianism and his low evaluation of the value of the lives of some severely disabled humans. The weaknesses of Morrison's ideological problem, as exemplified by analysis of the four points above, are that he tends to include the elements of various ethical theories that support his beliefs while excluding other aspects that would make his conclusions more debatable. For example, on one hand he criticizes the impartiality of utilitarian thinking (e.g. Singer), but then grounds the justification of animal research firmly within the principle of utility (no. 1). He adopts the concept of personhood as the criterion for moral standing (no. 2), but does not deal with the ethical implications of the scientific data coming to us about the nature of animal cognitive ability provided by ethologists and comparative cognitive psychologists. These data provide evidence of the existence in animals of many of the very cognitive characteristics that have traditionally served as the definition of human persons. Instead, he simply declares that evolutionary considerations do not apply to the domain of the mental (no. 4). The danger of Morrison's certainty is that it could result in some researchers being lulled into a sense of security about the clarity of the ethical debate. This contradicts a recent editorial in the July issue of the journal *Nature Neuroscience* (2002), which calls upon us as scientists to become increasingly sophisticated about the ethical issues involved with our work.

Except for the limited version of the Kantian position, there is wide agreement that animals matter morally. Utilitarians demand that we include the consequences of our interactions with them into the justificatory process. Kantian-influenced arguments require that we access the implications of the cognitive abilities that we find in animals and determine whether they reach the level that requires that we modify or forebear from the invasive interactions that may follow from our work. Even those writers that exclude animals from membership in the moral community agree that our treatment of them for good purpose be marked by sensitivity and respect. There is also widespread agreement that research on animals should involve the fewest number, at the level of the least pain possible, and then only when there is no valid alternative. These agreements follow closely on the proposals of Russell and Burch which are referred to as the "three Rs" (reduction, refinement, replacement).

Others have pointed out that some of the very animals whose welfare researchers are required to protect, receive very different treatment if encountered outside the laboratory. Thus "pest" mice are exterminated brutally while the use of laboratory mice for research must be carefully justified with concern for minimizing their pain and distress clearly demonstrated. It is then argued that this paradox is clear evidence that the need for ethical justification of animal research is patently absurd. This criticism fails to recognize that in general, the application of broad ethical principles (e.g. "do no harm") must be made relevant to the details of a particular real life situation under consideration. Conduct appropriate to this principle in some contexts may require modification in other circumstances. Clearly our ethical obligations to animals (and humans for that matter) who pose a real danger to our well-being are justifiably different than when those same animals pose no such risk. Let us suppose that we were to discover that an official responsible for the extermination of mice for public health purposes was found to be slowly frying the animals alive in large skillets in order to prolong their suffering. Would we not find that to be objectionable? While the risk to the public health may justify extermination it certainly does not remove the animals from some basic forms of ethical consideration.

Regulatory Perspectives

There is no question that ethical theory has influenced the development of national regulatory approaches in that all such approaches provide certain limitations and protections for animals used in biomedical research. In so doing, they acknowledge that animals deserve ethical consideration. However, the extent of the consideration varies considerably. Looking broadly, 23 countries currently have some form of animal research legislation. The countries included in this group are Australia (some states), Austria, Belgium, Denmark, Finland, France, Germany, Greece, Iceland, Ireland, Italy, Luxembourg, the Netherlands, New Zealand, Norway, Poland, Portugal, Spain, Sweden, Switzerland,

Taiwan, the United Kingdom, and the United States. Orlans has developed a list of eight characteristics on which the various legislative attempts can be graded. She argues that a country with all eight characteristics represents the highest form of protection while not at the same time excluding the practice (the principality of Liechtenstein is the only country that currently outlaws all forms of animal research or testing). The characteristics are:

1. The provision of basic husbandry requirements and the regular inspection of facilities by an independent review group.
2. Requirements that mandate the control of pain and suffering.
3. Critical pre-review of research proposals.
4. Requirements for investigator competence.
5. Bans on certain procedures, levels of pain and distress, sources of animals, and use of some species.
6. Application of the three Rs.
7. The use of ethical criteria in the justification and decisional process.
8. Requirements that require investigators to rate the level of expected harm to the animals.

Orlans points out that as time passes, the tendency of national regulations is to incorporate more and more of this list and not less. When the United States Animal Welfare Act (AWA) is compared with European standards, the central difference is related to the question of whether there are any limits to what can be done to an experimental animal in the name of science (item no. 5). In the United States, other than for performing surgery with non-anesthetic paralytic agents, any investigative procedure producing any level of pain can conceivably be approved if the argument for benefits is sufficiently credible. In other words, there is no point where animal interests rise to the level of trumping the search for human benefit. On he other hand, in the United Kingdom the ethic has moved to the position that experimental procedures that produce extreme levels of pain and distress are not permitted regardless of the predicted benefits. In general, the standards of the overall European Community do not rise to that level of protection but do require that research where harms are not balanced by benefits must not proceed.

The Use of Animals in Psychopharmacological Research

Researchers involved in the process of developing pharmacological treatments for neuropsychiatric disorders by studying animal models face a daunting task from both the scientific and ethical realm. The scientific challenges involve the unraveling of the cognitive, behavioral and affective manifestations of complex disorders that often substantially exist in the realm of the subjective and are mediated by the most complex of all physiological systems. From an ethical perspective, as we have seen, it is becoming widely accepted that the existence of a sentient "mental" life leads to moral standing and, as the complexity increases, so does the level of deserved protection. This reflects directly on the use of animals as global models of these disorders, as the very characteristics that make them potentially useful brings them increasingly under the protection of ethical norms. What adds to the ethical difficulty is that the use of animals in the study of psychiatric disorders has a long history where the ethical issues that we now are beginning to appreciate were not significant factors in research planning. . . .

Issues of Validity and Ethical Justification

In the most fundamental sense, the ethical justification for the use of animals requires that their use result in benefits for humans and perhaps animals as well. Therefore, the assessment of the validity of animal models is crucial. Geyer and Markou have forcefully emphasized that justification must in the end focus on reliability and predictive validity. In other words, if the model does not lead to useful predictions about the human clinical condition, it ought to be abandoned no matter how conceptually appealing the model may be. . . .

These validity issues highlight the necessary mutual dependency of human and animal research in this area. Without extensive human clinical information, animal researchers cannot properly target their research models, and their scientific and ethical justification is thereby weakened. Therefore it is imperative that researchers and ethicists work through the ethical issues related to studying clinical populations where informed consent is problematic.

Choice of Species

While the choice of animals for use in model research has ethical implications, all too often the selection is based on factors such as ease of availability rather than the model-relevant characteristics. Overall and colleagues have shown that when investigators have broad expertise in animal behavior it can lead to the discovery of powerful naturally occurring models. These researchers capitalized on the clinical veterinary literature that strongly suggests that dogs suffer from a wide variety of anxiety disorders such as separation anxiety, obsessive-compulsive disorder, post-traumatic stress disorder, panic attacks, and thunderstorm or noise phobia. These models have begun to provide important information and insight into the complex neurobiological and genetic elements leading to anxiety behaviors. Importantly, the research has also benefited many companion animals that suffer from anxiety problem. . . .

Conclusions

In summary, regardless of the ethical perspective one favors, there is strong agreement that animals matter morally and that at a minimum their welfare must be considered in the design of research, not just out of personal sense of caring, but from ethical obligation and duty. This position is supported by the ever-expanding proliferation of national regulatory schemes which are primarily based in the three Rs. Researchers must not leave the analysis of these issues solely to others whose positions seem to capture our preferences, for they turn out on close examination to be questionable prejudices. . . . Researchers must become more sophisticated about issues of model validation and the nature of the animals they use.

Tom Regan  **NO**

The Rights of Humans
and Other Animals

Because the theme of this issue lends itself to emphasizing the differences that exist between the participating philosophers, it seems especially important to make a few observations about some fundamental points on which we are all agreed. As will be clear momentarily, our unanimity concerns what we all think is false rather than what we think is true.

Points of Agreement

We all agree that moral judgments—judgments about what is right and wrong, good and bad, just and unjust—are not simply and solely expressions of individual feeling or attitude. Some of the things we say are simply and solely of this sort. For example, if I say "I like coffee," and you say "I like tea," each of us has expressed our personal preference regarding what we like to drink. And about such matters there is, of course, no right or wrong, no true or false, and no thought of justifying or supporting or validating what is said. About matters of taste, things just are the way they are, with different people liking different things.

Moral judgments are not like this. When two people make conflicting judgments about a controversial moral issue—about the morality of abortion, for example—they are not simply and solely saying what they like or dislike, as a matter of personal preference. They are saying something *about abortion*, not something *about their individual response* to abortion. And the person who says that abortion is always wrong is saying something about abortion that contradicts what is said by someone who says that abortion is sometimes morally permissible. As such, and unlike the situation in which different people simply and solely express their feelings or preferences, moral judgments do need to be defended, do need to be justified, do need to be validated. *How* to do this is a question whose possible answer divides the philosophers taking part in this discussion. But *that* this needs to be done—that moral judgments need to be justified, defended, validated—is common ground between all of us.

A second important agreement concerns a second falsehood. Just as some people think (mistakenly, in our view) that moral judgments are simply and solely expressions of personal feelings or attitudes, others think they are statements about a culture's mores. On this view, moral right and wrong are defined by the dominant customs of a culture, at any given period of its history; and because different cultures have different customs, this view, which usually is referred to as *cultural relativism,* concludes that there is no universal right and wrong; rather, there are as many rights and wrongs as there are different cultures with different customs.

The philosophers here, without exception, reject cultural relativism. When Frey denies that human beings have moral rights, he does not think he can be shown to be mistaken if we point out that most Americans disagree with him, any more than the rest of us are inclined to agree that slavery was not wrong among White citizens of the antebellum South, given the prevailing customs of that time and place. Even if it is an exaggeration to say, as Henrik Ibsen is said to have observed, that "the minority is always right," it is too obvious to need argument that the majority sometimes is wrong. We do not defend, justify, or validate a moral judgment by doing cultural anthropology.

Neither do we do this—and here I come to the third and final point of agreement among all of us—by consulting some holy book or by taking instruction from God's will. In saying this, I am not saying that no books are holy or that there is no God. I am only saying that, among the philosophers writing here, we all agree that judgments about moral right and wrong, good or bad, the just and the unjust must be defended, justified, or validated independently of what any God says or wills.

The Nature and Importance of Human Rights

As for our disagreements, it is important to realize that it is not only our respective views about animal rights that divide us. We also are divided when it comes to human rights. Cohen, Beauchamp, and I seem to be of one mind concerning the nature of human rights. (Let me add parenthetically that when I speak of human rights this is shorthand for human *moral* rights; and the same is true when I speak of animal rights: I am referring to their moral rights. Questions involving human or animal legal rights are an entirely separate matter.) Here, briefly, are those points on which I think the three of us agree.

Human rights place justified limits on what people are free to do to one another. For example, the right to bodily integrity disallows physically assaulting another person's body simply on the grounds that others might benefit as a result. To use Cohen's example, one cannot justify the Nazi hypothermia research because what was learned might help other people who suffer from exposure. . . .

There are some things that *morally cannot be done* to the individual even if others stand to benefit as a result of doing it. As Ronald Dworkin said, the rights of the individual "trump" the collective interest. In the moral game, the rights card is the trump card.

Even with these very few comments about rights on the table, I think we should be able to see why Cohen is correct when he says that the idea of animal rights is a very important idea, one fraught with massive potential practical significance. Because if animals have rights—including, for example, the right to bodily integrity and the right not to be made to suffer gratuitously—it is difficult to see how anything less than the total abolition of animal model research could be morally acceptable. In particular, if animals have rights, certain familiar ways of defending animal model research will be silenced. No longer will we want to listen to the long list of benefits attributed to research of this kind. If animals have rights, and if rights are the trump card in the moral game, their rights override any benefits, real or imagined, we have gained, or stand to gain, from using them in biomedical research. So, yes, Cohen is on the money when he states that animal rights is an important idea.

Now, Cohen, Beauchamp, and I agree that humans have rights. And Beauchamp and I agree that animals have rights (although we disagree over what rights they have). It is Frey who disagrees with all of us, maintaining, as he does, that neither animals nor humans have rights. Before going on to state my views concerning animal rights, I want to say something about his views concerning human rights.

Frey's Utilitarianism

Frey is a utilitarian, and a utilitarian of a certain stripe. All utilitarians think that the morality of what we do—whether our acts are morally right or wrong—depends on what happens as a result of the choices we make. Utilitarianism is a forward-looking view. The consequences, results, or effects of our actions determine their morality. And by our actions we should be trying to make the world better, to bring about the best possible consequences or results, in any given situation.

What is best [for] all considered, however, is not necessarily what is best for each individual. Utilitarians are committed to aggregating—to adding and subtracting—the positive and negative consequences experienced by different individuals. This means that one person might lose a lot so that another might gain. . . .

[T]he essential point is that his utilitarianism is, in my view, a fundamentally mistaken way to think about morality. Here is a simple test case that I think makes my point. Some time back four teenage boys raped and in other ways sexually abused a seriously retarded teenage girl. Among other things, as I recall, the boys took special pleasure in invading her body with a broom handle and a Coke bottle.

I assume that no one will question that the abuse this poor girl suffered was wrong. But I hope you will notice that Frey's theory cannot easily explain why it is wrong. After all, there were four boys and just the one girl, and the boys evidently had a very good time. Shuffling along, Frey might suggest that there are other consequences that need to be taken into account—for example, the insecurity experienced by other young girls as a result of what happened to this one, and so on.

But this is not the central point. The central point is that, *before* Frey can pass a moral judgment in this case, his theory requires that we take the pleasures the four boys experienced into account—that we count *their* equal interests equally. By my lights, however, the pleasures experienced by these four boys are *totally irrelevant* to assessing the morality of their actions. More generally, the interests of those who do what is morally wrong have no bearing on the determination of the wrong they do. It is because Frey's view requires that we count these interests, *and weigh them equally with those of the victims of wrongdoing,* that I think his way of thinking is fundamentally mistaken.

Thus, the importance of human rights, in my view. Because if we suppose that this young girl has rights, then the good time had by the boys—the benefits they derived from abusing her—emerges as beside the moral point. Her rights trump their good time; indeed, their good time has no bearing whatsoever on assessing the morality of what they did. If there is a valid way of defending or justifying our moral judgments, I believe that it involves thinking along the lines I have just sketched, crude as that sketch is.

Animal Welfare and Animal Rights

I turn now to the topic of animal rights, beginning with some comments on the distinction between animal welfarists and animal rightists. As the name suggests, animal welfarists are in theory committed to taking the welfare of animals seriously. Animals should not be caused gratuitous physical pain; their psychological wellbeing should not be diminished unnecessarily. These are among the principles that guide a conscientious welfarist.

As such, welfarists can, and some of them sometimes do, call for important reforms, in the name of humane improvements, regarding how humans utilize nonhuman animals. Provided, however, that the welfare interests of these animals are taken into account and counted fairly, we do nothing wrong in principle by utilizing them to advance human interests. In particular, the use of nonhuman animals in biomedical research is in principle morally right, from a welfarist perspective, even if this human endeavor occasionally goes wrong in practice, as when a particular researcher neglects or otherwise mistreats animals in his laboratory.

Animal welfarism, therefore, can be seen to embody the utilitarianism championed by someone like Frey. The many benefits allegedly derived from animal model research outweigh the many harms experienced by the animals. Indeed, if the biomedical community is looking for a coherent spokesperson to defend their activities philosophically, it could well be true that they will not be able to find anyone better than Frey and his utilitarianism.

Animal rightists differ from animal welfarists. Although animal welfarists can have reformist aspirations, animal rightists are necessarily abolitionists. From their perspective, the use of nonhuman animals in scientific research is wrong in principle, not simply occasionally wrong in practice. These animals do not belong in laboratories in the first place: They do not belong there because placing them there, in the hope of gaining benefits for others, violates their rights. Rights being the trump card in the moral game, it is not larger cages, but empty cages, that animal rightists call for.

Whatever we might think of the animal rights–animal welfare debate, it is important to realize that it represents a type of debate that has many logical cousins. The ongoing debate over the justice of the death penalty is an example. Some people believe there is nothing wrong with capital punishment in principle, even as they acknowledge there certainly have been some things wrong with it in practice. It was not too long ago that convicted criminals were hanged in public, burnt to death, or drowned for offenses that included such crimes as (here I cite North Carolina law) breaking a fish pond, stealing apples, dueling if death ensued, and (most remarkable of all) growing tobacco plants. Over the years, reformers of the death penalty sought to make the setting of the punishment more dignified and the method of execution more humane. Death by lethal injection, carried out in a sterile, hospital-like setting, would seem to represent as far as we might be able to go in the direction of such reforms.

This is not far enough for death penalty abolitionists. Think what one might of their arguments, these critics of capital punishment believe that it is wrong in principle, not merely sometimes grotesquely immoral in practice, and they therefore call for its complete abolition, not merely various "humane" reforms.

Thus does the logic of the animal rights–animal welfare debate mirror the logic of other important, divisive, and enduring social controversies. Other examples include the debates over reforming or abolishing slavery, child labor, and legal access to abortion. That all these controversies differ in important ways from the animal rights–animal welfare debate is too obvious to be denied. My point is not that this debate is like these other controversies in each and every way; mine is the far more modest point that they share a common logic.

Animal Rights

But *do* animals have rights? And if they do, what rights do they have? My answers to these questions are explained in my book, *The Case for Animal Rights* (1983), and it is this work that I recommend to anyone who is interested seriously in what my answers are and why I answer as I do. Concerning the latter point, let me remind you that all the philosophers writing in this issue agree that we do not offer answers to moral questions just by saying how we happen to feel or what we happen to like, or by making reference to the dominant customs in America today, or by citing selected passages in the Bible or some other sacred book. Our moral thinking needs to move in a different direction than those these paths open up to us.

But if not in these ways, how? No easy question, this; certainly not for the philosophically faint of heart. But here is *a* way, although certainly not the only way, to proceed.

Suppose we begin by assuming that humans have rights and ask how we might be able to illuminate or explain why we do. Of course, Frey will protest.

You will recall that he denies *both* animal *and* human rights. But you also will recall where, in my opinion, his utilitarianism-without-rights lands him. So, although beginning with the assumption that humans have rights is certainly not noncontroversial, it is a place we can defend using on this occasion—one that, by the way, Beauchamp and Cohen can be counted on as approving, given their agreement that humans do indeed have rights.

If humans have rights, there must be something about being human that helps explain or illuminates why we have them. Put another way, there must be some characteristic or set of characteristics (for brevity's sake, I refer to these possibilities as *C*) that makes the attribution of rights plausible in our case and implausible in the case of, for example, clouds, negative afterimages, and microfungi. The question is: What could this C be?

Possible answers are many. Some, although possibly widely believed, will not pass muster with my fellow philosophers. The idea that C is the soul, and that God endowed us with rights when he endowed us with a soul, rests on a religious basis that we agree is unsatisfactory. A more promising, nonreligious candidate is rational autonomy. It is because humans are rational autonomous agents, and because clouds, negative afterimages, and microfungi are not, that we have rights and they do not.

Suppose we grant this candidate for C for the moment; then we can ask how nonhuman animals would fare. In other words, we can ask, Are any nonhuman animals rational and autonomous? Because if some are, it would smack of prejudice to deny that they have rights but to affirm that we do.

Whether any nonhuman ananimals are rational and autonomous is a very difficult empirical question, one that we are unlikely to settle on this occasion. My own view, for what it is worth, is that there are many species of animals whose members satisfy these conditions. Nonhuman primates are the most obvious example. Next are the great whales and other mammals. Obviously, where we draw the line that separates those animals who are rational and autonomous from those who are not will be neither easy nor free of controversy. Indeed, it may be that there is no clearly defined line we can draw with confidence, given the abundance of our individual and collective ignorance. However, it is enough for our purposes to recognize that *some* nonhuman animals are like humans in being rational and autonomous. So if rational autonomy explains or illuminates why we have rights, consistency requires that we make the same judgment in the case of these other animals: They, too, would have rights.

There is, however, a problem. Not all human beings are rational, autonomous agents. Infants are not, although most of them some day will be, and older people who suffer from serious mental deterioration are not, although most of them once were. Plus there are those many thousands of humans who, like the young woman raped by the four teenage boys, are seriously mentally retarded throughout their entire lives. In any or all of these cases we have individuals who *are* human beings but who are *not* rational and autonomous. So if C is rational autonomy, it appears that billions of human beings lack rights and, in lacking them, lack the most important card in the moral game. In their case, we cannot say that it would be wrong to harm them in the hope of benefiting others because their rights trump the collective interest. In the nature of the case, they have no rights.

This problem can be avoided by putting forth a different candidate for C. Instead of using what Beauchamp refers to as "cognitive criteria," . . . criteria such as rationality, we might instead rely on noncognitive criteria, criteria such as sentience (the capacity to be able to experience pain and pleasure) or emotion. And this does seem to be a more promising way to think about C, especially because all those humans who were denied rights, given the criterion of rational autonomy, seem to satisfy these noncognitive criteria.

Noncognitive criteria do more than increase the number of human beings who qualify as rights holders. These same criteria also increase the number of nonhuman animals who qualify. Line drawing problems doubtless will persist, but, wherever one reasonably draws the line, it seems evident that there are many more nonhuman animals who are sentient or who feel emotions than there are nonhuman animals who are rational and autonomous.

Although much more needs to be said to complete the argument for animal rights, some features of the central plot emerge from the little that has been said here. We face a choice: *Either* we can set the criteria of rights possession (C) rather high, so to speak, requiring capacities such as rationality and autonomy, *or* we can set the criteria of rights possession lower, requiring noncognitive capacities such as sentience. If we choose the former, some (but not a great many) nonhuman animals arguably will qualify as possessors of rights; but many human beings also will fail to qualify. If we choose the latter alternative, these humans will be enfranchised within the class of rights holders; but so will many nonhuman animals. Rationally, we cannot have it both ways—cannot, that is, rationally defend the view that all and only human beings have rights. Cohen may think he can do this. But for reasons I hope to explain in the future, I believe he is seriously confused and mistaken.

Which choice should we make? Informed people of good will can answer this question differently. I favor a view of rights that enfranchises the most vulnerable humans among us. Infants and young children, the elderly who suffer from degenerative diseases of the brain, the seriously mentally retarded of all ages are the most obvious examples. I do not think those of us who are more fortunate should be free to utilize these human beings—in biomedical research, for example—in the hope that we might learn something that will benefit us or others. Frey's utilitarianism certainly could allow this, which in my opinion is all the more reason not to accept his moral philosophy. If we recognize the rights of these humans, however, we recognize that they hold trump cards that have greater ethical force than what is in the general interest. And that certainly is the position I hold and recommend in their case.

I also recognize, however, that any plausible criterion that would enfranchise these humans within the class of rights holders will spill over the species boundary, so to speak, and enfranchise many hundreds, possibly many thousands of species of animals. That being the case, these animals also must be viewed as holding the trump card in the moral game. And because the rights they have should not be overridden in the name of seeking benefits for ourselves or others, it follows that none of these animals should be in any laboratory for that purpose. From an animal rights perspective, as noted earlier, it is not larger cages, it is empty cages that recognition of animal rights requires.

POSTSCRIPT

Is the Use of Animals in Research Justified?

Much debate about the lethal experiments that were conducted on nonconsenting human subjects by the Nazis during World War II, as well as the ensuing trials of the Nazi physicians in Nuremburg, Germany, has established a consensus that no scientist can treat people the way the Nazis did. Informed consent is essential, and research on humans must aim to benefit those same humans.

As these ideas have gained currency, some people have tried to extend them to say that, just as scientists cannot do whatever they wish to humans, they cannot do whatever they wish to animals. Harriet Ritvo, in "Toward a More Peaceable Kingdom," *Technology Review* (April 1992), says that the animal rights movement "challenges the ideology of science itself . . . forcing experimenters to recognize that they are not necessarily carrying out an independent exercise in the pursuit of truth—that their enterprise, in its intellectual as well as its social and financial dimensions, is circumscribed and defined by the culture of which it is an integral part." The result is a continuing debate, driven by the periodic discovery of researchers who seem quite callous (at least to the layperson's eye) in their treatment of animals (see Kathy Snow Guillermo, *Monkey Business: The Disturbing Case That Launched the Animal Rights Movement* [National Press, 1993]), by the charge that animal rights advocates just do not understand nature or research, and by the counter-charge that animal research is irrelevant (see Peter Tatchell, "Why Animal Research Is Bad Science?" *New Statesman* (August 9, 2004).

In the February 1997 issue of *Scientific American,* Andrew N. Rowan presents a debate entitled "The Benefits and Ethics of Animal Research." The opposing articles are Neal D. Barnard and Stephen R. Kaufman, "Animal Research Is Wasteful and Misleading" and Jack H. Botting and Adrian R. Morrison, "Animal Research Is Vital to Medicine." Among books that are pertinent to this issue are F. Barbara Orlans, *In the Name of Science: Issues in Responsible Animal Experimentation* (Oxford University Press, 1993); Rod Strand and Patti Strand, *The Hijacking of the Humane Movement* (Doral, 1993); and Deborah Blum, *The Monkey Wars* (Oxford University Press, 1994). Adrian R. Morrison provides a guide to responsible animal use in "Ethical Principles Guiding the Use of Animals in Research," *American Biology Teacher* (February 2003). Barry Yeoman, "Can We Trust Research Done with Lab Mice," *Discover* (July 2003), notes that the conditions in which animals are kept can make a huge difference in their behavior and in their responses to experimental treatments.

Reviewing recent developments in the animal rights movement, Damon Linker, in "Rights for Rodents," *Commentary* (April 2001), concludes, "Can anyone really doubt that, were the misanthropic agenda of the animal-rights movement actually to succeed, the result would be an increase in man's inhumanity, to man and animal alike? In the end, fostering our age-old 'prejudice' in favor of human dignity may be the best thing we can do for animals, not to mention for ourselves." An editorial in *Lancet* (September 4, 2004), "Animal Research Is a Source of Human Compassion, Not Shame," insists that the use of animals in biomedical research is both an essentially humanistic endeavor and necessary.

Charles Colson and Anne Morse agree that the animal rights movement assaults human dignity in "Taming Beasts," *Christianity Today* (April 2003). Yet the idea that animals have rights too continues to gain ground. Steven M. Wise finds in *Drawing the Line: Science and the Case for Animal Rights* (Perseus, 2002) that there is a spectrum of mental capacities for different species, which supports the argument for rights. Niall Shanks, in "Animal Rights in the Light of Animal Cognition," *Social Alternatives* (Summer 2003) considers the moral/ philosophical justifications for animal rights and stresses the question of consciousness. Jim Motavalli, in "Rights from Wrongs," *E Magazine* (March/April 2003), describes with approval the movement toward giving animals legal rights (though not necessarily human rights). John Gray takes a more jaundiced view in "The Best Hope for Animal Liberation Is that Humans Kill Each Other in Wars," *New Statesman* (February 9, 2004).

You can find the benefits of the use of animals discussed on a number of Web sites. Begin with Americans for Medical Progress (http:// www.amprogress.org/About/aboutmain.cfm). For lists of specific benefits, visit Michigan State University at http://www.msu.edu/unit/ular/ biomed/biomed_index.htm and the Pennsylvania Society for Biomedical Research at http://www.psbr.org/society/ABOUT.htm.

ISSUE 18

Should Genetically Modified Foods Be Banned?

YES: Martin Teitel and Kimberly A. Wilson, from *Genetically Engineered Food: Changing the Nature of Nature* (Park Street Press, 2001)

NO: Henry I. Miller and Gregory Conko, from "Agricultural Biotechnology: Overregulated and Underappreciated," *Issues in Science and Technology* (Winter 2005)

ISSUE SUMMARY

YES: Activists Martin Teitel and Kimberly A. Wilson argue that genetically modified foods should be banned until their safety for human consumption has been demonstrated.

NO: Henry I. Miller and Gregory Conko argue that the acceptance of genetically modified foods has been blocked by activists' alarming messages and excessive regulation. Regulation should be based on genuine risk, not on the process by which a product is made.

In the early 1970s scientists first discovered that it was technically possible to move genes—biological material that determines a living organism's physical makeup—from one organism to another and thus (in principle) to give bacteria, plants, and animals new features and to correct genetic defects of the sort that cause many diseases, such as cystic fibrosis. Most researchers in molecular genetics were excited by the potentialities that suddenly seemed within their grasp. However, a few researchers—as well as many people outside the field—were disturbed by the idea; they thought that genetic mix-and-match games might spawn new diseases, weeds, and pests. Some people even argued that genetic engineering should be banned at the outset, before unforeseeable horrors were unleashed.

Researchers in support of genetic experimentation responded by declaring a moratorium on their own work until suitable safeguards could be devised. Once those safeguards were in place in the form of government regulations, work resumed. James D. Watson and John Tooze document the early years of this research in *The DNA Story: A Documentary History of Gene Cloning* (W. H. Freeman, 1981). For a shorter, more recent review of the story, see

Bernard D. Davis, "Genetic Engineering: The Making of Monsters?" *The Public Interest* (Winter 1993).

By 1989 the technology had developed tremendously: researchers could obtain patents for mice with artificially added genes ("transgenic" mice); firefly genes had been added to tobacco plants to make them glow (faintly) in the dark; and growth hormone produced by genetically engineered bacteria was being used to grow low-fat pork and increase milk production by cows. Critics argued that genetic engineering was unnatural and violated the rights of both plants and animals to their "species integrity"; that expensive, high-tech, tinkered animals gave the competitive advantage to big agricultural corporations and drove small farmers out of business; and that putting human genes into animals, plants, or bacteria was downright offensive. See Betsy Hanson and Dorothy Nelkin, "Public Responses to Genetic Engineering," *Society* (November/December 1989).

Thoughts of tinkering with humans themselves have prompted such comments as the following from Richard Hayes, "In the Pipeline: Genetically Modified Humans?" *Multinational Monitor* (January/February 2000): "No one can be sure how the technology will evolve, but a techno-eugenic future appears ever more likely unless an organized citizenry demands such visions be consigned to science fiction dystopias."

Skepticism about the benefits remains, but agricultural genetic engineering has proceeded at a breakneck pace largely because, as Robert Shapiro, CEO of Monsanto Corporation, said in June 1998, it "represents a potentially sustainable solution to the issue of feeding people." Between 1996 and 1998 the area planted with genetically engineered crops jumped from 1.7 million hectares to 27.8 million hectares. Also, sales of genetically engineered crop products are expected to reach $25 billion by 2010. See Brian Halweil, "The Emperor's New Crops," *WorldWatch* (July/August 1999).

Many people are not reassured by such data. They see potential problems in nutrition, toxicity, allergies, and ecology. In protest, some people even destroy research labs and test plots of trees, strawberries, and corn. Other people lobby for stringent regulations and even outright bans on the basis of their fears, while others insist that regulation should be based on sound science. See Karen A. Goldman, "Bioengineered Food—Safety and Labeling," *Science* (October 20, 2000) and Henry I. Miller and Gregory Conko, "The Science of Biotechnology Meets the Politics of Global Regulation," *Issues in Science and Technology* (Fall 2000).

In the following selections, Martin Teitel and Kimberly A. Wilson urge caution. They argue that genetically modified foods have not yet been proven to be safe for human consumption and that, until they are, these foods should be banned. Since they are also not necessary, they maintain, consumers should avoid them. Henry I. Miller and Gregory Conko argue that largely because of the alarmism of anti-technology and anti-agribusiness activists and despite the scientific evidence, regulatory policy in regard to genetic modification (recombinant DNA technology) has been based on the notion that the technology is inherently risky and in need of intensive oversight and control. As a result, the acceptance and further development of genetically modified foods has been blocked. Regulation should be based on genuine risk, not on the process by which a product is made.

**Martin Teitel and
Kimberly A. Wilson**

 **YES**

You Are What You Eat

Throughout history monarchs have employed food tasters. This rather high-risk line of work was invented not for gastronomic reasons, but out of a recognition that when we eat food we are placing a great deal of trust in whomever provides that meal. In societies where people grow their own food one has a pretty good idea of the origins of the food, what was sprayed on the crop as it grew, and how it was cooked. When food is produced locally, just keep the peace with the farmer and the chef and you can eat your dinner with no worries.

In nearly all societies nowadays, even monarchies, most people no longer grow their own food. We eat our meals each day with the assumption that what is sold is safe, both because we choose to trust the farmers and food sellers and because we have some degree of faith in government regulators and food inspectors. If this system of trust breaks down, people would understandably be frightened.

Recently, one of the authors was preparing a huge pot of vegetarian chili for a group of friends. Opening a large can of red kidney beans from a local supermarket, he was surprised to find the can full of peeled, white potatoes. Opening another can of beans from the same store, he found the same unexpected contents. Every person at the chili party had the same reaction: "Don't ever shop at that place again." Even though this one error in labeling some cans of beans produced no illness and was presumably an isolated incident, every person seeing the mislabeled cans had the same unequivocal reaction: their assumptions that food is carefully monitored all the way into their grocery carts were temporarily destroyed.

The genfood industry knows of the tendency of people to have a short fuse when it comes to food safety issues. A Monsanto spokesman told one of the authors that the firestorm of protest over genfoods in Great Britain in 1998 and 1999 was probably strongly propelled by the recent scare over mad-cow disease in that country. This statement recognizes that even though mad cow had little to do with genetically engineered food—any more than a mislabeled can of red beans has anything to do with a store's fish or lettuce—when trust in food purity and safety is shattered, people become *very* conservative.

And so they should. In the United States, up to 80 million people are estimated to become sick from food-caused illness each year. Nine thousand of them die. Statistics from other countries, when they are available, are comparable. The real incidence of illness is probably much higher: many of us have come home from a barbecue featuring sun-baked potato salad, or tried out a new restaurant that looked a bit seedy, and then attributed that night's sickness to the food we just ate. These relatively minor instances of food-related illness never get reported to the collectors of statistics. We just take some pinkish medicine and wait for the bad time to pass.

Other food-connected illnesses are less benign. So far, more than eighty deaths are attributed to mad-cow disease in Great Britain, and the number of people ultimately affected by this slow-moving disease won't be known for some time. A whole class of deadly illnesses that might be related to some food is cancer, possibly arising from the residue of added chemicals on or in the food. Because studies linking slow-onset diseases that have complex causes are still underway, contradictory, or not readily available, some people choose to ignore the possibility of risk until better information is available. Others decide on a more cautious approach and go to the extra trouble and expense of purchasing foods labeled "organic" to avoid consuming those chemicals. . . .

. . . [W]e are going to look at the human health issues associated with genetically engineered food. Is it safe to eat genfood? Let's look at the information available, and then see what actions a person might take.

Allergies

As we discussed [elsewhere], each gene contributes a single protein to the genetic "soup" that comprises a living organism. Proteins are crucial substances that play many roles in human physiology. One clear association with proteins involves allergies. When a person exhibits an allergic reaction, what her body is reacting to is a protein, most often a "foreign" or introduced protein.

This leads us to a serious issue that arises in connection to genetically engineered foods. If allergies are associated with introduced proteins, and if genfood is by definition characterized by introduced genes that produce proteins, then we have a situation in which caution about allergies is justified. . . . [A]llergies have already been proved to pass from one type of food into another via gene transfers. The fear of introduced genes triggering dangerous and even fatal allergic reactions is based on sound science.

Allergies are common in people, ranging from extreme reactions to exotic fish to a mild sensitivity to airborne pollen in the springtime. The amount of a given protein that might trigger an allergic reaction is highly variable. Some people are allergic to common foods such as wheat or eggs, while others are able to eat them with no ill effects. Most of us eat peanuts with pleasure, while a few people can find themselves fighting for their lives when they consume even a minuscule quantity of peanut protein. Because of this, most allergy specialists do not advise patients with food allergies to cut down on the food that they are sensitive to. Instead, they sternly admonish their patients to avoid *any* ingestion of that food in even the tiniest, most insignificant-seeming quantity.

The great solace—and safety—for people with food allergies is the labeling of ingredients. In the United States and in many other countries, food producers are obligated to list the ingredients of any prepared or processed food. People with allergies avoid frantic trips to the emergency room by learning to read package labels carefully. Food manufacturers and distributors avoid costly liability by this same disclosure of contents. Our laws tend to say that if an ingredient is revealed, that constitutes fair warning. So if people suffer ill effects from eating something that was properly labeled, they cannot sue the food producer.

This is not so with genetically engineered food. Even in countries that require genfood labeling, the labels will most often just say that genetically modified substances are in the food container. Because there is no requirement to say which gene has been inserted, people must avoid all genfood if they have allergic sensitivities and want to be totally prudent.

It is important to note that, unlike mad-cow disease, there have been no documented cases of deaths due to genfood-caused allergic reactions. However, because an autopsy for a death from allergic shock does not normally test for the presence of genetically engineered food, there is no reliable way of gathering data on genfood allergic reactions.

Genetically modified foods available around the world do not present enhancements to the buyer and consumer of those foods. The foods do not taste better, provide more nutrition, cost less, or look nicer. Why, then, would a person with a food allergy run the risk, however large or small it might be, of a life-threatening reaction when safe alternatives are available?

We just need to make sure that those alternatives *remain* available.

Nutrition

The assumption that many of us would make is that genfood is nutritionally equivalent to nonmodified food. In 1999 the California-based Center for Ethics and Toxics (CETOS) set out to see if this was the case. The people at the center noticed that the research submitted to, and accepted by, the U.S. government to demonstrate the safety of Monsanto's genetically engineered soybeans had been conducted by Monsanto's own scientists. A conflict of interest doesn't necessarily mean that people with the conflict are dishonest, only that, as in this case, their associations automatically put the objectivity of their work into question. The CETOS staff, Britt Bailey and toxicologist Marc Lappé, observed that the soybeans Monsanto tested were not an accurate representation of the soy that appears in stores as food because they were not treated with the herbicide Roundup, as they would be in real life. So Bailey and Lappé hired a reputable testing firm to conduct tests that would accurately compare Roundup Ready soybeans, treated with Roundup, to conventional soybeans that were identical to the Roundup Ready ones except for the missing engineered gene. The tests were also carefully designed to produce results that reflected real-world conditions. This sort of objectively designed science is what we need to be able to make good decisions about what we buy and eat.

The study was published in a peer-reviewed scientific journal in 1999. The process of peer review is important in science. It means that independent scientists looked at the CETOS study and found it to be based on sound and acceptable methods of scientific investigation. In their study, CETOS found that there was a 12 to 14 percent decline in types of plant-based estrogens called phytoestrogens. Phytoestrogens are associated with protection against heart disease, osteoporosis (bone loss), and breast cancer. A drop in phytoestrogens of 12 to 14 percent is a significant nutritional difference.

The CETOS study was attacked by the American Soybean Association, whose attack was in turn answered by CETOS. Monsanto also conducted new studies that did not show the same changes in phytoestrogens. The new Monsanto study is difficult to compare with the CETOS study, however, because Monsanto inexplicably used a different, older method in some of its research. Meanwhile, CETOS stands by its study, which the researchers point out at the very least raises some important questions about nutritional variances in this particular food.

While scientists sling studies and journal articles at each other, what's a food shopper to do? We can't all be expected to become experts on obscure scientific methods or substances we never knew existed, such as phytoestrogens. The government, which chose to accept the original Monsanto-paid tests as the basis for approval of this food, has been of no use in helping us to make prudent decisions.

Further, we have no way of knowing if differences in plant hormones in soybeans mean much for human health. More important, if CETOS, a nonprofit organization, can garner sufficient support to conduct more scientific experiments, we can find out if this study was a fluke.

What can we conclude about nutrition and genfoods from this example?

Soy products appear in many processed and prepared foods. No one knows just how many, but the words *soybean oil, soy flour, soy lecithin, isolated soy protein, textured vegetable protein, functional or nonfunctional soy protein concentrates,* and *textured soy protein concentrates* on the label are good tipoffs. As much as 60 percent of all prepared food in a typical U.S. supermarket contains genetically engineered ingredients. Further, many people who do not eat meat rely heavily on soy-based food for important nutritional components of their diet, including proteins, some fats—and phytoestrogens.

As with allergies and genfood, we are left with more questions than answers. Is genetically modified food more nutritious? There is no evidence for a claim of this type. Is genetically modified food less nutritious? We do not know for certain, yet. Is genetically modified food perhaps more variable in its nutritional value? We have at least one reputable study that suggests yes.

The conclusions we can draw from what is known, and not known, seem to be fairly straightforward. First, there is clearly a great need for many further studies of possible nutritional changes in genetically engineered food, based on the CETOS study. Second, there should be clear, unequivocal labeling of genfood so that people can make their own decisions about their nutrition.

Pesticides and Herbicides

A potential problem arising from herbicide resistant GM crops that is largely being ignored is what is the fate of these chemicals within the plant? Are they stable? If they are degraded, what are the products that are produced? And what health risks do they pose?

—Michael Antoniou

It should be no surprise to us that in discussing genetically modified food we need to pay attention to chemicals that are designed to kill plants or animals. Many of the significant genfood crops are engineered to either tolerate higher than usual amounts of herbicides or to contain pesticides inside each cell. . . . [M]any of the purveyors of genfood are companies that market agricultural chemicals. Engineering plants to require what a company already sells makes business sense to these corporations.

The pesticide most in question is *Bacillus thuringiensis,* Bt. This bacterium was isolated one hundred years ago, although it did not become commercially available in the United States until 1958. While this bacterium is related to a common bacterium that causes food poisoning and is also a close relative of the organism that causes anthrax, Bt itself is considered relatively safe, especially when compared with synthetic bug-killing chemicals.

Yet Bt *is* a poison. In its purified form it can be extremely toxic to mammals, including humans, and even in its more usual, nonpurified state there are numerous reports of poisonings and various negative health effects. The chemical may be particularly hazardous to people with compromised immune systems. Yet because the EPA has already established that Bt (as a spray *on* crops) is safe, it assumes the toxin is safe to eat *in* crops and does not require testing for human health effects.

When Bt is used by organic growers, it is sprayed on plants. It breaks down rapidly in the environment after killing the target bugs. While there may be health risks to the person applying the pesticide, there is no clear evidence of health problems resulting from people eating food that has been sprayed properly with Bt.

When Bt is engineered into a plant, it may remain present in the plant, and the resulting food, much longer than is the case with conventionally used Bt. There is even evidence that Bt engineered into plants remains after the harvest, so that plant leaves that drop to the ground or plant residue that is plowed under have an effect on the living organisms in the soil.

What we do not have is a series of clear, independent studies on the long- or short-term health effects of eating food containing the pesticide Bt. According to CETOS, from 1987 through 1998, 24 percent of genetically engineered crops released into the environment contained insect-resistant genes. According to this same source, Bt crops are grown in the United States, Brazil, Argentina, China, India, Australia, Canada, South Africa, and Japan. Yet we do not have information in hand to establish the safety of this pesticide for human health. The EPA does not test the plant with Bt in it; it only tests the bacteria in isolation. Essentially, the EPA is not testing the product that humans will be consuming. The Bt toxin produced by the plant and the toxin produced by the bacteria could be different. Until both are properly tested for human health effects, no one will know the effect of eating Bt food crops.

In a case that gained some notoriety in early 1999, a scientist at the Rowett Research Institute named Arpad Pusztai tested genetically engineered potatoes on rats. After only ten days the animals suffered substantial health effects, including weakened immune systems and changes in the development of their hearts, livers, kidneys, and brains.

When Dr. Pusztai went public with his findings, he was summarily fired and a commission was convened by his former employers to investigate his work. The commission found Dr. Pusztai's work deficient, yet another panel of twenty independent scientists confirmed both his data and his findings. More recent research by another U.K.-based scientist showing enlarged stomach walls in rats fed genetically engineered potatoes seems to support Dr. Pusztai, who has stated publicly that he will not eat genfood.

Aside from Bt crops, the other major genetically engineered plant chemical involves herbicide-tolerant plants, primarily the Roundup Ready series of plants from Monsanto. These genetically modified plants include corn and soy as well as oil-producing canola (rapeseed) and cotton. As we saw, the plants are engineered to withstand the plant-killing effects of the chemical glyphosate, the main ingredient in Roundup. Monsanto claims that this herbicide tolerance means that farmers can spray the plant-killing poison on their fields more precisely and thus use less of it, but there are serious concerns about how much herbicide is actually being sprayed.

What about the health effects of herbicide-tolerant crops? Scientists have already linked the herbicides containing glyphosate to cancer. Non-Hodgkins lymphoma, which is one of the fastest-rising cancers in the Western world, increasing 73 percent since 1973, has been connected to exposure to glyphosate and MCPA, another common herbicide.

Since even proximity to such chemicals has been linked to cancer, what are the health risks of eating crops sprayed with glyphosate or genetically engineered with Roundup resistance? While the maker of Roundup insists that when used properly the herbicide is safe, independent studies raise a long list of questions about the long- and short-term health effects of human ingestion of glyphosate.

Bottom line: Genetically engineered food hasn't been proved safe. Since wholesome alternatives exist, why not suspend production of genfood until *it* is shown to be wholesome? . . .

Bovine Growth Hormone

Sold in the United States under the Monsanto brand name Posilac, rBGH is injected into cows to increase milk production. Few people would argue that the drug does increase milk production, although in a country that periodically gives away dairy products to deal with the milk surplus it is difficult to understand why we need even more. Aside from well-documented health problems for the cows, including increases in udder infections, there are a series of health issues for humans.

As early as 1995, at a National Institutes for Health conference, the following adverse effects of rBGH were identified:

1. Strong role in breast cancer
2. Special risk of colon cancer due to local effects of rBGH on the GI tract
3. May play a role in osteosarcoma, the most common bone tumor in children, usually occurring during the adolescent growth spurt
4. Implicated in lung cancer
5. Possesses angiogenic properties—important to tumors, some of which secrete their own growth factors to promote angiogenesis
6. Lastly, the 1995 NIH conference recommended that the acute and chronic effects of IGF-1 in the upper GI tract be determined.

Americans have been drinking milk from cows treated with rBGH for several years now. When the hormone was approved by the U.S. government, the approval was based on studies of rats fed rBGH that showed no toxicological changes. Had there been any such changes, further human studies would have been mandated.

In the well-publicized 1998 Canadian Gaps Report . . . , we learn that in fact a large proportion of the rBGH-fed rats, between 20 and 30 percent, showed distinct immunological changes, while some male rats showed the formation of cysts of the thyroid and infiltration of the prostate. These are warning signs for possible immune system effects—and possible carcinogenic effects as well.

The Center for Food Safety and more than two dozen other organizations filed a petition in December of 1998 to reverse FDA approval of rBGH/rBST: "We're going to go to the courts and say—you were lied to," said Andrew Kimbrell of the Center for Food Safety. "Essentially it was fraud by the agency and fraud by Monsanto in telling the court that there were no human health effects possible from consuming these products made with rBGH-treated milk. We now know that not to be true."

The Canadian Gaps Report, the banning of rBGH in many countries around the globe, and the findings of a number of studies in the United States and in Europe all point to real, concrete health concerns about bovine growth hormone.

Estimates are that 15 to 30 percent of the milk supply of the United States comes from rBGH-injected cows. Since rudimentary labeling of rBGH milk exists in some communities, including direct labeling as well as the labeling of some milk as "organic," people can avoid feeding their families dairy products containing genetically engineered growth hormones. When such labeling or alternatives do not exist, there is little choice for people other than . . . becoming active in nationwide efforts to provide people with the option to consume only the food that they feel is safe for their families.

Is Genetically Engineered Food Safe?

. . . [W]e have examined a number of different possible health issues with genetically modified foods. In some instances, such as phytoestrogen decline in genetically engineered soy, or a variety of health questions arising from animal studies of bovine growth hormone, there are ample reasons for people to decide to avoid genetically modified food. In other instances, such as the health effects of ingesting herbicide-tolerant engineered food, there just isn't enough good science yet to be sure.

If the FDA does not require labels, and safety testing is the exception rather than the rule, just what is the U.S. government doing to protect the public? The Hoover Institute's Henry Miller, a fan of genetic engineering, writes, "The FDA does not routinely subject foods from new plant varieties to premarket review or to extensive scientific safety tests." Later he notes that the FDA only follows "the development of foods made with new biotechnology via noncompulsory informal consultation procedures."

The conclusion to all of this is clear. There is no genetically engineered food product on the market now—not one—that is necessary. Each product, which may confer financial benefit to its producers, can be shown to have an alternative that from the consumer's point of view is at least equivalent if not superior. If genfoods do not provide a benefit to consumers, and may be shown to have health hazards now or in the future, why take any risk with your health or your family's health?

Since safety has not been demonstrated and our health is precious, avoid eating all genfood.

Henry I. Miller and
Gregory Conko

 **NO**

Agricultural Biotechnology:
Overregulated and Underappreciated

The application of recombinant DNA technology, or gene splicing, to agriculture and food production, once highly touted as having huge public health and commercial potential, has been paradoxically disappointing. Although the gains in scientific knowledge have been stunning, commercial returns from two decade of R&D have been meager. Although the cultivation of recombinant DNA-modified crops, first introduced in 1995, now exceeds 100 million acres, and such crops are grown by 7 million farmers in 18 countries, their total cultivation remains but a small fraction of what is possible. Moreover, fully 99 percent of the crops are grown in only six countries—the United States, Argentina, Canada, Brazil, China, and South Africa—and virtually all the worldwide acreage is devoted to only four commodity crops: soybeans, corn, cotton, and canola.

Attempts to expand "agbiotech" to additional crops, genetic traits, and countries have met resistance from the public, activists, and governments. The costs in time and money to negotiate regulatory hurdles make it uneconomical to apply molecular biotechnology to any but the most widely grown crops. Even in the best of circumstances—that is, where no bans or moratoriums are in place and products are able to reach the market—R&D costs are prohibitive. In the United States, for example, the costs of performing a field trial of a recombinant plant are 10 to 20 times that of the same trial with a virtually identical plant that was crafted with conventional techniques, and regulatory expenditures to commercialize a plant can run tens of millions dollars more than for a conventionally modified crop. In other words, regulation imposes a huge punitive tax on a superior technology.

Singled Out for Scrutiny

At the heart of the problem is the fact that during the past two decades, regulators in the United States and many other countries have created a series of rules specific for products made with recombinant DNA technology. Regulatory policy has consistently treated this technology as though it were inherently risky and in need of unique, intensive oversight and control. This has happened despite the fact that a broad scientific consensus holds that agbiotech is merely an extension, or refinement, of less precise and less predictable technologies that have long been used for similar purposes, and the products of which are generally exempt from case-by-case review. All of the grains, fruits, and vegetables grown commercially in North America, Europe, and elsewhere (with the exception of wild berries and wild mushrooms) come from plants that have been genetically improved by one technique or another. Many of these "classical" techniques for crop improvement, such as wide-cross hybridization and mutation breeding, entail gross and uncharacterized modifications of the genomes of established crop plants and commonly introduce entirely new genes, proteins, secondary metabolites, and other compounds into the food supply.

Nevertheless, regulations in the United States and abroad, which apply only to the products of gene splicing, have hugely inflated R&D costs and made it difficult to apply the technology to many classes of agricultural products, especially ones with low profit potential, such as noncommodity crops and varieties grown by subsistence farmers. This is unfortunate, because the introduced traits often increase productivity far beyond what is possible with classical methods of genetic modification. Furthermore, many of the recombinant traits that have been introduced commercially are beneficial to the environment. These traits include the ability to grow with lower amounts of agricultural chemicals, water, and fuel, and under conditions that promote the kind of no-till farming that inhibits soil erosion. Society as a whole would have been far better off if, instead of implementing regulation specific to the new biotechnology, governments had approached the products of gene splicing in the same way in which they regulate similar products—Pharmaceuticals, pesticides, and new plant varieties—made with older, less precise, and less predictable techniques.

But activist groups whose members appear to fear technological progress and loathe big agribusiness companies have egged on regulators, who need little encouragement to expand their empires and budgets. The activists understand that overregulation advances their antibiotechnology agenda by making research, development, and commercialization prohibitively expensive and by raising the barriers to innovation.

Curiously, instead of steadfastly demanding scientifically sound, risk-based regulation, some corporations have risked their own long-term best interests, as well as those of consumers, by lobbying for excessive and discriminatory government regulation in order to gain short-term advantages. From the earliest stages of the agbiotech industry, those firms hoped that superfluous regulation would act as a type of government stamp of approval for their products, and they knew that the time and expense engendered by overregulation would also act as a barrier to market entry by smaller competitors. Those companies, which include Monsanto, DuPont-owned Pioneer Hi-Bred, and Ciba-Geigy (now reorganized as Syngenta), still seem not to understand the ripple effect of overly restrictive regulations that are based on, and reinforce, the false premise that there is something uniquely worrisome and risky about the use of recombinant DNA techniques.

The consequences of this unwise, unwarranted regulatory policy are not subtle. Consider, for example, a recent decision by Harvest Plus, an alliance of public-sector and charitable organizations devoted to producing and disseminating staple crops rich in such micronutrients as iron, zinc, and vitamin A. According to its director, the group has decided that although it will continue to investigate the potential for biotechnology to raise the level of nutrients in target crops above what can be accomplished with conventional breeding, "there is no plan for Harvest Plus to disseminate [gene-spliced] crops, because of the high and difficult-to-predict costs of meeting regulatory requirements in countries where laws are already in place, and because many countries as yet do not have regulatory structures." And in May 2004, Monsanto announced that it was shelving plans to sell a recombinant DNA-modified wheat variety, attributing the decision to changed market conditions. However, that decision was forced on the company by the reluctance of farmers to plant the variety and of food processors to use it as an ingredient: factors that are directly related to the discriminatory overregulation of the new biotechnology in important export markets. Monsanto also announced in May that it has abandoned plans to introduce its recombinant canola into Australia, after concerns about exportability led several Australian states to ban commercial planting and, in some cases, even field trials.

Other companies have explicitly acknowledged giving up plans to work on certain agbiotech applications because of excessive regulations. After receiving tentative approval in spring 2004 from the British government for commercial cultivation of a recombinant maize variety, Bayer CropScience decided not to sell it because the imposition of additional regulatory hurdles would delay commercialization for several more years. And in June 2004, Bayer followed Monsanto's lead in suspending plans to commercialize its gene-spliced canola in Australia until its state governments "provide clear and consistent guidelines for a path forward."

Another manifestation of the unfavorable and costly regulatory milieu is the sharp decline in efforts to apply recombinant DNA technology to fruits and vegetables, the markets for which are minuscule compared to crops such as corn and soybeans. Consequently, the number of field trials in the United States involving gene-spliced horticulture crops plunged from approximately 120 in 1999 to about 20 in 2003.

Setting Matters Aright

The public policy miasma that exists today is severe, worsening, and seemingly intractable, but it was by no means inevitable. In fact, it was wholly unnecessary. From the advent of the first recombinant DNA-modified microorganisms and plants a quarter century ago, the path to rational policy was not at all obscure. The use of molecular techniques for genetic modification is no more than the most recent step on a continuum that includes the application of far less precise and predictable techniques for genetic improvement. It is the combination of phenotype and use that determines the risk of agricultural plants, not the process or breeding techniques used to develop them.

Conventional risk analysis, supplemented with assessments specific to the new biotechnology in those very rare instances where they were needed, could easily have been adapted to craft regulation that was risk-based and scientifically defensible. Instead, most governments defined the scope of biosafety regulations to capture all recombinant organisms but practically none developed with classical methods.

In January 2004, the U.S. Department of Agriculture (USDA) announced that it would begin a formal reassessment of its regulations for gene-spliced plants. One area for investigation will include the feasibility of exempting "low-risk" organisms from the permitting requirements, leading some observers to hope that much needed reform may be on the horizon. However, regulatory reform must include more than a simple carve-out for narrowly defined classes of low-risk recombinant organisms.

An absolutely essential feature of genuine reform must be the replacement of process-oriented regulatory triggers with risk-based approaches. Just because recombinant DNA techniques are involved does not mean that a field trial or commercial product should be subjected to case-by-case review. In fact, the introduction of a risk-based approach to regulation is hardly a stretch; it would merely represent conformity to the federal government's official policy, articulated in a 1992 announcement from the White House Office of Science and Technology Policy, which calls for "a risk-based, scientifically sound approach to the oversight of planned introductions of biotechnology products into the environment that focuses on the characteristics of the . . . product and the environment into which it is being introduced, not the process by which the product is created."

One such regulatory approach has already been proposed by academics. It is, ironically, based on the well-established model of the USDA's own plant quarantine regulations for nonrecombinant organisms. Almost a decade ago, the Stanford University Project on Regulation of Agricultural Introductions crafted a widely applicable regulatory model for the field testing of any organism, whatever the method employed in its construction. It is a refinement of the "yes or no" approach of national quarantine systems, including the USDA's Plant Pest Act regulations; under these older regimens, a plant that a researcher might wish to introduce into the field is either on the proscribed list of plant pests, and therefore requires a permit, or it is exempt.

The Stanford model takes a similar, though more stratified, approach to field trials of plants, and it is based on the ability of experts to assign organisms to one of several risk categories. It closely resembles the approach taken in the federal government's handbook on laboratory safety, which specifies the procedures and equipment that are appropriate for research with microorganisms, including the most dangerous pathogens known. Panels of scientists had stratified these microorganisms into risk categories, and the higher the risk, the more stringent the procedures and isolation requirements. In a pilot program, the Stanford agricultural project did essentially the same thing for plants to be tested in the field: A group of scientists from five nations evaluated and, based on certain risk-related characteristics, stratified a number of crops into various risk categories. Importantly, assignment to one or another risk category had nothing to do with the use of a particular process for modification or even whether the plant was modified at all. Rather, stratification depended solely on the intrinsic properties of a cultivar, such as potential for weediness, invasiveness, and out-crossing with valuable local varieties.

What are the practical implications of an organism being assigned to a given risk category? The higher the risk, the more intrusive the regulators' involvement. The spectrum of regulatory requirements could encompass complete exemption; a simple "postcard notification" to a regulatory authority (without prior approval required); premarket review of only the first introduction of a particular gene or trait into a given crop species; case-by-case review of all products in the category; or even prohibition (as is the case currently for experiments with foot-and-mouth disease virus in the United States).

Under such a system, some currently unregulated field trials of organisms modified with older techniques would likely become subject to regulatory review. whereas many recombinant organisms that now require case-by-case review would be regulated less stringently. This new approach would offer greater protection and, by decreasing research costs and reducing unpredictability for low-risk organisms, encourage more R&D, especially on noncommodity crops.

The Stanford model also offers regulatory bodies a highly adaptable, scientific approach to the oversight of plants, microorganisms, and other organisms, whether they are naturally occurring or "non-coevolved" organisms or have been genetically improved by either old or new techniques. The outlook for the new biotechnology applied to agriculture, especially as it would benefit the developing world, would be far better if governments and international organizations expended effort on perfecting such a model instead of clinging to unscientific, palpably flawed regulatory regimes. It is this course that the USDA should pursue as it reevaluates its current policies.

At the same time as the U.S. government begins to rationalize public policy at home, it must stand up to the other countries and organizations that are responsible for unscientific, debilitating regulations abroad and internationally. U.S. representatives to international bodies such as the Codex Alimentarius Commission, the United Nations' agency that sets food-safety standards, must be directed to support rational science-based policies and to work to dismantle politically motivated unscientific restrictions. All science and economic attachés in every U.S. embassy and consulate around the world should have biotechnology policy indelibly inscribed on their diplomatic agendas. Moreover, the U.S. government should make United Nations agencies and other international bodies that implement, collude, or cooperate in any way with unscientific policies ineligible to receive funding or other assistance from the United States. Flagrantly unscientific regulation should be made the "third rail" of U.S. domestic and foreign policy.

Uncompromising? Aggressive? Yes, but so is the virtual annihilation of entire areas of R&D; the trampling of individual and corporate freedom; the disuse of a critical, superior technology; and the disruption of free trade.

Strategies for Action

Rehabilitating agbiotech will be a long row to hoe. In order to move ahead, several concrete strategies can help to reverse the deteriorating state of public policy toward agricultural biotechnology.

First, individual scientists should participate more in the public dialogue on policy issues. Perhaps surprisingly, few scientists have demanded that policy be rational; instead, most have insisted only on transparency or predictability, even if that delivers only the predictability of research delays and unnecessary expense. Others have been seduced by the myth that just a little excess regulation will assuage public anxiety and neutralize activists' alarmist messages. Although defenders of excessive regulation have made those claims for decades, the public and activists remain unappeased and technology continues to be shackled.

Scientists are especially well qualified to expose unscientific arguments and should do so in every possible way and forum, including writing scientific and popular articles, agreeing to be interviewed by journalists, and serving on advisory panels at government agencies. Scientists with mainstream views have a particular obligation to debunk the claims of their few rogue colleagues, whose declarations that the sky is falling receive far too much attention.

Second, groups of scientists—professional associations, faculties, academies, and journal editorial boards—should do much more to point out the flaws in current and proposed policies. For example, scientific societies could include symposia on public policy in their conferences and offer to advise government bodies and the news media.

Third, reporters and their editors can do a great deal to explain policy issues related to science. But in the interest of "balance," the news media often give equal weight to all of the views on an issue, even if some of them have been discredited. All viewpoints are not created equal, and not every issue has "two sides." Journalists need to distinguish between honest disagreement among experts, on the one hand, and unsubstantiated extremism or propaganda, on the other. They also must be conscious of recombinant DNA technology's place in the context of overall crop genetic improvement. When writing about the possible risks and benefits of gene-spliced herbicide-tolerant plants, for example, it is appropriate to note that herbicide-tolerant plants have been produced for decades with classical breeding techniques.

Fourth, biotechnology companies should eschew short-term advantage and actively oppose unscientific discriminatory regulations that set dangerous precedents. Companies that passively, sometimes eagerly, accept government oversight triggered simply by the use of recombinant DNA techniques, regardless of the risk of the product, ultimately will find themselves the victims of the law of unintended consequences.

Fifth, venture capitalists, consumer groups, patient groups, philanthropists, and others who help to bring scientific discoveries to the marketplace or who benefit from them need to increase their informational activities and advocacy for reform. Their actions could include educational campaigns and support for organizations such as professional associations and think tanks that advocate rational science-based public policy.

Finally, governments should no longer assume primary responsibility for regulation. Nongovernmental agencies already accredit hospitals, allocate organs for transplantation, and certify the quality of consumer products ranging from seeds to medical devices. Moreover, in order to avoid civil legal liability for damages real or alleged, the practitioners of agricultural biotechnology already face strong incentives to adhere to sound practices. Direct government oversight may be appropriate for products with high-risk characteristics, but government need not insinuate itself into every aspect of R&D with recombinant DNA-modified organisms.

The stunted growth of agricultural biotechnology worldwide stands as one of the great societal tragedies of the past quarter century. The nation and the world must find more rational and efficient ways to guarantee the public's safety while encouraging new discoveries. Science shows the path, and society's leaders must take us there.

POSTSCRIPT

Should Genetically Modified Foods Be Banned?

At first, most of the attention aimed at genetic engineering focused first on its use to modify bacteria and other organisms to generate drugs needed to fight human disease, and second on its potential to modify human genes and attack hereditary diseases at their roots. See Eric B. Kmiec, "Gene Therapy," *American Scientist* (May–June 1999).

Despite some successes, gene therapy has not yet become a multimillion-dollar industry. Pharmaceutical applications of genetic engineering have been much more successful. According to Brian Halweil, in "The Emperor's New Crops," *World Watch* (July/August 1999), so have agricultural applications. Halweil is skeptical, saying that genetically modified foods have potential benefits but that they may also have disastrous effects on natural ecosystems and—because high-tech agriculture is controlled by major corporations such as Monsanto—on less-developed societies. He argues that "ecological" agriculture (e.g., using organic fertilizers and natural enemies instead of pesticides) offers much more hope for the future. Similar arguments are made by those who demonstrate against genetically modified foods and lobby for stringent labeling requirements or for outright bans on planting and importing these crops (as in Europe). See Capulalpum, "Risking Corn, Risking Culture," *WorldWatch* (November–December 2002).

Many researchers see more hope in genetically modified foods. In July 2000, for example, the Royal Society of London, the U.S. National Academy of Sciences, the Brazilian Academy of Sciences, the Chinese Academy of Sciences, the Indian Academy of Sciences, the Mexican Academy of Sciences, and the Third World Academy of Sciences issued a joint report entitled "Transgenic Plants and World Agriculture" (available at `http://www.royalsoc.ac.uk`). This report stresses that during the twenty-first century, both population and the need for food are going to increase dramatically, especially in developing nations. According to the report, "Foods can be produced through the use of GM [genetic modification] technology that are more nutritious, stable in storage and in principle, health promoting. . . . New public sector efforts are required for creating transgenic crops that benefit poor farmers in developing nations and improve their access to food. . . . Concerted, organised efforts must be undertaken to investigate the potential environmental effects, both positive and negative, of GM technologies [compared to those] from conventional agricultural technologies. . . . Public health regulatory systems need to be put in place in every country to identify and monitor any potential adverse human health effects."

The worries surrounding genetically modified foods and the scientific evidence to support them are summarized by Kathryn Brown, in "Seeds of Concern," and Karen Hopkin, in "The Risks on the Table," both in *Scientific American* (April 2001). In the same issue, Sasha Nemecek poses the question "Does the World Need GM Foods?" to two prominent figures in the debate: Robert B. Horsch, a Monsanto vice president and recipient of the 1998 National Medal of Technology for his work on modifying plant genes, who says yes, and Margaret Mellon, of the Union of Concerned Scientists, who says no, adding that much more work needs to be done on safety. Jeffrey M. Smith, *Seeds of Deception: Exposing Industry and Government Lies about the Safety of the Genetically Engineered Foods You're Eating* (Chelsea Green, 2003), argues that the dangers of GM foods have been deliberately concealed. Henry I. Miller and Gregory Conko, in *The Frankenfood Myth: How Protest and Politics Threaten the Biotech Revolution* (Praeger, 2004), address at length the fallacy that GM foods are especially risky. Harihara M. Mehendale, "Genetically Modified Foods: Why the Public Frenzy? Role of Mainstream News Media," *International Journal of Toxicology* (September 2004), blames "the role of the press in spreading misleading facts related to the technology." Walter F. Deal and Stephen L. Baird, in "Genetically Modified Foods: A Growing Need," *Technology Teacher* (April 2003), contend that GM foods "can help overcome the world's concern for feeding its ever-growing population."

Is the issue safety? Human welfare? Or economics? When genetically modified corn and other foods were offered as relief supplies to African nations threatened by famine, some accepted the aid. Others, pressured by European activists, turned it down. Robert L. Paarlberg discusses what the U.S. can do to counter resistance to GM foods in "Reinvigorating Genetically Modified Crops," *Issues in Science and Technology* (Spring 2003); he favors addressing the needs of developing countries.

And is the issue only genetically modified food? The July/August 2002 issue of *WorldWatch* magazine bore the overall title of "Beyond Cloning: The Risks of Rushing into Human Genetic Engineering." The editorial says that human genetic engineering poses "profound and medical social risks." Contributors object to it as unnatural, commercial, a violation of human integrity, potentially racist, and more. Francis Fukuyama, "In Defense of Nature, Human and Non-Human," says, "Anyone who feels strongly about defending non-human nature from technological manipulation should feel equally strongly about defending human nature as well. . . . Nature—both the natural environment around us, and our own—deserves an approach based on respect and stewardship, not domination and mastery."

ISSUE 19

Is It Ethically Permissible to Clone Human Beings?

YES: Julian Savulescu, from "Should We Clone Human Beings? Cloning as a Source of Tissue for Transplantation," *Journal of Medical Ethics* (April 1, 1999)

NO: Leon R. Kass, from "The Wisdom of Repugnance," *The New Republic* (June 2, 1997)

ISSUE SUMMARY

YES: Julian Savulescu, director of the Ethics Program of the Murdoch Institute at the Royal Children's Hospital in Melbourne, Australia, argues that it is not only permissible but morally required to use human cloning to create embryos as a source of tissue for transplantation.

NO: Biochemist Leon R. Kass argues that human cloning is "so repulsive to contemplate" that it should be prohibited entirely.

In February 1997 Ian Wilmut and Keith H. S. Campbell of the Roslin Institute in Edinburgh, Scotland, announced that they had cloned a sheep by transferring the gene-containing nucleus from a single cell of an adult sheep's mammary gland into an egg cell whose own nucleus had been removed and discarded. The resulting combination cell then developed into an embryo and eventually a lamb in the same way a normal egg cell does after being fertilized with a sperm cell. That lamb, named Dolly, was a genetic duplicate of the ewe from which the udder cell's nucleus was taken. Similar feats had been accomplished years before with fish and frogs, and mammal embryos had previously been split to produce artificial twins. And in March researchers at the Oregon Regional Primate Research Center announced that they had cloned monkeys by using cells from monkey embryos (not adults). In July the Roslin researchers announced the cloning of lambs from fetal cells—this time cells including human genes. But the reactions of the media, politicians, ethicists, and laypeople have been largely negative. Dr. Donald Bruce, director of the Church of Scotland's Society, Religion and Technology Project, for example, has argued at some length about how "nature is not ours to do exactly what we like with."

Many people seem to agree. In 1994 the U.S. National Advisory Board on Ethics in Reproduction called the whole idea of cloning oneself "bizarre . . . narcissistic and ethically impoverished." Arthur Caplan, director of the Center for Bioethics at the University of Pennsylvania, wonders, "What is the ethical purpose of even trying?" Conservative columnist George Will asks whether humans are now uniquely endangered since "the great given—a human being is the product of the union of a man and a woman—is no longer a given" and "humanity is supposed to be an endless chain, not a series of mirrors."

Others go further. President Bill Clinton asked the National Bioethics Advisory Commission (see http://bioethics.georgetown.edu/nbac/), chaired by Harold T. Shapiro, president of Princeton University, to investigate the implications of this "stunning" research and to issue a final report by the end of May 1997. He also barred the use of U.S. funds to support work on human cloning. The commission's report called for extending the ban and called any attempt to clone a human "morally unacceptable" for now. Many countries besides the United States agreed, and bans on cloning research were widely imposed.

Yet, says J. Madeleine Nash in "The Case for Cloning," *Time* (February 9, 1998), "hasty legislation could easily be too restrictive." Cloning could serve a great many useful purposes, and further development of the technology could lead to much less alarming procedures, such as growing replacement organs within a patient's body. See Arlene Judith Klotzko, "We Can Rebuild . . . ," *New Scientist* (February 27, 1999). Some of these benefits were considered when George Washington University researchers, using nonviable embryos, demonstrated that single cells could be removed from human embryos and induced to grow into new embryos. If permitted to develop normally, the cells would grow into genetically identical adults. The resulting adults would be duplicates, but only of each other (like identical twins), not of some preexisting adult.

Did Dolly represent something entirely new? For the very first time, it seemed more than science fiction to say it might soon be possible to duplicate an adult human, not just an embryo. But when ethicist John A. Robertson spoke at the National Bioethics Advisory Commission conference held in Washington, D.C., March 13–14, 1997, he said, "At this early stage in the development of mammalian cloning a ban on all human cloning is both imprudent and unjustified. Enough good uses can be imagined that it would be unwise to ban all cloning and cloning research because of vague and highly speculative fears."

In the following selection, Julian Savulescu argues, in part, that because cloned embryos have no moral value beyond that of the cells from which they are cloned, and because human suffering can be relieved, it is not only permissible but morally required to use human cloning to create embryos as a source of tissue for transplantation.

In the second selection, Leon R. Kass contends that people should trust their initial repugnance about human cloning because it threatens important human values, such as the profundity of sex, the sacredness of the human body, and the value of individuality. Human reproduction must not be debased by turning it into mere willful manufacturing. Kass concludes that human cloning is "so repulsive to contemplate" that it should be prohibited entirely.

YES

Julian Savulescu

Should We Clone Human Beings?

Introduction

When news broke in 1997 that Ian Wilmut and his colleagues had successfully cloned an adult sheep, there was an ill-informed wave of public, professional and bureaucratic fear and rejection of the new technique. Almost universally, human cloning was condemned. Germany, Denmark and Spain have legislation banning cloning; Norway, Slovakia, Sweden and Switzerland have legislation implicitly banning cloning. Some states in Australia, such as Victoria, ban cloning. There are two bills before congress in the US which would comprehensively ban it. There is no explicit or implicit ban on cloning in England, Greece, Ireland or the Netherlands, though in England the Human Embryology and Fertilisation Authority, which issues licences for the use of embryos, has indicated that it would not issue any licence for research into "reproductive cloning." This is understood to be cloning to produce a fetus or live birth. Research into cloning in the first 14 days of life might be possible in England.

There have been several arguments given against human reproductive cloning:

1. It is liable to abuse.
2. It violates a person's right to individuality, autonomy, selfhood, etc.
3. It violates a person's right to genetic individuality (whatever that is— identical twins cannot have such a right).
4. It allows eugenic selection.
5. It uses people as a means.
6. Clones are worse off in terms of wellbeing, especially psychological wellbeing.
7. There are safety concerns, especially an increased risk of serious genetic malformation, cancer or shortened lifespan.

There are, however, a number of arguments in favour of human reproductive cloning. These include:

1. General liberty justifications.
2. Freedom to make personal reproductive choices.
3. Freedom of scientific enquiry.

4. Achieving a sense of immortality.
5. Eugenic selection (with or without gene therapy/enhancement).
6. Social utility—cloning socially important people.
7. Treatment of infertility (with or without gene therapy/enhancement).
8. Replacement of a loved dead relative (with or without gene therapy/ enhancement).
9. "Insurance"—freeze a split embryo in case something happens to the first: as a source of tissue or as replacement for the first.
10. Source of human cells or tissue.
11. Research into stem cell differentiation to provide an understanding of aging and oncogenesis.
12. Cloning to prevent a genetic disease.

The arguments against cloning have been critically examined elsewhere and I will not repeat them here. Few people have given arguments in favour of it. Exceptions include arguments in favour of 7–12, with some commentators favouring only 10–11 or 11–12. Justifications 10–12 (and possibly 7) all regard cloning as a way of treating or avoiding disease. These have emerged as arguably the strongest justifications for cloning. This paper examines 10 and to some extent 11.

Human Cloning as a Source of Cells or Tissue

Cloning is the production of an identical or near-identical genetic copy. Cloning can occur by fission or fusion. Fission is the division of a cell mass into two equal and identical parts, and the development of each into a separate but genetically identical or near-identical individual. This occurs in nature as identical twins.

Cloning by fusion involves taking the nucleus from one cell and transferring it to an egg which has had its nucleus removed. Placing the nucleus in the egg reprogrammes the DNA in the nucleus to replicate the whole individual from which the nucleus was derived: nuclear transfer. It differs from fission in that the offspring has only one genetic parent, whose genome is nearly identical to that of the offspring. In fission, the offspring, like the offspring of normal sexual reproduction, inherits half of its genetic material from each of two parents. Henceforth, by "cloning," I mean cloning by fusion.

Human cloning could be used in several ways to produce cells, tissues or organs for the treatment of human disease.

Human Cloning as a Source of Multipotent Stem Cells

In this paper I will differentiate between totipotent and multipotent stem cells. Stem cells are cells which are early in developmental lineage and have the ability to differentiate into several different mature cell types. Totipotent stem cells are very immature stem cells with the potential to develop into any of the mature cell types in the adult (liver, lung, skin, blood, etc). Multipotential stem cells are more mature stem cells with the potential to develop into different mature forms of a particular cell lineage, for example, bone marrow stem cells can form either white or red blood cells, but they cannot form liver cells.

Multipotential stem cells can be used as

1. a vector for gene therapy.
2. cells for transplantation, especially in bone marrow.

Attempts have been made to use embryonic stem cells from other animals as vectors for gene therapy and as universal transplantation cells in humans. Problems include limited differentiation and rejection. Somatic cells are differentiated cells of the body, and not sex cells which give rise to sperm and eggs. Cloning of somatic cells from a person who is intended as the recipient of cell therapy would provide a source of multipotential stem cells that are not rejected. These could also be vectors for gene therapy. A gene could be inserted into a somatic cell from the patient, followed by selection, nuclear transfer and the culture of the appropriate clonal population of cells in vitro. These cells could then be returned to the patient as a source of new tissue (for example bone marrow in the case of leukaemia) or as tissue without genetic abnormality (in the case of inherited genetic disease). The major experimental issues which would need to be addressed are developing clonal stability during cell amplification and ensuring differentiation into the cell type needed. It should be noted that this procedure does not necessarily involve the production of a multicellular embryo, nor its implantation in vivo or artificially. (Indeed, cross-species cloning—fusing human cells with cow eggs—produces embryos which will not develop into fetuses, let alone viable offspring.)

A related procedure would produce totipotent stem cells which could differentiate into multipotent cells of a particular line or function, or even into a specific tissue. This is much closer to reproductive cloning. Embryonic stem cells from mice have been directed to differentiate into vascular endothelium, myocardial and skeletal tissue, haemopoietic precursors and neurons. However, it is not known whether the differentiation of human totipotent stem cells can be controlled in vitro. Unlike the previous application, the production of organs could involve reproductive cloning (the production of a totipotent cell which forms a blastomere), but then differentiates into a tissue after some days. Initially, however, all early embryonic cells are identical. Producing totipotent stem cells in this way is equivalent to the creation of an early embryo.

Production of Embryo/Fetus/Child/ Adult as a Source of Tissue

An embryo, fetus, child or adult could be produced by cloning, and solid organs or differentiated tissue could be extracted from it.

Cloning as Source of Organs, Tissue and Cells for Transplantation

The Need for More Organs and Tissues

Jeffrey Platts reports: "So great is the demand that as few as 5% of the organs needed in the United States ever become available." According to David K C Cooper, this is getting worse: "The discrepancy between the number of potential recipients and donor organs is increasing by approximately 10–15% annually." Increasing procurement of cadaveric organs may not be the solution. Anthony Dorling and colleagues write:

> "A study from Seattle, USA, in 1992 identified an annual maximum of only 7,000 brain dead donors in the USA. Assuming 100% consent and suitability, these 14,000 potential kidney grafts would still not match the numbers of new patients commencing dialysis each year. The clear implication is that an alternative source of organs is needed."

Not only is there a shortage of tissue or organs for those with organ failure, but there remain serious problems with the compatibility of tissue or organs used, requiring immunosuppressive therapy with serious side effects. Using cloned tissue would have enormous theoretical advantages, as it could be abundant and there is near perfect immunocompatibility.

There are several ways human cloning could be used to address the shortfall of organs and tissues, and each raises different ethical concerns.

1. Production of Tissue or Cells Only by Controlling Differentiation

I will now give an argument to support the use of cloning to produce cells or tissues through control of cellular differentiation.

The fate of one's own tissue.   Individuals have a strong interest or right in determining the fate of their own body parts, including their own cells and tissues, at least when this affects the length and quality of their own life. A right might be defended in terms of autonomy or property rights in body parts.

This right extends (under some circumstances) both to the proliferation of cells and to their transmutation into other cell types (which I will call the Principle of Tissue Transmutation).

Defending the Principle of Tissue Transmutation
Consider the following hypothetical example:

Lucas I   Lucas is a 22-year-old man with leukaemia. The only effective treatment will be a bone marrow transplant. There is no compatible donor. However, there is a drug which selects a healthy bone marrow cell and causes it to multiply. A doctor would be negligent if he or she did not employ such a drug for the treatment of Lucas's leukaemia. Indeed, there is a moral imperative to develop such drugs if we can and use them. Colony-stimulating factors, which cause blood cells to multiply, are already used in the treatment of leukaemia, and with stored marrow from those in remission in leukaemia before use for reconstitution during relapse.

Lucas II   In this version of the example, the drug causes Lucas's healthy skin cells to turn into healthy bone marrow stem cells. There is no relevant moral difference between Lucas I and II. We should develop such drugs and doctors would be negligent if they did not use them.

If this is right, there is nothing problematic about cloning to produce cells or tissues for transplantation by controlling differentiation. All we would be doing is taking, say, a skin cell and turning on and off some components of the total genetic complement to cause the cell to divide as a bone marrow cell. We are causing a differentiated cell (skin cell) to turn directly into a multipotent stem cell (bone marrow stem cell).

Are there any objections? The major objection is one of practicality. It is going to be very difficult to cause a skin cell to turn *directly* into a bone marrow cell. There are also safety considerations. Because we are taking a cell which has already undergone many cell divisions during terminal differentiation to give a mature cell such as a skin cell, and accumulated mutations, there is a theoretical concern about an increased likelihood of malignancy in that clonal population. However, the donor cell in these cases is the same age as the recipient (exactly), and a shorter life span would not be expected. There may also be an advantage in some diseases, such as leukaemia, to having a degree of incompatibility between donor and recipient bone marrow so as to enable the donor cells to recognise and destroy malignant recipient cells. This would not apply to non-malignant diseases in which bone marrow transplant is employed, such as the leukodystrophies. Most importantly, all these concerns need to be addressed by further research.

Lucas IIA   In practice, it is most likely that skin cells will not be able to be turned directly into bone marrow cells: there will need to be a stage of totipotency in between. The most likely way of producing cells to treat Lucas II is via the cloning route, where a skin cell nucleus is passed through an oocyte to give a totipotent cell. The production of a totipotent stem cell is the production of an embryo.

Production of an embryo as a source of cells or tissues.   There are two ways in which an embryo could be a source of cells and tissues. Firstly, the early embryonic cells could be made to differentiate into cells of one tissue type, for example, bone marrow. Secondly, differentiated cells or tissues from an older embryo could be extracted and used directly.

Are these permissible?

In England, the Royal Society has given limited support to cloning for the purposes of treating human disease. The Human Genetics Advisory Commission (HGAC) defines this as "therapeutic cloning," differentiating it from "reproductive cloning." Both bodies claim that embryo experimentation in the first 14 days is permitted by English law, and question whether cloning in this period would raise any new ethical issues.

Cloning in this circumstance raises few ethical issues. What is produced, at least in the first few days of division after a totipotent cell has been produced from an adult skin cell, is just a skin cell from that person with an altered gene expression profile (some genes turned on and some turned off). In one way, it is just an existing skin cell behaving differently from normal skin cells, perhaps more like a malignant skin cell. The significant processes are ones of *cellular multiplication* and later, *cellular differentiation*.

If this is true, why stop at research at 14 days? Consider the third version of the Lucas case:

Lucas III   The same as Lucas IIA, but in this case, Lucas also needs a kidney transplant. Therefore, in addition to the skin cell developing blood stem cells (via the embryo), the process is adjusted so that a kidney is produced.

The production of another tissue type or organ does not raise any new relevant ethical consideration. Indeed, if Lucas did not need the kidney, it could be used for someone else who required a kidney (if, of course, in vitro maturation techniques had been developed to the extent that a functioning organ of sufficient size could be produced).

Consider now:

Lucas IV   In addition to the blood cells, all the tissue of a normal human embryo is produced, organised in the anatomical arrangement of an embryo. This (in principle) might or might not involve development in a womb. For simplicity, let us assume that this occurs in vitro (though this is impossible at present).

Is there any morally relevant difference from the previous versions? It is not relevant that many different tissues are produced rather than one. Nor is the size of these tissues or their arrangement morally relevant. If there is a difference, it must be that a special kind of tissue has been produced, or that some special relationship develops between existing tissues, and that a morally significant entity then exists. When does this special point in embryonic development occur?

The most plausible point is some point during the development of the brain. There are two main candidates:

1. when tissue differentiates and the first identifiable brain structures come into existence as the neural plate around day 19.
2. when the brain supports some morally significant function: consciousness or self-consciousness or rational self-consciousness. The earliest of these, consciousness, does not occur until well into fetal development.

On the first view, utilisation of cloning techniques in the first two weeks to study cellular differentiation is justifiable. The most defensible view, I believe, is that our continued existence only becomes morally relevant when we become self-conscious. (Of course, if a fetus can feel pain at some earlier point, but is not self-conscious, its existence is morally relevant in a different way: we ought not to inflict unnecessary pain on it, though it may be permissible to end its life painlessly.) On this view, we should use the drug to cause Lucas IV's skin cells to transmutate and remove bone marrow from these. What is going on in Lucas IV is no different, morally speaking, from cloning. If this is right, it is justifiable to extract differentiated tissues from young fetuses which have been cloned. . . .

I cannot see any intrinsic morally significant difference between a mature skin cell, the totipotent stem cell derived from it, and a fertilised egg. They are all cells which could give rise to a person if certain conditions obtained. (Thus, to claim that experimentation on cloned embryos is acceptable, but the same experimentation on non-cloned embryos is not acceptable, because the former are not embryos but totipotent stem cells, is sophistry.)

Looking at cloning this way exposes new difficulties for those who appeal to the potential of embryos to become persons and the moral significance of conception as a basis for opposition to abortion. If all our cells could be persons, then we cannot appeal to the fact that an embryo could be a person to justify the special treatment we give it. Cloning forces us to abandon the old arguments supporting special treatment of fertilised eggs.

Production of a Fetus

If one believes that the morally significant event in development is something related to consciousness, then extracting tissue or organs from a cloned fetus up until that point at which the morally relevant event occurs is acceptable. Indeed, in law, a legal persona does not come into existence until birth. At least in Australia and England, abortion is permissible throughout fetal development.

Production of a Child or Adult as a Source of Cells or Tissues

Like the production of a self-conscious fetus, the production of a cloned child or adult is liable to all the usual cloning objections, together with the severe limitations on the ways in which tissue can be taken from donors for transplantation.

Many writers support cloning for the purposes of studying cellular differentiation because they argue that cloning does not raise serious new issues above those raised by embryo experimentation. Such support for cloning is too limited. On one view, there is no relevant difference between early embryo research and later embryo/early fetal research. Indeed, the latter stand more chance of providing viable tissue for transplantation, at least in the near future. While producing a cloned live child as a source of tissue for transplantation would raise new and important issues, producing embryos and early fetuses as a source of tissue for transplantation may be morally obligatory.

Consistency

Is this a significant deviation from existing practice?

1. Fetal Tissue Transplantation

In fact, fetal tissue has been widely used in medicine. Human fetal thymus transplantation is standard therapy for thymic aplasia or Di George's syndrome. It has also been used in conjunction with fetal liver for the treatment of sub-acute combined immunodeficiency.

Human fetal liver and umbilical cord blood have been used as a source of haematopoietic cells in the treatment of acute leukaemia and aplastic anaemia. Liver has also been used for radiation accidents and storage disorders. The main problem has been immune rejection.

One woman with aplastic anaemia received fetal liver from her own 22-week fetus subsequent to elective abortion over 20 years ago.

Fetal brain tissue from aborted fetuses has been used as source of tissue for the treatment of Parkinson's disease. Neural grafts show long term survival and function in patients with Parkinson's disease, though significant problems remain.

Fetal tissue holds promise as treatment for Huntington's disease, spinal cord injuries, demyelinating disorders, retinal degeneration in retinitis pigmentosa, hippocampal lesions associated with temporal lobe epilepsy, cerebral ischaemia, stroke and head injury, and beta thalassemia in utero using fetal liver. Fetal pancreas has also been used in the treatment of diabetes.

Fetal Tissue Banks

Indeed, in the US and England, fetal tissue banks exist to distribute fetal tissues from abortion clinics for the purposes of medical research and treatment. In the US, the Central Laboratory for Human Embryology in Washington, the National Diseases Research Interchange, and the International Institute for the Advancement of Medicine and the National Abortion Federation, all distribute fetal tissue.

In the UK, the Medical Research Council's fetal tissue bank was established in 1957 and disperses about 5,000 tissues a year.

2. Conception of a Non-Cloned Child as a Source of Bone Marrow: Ayala Case

Not only has fetal tissue been used for the treatment of human disease, but human individuals have been deliberately conceived as a source of tissue for transplantation. In the widely discussed Ayala case, a 17-year-old girl, Anissa, had leukaemia. No donor had been found in two years. Her father had his vasectomy reversed with the intention of having another child to serve as a bone marrow donor. There was a one in four chance the child would be compatible with Anissa. The child, Marissa, was born and was a compatible donor and a successful transplant was performed.

A report four years later noted: "Marissa is now a healthy four-year-old, and, by all accounts, as loved and cherished a child as her parents said she would be. The marrow transplant was a success, and Anissa is now a married, leukaemia-free, bank clerk."

Assisted reproduction (IVF) has been used to produce children to serve as bone marrow donors. It is worth noting that had cloning been available, there would have been a 100% chance of perfect tissue compatibility and a live child need not have been produced.

Objections

While there are some precedents for the proposal to use cloning to produce tissue for transplantation, what is distinctive about this proposal is that human tissue will be: (i) cloned and (ii) deliberately created with abortion in mind. This raises new objections.

Abortion Is Wrong

Burtchaell, a Catholic theologian, in considering the ethics of fetal tissue research, claims that abortion is morally wrong and that fetal tissue cannot be used for research because no one can give informed consent for its use and to use it would be complicity in wrongful killing. He claims that mothers cannot consent: "The flaw in this claim [that mothers can consent] is that the tissue is from within her body but is the body of another, with distinct genotype, blood, gender, etc." Claims such as those of Burtchaell are more problematic in the case of cloning. If the embryo were cloned from the mother, it would be of the same genotype as her, and, arguably, one of her tissues. Now at some point a cloned tissue is no longer just a tissue from its clone: it exists as an individual in its own right and at some point has interests as other individuals do. But the latter point occurs, I believe, when the cloned individual becomes self-conscious. The presence or absence of a distinct genotype is irrelevant. We are not justified in treating an identical twin differently from a non-identical twin because the latter has a distinct genotype.

In a society that permits abortion on demand, sometimes for little or no reason, it is hard to see how women can justifiably be prevented from aborting a fetus for the purpose of saving someone's life. And surely it is more respectful of the fetus, if the fetus is an object of respect, that its body parts be used for good rather than for no good purpose at all.

It Is Worse to Be a Clone

Some have argued that it is worse to be a clone. This may be plausible in the sense that a person suffers in virtue of being a clone—living in the shadow of its "parent," feeling less like an individual, treated as a means and not an end, etc. Thus cloning in the Ayala case would raise some new (but I do not believe overwhelming) issues which need consideration. But cloning followed by abortion does not. I can't make any sense of the claim that it is worse to be a cloned cell or tissue. These are not the things we ascribe these kinds of interests to. Cloning is bad when it is bad for a person. Likewise, arguments regarding "instrumentalisation" apply to persons, and not to tissues and cells.

Creating Life with the Intention of Ending It to Provide Tissue

Using cloning to produce embryos or fetuses as a source of tissue would involve deliberately creating life for the purposes of destroying it. It involves intentionally killing the fetus. This differs from abortion where women do not intend to become pregnant for the purpose of having an abortion.

Is it wrong deliberately to conceive a fetus for the sake of providing tissue? Most of the guidelines on the use of fetal tissue aim to stop women having children just to provide tissues. The reason behind this is some background belief that abortion is itself wrong. These guidelines aim to avoid moral taint objections that we cannot benefit from wrong-doing. More importantly, there is a concern that promoting some good outcome from abortion would encourage abortion. However, in this case, abortion would not be encouraged because this is abortion in a very special context: it is abortion of a *cloned* fetus for medical purposes.

But is it wrong deliberately to use abortion to bring about some good outcome?

In some countries (for example those in the former Eastern bloc), abortion is or was the main available form of birth control. A woman who had intercourse knowing that she might fall pregnant, in which case she would have an abortion, would not necessarily be acting wrongly in such a country, if the alternative was celibacy. When the only way to achieve some worthwhile end—sexual expression—is through abortion, it seems justifiable.

The question is: is the use of cloned fetal tissue the best way of increasing the pool of transplantable tissues and organs?

An Objection to the Principle of Tissue Transmutation

Another objection to the proposal is that we do not have the right to determine the fate of all our cells. For example, we are limited in what we can do with our sex cells. However, we should only be constrained in using our own cells when that use puts others at risk. This is not so in transmutation until another individual with moral interests comes into existence.

Surrogacy Concerns

At least at present, later embryonic and fetal development can only occur inside a woman's uterus, so some of the proposals here would require a surrogate. I have assumed that any surrogate would be freely consenting. Concerns with surrogacy have been addressed elsewhere, though cloning for this purpose would raise some different concerns. There would be no surrogacy concerns if the donor cell were derived from the mother (she would be carrying one of her own cells), from the mother's child (she would be carrying her child again) or if an artificial womb were ever developed.

Should We Give Greater Importance to Somatic Cells?

I have claimed that the totipotent cells of the early embryo, and indeed the embryo, do not have greater moral significance than adult skin cells (or indeed lung or colon or any nucleated cells). I have used this observation to downgrade the importance we attach to embryonic cells. However, it might be argued that we should upgrade the importance which we attach to somatic cells.

This is a *reductio ad absurdum* of the position which gives importance to the embryo, and indeed which gives weight to anatomical structure rather than function. If we should show special respect to all cells, surgeons should be attempting to excise the very minimum tissue (down to the last cell) necessary during operations. We should be doing research into preventing the neuronal loss which occurs normally during childhood. The desquamation of a skin cell should be as monumental, according to those who believe that abortion is killing persons, as the loss of a whole person. These claims are, I think, all absurd.

Yuk Factor

Many people would find it shocking for a fetus to be created and then destroyed as a source of organs. But many people found artificial insemination abhorrent, IVF shocking and the use of animal organs revolting. Watching an abortion is horrible. However, the fact that people find something repulsive does not settle whether it is wrong. The achievement in applied ethics, if there is one, of the last 50 years has been to get people to rise above their gut feelings and examine the reasons for a practice.

Permissive and Obstructive Ethics

Many people believe that ethicists should be merely moral watch-dogs, barking when they see something going wrong. However, ethics may also be permissive. Thus ethics may require that we stop interfering, as was the case in the treatment of homosexuals. Ethics should not only be obstructive but constructive. To delay unnecessarily a good piece of research which will result in a life-saving drug is to be responsible for some people's deaths. It is to act wrongly. This debate about cloning illustrates a possible permissive and constructive role for ethics.

Conclusion

The most justified use of human cloning is arguably to produce stem cells for the treatment of disease. I have argued that it is not only reasonable to produce embryos as a source of multipotent stem cells, but that it is morally required to produce embryos and early fetuses as a source of tissue for transplantation. This argument hinges on:

1. The claim that the moral status of the cloned embryo and early fetus is no different from that of the somatic cell from which they are derived.
2. The claim that there is no morally relevant difference between the fetus and the embryo until some critical point in brain development and function.
3. The fact that the practice is consistent with existing practices of fetal tissue transplantation and conceiving humans as a source of tissue for transplantation (the Ayala case).
4. An argument from beneficence. This practice would achieve much good.
5. An argument from autonomy. This was the principle of tissue transmutation: that we should be able to determine the fate of our own cells, including whether they change into other cell types.

This proposal avoids all the usual objections to cloning. The major concerns are practicality and safety. This requires further study.

The HGAC and The Royal Society have broached the possibility of producing clones for up to 14 days: "therapeutic cloning." Those bodies believe that it is acceptable to produce and destroy an embryo but not a fetus. Women abort fetuses up to 20 weeks and later. We could make it mandatory that women have abortions earlier (with rapid pregnancy testing). However, we do not. Moreover, while the decision for most women to have an abortion is a momentous and considered one, in practice, we allow women to abort fetuses regardless of their reasons, indeed occasionally for no or bad reasons. If a woman could abort a fetus because she wanted a child with a certain horoscope sign, surely a woman should be able to abort a fetus to save a person's life.

I have been discussing cloning for the purposes of saving people's lives or drastically improving their quality. While we beat our breasts about human dignity and the rights of cells of different sorts, people are dying of leukaemia and kidney disease. If a woman wants to carry a clone of her or someone else's child to save a life, it may not be society's place to interfere.

NO

Leon R. Kass

The Wisdom of Repugnance

Our habit of delighting in news of scientific and technological break-throughs has been sorely challenged by the birth announcement of a sheep named Dolly. Though Dolly shares with previous sheep the "softest clothing, woolly, bright," William Blake's question, "Little Lamb, who made thee?" has for her a radically different answer: Dolly was, quite literally, made. She is the work not of nature or nature's God but of man, an Englishman, Ian Wilmut, and his fellow scientists. What's more, Dolly came into being not only asexually—ironically, just like "He [who] calls Himself a Lamb"—but also as the genetically identical copy (and the perfect incarnation of the form or blueprint) of a mature ewe, of whom she is a clone. This long-awaited yet not quite expected success in cloning a mammal raised immediately the prospect—and the specter—of cloning human beings: "I a child and Thou a lamb," despite our differences, have always been equal candidates for creative making, only now, by means of cloning, we may both spring from the hand of man playing at being God.

After an initial flurry of expert comment and public consternation, with opinion polls showing overwhelming opposition to cloning human beings, President Clinton ordered a ban on all federal support for human cloning research (even though none was being supported) and charged the National Bioethics Advisory Commission to report in ninety days on the ethics of human cloning research. The commission (an eighteen-member panel, evenly balanced between scientists and non-scientists, appointed by the president and reporting to the National Science and Technology Council) invited testimony from scientists, religious thinkers and bioethicists, as well as from the general public. It is now deliberating about what it should recommend, both as a matter of ethics and as a matter of public policy.

Congress is awaiting the commission's report, and is poised to act. Bills to prohibit the use of federal funds for human cloning research have been introduced in the House of Representatives and the Senate; and another bill, in the House, would make it illegal "for any person to use a human somatic cell for the process of producing a human clone." A fateful decision is at hand. To clone or not to clone a human being is no longer an academic question.

From Leon R. Kass, "The Wisdom of Repugnance," *The New Republic* (June 2, 1997). Copyright © 1997 by The New Republic, Inc. Reprinted by permission.

. . . [S]ome cautions are in order and some possible misconceptions need correcting. For a start, cloning is not Xeroxing. As has been reassuringly reiterated, the clone of Mel Gibson, though his genetic double, would enter the world hairless, toothless and peeing in his diapers, just like any other human infant. Moreover, the success rate, at least at first, will probably not be very high: the British transferred 277 adult nuclei into enucleated sheep eggs, and implanted twenty-nine clonal embryos, but they achieved the birth of only one live lamb clone. For this reason, among others, it is unlikely that, at least for now, the practice would be very popular, and there is no immediate worry of mass-scale production of multicopies. The need of repeated surgery to obtain eggs and, more crucially, of numerous borrowed wombs for implantation will surely limit use, as will the expense; besides, almost everyone who is able will doubtless prefer nature's sexier way of conceiving.

Still, for the tens of thousands of people already sustaining over 200 assisted-reproduction clinics in the United States and already availing themselves of in vitro fertilization, intracytoplasmic sperm injection and other techniques of assisted reproduction, cloning would be an option with virtually no added fuss (especially when the success rate improves). . . .

In anticipation of human cloning, apologists and proponents have already made clear possible uses of the perfected technology, ranging from the sentimental and compassionate to the grandiose. They include: providing a child for an infertile couple; "replacing" a beloved spouse or child who is dying or has died; avoiding the risk of genetic disease; permitting reproduction for homosexual men and lesbians who want nothing sexual to do with the opposite sex; securing a genetically identical source of organs or tissues perfectly suitable for transplantation; getting a child with a genotype of one's own choosing, not excluding oneself; replicating individuals of great genius, talent or beauty—having a child who really could "be like Mike"; and creating large sets of genetically identical humans suitable for research on, for instance, the question of nature versus nurture, or for special missions in peace and war (not excluding espionage), in which using identical humans would be an advantage. Most people who envision the cloning of human beings, of course, want none of these scenarios. That they cannot say why is not surprising. What is surprising, and welcome, is that, in our cynical age, they are saying anything at all.

The Wisdom of Repugnance

"Offensive." "Grotesque." "Revolting." "Repugnant." "Repulsive." These are the words most commonly heard regarding the prospect of human cloning. Such reactions come both from the man or woman in the street and from the intellectuals, from believers and atheists, from humanists and scientists. Even Dolly's creator has said he "would find it offensive" to clone a human being.

People are repelled by many aspects of human cloning. They recoil from the prospect of mass production of human beings, with large clones of lookalikes, compromised in their individuality; the idea of father-son or mother-daughter twins; the bizarre prospects of a woman giving birth to and rearing a genetic copy of herself, her spouse or even her deceased father or mother; the grotesqueness of conceiving a child as an exact replacement for another who has died; the utilitarian creation of embryonic genetic duplicates of oneself, to be frozen away or created when necessary, in case of need for homologous tissues or organs for transplantation; the narcissism of those who would clone themselves and the arrogance of others who think they know who deserves to be cloned or which genotype any child-to-be should be thrilled to receive; the Frankensteinian hubris to create human life and increasingly to control its destiny; man playing God. Almost no one finds any of the suggested reasons for human cloning compelling; almost everyone anticipates its possible misuses and abuses. Moreover, many people feel oppressed by the sense that there is probably nothing we can do to prevent it from happening. This makes the prospect all the more revolting.

◈

Revulsion is not an argument; and some of yesterday's repugnances are today calmly accepted—though, one must add, not always for the better. In crucial cases, however, repugnance is the emotional expression of deep wisdom, beyond reason's power fully to articulate it. Can anyone really give an argument fully adequate to the horror which is father-daughter incest (even with consent), or having sex with animals, or mutilating a corpse, or eating human flesh, or even just (just!) raping or murdering another human being? Would anybody's failure to give full rational justification for his or her revulsion at these practices make that revulsion ethically suspect? Not at all. On the contrary, we are suspicious of those who think that they can rationalize away our horror, say, by trying to explain the enormity of incest with arguments only about the genetic risks of inbreeding.

The repugnance at human cloning belongs in this category. We are repelled by the prospect of cloning human beings not because of the strangeness or novelty of the undertaking, but because we intuit and feel, immediately and without argument, the violation of things that we rightfully hold dear. Repugnance, here as elsewhere, revolts against the excesses of human willfulness, warning us not to transgress what is unspeakably profound. . . .

◈

Typically, cloning is discussed in one or more of three familiar contexts, which one might call the technological, the liberal and the meliorist. Under the first, cloning will be seen as an extension of existing techniques for assisting reproduction and determining the genetic makeup of children. Like them, cloning is to be regarded as a neutral technique, with no inherent meaning or goodness, but subject to multiple uses, some good, some bad. The morality of cloning thus depends absolutely on the goodness or badness of the motives and intentions of the cloners. . . .

The liberal (or libertarian or liberationist) perspective sets cloning in the context of rights, freedoms and personal empowerment. Cloning is just a new option for exercising an individual's right to reproduce or to have the kind of child that he or she wants. Alternatively, cloning enhances our liberation (especially women's liberation) from the confines of nature, the vagaries of change, or the necessity for sexual mating. Indeed, it liberates women from the need for men altogether. . . .

The meliorist perspective embraces valetudinarians and also eugenicists. . . . These people see in cloning a new prospect for improving human beings—minimally, by ensuring the perpetuation of healthy individuals by avoiding the risks of genetic disease inherent in the lottery of sex, and maximally, by producing "optimum babies," preserving outstanding genetic material, and (with the help of soon-to-come techniques for precise genetic engineering) enhancing inborn human capacities on many fronts. Here the morality of cloning as a means is justified solely by the excellence of the end. . . .

∙◉∙

These three approaches, all quintessentially American and all perfectly fine in their places, are sorely wanting as approaches to human procreation. It is, to say the least, grossly distorting to view the wondrous mysteries of birth, renewal and individuality, and the deep meaning of parent-child relations, largely through the lens of our reductive science and its potent technologies. Similarly, considering reproduction (and the intimate relations of family life!) primarily under the political-legal, adversarial and individualistic notion of rights can only undermine the private yet fundamentally social, cooperative and duty-laden character of child-bearing, child-rearing and their bond to the covenant of marriage. . . .

The technical, liberal and meliorist approaches all ignore the deeper anthropological, social and, indeed, ontological meanings of bringing forth new life. To this more fitting and profound point of view, cloning shows itself to be a major alteration, indeed, a major violation, of our given nature as embodied, gendered and engendering beings—and of the social relations built on this natural ground. Once this perspective is recognized, the ethical judgment on cloning can no longer be reduced to a matter of motives and intentions, rights and freedoms, benefits and harms, or even means and ends. It must be regarded primarily as a matter of meaning: Is cloning a fulfillment of human begetting and belonging? Or is cloning rather, as I contend, their pollution and perversion? To pollution and perversion, the fitting response can only be horror and revulsion; and conversely, generalized horror and revulsion are prima facie evidence of foulness and violation. The burden of moral argument must fall entirely on those who want to declare the widespread repugnances of humankind to be mere timidity or superstition.

Yet repugnance need not stand naked before the bar of reason. The wisdom of our horror at human cloning can be partially articulated, even if this is finally one of those instances about which the heart has its reasons that reason cannot entirely know. . . .

The Perversities of Cloning

First, an important if formal objection: any attempt to clone a human being would constitute an unethical experiment upon the resulting child-to-be. As . . . animal experiments . . . indicate, there are grave risks of mishaps and deformities. Moreover, because of what cloning means, one cannot presume a future cloned child's consent to be a clone, even a healthy one. Thus, ethically speaking, we cannot even get to know whether or not human cloning is feasible.

I understand, of course, the philosophical difficulty of trying to compare a life with defects against nonexistence. Several bioethicists, proud of their philosophical cleverness, use this conundrum to embarrass claims that one can injure a child in its conception, precisely because it is only thanks to that complained-of conception that the child is alive to complain. But common sense tells us that we have no reason to fear such philosophisms. For we surely know that people can harm and even maim children in the very act of conceiving them, say, by paternal transmission of the AIDS virus, maternal transmission of heroin dependence or, arguably, even by bringing them into being as bastards or with no capacity or willingness to look after them properly. And we believe that to do this intentionally, or even negligently, is inexcusable and clearly unethical. . . .

⋅≪◉≫⋅

Cloning creates serious issues of identity and individuality. The cloned person may experience concerns about his distinctive identity not only because he will be in genotype and appearance identical to another human being, but, in this case, because he may also be twin to the person who is his "father" or "mother"—if one can still call them that. What would be the psychic burdens of being the "child" or "parent" of your twin? The cloned individual, moreover, will be saddled with a genotype that has already lived. He will not be fully a surprise to the world. People are likely always to compare his performances in life with that of his alter ego. True, his nurture and his circumstance in life will be different; genotype is not exactly destiny. Still, one must also expect parental and other efforts to shape this new life after the original—or at least to view the child with the original version always firmly in mind. . . .

Since the birth of Dolly, there has been a fair amount of doublespeak on this matter of genetic identity. Experts have rushed in to reassure the public that the clone would in no way be the same person, or have any confusions about his or her identity: as previously noted, they are pleased to point out that the clone of Mel Gibson would not be Mel Gibson. Fair enough. But one is shortchanging the truth by emphasizing the additional importance of the intrauterine environment, rearing and social setting: genotype obviously matters plenty. That, after all, is the only reason to clone, whether human beings or sheep. The odds that clones of Wilt Chamberlain will play in the NBA are, I submit, infinitely greater than they are for clones of Robert Reich. . . .

Genetic distinctiveness not only symbolizes the uniqueness of each human life and the independence of its parents that each human child rightfully attains. It can also be an important support for living a worthy and dignified life. Such arguments apply with great force to any large-scale replication of human individuals. But they are sufficient, in my view, to rebut even the first attempts to clone a human being. One must never forget that these are human beings upon whom our eugenic or merely playful fantasies are to be enacted.

Troubled psychic identity (distinctiveness), based on all-too-evident genetic identity (sameness), will be made much worse by the utter confusion of social identity and kinship ties. . . .

Social identity and social ties of relationship and responsibility are widely connected to, and supported by, biological kinship. Social taboos on incest (and adultery) everywhere serve to keep clear who is related to whom (and especially which child belongs to which parents), as well as to avoid confounding the social identity of parent-and-child (or brother-and-sister) with the social identity of lovers, spouses and co-parents. True, social identity is altered by adoption (but as a matter of the best interest of already living children: we do not deliberately produce children for adoption). True, artificial insemination and in vitro fertilization with donor sperm, or whole embryo donation, are in some way forms of "prenatal adoption"—a not altogether unproblematic practice. Even here, though, there is in each case (as in all sexual reproduction) a known male source of sperm and a known single female source of egg—a genetic father and a genetic mother—should anyone care to know (as adopted children often do) who is genetically related to whom.

In the case of cloning, however, there is but one "parent." The usually sad situation of the "single-parent child" is here deliberately planned, and with a vengeance. In the case of self-cloning, the "offspring" is, in addition, one's twin; and so the dreaded result of incest—to be parent to one's sibling—is here brought about deliberately, albeit without any act of coitus. Moreover, all other relationships will be confounded. . . .

⁂

Human cloning would also represent a giant step toward turning begetting into making, procreation into manufacture (literally, something "handmade"), a process already begun with in vitro fertilization and genetic testing of embryos. With cloning, not only is the process in hand, but the total genetic blueprint of the cloned individual is selected and determined by the human artisans. . . . In clonal reproduction, . . . and in the more advanced forms of manufacture to which it leads, we give existence to a being not by what we are but by what we intend and design. As with any product of our making, no matter how excellent, the artificer stands above it, not as an equal but as a superior, transcending it by his will and creative prowess. Scientists who clone animals make it perfectly clear that they are engaged in instrumental making; the animals are, from the start, designed as means to serve rational human purposes. In human cloning, scientists and prospective "parents" would be adopting the same technocratic mentality to human children: human children would be their artifacts.

Such an arrangement is profoundly dehumanizing, no matter how good the product. Mass-scale cloning of the same individual makes the point vividly; but the violation of human equality, freedom and dignity are present even in a single planned clone. . . .

⋅⦿⋅

Finally, and perhaps most important, the practice of human cloning by nuclear transfer—like other anticipated forms of genetic engineering of the next generation—would enshrine and aggravate a profound and mischievous misunderstanding of the meaning of having children and of the parent-child relationship. When a couple now chooses to procreate, the partners are saying yes to the emergence of new life in its novelty, saying yes not only to having a child but also, tacitly, to having whatever child this child turns out to be. In accepting our finitude and opening ourselves to our replacement, we are tacitly confessing the limits of our control. In this ubiquitous way of nature, embracing the future by procreating means precisely that we are relinquishing our grip, in the very activity of taking up our own share in what we hope will be the immortality of human life and the human species. This means that our children are not *our* children: they are not our property, not our possessions. Neither are they supposed to live our lives for us, or anyone else's life but their own. To be sure, we seek to guide them on their way, imparting to them not just life but nurturing, love, and a way of life; to be sure, they bear our hopes that they will live fine and flourishing lives, enabling us in small measure to transcend our own limitations. Still, their genetic distinctiveness and independence are the natural foreshadowing of the deep truth that they have their own and never-before-enacted life to live. They are sprung from a past, but they take an uncharted course into the future. . . .

Meeting Some Objections

The defenders of cloning, of course, are not wittingly friends of despotism. Indeed, they regard themselves mainly as friends of freedom: the freedom of individuals to reproduce, the freedom of scientists and inventors to discover and devise and to foster "progress" in genetic knowledge and technique. They want large-scale cloning only for animals, but they wish to preserve cloning as a human option for exercising our "right to reproduction"—our right to have children, and children with "desirable genes." As law professor John Robertson points out, under our "right to reproduce" we already practice early forms of unnatural, artificial and extramarital reproduction, and we already practice early forms of eugenic choice. For this reason, he argues, cloning is no big deal.

We have here a perfect example of the logic of the slippery slope, and the slippery way in which it already works in this area. Only a few years ago, slippery slope arguments were used to oppose artificial insemination and in vitro fertilization using unrelated sperm donors. Principles used to justify these practices, it was said, will be used to justify more artificial and more eugenic practices, including cloning. Not so, the defenders retorted, since we can make the necessary distinctions. And now, without even a gesture at making the necessary distinctions, the continuity of practice is held by itself to be justificatory.

The principle of reproductive freedom as currently enunciated by the proponents of cloning logically embraces the ethical acceptability of sliding down the entire rest of the slope—to producing children ectogenetically from sperm to term (should it become feasible) and to producing children whose entire genetic makeup will be the product of parental eugenic planning and choice. If reproductive freedom means the right to have a child of one's own choosing, by whatever means, it knows and accepts no limits.

But, far from being legitimated by a "right to reproduce," the emergence of techniques of assisted reproduction and genetic engineering should compel us to reconsider the meaning and limits of such a putative right. In truth, a "right to reproduce" has always been a peculiar and problematic notion. Rights generally belong to individuals, but this is a right which (before cloning) no one can exercise alone. Does the right then inhere only in couples? Only in married couples? Is it a (woman's) right to carry or deliver or a right (of one or more parents) to nurture and rear? Is it a right to have your own biological child? Is it a right only to attempt reproduction, or a right also to succeed? Is it a right to acquire the baby of one's choice? . . .

Ban the Cloning of Humans

What, then, should we do? We should declare that human cloning is unethical in itself and dangerous in its likely consequences. In so doing, we shall have the backing of the overwhelming majority of our fellow Americans, and of the human race, and (I believe) of most practicing scientists. Next, we should do all that we can to prevent the cloning of human beings. We should do this by means of an international legal ban if possible, and by a unilateral national ban, at a minimum. Scientists may secretly undertake to violate such a law, but they will be deterred by not being able to stand up proudly to claim the credit for their technological bravado and success. Such a ban on clonal baby-making, moreover, will not harm the progress of basic genetic science and technology. On the contrary, it will reassure the public that scientists are happy to proceed without violating the deep ethical norms and intuitions of the human community. . . .

I appreciate the potentially great gains in scientific knowledge and medical treatment available from embryo research, especially with cloned embryos. At the same time, I have serious reservations about creating human embryos for the sole purpose of experimentation. There is something deeply repugnant and fundamentally transgressive about such a utilitarian treatment of prospective human life. This total, shameless exploitation is worse, in my opinion, than the "mere" destruction of nascent life. But I see no added objections, as a matter of principle, to creating and using *cloned* early embryos for research purposes, beyond the objections that I might raise to doing so with embryos produced sexually.

And yet, as a matter of policy and prudence, any opponent of the manufacture of cloned humans must, I think, in the end oppose also the creating of cloned human embryos. . . . We should allow all cloning research on animals to go forward, but the only safe trench that we can dig across the slippery slope, I suspect, is to insist on the inviolable distinction between animal and human cloning.

Some readers, and certainly most scientists, will not accept such prudent restraints, since they desire the benefits of research. They will prefer, even in fear and trembling, to allow human embryo cloning research to go forward.

Very well. Let us test them. If the scientists want to be taken seriously on ethical grounds, they must at the very least agree that embryonic research may proceed if and only if it is preceded by an absolute and effective ban on all attempts to implant into a uterus a cloned human embryo (cloned from an adult) to produce a living child. Absolutely no permission for the former without the latter.

The National Bioethics Advisory Commission's recommendations regarding this matter should be watched with the greatest care. Yielding to the wishes of the scientists, the commission will almost surely recommend that cloning human embryos for research be permitted. To allay public concern, it will likely also call for a temporary moratorium—not a legislative ban—on implanting cloned embryos to make a child, at least until such time as cloning techniques will have been perfected and rendered "safe" (precisely through the permitted research with cloned embryos). But the call for a moratorium rather than a legal ban would be a moral and a practical failure. Morally, this ethics commission would (at best) be waffling on the main ethical question, by refusing to declare the production of human clones unethical (or ethical). Practically, a moratorium on implantation cannot provide even the minimum protection needed to prevent the production of cloned humans.

Opponents of cloning need therefore to be vigilant. Indeed, no one should be willing even to consider a recommendation to allow the embryo research to proceed unless it is accompanied by a call for *prohibiting* implantation and until steps are taken to make such a prohibition effective.

⋅⟨◉⟩⋅

Technically, the National Bioethics Advisory Commission can advise the president only on federal policy, especially federal funding policy. But given the seriousness of the matter at hand, and the grave public concern that goes beyond federal funding, the commission should take a broader view. (If it doesn't, Congress surely will.) . . .

The proposal for such a legislative ban is without American precedent, at least in technological matters, though the British and others have banned cloning of human beings, and we ourselves ban incest, polygamy and other forms of "reproductive freedom." Needless to say, working out the details of such a ban, especially a global one, would be tricky, what with the need to develop appropriate sanctions for violators. Perhaps such a ban will prove ineffective; perhaps it will eventually be shown to have been a mistake. But it would at least place the burden of practical proof where it belongs: on the proponents of this horror, requiring them to show very clearly what great social or medical good can be had only by the cloning of human beings. . . .

The president's call for a moratorium on human cloning has given us an important opportunity. In a truly unprecedented way, we can strike a blow for the human control of the technological project, for wisdom, prudence and human dignity. The prospect of human cloning, so repulsive to contemplate, is the occasion for deciding whether we shall be slaves of unregulated progress, and ultimately its artifacts, or whether we shall remain free human beings who guide our technique toward the enhancement of human dignity.

POSTSCRIPT

Is It Ethically Permissible
to Clone Human Beings?

Have humans already been cloned? At the end of 2002, Clonaid, founded by members of the Raelian religious cult, announced that it had succeeded. However, it neither produced the so-called clone baby nor permitted it to be tested. Most scientists believe the claims were lies at best.

The cloning technique has been shown to work with sheep, cattle, cats, rabbits, mules, pigs, and other animals. Early in 2003, researchers reported that the technique appears to be impossible in primates (including humans) because of the way certain proteins are arranged in egg cells (Calvin Simerly, et al., "Molecular Correlates of Primate Nuclear Transfer Failures," *Science,* April 11, 2003). However, useful applications of cloning are already being developed (see Ian Wilmut, "Cloning for Medicine," *Scientific American,* December 1998) and the debate over whether we should even try to clone humans and human stem cells continues to rage. Ian Wilmut, "The Case for Cloning Humans," *The Scientist* (April 25, 2005), argues that cloning human embryos may offer the best way to understand and treat difficult diseases; Wilmut's team received a license to clone human embryos in February 2005. For a good overview of the stem cell issue, see Rick Weiss, "The Power to Divide," *National Geographic* (July 2005). See also Ronald Bailey, *Liberation Biology: The Scientific and Moral Case for the Biotech Revolution* (Prometheus, 2005).

Leon Kass develops his objections further in "Preventing a Brave New World," *The Human Life Review* (July 2001), and *Life, Liberty and the Defense of Dignity: The Challenge for Bioethics* (Encounter, 2002). He gains support from Mary Midgley, who in "Biotechnology and Monstrosity: Why We Should Pay Attention to the 'Yuk Factor'," *Hastings Center Report* (September–October 2000), argues that intuitive, emotional responses to things such as cloning have a significance that must not be dismissed out of hand. In *Our Posthuman Future: Consequences of the Biotechnological Revolution* (Farras, Strauss & Giroux, 2002; paperback Picador, 2003), Francis Fukuyama argues for limits on cloning and genetic engineering in order to protect human nature and dignity. David Gurnham, "The Mysteries of Human Dignity and the Brave New World of Human Cloning," *Social & Legal Studies* (June 2005), agrees that cloning threatens human dignity. As a result of such arguments, the United States has banned the use of federal funds for reproductive cloning and severely limited the cloning of embryos to obtain stem cells for either research or treatment purposes. However, some states (e.g., California; see Nigel Williams, "California Ramps Up Stem Cell Plans," *Current Biology* [March 2005]) have chosen to develop their own state-funded research programs. In May 2005, President Bush was threatening to veto a proposed bill that would provide federal funding for stem-cell research; see "Bush Says He Would Veto Stem Cell Bill," *CongressDaily* (May 20, 2005). In other countries, progress has been more rapid. See Susan Mayor, "UK and Korean Teams Refine Techniques for Human Cloning," *BMJ: British Medical Journal* (May 28, 2005).

Speaking to the National Bioethics Advisory Commission (whose report was summarized by chair Harold T. Shapiro in the July 11, 1997, issue of *Science*), Ruth Macklin, of the Albert Einstein College of Medicine, said, "It is absurd to maintain that the proposition 'cloning is morally wrong' is self-evident. . . . If I cannot point to any great benefits likely to result from cloning, neither do I foresee any probable great harms, provided that a structure of regulation and oversight is in place. If objectors to cloning can identify no greater harm than a supposed affront to the dignity of the human species, that is a flimsy basis on which to erect barriers to scientific research and its applications." Nathan Myhrvold argues in "Human Clones: Why Not? Opposition to Cloning Isn't Just Luddism—It's Racism," *Slate* (March 13, 1997), that "Calls for a ban on cloning amount to discrimination against people based on another genetic trait—the fact that somebody already has an identical DNA sequence." There are reasons why cloning—at least of embryonic cells— should be permitted. According to Thomas B. Okarma (interviewed by Erika Jonietz, "Cloning, Stem Cells, and Medicine's Future," *Technology Review*, June 2003), they hold great hope for new and useful medical treatments. And according to Robin Marantz Henig, "Pandora's Baby," *Scientific American* (June 2003), when other reproductive technologies such as *in vitro* fertilization were new, they faced similar objections; now they are routine, and it is likely that someday cloning will be too. Daniel J. Kevles agrees; in "Cloning Can't Be Stopped," *Technology Review* (June 2002), he said that if human cloning can but succeed, it will "become commonplace . . . a new commodity in the growing emporium of human reproduction." Seymour W. Itzkoff, in "Intervening with Mother Nature: The Ethics of Human Cloning," *The Mankind Quarterly* (Fall 2003), calls objections to cloning and related issues "reactionary" and notes that "The cloning of humans and the stem cell production issue are . . . the tip of the iceberg, the slippery slope, or any other metaphor that points to the growing impact of scientific research that could undercut the twentieth-century ideological opposition to viewing human behavior as biologically/genetically determined."

Contributors to This Volume

EDITOR

THOMAS A. EASTON is Professor of Science at Thomas College in Waterville, Maine, where he has been teaching since 1983. He received a B.A. in biology from Colby College in 1966 and a Ph.D. in theoretical biology from the University of Chicago in 1971. He has also taught at Unity College, Husson College, and the University of Maine. He is a prolific writer, and his articles on scientific and futuristic issues have appeared in the scholarly journals *Experimental Neurology* and *American Scientist,* as well as in such popular magazines as *Astronomy, Consumer Reports,* and *Robotics Age.* His publications include *Focus on Human Biology,* 2d ed., coauthored with Carl E. Rischer (HarperCollins, 1995), *Careers in Science,* 4th ed. (VGM, 2004), and *Taking Sides: Clashing Views on Controversial Environmental Issues,* 11th ed. (McGraw-Hill Dushkin, 2005). Dr. Easton is also a well-known writer and critic of science fiction.

STAFF

Larry Loeppke	Managing Editor
Jill Peter	Senior Developmental Editor
Nichole Altman	Developmental Editor
Beth Kundert	Production Manager
Jane Mohr	Project Manager
Tara McDermott	Design Coordinator
Bonnie Coakley	Editorial Assistant
Lori Church	Permissions

AUTHORS

MICHAEL BEHAR is a freelance writer and editor based in Washington, D.C. His beat includes environmental issues and scientific innovations.

JORDAN BELL is a graduate student in the department of psychology at the University of New Mexico.

LEWIS M. BRANSCOMB is the Aetna professor of public policy and corporate management emeritus and former director of the Science, Technology, and Public Policy Program in the Center for Science and International Affairs at Harvard University's Kennedy School of Government.

JOSEPH BURNS, IRVING PORTER Church Professor of Engineering and Professor of Astronomy at Cornell University, is a member of the National Research Council's Solar System Exploration Survey Committee.

BRIAN BUTLER is an assistant professor of business administration at the University of Pittsburgh.

GEORGE CARLO is a public health scientist, epidemiologist, lawyer, and founder of the Health Risk Management Group. He is chairman of the Carlo Institute and a fellow of the American College of Epidemiology, and he serves on the faculty of the George Washington University School of Medicine. Dr. Carlo has published numerous research articles, commentaries, chapters in books, and health policy papers addressing issues in the health sciences, and he is frequently consulted for television, radio, and newspaper interviews pertaining to public health issues.

RICHARD J. CLIFFORD is a professor of biblical studies at Weston Jesuit School of Theology in Cambridge, Massachusetts, and a former president of the Catholic Biblical Association of America. He is the author of *Creation Accounts in the Ancient Near East and in the Bible* (Catholic Biblical Association of America, 1994).

GREGORY CONKO is the director of food safety policy at the Competitive Institute. He is the coauthor, with Henry I. Miller, of *The Frankenfood Myth: How Protest and Politics Threaten the Biotech Revolution* (Praeger, 2004).

SIMON COOPER is a writer-at-large for the science/culture magazine *Seed* and a contributing editor for *Rolling Stone* and *Playboy*.

JONATHAN N. CUMMINGS is an assistant professor of management at the Massachusetts Institute of Technology.

STEVE DITLEA, a journalist based in Spuyten Duyvil, New York, is a contributing writer to *Technology Review.*

JOHN P. GLUCK is professor of psychology and psychiatry at the University of New Mexico and an affiliate faculty member at the Kennedy Institute of Ethics, Georgetown University.

ALEXANDER GOUREVITCH was an *American Prospect* writing fellow for 2002–2003.

KARL GROSSMAN is professor of journalism at the State University of New York/College at Old Westbury. He has specialized in investigative and environmental journalism for over 35 years and is the author of *Cover Up: What You*

Are NOT Supposed to Know about Nuclear Power (The Permanent Press, 1994). He also hosts documentaries and interview shows for New York–based EnviroVideo.

JOHN B. HORRIGAN is a senior researcher with the Pew Internet & American Life Project. Prior to joining the Project, he was a staff officer for the Board on Science, Technology, and Economic Policy at the National Research Council.

INTERGOVERNMENTAL PANEL ON CLIMATE CHANGE was established by the World Meteorological Organization and the United Nations Environment Programme to assess the scientific, technical, and socioeconomic information relevant to the understanding of the risk of human-induced climate change. It bases its assessments mainly on peer-reviewed and published scientific/technical literature.

LEON R. KASS is the Addie Clark Harding Professor in the College and the Committee on Social Thought at the University of Chicago and an adjunct scholar at the American Enterprise Institute. A trained physician and biochemist, he is the author of *Toward a More Natural Science: Biology and Human Affairs* (Free Press, 1985), and *Life Liberty and the Defense of Dignity: The Challenge for Bioethics* (Encounter, 2002).

ROBERT KRAUT is the Herbert A. Simon Professor of Human Computer Interaction at Carnegie Mellon University.

DR. JOHN H. MARBURGER, III, is the science adviser to the president and director of the Office of Science and Technology Policy. He has also served as director of Brookhaven National Laboratory, the third president of the State University of New York at Stony Brook, and a University of Southern California professor of physics and electrical engineering.

ANNE PLATT McGINN is a senior researcher at the Worldwatch Institute and the author of "Why Poison Ourselves? A Precautionary Approach to Synthetic Chemicals," *Worldwatch Paper 153* (November 2000).

MICHAEL MEYER, the European editor for *Newsweek International,* is a member of the New York Council on Foreign Relations and was an Inaugural Fellow at the American Academy in Berlin. He won the Overseas Press Club's Morton Frank Award for business/economic reporting from abroad in 1986 and 1988 and was a member of the *Newsweek* team that won a 1993 National Magazine Award for its coverage of the Los Angeles riots. He is the author of *The Alexander Complex* (Times Books, 1989), an examination of the psychology of American empire-builders.

HENRY I. MILLER is a research fellow at Stanford University's Hoover Institution. His research focuses on public policy toward science and technology, especially biotechnology. He is the coauthor, with Gregory Conko, of *The Frankenfood Myth: How Protest and Politics Threaten the Biotech Revolution* (Praeger, 2004).

PETER MONTAGUE is executive director of the New Brunswick, New Jersey–based Environmental Research Foundation, and editor of *Rachel's Environment and Health News.*

DAVID NICHOLSON-LORD is an environmental writer, formerly with *The Times, The Independent,* and *The Independent on Sunday,* where he was environment editor. He is the author of *The Greening of the Cities* (Routledge, 1987) and of *Green Cities—And Why We Need Them* (New Economics Foundation, 2003), a member of UNESCO's UK Man and the Biosphere Urban Forum and of the Urban Wildlife Network executive and a trustee of the National Wildflower Centre. He also teaches environment in the journalism faculty at City University, London.

EVAN RATLIFF is a contributing editor to *Wired Magazine* and a coauthor of *SAFE: The Race to Protect Ourselves in a Newly Dangerous World* (Harper-Collins, 2005), a book on the science and technology of antiterrorism.

TOM REGAN, emeritus professor of philosophy at North Carolina State University, is considered the philosophical leader of the animal rights movement in the United States. His latest book is *Empty Cages: Facing the Challenge of Animal Rights* (Rowman & Littlefield, 2004).

SPENCER REISS is a contributing editor to *Wired Magazine*. He specializes in energy issues and the human impact of technology.

JEREMY RIFKIN is the president of the Foundation on Economic Trends in Washington, D.C., and author of *The Hydrogen Economy: The Creation of the World Wide Energy Web and the Redistribution of Power on Earth* (Tarcher/Putnam, 2002).

THE ROYAL SOCIETY is the United Kingdom's national academy of science.

JULIAN SAVULESCU is director of the Ethics Unit of the Murdoch Institute at the Royal Children's Hospital in Melbourne, Australia, and an associate professor in the Centre for the Study of Health and Society at the University of Melbourne. He has also worked as a clinical ethicist at the Oxford Radcliffe Hospitals, and he helped set up the Oxford Institute for Ethics and Communication in Health Care Practice.

MARTIN SCHRAM is a syndicated columnist, television commentator, and author. His publications include *Mandate for Change,* coedited with Will Marshall (Berkley Books, 1993) and *Speaking Freely: Former Members of Congress Talk About Money in Politics* (Center for Responsive Politics, 1995).

PETER SCHWARTZ is chair and cofounder of the Global Business Network, a scenario-planning firm. His books include *Inevitable Surprises* (Gotham, 2003) and *The Art of the Long View* (Doubleday Currency, 1991).

SETH SHOSTAK is a senior astronomer at the SETI Institute and the author of *Sharing the Universe: Perspectives on Extraterrestrial Life* (Berkeley Hills Books, 1998).

STEPHEN SOTTONG is Engineering, Technology, and Computer Science Librarian and Leader of the Library Information Technology Team, California State University, Los Angeles.

STUART TAYLOR, JR., is a senior writer and columnist for *National Journal* and a contributing editor at *Newsweek*.

MARTIN TEITEL is executive director of the Council for Responsible Genetics, a nonprofit organization of concerned scientists, doctors, and activists founded in 1983 to foster public debate about the social, ethical, health, economic, and environmental implications of genetic technology. He is the author of *Rain Forest in Your Kitchen: The Hidden Connection Between Extinction and Your Supermarket* (Island Press, 1992).

MIKE TREDER is executive director of the Center for Responsible Nanotechnology, a nonprofit research and policy group based in New York City.

WILLIAM TUCKER is a New York City journalist who has written books on environmentalism, crime, and housing.

THE UNION OF CONCERNED SCIENTISTS (UCS) is an independent nonprofit alliance of more than 100,000 concerned citizens and scientists. It was founded in 1969 by faculty members and students at the Massachusetts Institute of Technology who were concerned about the misuse of science and technology in society. Their statement called for the redirection of scientific research to pressing environmental and social problems. From that beginning, UCS has become a powerful voice for change.

THE UNITED KINGDOM'S NATIONAL RADIATION PROTECTION BOARD JOINED THE HEALTH PROTECTION AGENCY (HPA) as its Radiation Protection Division (http://www.hpa.org.uk/radiation/) on April 1, 2005. The mission of the HPA is to provide better protection in the UK against infectious diseases and other dangers to health, including chemical hazards, poisons, and radiation.

STEPHEN WEBB is a theoretical physicist who investigates how technology can help college students understand physical and mathematical concepts. He was an author on the team that developed "Software Teaching of Modular Physics," a hypermedia package that won the European Academic Software Award. His latest book is *Out of This World: Colliding Universes, Branes, Strings, and Other Wild Ideas of Modern Physics* (Springer, 2004).

EDWARD WEILER is NASA's Associate Administrator for space science.

STEVEN WEINBERG holds the Josey Regental Chair in Science at the University of Texas at Austin, where he is a member of the physics and astronomy departments. His research has earned him the Nobel Prize in Physics (1979), the National Medal of Science (1991), and the Benjamin Franklin Medal of the American Philosophical Society (2004). He is a member of the U.S. National Academy of Sciences, Britain's Royal Society, the American Philosophical Society, and the American Academy of Arts and Sciences. He has written over 300 articles on elementary particle physics and numerous books, of which the latest is *Glory and Terror—The Growing Nuclear Danger* (New York Review Books, 2004).

THE WELLCOME TRUST is a charitable organization whose mission is "to foster and promote research with the aim of improving human and animal health."

KIMBERLY A. WILSON, former director of the Commercial Biotechnology and the Environment program of the Council for Responsible Genetics, works with the Greenpeace biotechnology campaign.

Index